Gall

Gall (1840–1894) during his reservation years. Courtesy of Glen Swanson.

Gall

Lakota War Chief

Robert W. Larson

University of Oklahoma Press : Norman

ALSO BY ROBERT LARSON

New Mexico's Quest for Statehood, 1846–1912 (Albuquerque, 1968)
New Mexico Populism: A Study of Radical Protest in a Western Territory
    (Boulder, Colo., 1974)
Populism in the Mountain West (Albuquerque, 1986)
*Shaping Educational Change: The First Century of the University of Northern
    Colorado at Greeley* (Boulder, Colo., 1989)
Red Cloud: Warrior-Statesman of the Lakota Sioux (Norman, 1997)

Library of Congress Cataloging-in-Publication Data

Larson, Robert W., 1927–
    Gall : Lakota war chief / By Robert W. Larson.
        p.   cm.
    Includes bibliographical references and index.
    ISBN 978-0-8061-3830-5 (hardcover : alk. paper)
    1. Gall, ca. 1840–1894.   2. Hunkpapa Indians—Kings and rulers—
Biography.   3. Hunkpapa Indians—Wars.   4. Hunkpapa Indians—
Government relations.   5. Standing Rock Indian Reservation (N.D.
and S.D.)—History.   I. Title.
    E99.H795.G355   2007
    978.004'975244—dc22
    [B]   2006102745

2 3 4 5 6 7 8 9 10

For my wife, Peggy,
who has been such a source
of help and encouragement

Contents

Illustrations

Figures

Maps

Preface

When Gall died over a century ago, he was almost as famous as his mentor, Sitting Bull. They had been comrades-in-arms for many years. In 1864 Gall fought with Sitting Bull against an especially large force of blue-coated soldiers under Brigadier General Alfred Sully at the Battle of Killdeer Mountain. When Sitting Bull was wounded in an attack on a wagon train protected by Captain James L. Fisk shortly thereafter, Gall and other Hunkpapa warriors finished the assault.

Gall was also the Hunkpapa Sioux warrior who terrified Colonel David S. Stanley's men during the U.S. Army's 1872 Yellowstone Expedition when he waved the scalps of expedition members from a nearby hillock. Gall's ferocity during the 1872 campaign and the death of a first cousin of Julia Dent Grant (Ulysses S. Grant's wife) at the hands of Gall's followers led to an even larger troop escort in 1873 for the Northern Pacific Railroad's surveyors. Determined to prevent surveying of the rail route through the Yellowstone country, Gall would face Lieutenant Colonel George Armstrong Custer in battle for the first time when he engaged the 1873 Yellowstone Expedition.

Three years later, Gall confronted Custer and his command at the Battle of the Little Bighorn. He became the first major participant of that battle to tell the Indian side. Gall had taken an active part in that fight, and many historians have regarded him as the bellwether of what was a decisive Indian victory. Gall fought alongside Sitting Bull in succeeding months and then accompanied him to Canada, where many Lakotas would remain in exile for four years. In fact, Chief Gall was involved in so many battles and skirmishes with the U.S. Army that soldiers dubbed him the "Fighting Cock of the Sioux."

Gall's fame was based on controversy as well as demonstrated prowess. He was the first major Hunkpapa leader to ratify the 1868 Treaty of Fort Laramie, at first denouncing it at a peace conference at Fort Rice but later approving it in return for federal gifts granted to him and other Indian conferees. The veteran war chief broke with Sitting Bull over the question of surrender in 1881 when he led the many near-starving Lakotas of his band back to the United States and a much dreaded life on the reservation.

After his surrender at the Battle of Poplar River, Gall's character and personality underwent a significant transformation. He grew more cooperative and adapted to the white man's way of life. His service as a district farmer teaching the latest agricultural methods to his people, and as a judge on the Court of Indian Offenses to bring them justice, angered Sitting Bull and the more traditional Indians at Standing Rock. Notwithstanding his diligent efforts to reconcile the two cultures, Gall remained loyal to his *tiospaye*, or band. He believed that assimilation of his people was inevitable, given the decisive outcome of the Great Sioux War.

Gall's leadership of the most cooperative Indian faction on the Standing Rock Reservation greatly pleased Indian agent Major James McLaughlin. McLaughlin, along with many prominent federal authorities and politicians in Dakota Territory, praised Gall's virtues throughout the country, while denigrating those of the less flexible Sitting Bull. At the time of his death in 1894, Gall was one of the best-known American Indian leaders in the country, yet his fame would eventually fade. Today, those who study the high-plains Indian wars know him well, but he is almost unknown among Americans generally.

When Gall first drew my interest, I was surprised to learn that no full-length biographical study of him had ever been published. The name of Sitting Bull, by contrast, for whom two major biographies have been written, is almost a household word. Crazy Horse has inspired a number of biographies; Red Cloud, at least two. Even Gall's implacable Arikara enemy, Bloody Knife, Custer's favorite scout, has received full biographical treatment, but not Gall.

I feared that the primary and secondary sources that contain Gall's past might be too few or too contradictory. My early research showed there is ample material, however, although some of it is contradictory. One problem in doing an Indian biography, especially about a Native leader deeply involved in the Indian wars, lies in finding enough information to do justice to both sides of this long struggle. Non-Indian sources may also be so plentiful that they overwhelm those that present the Indian point of view. These concerns, too, were soon dispelled. Published studies by historians Robert M. Utley, Jerome A. Greene, Paul L. Hedren, Gregory F. Michno, Richard G. Hardorff, Lawrence A. Frost, M. John Lubetkin, Charles Robinson III, R. Eli Paul, Neill C. Mangum, and others do recognize the fighting abilities both of Indians and of soldiers from the frontier army.

To better understand Gall's role as a headman for his band, I found a number of ethnohistorical and anthropological accounts that reveal the beliefs and practices of the Lakota tribes on the western plains and of other Sioux tribes to the east. Such scholars as Raymond J. DeMallie, William K. Powers, Herbert T. Hoover, Michael Steltenkamp, Royal B. Hassrick, David Rich Lewis, Catherine Price, Margaret Connell Szasz, William T. Hagan, Father Francis Paul Prucha, Carole Barrett, Richard White, and Donald E. Worster clarified my perception of the Lakota and other western tribes that had to adjust to the new lifestyle imposed on them by the federal government. Adding to these revelations was a master's thesis about the leadership roles of Gall and John Grass at Standing Rock by James R. Frank, and a published study by Gary Clayton Anderson about Sioux kinship patterns and the tenuous relations between settlers and the eastern Sioux during the Minnesota Uprising, which led to the Indian wars.

Although it sometimes proved more difficult to find relevant *primary* sources about the Indians, I did discover a gratifying number of them in state and federal archives and libraries throughout the Great Plains and Mountain West. The State Historical Society of North Dakota, where I began my archival research, proved bountiful. The Major James McLaughlin Papers (consisting largely of military files from Record Group 393 of the National Archives and Records Administration), the Frank B. Fiske Papers, the Frank Zahn Collection, and the D. F. Barry Papers, along with census and other public records, proved most valuable. The help I received from Richard E. Collin, communications director for the North Dakota historical society, was outstanding; there is no other word for it. Also of great assistance were Mark J. Halvorson, curator of collections research; James A. Davis, reference specialist; Jenny D. Yearous, curator of collections management; and Sharon Silengo, photo archivist. At Fort Buford, the state-managed historical site where both Gall and Sitting Bull surrendered, Charles Stalnaker, site supervisor, and Diane Avans, maintenance supervisor, were of important assistance.

At the Standing Rock Reservation, Tim Metz, Sr. (Red Bull), tribal historic preservation officer, gave unselfishly of his time to explain the culture of his people. Also helpful were Gall's great-grandchildren, Vernon Iron Cloud and his wife, Theo, and the late Lavora Jones. Linda Jones, who is married to Lavora Jones's son, Wilferd, also provided me with good insights into Gall's lineage. Other Gall descendants who enlightened me were Gladys Hawk, Mike Her-Many-Horses, and Leo Her-Many-Horses. I interviewed a number of people, both Indian and non-Indian, who were excellent sources of knowledge about the Hunkpapa experience at Standing Rock. Of particular importance was Carole Barrett, associate professor of Indian Studies at the University of Mary in Bismarck. Two of her studies, sponsored by the North Dakota Humanities Council, deal with Agent McLaughlin and the St. Elizabeth Episcopal Mission, where Gall worshiped. In a series of interviews, Professor Barrett also shared useful information regarding Standing Rock. Beneficial, too, was the solid advice given to me at the beginning of my research travels by Christopher Dill, curator at the Greeley Museum.

Most of the federal records for Standing Rock during Gall's time are now kept at the National Archives and Record Administration (NARA), Central Plains Region, Kansas City. Gall's appointment papers as a district farmer and as a judge on the Court of Indian Offenses were made available to me through the diligent efforts of archives technician Barbara J. Larsen. Larsen's associates at the Kansas City archives, Lori Cox-Paul and Tim Rives, made a special effort to cull the archival documents dealing with the controversy over the execution of Brave Bear that helped to stall federal efforts to partition the Great Sioux Reservation. Also helpful in my research were Scott M. Forsythe, archivist for NARA, Great Lakes Region, Chicago; and Joel Barker, Mark Ferguson, William Eric Bittner, Eileen Bolger, and Richard "Rick" Martinez, from NARA, Rocky Mountain Region, Denver.

Other pertinent research materials are located at the South Dakota State Historical Society in Pierre. The Doane Robinson Papers were crucial in providing overall insights into the seven Lakota tribes. I greatly appreciate the help of Kenneth Stewart, research administrator there, and Virginia Hanson, archivist. Also supportive was Joe Edelen, head of content management and systems in the I. D. Weeks Library at the University of South Dakota in Vermillion. Episcopal Church records validating Gall's birth, death, baptism, and marriage were provided by Harry F. Thompson, director of research collections and publications for Western Studies at Augustana College in Sioux Falls. In Nebraska the State Historical Society in Lincoln made available the extensive Eli S. Ricker Collection, which comprises early-twentieth-century interviews with important Lakota leaders, soldiers, and federal authorities. Also in Nebraska is the Museum of the Fur Trade at Chadron, where the Josephine Waggoner Papers are kept. These papers include numerous biographies of Lakota warriors and chiefs that Waggoner compiled largely from personal interviews. The Waggoner Papers are maintained by Gail DeBuse Potter, the director of the museum, with assistance from her husband, James E. Potter, senior research historian for the Nebraska State Historical Society. I am also grateful to James Stroud of Golden, Colorado, and R. Eli Paul, curator of the Liberty Memorial Museum in Kansas City, for providing me with copies of some of Waggoner's biographies.

The University of Oklahoma Library's Western History Collections were another critical source for research on Gall's life. The services rendered by John R. Lovett, assistant curator, were especially appreciated. The library's Walter S. Campbell Collection is rich in material dealing with many aspects of Hunkpapa life. Although a preponderance of its materials deal with Sitting Bull, there is useful information about Gall. Campbell's chief informants were Sitting Bull's nephews White Bull and One Bull, along with Old Bull and Robert Higheagle. Given the bitter break between Gall and Sitting Bull during their Canadian exile, Campbell's Indian sources treat Gall with reasonable fairness. Campbell used these materials for his 1932 biography of Sitting Bull, which Campbell wrote under the name of Stanley Vestal. Much more valuable to the historian, however, is his *New Sources of Indian History*, also published under the name of Vestal. It includes valuable correspondence and an informative narrative replete with strong opinions.

One high-plains organization that has focused on the Indian wars through its archeological work and historical research is the Frontier Heritage Alliance. New information about Baker's Battle on the Yellowstone in 1872 was supplied by the organization's president, Gerald Groenewold of the University of North Dakota. Particularly helpful was the testimony of Howard Boggess, project director, and of Mary Ellen McWilliams, coordinator, and Richard E. Collin of the State Historical

Society of North Dakota. Eloise Ogden, regional editor of the *Minot Daily News*, has promoted knowledge about the Indian tribes on the Upper Missouri during Gall's time.

One of the best sources of research information close to home is the Western History/Genealogy Department of the Denver Public Library. In addition to its collection of old and rare books and articles, the library has the David F. Barry Papers and many photographs Barry took of frontier figures such as Gall, Sitting Bull, and Custer. The staff at the Denver Public Library was exceptionally helpful; Phil Panum, Bruce Harmon, Rose Ann Taht, Kay Wisnia, Trina Purcell, Rob Jackson, Janice Prater, and Joan Harms, among others, were always cooperative. The library's Frontier Newspaper Collection also proved valuable. Another nearby archival source I was able to utilize was the collection of governmental documents at the University of Denver. Government documents librarian Christopher C. Brown was diligent in locating the pertinent ones for me.

Also crucial to this project was my wife, Peggy, who traveled with me to the various archives and libraries throughout the Great Plains. Indeed her computer skills significantly cut the time expended on my research and writing. My sister, Sally Cumine, made some good suggestions about organizing the Gall study. My daughter, Helen Carlson, and her family and my son, Matthew, and his family from nearby Greeley may have wondered why I was so occupied during the past six years, but they were patient nonetheless. Also supportive were Jamie, Tracy, Schelly, Keith, Chris, and their families. I would be remiss if I did not mention Mark Gray, another Denver resident who searched diligently for Gall material on his computer, and Jeff Broome, the organizer of the annual Custer Symposium in Denver. I am also grateful to the members of the Denver Posse of Westerners for their strong interest and support.

Throughout the preparation of this manuscript, I was ably assisted by the staff of the University of Oklahoma Press. Especially helpful were Charles E. Rankin, the editor-in-chief; Bobbie J. Canfield and Christi A. Madden, his editorial assistants; Steven B. Baker, assistant managing editor; and Marian M. "Emmy" Ezzell, the production manager. The editorial help and copyediting of Melanie Mallon was invaluable as was the advice, from the start of my project, of Richard W. Etulain.

Robert W. Larson
Denver, Colorado

Gall

CHAPTER ONE

Like a Roman Warrior

On January 10, 1881, a large party of soldiers escorting a destitute group of Lakota captives reached Fort Buford in the remote northwestern corner of Dakota Territory. The tired troopers, who were struggling against the bitter cold as much as their prisoners were, served under the determined command of Major Guido Ilges. Ilges's captives numbered more than three hundred, including seventy-four seasoned warriors whom the major caustically called "full grown bucks." One of the intransigent warriors, Black Horn, was in shackles, but the best known and most prized of Ilges's prisoners was the Hunkpapa Sioux leader Gall. He, along with most of the other able-bodied men, trudged alongside the sturdy wagons that carried his band's women, children, and old people to their new destination. Their snowy midwinter trip from the Poplar River Agency had taken four days; indeed, when it started on the morning of January 6, the temperature had been twenty-eight degrees below zero.[1]

Even General William Tecumseh Sherman, who had shown little sympathy for the stubborn Lakotas holding out against the federal government, was anxious about the weather. He felt a genuine concern for the blue-coated soldiers stationed in the frigid northern plains; they, like the Sioux, had to face "the rigors of this winter."[2]

When Gall entered the large compound at Fort Buford, he had little reason to be happy. In early October 1880, he had made a promise to Edwin H. Allison, sometime emissary of Major David Hammet Brotherton, Fort Buford's commander. He had assured Allison that by December he

3

would bring his people from their Canadian exile to the Poplar River Agency, in Montana Territory. He now had second thoughts about this promise. In fact, he and his people had categorically refused to surrender when they had arrived at Poplar River on November 26. Instead of encamping at the agency, they had chosen a site in a wooded area across the Missouri River from the agency.

The situation worsened during the ensuing two weeks. Gall's Hunkpapas were joined by another Lakota Sioux band, the Sans Arcs, under the leadership of Chief Spotted Eagle. With Spotted Eagle's arrival and the arrival of other Lakotas, Gall's encampment grew from thirty-eight lodges to seventy-three. The U.S. Army and many of the agency employees at Poplar River, all of whom were familiar with Gall's reputation as the Fighting Cock of the Sioux, grew increasingly wary.[3] As for Gall, his ambivalence grew in proportion to the increasing number of tipis dotting the willow thickets and cottonwoods along the Missouri.

The last five years had been difficult for the forty-year-old warrior, whose strength and vigor belied his age; few warriors could demonstrate the physical prowess Gall did as they reached middle age. During the months after the Little Bighorn, Gall had remained one of Sitting Bull's most trusted war lieutenants, but he and Sitting Bull's followers, being separated from Crazy Horse's elusive band by army forces under Colonel Nelson A. Miles, had been compelled to cross the Canadian border in May 1877.[4]

Throughout their four-year stay in Grandmother's Land, Gall continued to support Sitting Bull.[5] Life had been better at first. The Canadian government was much more sympathetic toward them than the United States government had been, allowing the Lakotas to settle in a still bountiful area of hills, trees, and grasslands stretching west from Wood Mountain in present-day Saskatchewan. But there had been problems, such as the increasing scarcity of buffalo and the hostility of such Canadian tribes as the Crees, Bloods, Blackfeet, and Piegans. Moreover, the United States government exerted strong pressure on Canada to expel the Lakotas from their sanctuary in Saskatchewan. With near starvation becoming a reality among most of these Lakota bands, Gall finally broke with Sitting Bull and allowed supporters from approximately twenty of his lodges to return to the United States.[6] Sitting Bull's anger over this move only compounded the tensions between these two old friends. This schism was undoubtedly on Gall's mind as he encamped near the Poplar River Agency, debating his decision to surrender.

In response to the ominous gathering of Lakota Sioux bands at the Poplar River Agency, Major Ilges, in command of some four hundred men, was sent to the agency from Fort Keogh, a new post Colonel Miles's men had built on the Yellowstone River in 1877.[7] Ilges made the difficult 192-mile journey to the agency in nine days, traveling through deep snow, with temperatures ranging from 10 to 35 degrees below zero. Upon his arrival at Poplar River in late December, Gall took the initiative and asked for a conference with the major. In the tense meeting that followed, the Hunkpapa war chief revealed his strong ambivalence toward giving up the free and nomadic life his people had long enjoyed. He told Major Ilges that, while he was ready to surrender, his people were not prepared to do so until the advent of spring. Then they "would elect whether or not . . . to remain at this agency or go to Fort Keogh or Buford."[8] Gall's sensitivity to the needs of his band had characterized his leadership role during the years of struggle that had marked the Indian wars of the 1860s and 1870s. The veteran chief also wanted to visit Fort Buford before he made any final decision; in fact, his request for such a visit was coupled with a demand that Ilges provide him with both transportation and a military escort.

The major was exasperated by Gall's forceful manner throughout their meeting, and he lacked specific instructions from his superiors for how to handle Gall's demands in a decisive way. He did know, however, that the army was anxious to solve the Sioux problem, and the surrender of Gall and Sitting Bull was essential to that solution. He gave Gall and his people three days to reach a consensus, but he made it clear that after three days, Gall was going to Fort Buford and his followers were going with him.[9]

Despite Gall's reservations, he was probably ready to submit if he could get the right terms. He had said as much to Major Brotherton's emissary Edwin Allison three months earlier. Allison, an experienced scout who spoke Gall's language fluently, was a longtime friend of the Hunkpapa warrior. Indeed, Gall respected the controversial Allison, often called Fish by the Sioux, even though many of Gall's friends did not. Even more convincing proof that Gall was ready to surrender were the lodges Gall had brought from Canada as a token of good faith. Consequently, although Sitting Bull was still pondering his future, Gall was in the process of luring almost two-thirds of Sitting Bull's supporters southward across the international boundary. In the end, Sitting Bull was left with perhaps as few as two hundred loyal followers.[10]

Unfortunately Gall's leadership over these new Lakota followers was not very secure. Major Ilges's three-day ultimatum undoubtedly put

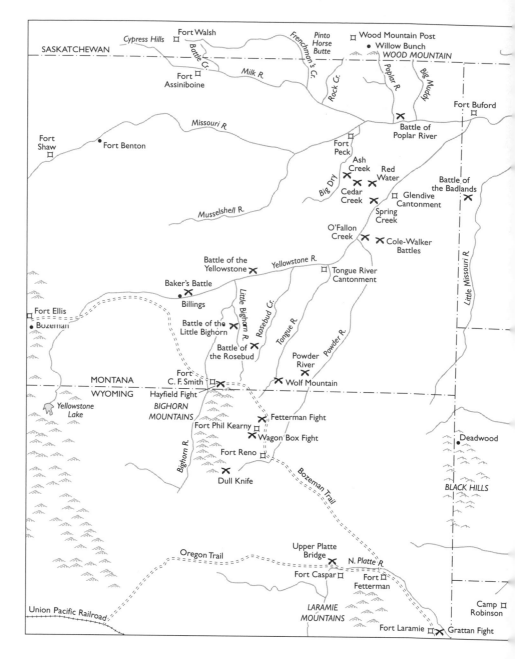

Gall country, 1840–1894

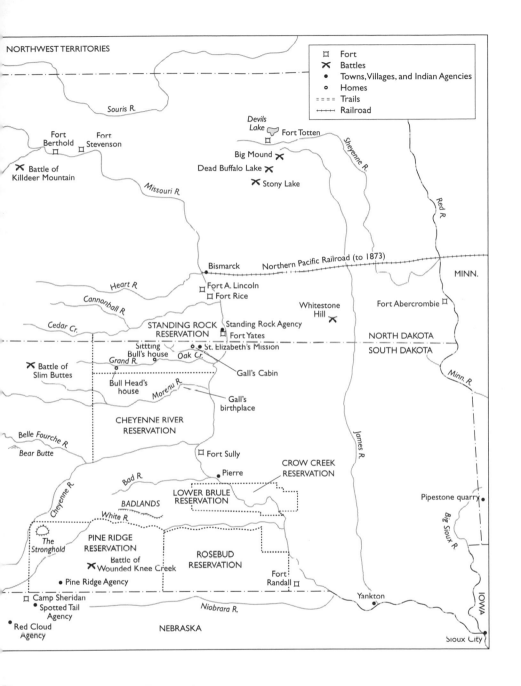

NORTHWEST TERRITORIES

	Fort
✕	Battles
•	Towns, Villages, and Indian Agencies
○	Homes
═ ═ ═ ═	Trails
┝━┿━┥	Railroad

Souris R.

Devils
Lake ▱ Fort Totten

Fort
Berthold
Fort
Stevenson

Big Mound ✕
Dead Buffalo Lake ✕
Stony Lake ✕

✕ Battle of
Killdeer Mountain

Missouri R.

Sheyenne R.

Red R.

Bismarck   Northern Pacific Railroad (to 1873)

MINN.

Heart R.
☐ Fort A. Lincoln
☐ Fort Rice

Cannonball R.

Whitestone
Hill ✕

Fort Abercrombie ☐

Cedar Cr.

STANDING ROCK   Standing Rock Agency
RESERVATION   ☐ Fort Yates

NORTH DAKOTA
SOUTH DAKOTA

Sitting   ○ • St. Elizabeth's Mission
Bull's house   Oak Cr.
Grand R.   ○

✕ Battle of
Slim Buttes

Gall's Cabin

Bull Head's
house   Morenu R.

Gall's
birthplace

CHEYENNE RIVER
RESERVATION

James R.

Minn. R.

Belle Fourche R.
Bear Butte

☐ Fort Sully

• Pierre

CROW CREEK
RESERVATION

Cheyenne R.

Bad R.

BADLANDS

White R.

LOWER BRULE
RESERVATION

Pipestone quarry •

Big Sioux R.

The
Stronghold

PINE RIDGE
RESERVATION

Battle of
✕ Wounded Knee Creek

• Pine Ridge Agency

ROSEBUD
RESERVATION

Fort
Randall ☐

Yankton
•

IOWA

☐ Camp Sheridan
• Spotted Tail
Agency
• Red Cloud
Agency

Niobrara R.

NEBRASKA

Sioux City

uncomfortable pressure on Gall because about sixty warriors were present during his stormy conference with Ilges. One of them, Crow, requested another interview with the willful major. During this much more acrimonious meeting, Crow, accompanied by twelve headmen from his camp, insisted on waiting to see what action his "only chief" Sitting Bull would take, making it clear that they would abide by any decision Sitting Bull would make. Major Ilges, probably not that familiar with the legendary independence of most Lakota warriors, urged Crow to go to Fort Buford and reminded him of the desperate need for food and clothing among his people.

Following this stressful meeting, two important developments occurred. First, Ilges received a telegram from one of his superiors on December 28. In these new instructions he was authorized to "compel the surrender of 'the Gall' and his people by such means as to . . . [Ilges] may seem best adapted to that end."[11] The second development was Crow King's arrival at Poplar River. Crow King, a great Hunkpapa warrior in his own right, probably exercised as much influence on these proceedings as Gall did. About ten days earlier, Fish Allison had persuaded Crow King and two other warriors to meet Major Brotherton at Fort Buford. The war chief, after spending Christmas Eve at the fort, returned to the Poplar River Agency with glowing reports about the conditions at Fort Buford.

A meeting was convened by Major Ilges on December 31, 1880, which included Crow King, his two Indian comrades, Allison, the Indian agent at Poplar River, and approximately sixty warriors, including Gall and Crow. Crow King extolled the virtues of Fort Buford and urged Gall and Crow, along with their followers, to go there. He insisted that this was the wish of Sitting Bull "for whom he was acting and speaking." Although Sitting Bull would later clash with Crow King over these bold assumptions, he had undoubtedly made a great impression on the once dubious warriors at this gathering.[12] None of them declined to go to the fort. Some, however, insisted that it was too cold to leave as early as January 2, the date set by Major Ilges for their departure.

Crow was deeply disturbed by these new plans, and he abruptly terminated the meeting by telling Major Ilges he was tired of hearing the major talk. On the following evening, Crow went to the home of Major Ilges's interpreter, Joseph S. Culbertson, and asked him to tell Ilges "that he and his people would not move until spring." He then called the major's men cowards, saying they could not handle guns and were "afraid to fight." Crow warned Ilges that if the military forces stationed at Poplar River attempted to interfere, his people would fight. Later that evening, Gall, who also had a mercurial personality, approached the post trader at the agency. Not to be outdone by Crow, he advised the trader and his employees to "leave the agency at once as he liked them and did not like to see them killed." Gall, more so than most Lakota leaders during the wars leading up to his surrender, often traded at various forts and posts with both civilian traders and their Indian allies, many of whom he befriended and sincerely liked. He told these agency employees also that the Lakotas encamped near the agency would "fight and wipe out the soldiers and kill everybody at the soldier camp."[13]

Gall and Crow's intemperate conduct gave Major Ilges the pretext he needed to launch an attack. At 11 a.m. on January 2, 1881, soldiers from the Seventh and Eleventh infantries, sporting a Rodman three-inch gun and under the command of Captain Ogden B. Read, assembled approximately three miles below the vulnerable Indian encampments. At twelve o'clock, Major Ilges brought an even larger force, a battalion of soldiers primarily from the Fifth Infantry. These soldiers brought the total number under his command to three hundred. The infantry companies under Ilges would constitute the western column of an elaborate pincer movement designed to engulf these disgruntled Lakota camps. He also mustered into service nineteen Indian scouts and volunteers, including a group of Yanktonais, whom Ilges feared might join their Sioux brethren. A Howitzer gun increased the already enormous advantage enjoyed by Major Ilges's troops in what would become known as the Battle of Poplar River. Historian Robert M. Utley has characterized this conflict as a classic example of "military overkill."[14]

When Major Ilges's forces crossed the frozen Missouri, they encountered virtually no resistance. The first Lakota village, thirty-two lodges tucked in among the willows and thick underbrush along the river, was almost deserted. A "few superannuated bucks" came running toward Ilges's troops to deposit "a few worthless muskets," but the total number of weapons found in this Miniconjou Sioux camp amounted to sixteen rifles, plus "guns of different patterns" and two pistols.

A short time later, Ilges's command reached Gall's Hunkpapa Sioux village of forty lodges and was greeted by an almost perfect silence; not one Indian was to be seen. Ilges responded to this intimidating calm by putting his Howitzer into position and sending "a few shells" into the nearby woods to convince these defiant Indians that his men were determined to escort them to Fort Buford immediately. But it took a subsequent search of the village to prompt the first shot to be fired from the huddle of forlorn tipis. The solitary gunshot was met by an avalanche of return fire, but the results were meager at best. One Hunkpapa warrior was killed, and two were wounded, including a woman.

Shortly thereafter, Captain Read arrived with his infantrymen; they constituted the eastern arm of Ilges's pincer movement. Read, too, had crossed the icebound Missouri, meeting virtually no opposition. The joining of the two columns was marked by an artillery bombardment of these almost defenseless Sioux villages, accompanied by loud demands for their surrender. This strategy soon bore results. Weary Hunkpapas raised a white flag and, along with a few of their Lakota allies, trickled out of the adjacent thickets to surrender.[15] Among these chastened Indians was the proud Gall. According to Captain J. M. Bell, one of the officers on the scene, Gall "came riding out on his pony with his blanket wrapped around him and arms folded." Bell commented that Gall "looked around him as like an old Roman as any man I ever saw."[16] Whether Gall wore the red blanket that had become his trademark or carried his trusted Winchester 76 is not definitely known, but the seasoned war chief's appearance almost always created a little awe among his enemies.

The term "battle" is probably a misnomer for this encounter. The tired and underfed Indians were unable to offer any real resistance. Even so, they suffered eight casualties, compared with none for Major Ilges's well-armed soldiers. Crow, and to a lesser extent Gall, had undoubtedly provoked the army to take this aggressive action, and their own followers paid the biggest price for their provocative language. But the pleas of both men that Major Ilges should wait until spring before marching their people to Fort Buford were more than justified. The weather was bitterly cold, and the snow was deep along the wintry route across Montana to Fort Buford at the western edge of Dakota Territory.

Major Ilges and his superiors, however, did not want to delay this difficult journey. They were determined to place these stubborn Lakota Sioux holdouts under strict military supervision at an established military post, such as Fort Buford. Military leaders feared a last-minute reunification of all these restless Sioux bands, the majority of which had fought for years to maintain their traditional lifestyle. The military was also apprehensive about the more pliable Yanktonais at Poplar River uniting with the Hunkpapas, Miniconjous, Sans Arcs, and other Lakota tribes under Gall's shaky leadership.[17]

An even greater concern among the top generals campaigning in the West was the attitude of Sitting Bull and his approximately 150 warriors. They had migrated below the Canadian border some fifty miles northwest of the Poplar River Agency. General Alfred H. Terry hoped that the surrender of Gall's supporters would convince Sitting Bull to follow suit; the Battle of Poplar River, however, appeared to have the opposite effect. Sitting Bull's nervous camp hastily recrossed the international boundary; the charismatic Hunkpapa chief and medicine man now had even stronger reservations about surrendering.[18] Terry and other officers soon hatched plans to send Major Ilges northward for a campaign against Sitting Bull if further negotiations failed to materialize.[19]

Gall's surrender at Poplar River must have been both bitter and frustrating. He had left his Canadian exile without Sitting Bull because he and his supporters felt it was the only feasible option for a starving people living miles from their familiar hunting grounds in the United States. Too proud to be genuinely humble, Gall could exercise little influence over Major Ilges. The rigid army officer, whose instructions from his superiors were too brief and vague to give him much self-confidence, would not grant Gall any significant concessions. He would not even let Gall's followers postpone their military escort to Fort Buford until the weather improved. Gall's leadership was also imperiled by the tactless Crow, whose primary loyalty was still with Sitting Bull. Gall's role in this one-sided confrontation with the army and his mortifying surrender were in sharp contrast to his feats of valor along the Yellowstone in the early 1870s or those at the Little Bighorn or the other battle sites during the waning days of the Great Sioux War.

Perhaps the final outrage for this prideful Hunkpapa war chief was the penalty he paid for resisting Major Ilges's will, having to walk for four days alongside the Fort Buford–bound wagons. The weather was so cold that General Sherman had refused to subject his troops at Fort Assiniboine, in north-central Montana, to a comparable journey, even in full winter gear. When the three hundred unhappy Indian captives approached Fort Buford, Gall, although probably not fazed much by the cold and exhausting pace of the march, was a truly angry man.[20]

The garrison at Fort Buford was fully prepared for its weary new guests. The commandant, Major Brotherton of the Seventh Infantry, was ready to accommodate his new charges. Brotherton's main problem, however, was to maintain the security of his post. A worried General Terry, in a dispatch to Brotherton, mailed the day Gall had arrived, put it this way: "Until Ilges' operations come to a conclusion, you must do the best you can with your present force, and the cavalry must take their full share of guard duty."[21] Major Brotherton's men had been given a tough assignment. The post was manned by a relatively small force, fewer than 250 men from companies A, B, and E of the Seventh Infantry and Company F of the ill-fated Seventh Cavalry. Nevertheless, most of the infantrymen at the post were seasoned veterans of the Great Sioux War.

Typical of many frontier posts, the parade ground at the remote fort, although not especially commodious, was the focal point; it was surrounded by sixty buildings of various sizes and uses. On the east side were barracks, a single and two double, and on the west side were ten clapboard officer's quarters, including Major Brotherton's residence. On the north side was a twenty-four-bed hospital, and on the south side, a guard house, where Gall and the new prisoners were to be kept. The commissary and quartermaster's storehouse were located near Gall's place of incarceration. The buildings on the south edge of Fort Buford were only a quarter of a mile from a steamboat landing on the Missouri, the fort's lifeline to civilization.[22]

Locating Gall and his supporters near buildings provisioned with food, clothing, and other supplies was probably a logical decision for the garrison's outnumbered soldiers. The nature of their internment, however, remains a matter of keen debate today. The army would insist that these warriors and their families were just being "detained," but many of the warriors would insist, especially after Sitting Bull arrived at the fort seven months later, that their incarceration was both stern and intrusive.[23]

The soldiers may have been outnumbered by their prisoners, but they did receive invaluable assistance from the approximately one hundred civilians located there. Behind the officers' quarters, on the west side of the parade ground, for instance, was a complex of buildings belonging to Leighton and Jordan, the post traders at Fort Buford. These buildings included stables, warehouses, and stores.[24] One of the employees, a thirty-three-year-old Missouri-born trader named Charles Baldwin, was a particularly observant person. He caught Gall's agitated mood at the fort as well as anyone. Gall, in his opinion, was an "out-and[-]out hostile" during much of his unhappy stay at Fort Buford. "On his face," Baldwin once remarked, "was . . . a look of alarm and uncertainty, yet, withal, an expression of indifference, so characteristic of the Sioux when facing a situation of danger."

Baldwin also gave a detailed description of Gall's powerful physique. Using a characterization that many would soon embrace, he described Gall as being "a most magnificent specimen of the Sioux." Although not tall, Baldwin said, he "was masive [sic] in chest and shoulders. His well-formed head; piercing black eyes; and long, black hair, which he wore in braids, marked him as a distinguished Indian."[25] Baldwin's recognition that Gall was not a tall man—he was only about five feet seven inches—corrected what had become a popular misconception.[26] Many who had seen him fighting on horseback or heard the tales of his skill in combat were convinced that he was an enormous man. The experienced hunter and trapper Joseph Henry Taylor, for instance, was convinced that "Gall stood in his moccasins near six feet tall, a frame of bone, with full breast of a gladiator and [the] bearing of one born to command."[27]

One of the prominent visitors to the fort introduced Gall to the world outside the vast northern plains. David F. Barry, a rising western photographer, was particularly impressed with Gall's appearance. The small, mustachioed photographer, called the Little Shadow Catcher by many of his Indian subjects, wanted to photograph Gall as soon as he saw him. Apparently receiving Major Brotherton's permission, Barry used Captain Walter Clifford and a scout named George Finney as go-betweens to arrange a sitting for Gall in Barry's makeshift studio. The suspicious Hunkpapa warrior was given twenty-one dollars for his cooperation, a fairly tidy sum for that day.

Gall, still adjusting to his degrading status as a prisoner, proved to be a most independent subject: "Refusing to listen to suggestions as to pose[,] he stood before the camera as best suited him." Later, after Gall's sitting, Barry characterized his photograph of Gall as "the only one ever taken of him as he looked as a hostile." What is especially fascinating about this particular photo, probably the most treasured one taken of Gall, was its near-destruction.

Lakota prisoners at Fort Buford must have been granted some latitude in their movements, because Gall was able to return to Barry's gallery without an escort. The intimidating war chief wanted to see his photographic plate, which was not yet finished. Gall, still bitter about the circumstances of his surrender, declared that having his picture taken was a bad idea; he now insisted that the plate be destroyed. Anticipating Gall's negative reaction, Barry had put Gall's plate back in the dark room. When Gall tried to retrieve it, the Little Shadow Catcher pushed aside the temperamental warrior. An enraged Gall responded by drawing a knife, but his menacing gesture was quickly met by a revolver in Barry's nervous hand; the little photographer had wisely kept his gun on a nearby shelf. Surprised by Barry's sudden response and unable to fathom the extent of the photographer's determination, Gall slowly backed out of Barry's gallery; the photographer's first photo of Gall was saved.[28]

Ironically, after this lethal incident, the two became good friends. Barry would use representations of Gall's head and upper body on the top of his letterheads, business cards, and advertising copies.[29] Other photographers, such as Barry's rival Frank B. Fiske, also sought Gall for sittings at their studio. Gall soon became one of the symbols of the Old West, even as that romanticized concept of American history was nearing an end.[30] The Little Shadow Catcher, who also photographed Rain-in-the-Face, later immortalized in one of Henry Wadsworth Longfellow's poems, even wrote laudatory accounts of Gall's role at the Battle of the Little Bighorn.[31]

Barry even sent a photo of Gall to George Armstrong Custer's wife, Elizabeth, even though Gall was one of her late husband's most formidable adversaries. Libbie Custer had to admit that, as painful as it was for her "to look upon a pictured face of an Indian," she had never in her life "dreamed there could be in all the tribes so fine a specimen of a warrior as Gall."[32]

Although Gall's surrender and incarceration at Fort Buford marked a low point in his life, the fame he had achieved as the Fighting Cock of the Sioux would not end; rather, it would take a different form. He would become better known, if more controversial, as a reservation Indian on what was called in 1881 the Great Sioux Reservation. The accounts of his exploits as a war chief and the wide distribution of his photographic image would extend his fierce reputation throughout the final fourteen years of his life. But the forty years prior to 1881 must be understood to appreciate the last fourteen.

CHAPTER TWO

Little Cub Bear

Historians have speculated that Gall was born sometime between 1838 and 1846. Yet, when the once vigorous warrior was baptized in the Episcopal Church on July 4, 1892, he gave the month and the year of his birth as October 1840.[1] Gall was born along the Moreau River in present-day South Dakota, west of the Missouri River in a prairie region that appeared hillier as it sprawled northward into North Dakota. Today this stretch of the vast Great Plains encompasses the Cheyenne River Reservation. Located just above it, and comparable in size, was the Standing Rock Reservation, where Gall spent the last years of his life.[2]

The future war chief was probably reared in a small band, because the Hunkpapa tribe of the Lakota Sioux was never very large. The band was camping along the banks of the Moreau for shelter by trees, a scarce resource on the Great Plains. In October, just prior to an ordinarily severe Dakota winter, Gall's birth site was presumably his band's winter camp. If this was the case, the first six months of Gall's life would have been especially calm and uneventful.

Most of Gall's time would have been spent inside his parents' tipi, resting on buffalo robes for warmth during the cold, snowy days. The infant's usual resting place would have been his cradle, a cushioned board decorated with buckskin flaps on either side. The cradle was frequently hung on the family's tipi pole by a sturdy loop, especially during the long winter months, when most Lakota Sioux bands waited patiently for better weather. When spring came, however, Gall, like other Lakota infants, would have been carried on his mother's back much of the time; the days were longer, and his people were now engaged in their nomadic travels.[3]

These wanderings were not erratic nor were they without direction. They were based on previous experiences that had given the band a good understanding of the challenging environment of the Great Plains. In fact, the topography and the flora and fauna of this vast wilderness provided part of the curricula for young Lakota boys like Gall. Learning to be a warrior and a hunter was necessary for tribal survival, but knowing the land was also vital. Knowledge of where to locate their next campsite during the warmer months was crucial to all Hunkpapa bands living off buffalo and other game, as was being aware of the landmarks, the rivers and streams that often determined their travel routes. Knowing which plants along the way were good for medicinal purposes, and which were not, would be yet another factor in the education of both Hunkpapa boys and girls. The Oglala chief Red Cloud remarked in his autobiography that he rarely stayed in one place for more than two months except during the most severe winter weather. Gall and his people, living farther north than Red Cloud, probably had even longer winter encampments than the Oglalas, but they, too, needed to stay on the move whenever possible to find and remain close to the great bison herds that roamed the plains during Gall's youth.[4]

Not much is known about Gall's parents. His father, Iciskehan, went by at least two names, Making-Many-Sisters and Running Horse. His mother's name was Cajeotawin, or Walks-with-Many-Names. Their names signified the high esteem they enjoyed. The father's indicated that he had adopted many sisters, an important act because generosity was one of the four cardinal virtues of all Lakota people. The mother's indicated that she had been given special names by many women societies, such as the tribal quilling groups. The family was apparently well connected. Historian Walter S. Campbell, who wrote under the name Stanley Vestal, found evidence that one of Gall's parents was related to Black Moon, a major hereditary chief from one of the tribe's leading families.[5]

Sadly enough for a child born in a society where warriors and hunters were vital to its survival, Gall was not raised by his father during most of his formative years. According to Gall's great-great-granddaughter, Jeanine Standing Bear, both parents were forced to abandon Gall when he was a child because of an enemy tribe's attack on their Hunkpapa band.[6] Gall was raised almost as a younger brother to Sitting Bull, the famous Hunkpapa war chief and, later, *wicasa wakan* (holy man). But there is evidence that Gall's mother survived this alleged catastrophe and raised her son.[7]

Gall's great-grandson Vernon Iron Cloud, who was raised by one of Gall's daughters, Sarah Shoots (also called Red Hawk), would often hear stories about Gall's widowed mother. One of Vernon's most vivid remembrances of these stories was that Gall's mother called her infant son Little Cub Bear, an appropriate and affectionate name for a husky little boy who truly resembled a grizzly cub in constant motion.[8] Gall had other names, as a child and later as an adult, that would obviously remain with him longer than Little Cub Bear. One of them was Matohinshda, or Bear Shedding His Hair, another term of endearment used by Gall's mother. This name denoted the size and physical vigor of Gall as he grew into manhood; the bear was a symbol of strength among all Plains tribes.[9]

But the name that would best mark his permanent identity was Pizi, or Gall, given to him by Walks-with-Many-Names after she observed her son eating the gallbladder of a freshly killed buffalo. Her attribution eventually caught on with other tribal members; even as a reservation Indian during the last thirteen years of his life, Gall was known, at least in official and religious records, as Abraham Gall.[10] Of course, most Lakota Sioux, whether they be Hunkpapas, Oglalas, or Brulés, had more than one name.[11] Gall was also known as The-Man-That-Goes-in-the-Middle (his favorite name) and Walks-in-Red-Clothing (often translated as Red Walker). The latter sobriquet was the result of Gall's partiality for the color red; during his warrior years, his enemies would often see him riding on a war horse covered with a red saddle blanket. Indeed, red became an important trademark when this young boy became a great warrior.[12]

Adapting to severe weather on the upper Great Plains was one of the great challenges faced by all Lakota Sioux tribes. Like other tribes wandering the northern plains, they had to overcome the elements in order to survive and hunt the buffalo, the great food source in this hostile land. Young Gall, like most Hunkpapas, would in time learn to hunt, fight, and survive during the sizzling summers and harsh winters of this wilderness area.

Coping with the environment, however, was not a new experience for Gall's Hunkpapas. For almost two centuries their ancestors had migrated hundreds of miles across the northern plains from hunting grounds in central and northern Minnesota. Their old Minnesota home was a largely wooded area west of the Great Lakes. According to longstanding tradition, they lived there with groups of like-minded Indians who spoke a Siouan language dialect. This dialect, second only to the Algonquian in common usage, encouraged political ties among them. They eventually organized into seven tribes, joining with each other through an institution they called the Seven Council Fires. The seven tribes that obligated themselves to tend these council fires were called the Sisseton, Wahpeton, Mdewakantons, Wahpekute, Yanktons, Yanktonais, and Tetons.[13]

They were woodland Indians, primarily hunters and food gatherers. Wild game, such as deer, and nutritious cereal grass, such as the rice they gathered from the many marshlands in their forest habitat, constituted the bulk of their food supply. They probably employed a few rudimentary agricultural practices but certainly not to the degree that their future allies, the Cheyennes, did. A largely nomadic people, these early Sioux were frequently on the move, trudging along narrow woodland trails by foot or paddling their birch canoes on the waterways that crisscrossed this forest primeval.

The tribes of the Seven Council Fires comprised resolute warriors, whose warlike ways cast fear among their neighbors. Approximately two hundred miles to the east of the 132,000-acre lake Mille Lacs, where many of the Sioux were located, lived the Chippewa Indians (more accurately called Ojibwa today). Concentrated on Michigan's northern peninsula, these Indians, who spoke an Algonquian dialect, felt enormous pressure from at least two of their Indian neighbors. They were being squeezed by the powerful Iroquois Confederacy on their eastern and southern flanks and by the upstart tribes of the Seven Council Fires on their western flank.

The Chippewas dubbed the Iroquois the True Adders, and the Sioux, whom they particularly despised, the Lesser Adders. The word for Lesser Adder in the Chippewa language, incidentally, was Nadoweisiw. The French, who in the eighteenth century competed with the English for dominance in the Great Lakes fur trade, took the last syllable of this name and garbled it into the word "Sioux." This term soon fell into popular usage among both of these European intruders, but the keepers of the council fires deeply resented it, because it meant "enemy" in the Chippewa language.[14]

The Sioux, from the time of Gall to the present, never appreciated being known as "the enemy." They preferred the name Dakota (or a variation of that word), which means "ally" in their language. The Santee Sioux, comprising such ancestral tribes as the Sisseton, Wahpeton,

Mdewakantons, and Wahpekute, used the name Dakota to identify themselves. Most of them remained in Minnesota until the 1860s. Their allies, the Yanktonais and Yanktons, preferred to be called Dakota, but they pronounced it Nakota. They started their migration westward in the late seventeenth century, eventually settling in eastern South Dakota and in parts of Iowa and Minnesota. Finally the Tetons, or "dwellers on the prairie," who had migrated across the Missouri to hunt and roam in western Dakota, also insisted on being known as allies. Their pronunciation of the word, however, was Lakota, not Dakota or Nakota.[15]

The Sioux tribes were secure in their Minnesota woodlands until the Chippewas and Crees, both of whom were Algonquian speaking, got guns from the French and the English. Early possession of these firearms was decisive. All seven Sioux tribes were forced to give ground in Minnesota, and the Yanktonais, Yanktons, and Tetons ultimately left the Minnesota woodlands to migrate throughout the Dakotas and the prairie lands of Nebraska, Wyoming, and Montana.

The Tetons, or Lakotas, who were living near the present town of Sauk Rapids, Minnesota, as late as 1680, were compelled to move because of determined gun-bearing foes. According to historian George E. Hyde, they retreated down the Mississippi and up the adjoining Minnesota River. When they reached the elbow bend of the Minnesota River near Swan Lake, they, like the Yanktonais and Yanktons, had to make a choice. They were either to move into the prairie lands south of the river, where buffalo were still plentiful, or to travel up the Minnesota River, where deer and other game roamed along the river's wooded banks.[16]

The Yanktons and two of the Lakota tribes, the Oglalas and Brulés, migrated south of the Minnesota, reaching another prairie river called the Blue Earth, a major tributary of the Minnesota. The bison that dotted the land adjacent to this river quickly proved to be a good source of food and shelter, and these tribes soon became skilled buffalo hunters. The Yanktons ultimately occupied land between the Blue Earth and the famous pipestone quarry in southwestern Minnesota. The Oglalas, who became the vanguard for the westward-bound Lakotas, bypassed the buffalo-hunting grounds of the Yanktons and pushed into South Dakota. They ultimately reached the James River and later the east bank of the Missouri, where in 1760 they settled in appreciable numbers.

During their westward migration, the Yanktons, Oglalas, and Brulés pushed aside such smaller Siouan tribes as the Omahas, Otoes, and Iowas.

Moreover, European traders, impressed by the enterprise of these restless Sioux tribes, began holding trade fairs for them at the juncture of the Mississippi and Minnesota rivers. As more Sioux bands moved into eastern South Dakota, these traders also began holding fairs near the headwaters of the Minnesota, exchanging items such as beaver pelts, liquor, trinkets, and guns. Although liquor would often be lethal for the Sioux, guns would put them on a par with those enemy tribes who had gained possession of these crucial weapons decades earlier.[17]

Eventually both the Oglala and Brulé tribes crossed the Missouri. The Oglalas followed the Bad River north of the Badlands to the river's headwaters 120 miles east of the Black Hills, while the Brulés followed the White River south of the Badlands to its headwaters in northwestern Nebraska. As early as the 1770s, an Oglala leader named Standing Bull discovered the Black Hills, or Paha Sapa, soon to become sacred to all Lakotas.[18]

Eventually both the Oglalas and the Brulés would acquire horses, another European contribution to the life of the Sioux tribes. Horses were introduced into the American Southwest by the Spanish. Pueblo Indians were probably the first Native Americans to use them, but being a sedentary agricultural people, they were not as interested in the mobility provided by horses as were such nomadic neighbors as the Utes and Apaches; indeed these nomadic tribes became much more efficient in their raids against Pueblo villages once they had horses. Through persistent trading and raiding, the use of these horses spread northward, making every tribe that acquired them more efficient in their hunt for the buffalo.[19]

By 1690 horse trading had reached the Red River of the South, where tribes like the Oklahoma-based Wichitas acquired them in 1719. The Otoes, Omahas, and Iowas, after being displaced by the Sioux, also assimilated horses into their life and culture. Some tribes, such as the Pawnees, living along the Platte and Loup rivers in eastern Nebraska, developed a reputation as being excellent horsemen. They traded with the Wichitas for their steeds or stole from those Apaches who wandered too close to Pawnee settlements. Eventually the Oglalas and Brulés would demonstrate their skills as superb equestrians in their years of prolonged warfare with the Pawnees. Gall's Hunkpapas, living farther north, would eventually use horses for transportation and hunting with equal effectiveness.

Unlike the Oglalas and Brulés, the other five Lakota tribes followed the Minnesota River westward toward its source on the northern plains. This decision probably made them more vulnerable to attacks by the

Crees and their Siouan-speaking Assiniboine allies, but it also allowed them to continue their familiar life as woodland Indians. These five tribes were certainly more conservative than their Oglala and Brulé allies when it came to maintaining the Sioux's traditional way of life. Indeed, their more adventuresome Oglala and Brulé kinfolk began calling them Saones, or Shooters among the Trees, because they hunted and trapped almost exclusively along the Minnesota River. This nickname would remain with them until the late nineteenth century.[20]

According to ethnologist Harry Anderson, by the early nineteenth century the largest of these five tribes were the Miniconjous, or Those Who Plant by the Stream.[21] The other four were smaller in size. The Two Kettle Sioux, for instance, although growing proportionately faster than any of the other Lakota tribes during the mid-nineteenth century, had far fewer members than the Miniconjous.[22] This tribe, along with another, the Sans Arcs (or Without Bows), tended to follow the Miniconjous on their course westward along the Minnesota.

Migrating more gradually than these three were two rather small Lakota tribes. One was the Blackfoot Lakotas, or Sihasapas, and the other was Gall's tribe, the Hunkpapas. The Hunkpapas, despite their modest numbers, would one day enjoy enormous respect among all Lakotas. Their name, which meant Those Who Camp at the Entrance, was a particularly prestigious one, because in tribal lore, the entrance was always regarded as a place of honor in any circle-shaped Lakota encampment.[23] Although the Hunkpapas would later rival the Oglalas in their warlike reputation, they were surprisingly cautious during this great migration of Lakota tribes across the northern plains.

One especially formidable obstacle to the Sioux's westward trek was the powerful Arikara, or Ree, tribe. This tribe, like the Pawnees, spoke Caddoan; lived in mud villages; grew crops of corn, beans, and squash; and hunted buffalo, usually after the spring planting or the fall harvest. When the Oglalas and Brulés finally reached the Missouri River, the Arikaras were living in fortified villages that stretched from the present site of Pierre, South Dakota, to the mouth of Crow Creek.

For more than a generation the Oglalas and Brulés had a tempestuous relationship with the Arikaras, sometimes raiding the Arikaras' fields to steal corn and other foodstuffs. When buffalo were scarce, however, they would often return to them to beg for food. Even after the Oglalas and the Brulés acquired European guns at the trade fairs, they were still unable to overpower their Arikara rivals; in fact, the Arikaras denied them a safe crossing point along the Missouri River for many years. The Arikaras, as the largest of the river tribes, reached a population of about twenty-three thousand in 1760, about double that of the Sioux tribes, who continued to reach the banks of the Missouri throughout much of the eighteenth century.

These river dwellers had been supplied by the Kiowas, before this ubiquitous tribe was driven from the Black Hills by Oglala warriors. The Kiowas had traded Spanish horses and other goods with the Arikaras in exchange for corn and other items. Soon the Arikaras had enough horses to mount four thousand warriors, armed with Spanish saber blades attached to their buffalo lances. Their frightening display of power often allowed them to rout hungry Oglalas and Brulés even after the Lakotas had acquired guns. The result was a long stalemate during which Lakota tribes, including the Hunkpapas, would often trade with the Arikaras during times of peace. But the Lakotas were not above disrupting this busy commerce with force whenever they saw any vulnerability in the Arikaras.[24]

This early dominance by the Arikaras was destroyed by another European import, smallpox. Living along the Missouri River brought these Indians and other river dwellers into contact with European traders traveling up the great watercourse. Unfortunately, some of these traders carried smallpox, along with germs from such communicable diseases as measles and scarlet fever. The Arikaras were hit especially hard by smallpox; three epidemics from 1772 to 1780 resulted in the death of four-fifths of their people. Other tribes living in the upper Missouri country were hurt too; the Piegan Blackfeet lost more than half of their population because of smallpox.[25]

The more mobile Lakota tribes were not immune to smallpox and the other European diseases either. According to the winter counts of the Brulés, many Lakotas died as a result of smallpox epidemics in 1779–1780, 1780–1781, and 1801–1802.[26] The nomadic lifestyle of the Lakotas, however, resulted in modest losses compared to the stationary tribes along the Missouri, such as the Arikaras, Mandans, and Hidatsas. Roaming throughout the grasslands west of the Missouri isolated many Lakotas from these diseases. The Hunkpapas and Blackfoot Lakotas were particularly isolated from smallpox carriers and benefited accordingly. Indeed, because of their geographical dispersal, the Lakotas grew from about eighty-five hundred in 1805 to approximately twenty-two thousand in 1881.[27]

The Arikaras, weakened by their diminishing numbers, were compelled to move upriver, allowing the Brulés, Oglalas, and their Yankton allies to settle along the Missouri, just below its great bend in South Dakota. The Arikaras now had to deal with the Lakotas to the north. Although these northern Lakotas, or Saones, including the Hunkpapas, had not been as aggressive toward the Arikaras as the Oglalas and Brulés had been, their attitude would change by the mid-eighteenth century. Heretofore, warfare with raiding Crees and Assiniboines from about 1725 to 1750 had occupied much of their time. But now the Arikaras had become their main enemy, posing the most serious obstacle to any effort to cross the Missouri. In 1786, for instance, the Arikaras settled near the confluence of the Cheyenne and Missouri rivers, right in the pathway of the migrating Saones.[28]

As early as the 1770s, the delay in the westward trek of the five northern Lakota tribes became an increasingly frustrating one. Although distance prevented frequent contacts with the Oglala and Brulé tribes, the northern tribes were undoubtedly aware that the horses acquired by these two southern tribes were making them more successful in hunting buffalo west of the Missouri. The mobility provided by these reliable steeds was already well known, and the large stores of buffalo meat in the Oglala and Brulé lodges were impressive and much envied by the Hunkpapas and their Saone allies.[29]

The Oglala and Brulé tribes were also enjoying a much welcomed change in their everyday lives because of horses. The necessity of using women and children as porters to carry their heavy loads or dogs to pull their sturdy travois was becoming less a factor in their busy lives. Moreover, their horses could haul much larger poles than their dogs could, thus assuring taller, more commodious tipis. In fact, with horses being work animals as well as hunting animals, a Lakota band, carrying all the necessary baggage, could travel more than five miles a day.

Primarily because of a growing eagerness to join their more prosperous allies across the Missouri, the Saones in the summer of 1794 drove one band of Arikaras up the Missouri to seek sanctuary with the Mandans and another down the Missouri to join the Skidi Pawnees in Nebraska. But the embattled Arikaras, in their quest for survival, encountered some jolting disappointments. Those who went northward had a falling out with the Mandans, who, in league with the Hidatsas, compelled them to retreat southward. There, in 1799, they established three villages above the confluence of the Grand and Missouri rivers. They were located in an area not that far from where Gall would be born four decades later.

This new home for the beleaguered Arikaras was many miles north of where the Cheyenne River flowed into the Missouri. Thus, the Cheyenne River, with its tributaries originating in and around the Black Hills, became the main route for the five Saone tribes migrating across the trans-Missouri plains. Conditions along this river were so favorable that the northern Lakotas began calling it the Good River.[30] The large Miniconjou tribe boldly led the way, followed closely by Sans Arcs and Two Kettles. The Hunkpapas and Blackfoot Lakotas, however, lagged behind; one reason for the delay was their brisk trade with the Arikaras, which had developed throughout the years. As late as the mid-nineteenth century, Gall and his Hunkpapa band often traded with the Arikaras, despite the traditional rivalry that divided these two tribes. Moreover, both of these Lakota tribes seemed more content with the pristine prairie lands just west of the Missouri.

The Miniconjous and their two tribal allies, on the other hand, pushed southward and westward, coming into more frequent contact with the adventuresome Oglalas. In fact, the number of Saones who started to live and hunt with Oglalas became so large that, by 1840, approximately half the Oglalas had some Saone blood.[31] Oglala chief Red Cloud's mother, Walks-as-She-Thinks, for instance, was probably a Saone. Her kin, the Oglala chief Smoke, who may have been her brother, also had Saone blood.[32]

In the half century following the crossing of the Missouri by the five northern Lakota tribes, the Lakotas became dominant on the northern Great Plains. When Lewis and Clark reached the upper Missouri in 1804, the Lakotas did not appear formidable. When General Henry Atkinson reached the same area in 1825, he counted more than four times the number that Lewis and Clark had. By this time, the Lakotas had also become terrors along the Missouri, often forcing European and American traders to pay tribute in order to reach the Arikara villages, which had for many years been excellent trading sites for both Indians and white entrepreneurs.

Although the Lakotas were never strong enough to subdue the encroaching tide of white settlement, they enjoyed enormous success in dominating other tribes in this region. They not only drove the Kiowas out of the Black Hills but continued to pressure them, ultimately pushing them south toward the Red River country. There, along with southern

Cheyenne and Arapaho allies, they combined with Comanches and Kiowa Apaches to engage in widespread trade throughout the Great Plains.[33]

The Lakotas also put intense pressure on the Crows because they occupied hunting lands the Lakotas wanted, and thus they became bitter enemies of the Sioux. Lakota expansionism eventually encroached on established Crow hunting grounds to the west and the north of the Black Hills. Thus, the Powder River country, once dominated by the Crows, became a neutral hunting ground where no tribe could be completely dominant. Buffalo herds thrived there because the dangers of conflict had significantly limited the number of hunters. The Hunkpapas became particularly violent foes of the Crows, challenging them not only in the Powder River country but also in the neutral hunting grounds of eastern Montana.[34]

When Gall was born in the autumn of 1840, his people were near the height of their power. The geographical domain of the Lakotas included most of the western Dakotas, along with western Nebraska and eastern Wyoming. They were starting to exercise great pressure to bring the Powder River country and the plains of eastern Montana under their influence. They did, however, still have formidable rivals. The Pawnees vigorously contested the claims of the Oglala and Brulé tribes in Nebraska. Lakota probes into Wyoming brought them into conflict with the Shoshones and even the Utes. The Crows resisted the Lakotas in the game-rich Powder River, delaying their dominance for many years.[35] When Gall became a full-fledged warrior during his teens, he would fight against his people's on-again off-again rivals the Arikaras.[36] But much of his warlike energies would ultimately be expended against the Crows and Assiniboines to the west.

The Lakotas did have allies to help them maintain their new dominance. Although the Cheyenne Indians had started out as rivals, even enemies, they eventually became the Lakotas' staunchest friends. The Arapahoes, although fewer in number, would often make common cause with both the Lakotas and the Cheyennes. When the U.S. Army became the most formidable rival of all Plains tribes, the northern branches of the Cheyenne and Arapaho nations would become the Lakotas' best allies, fighting alongside them in such legendary encounters as the Battle of the Little Bighorn.[37] In these battles with the U.S. Army, Gall would acquire his reputation as being one of the most formidable warriors of the Great Plains Indian culture.

CHAPTER THREE

Proving Himself

By spring 1841, Gall, months away from his first birthday, began a life of nomadic travels that would last until his surrender to the U.S. Army in 1881. The mobility achieved by his parents' band, when the winter snows had melted, no doubt benefited the lively infant. Although Gall was still largely confined to his cradle, he would soon be on the move with his people. Carried on his mother's back part of the time, he was also tied to a horse-drawn travois at other times. It was a pretty safe arrangement; the cradle was securely tied to the two long poles that held the travois together. He was also protected from uncomfortable jolts by his cushioned cradleboard. Although given opportunities to play near his parents' tipi, when the band was encamped, he continued to sleep or squirm in his cradle when the band resumed its travels.[1]

The husky toddler was probably happiest at the end of the day. His mother could focus her attention on him only after she had disassembled their heavily laden travois, set up the family's tipi, and prepared the evening meal. Fortunately, Walks-with-Many-Names's cooking utensils were not cumbersome. Because pottery was simply not practical for the nomadic life, the Lakota women, who did virtually all the cooking, initially used the stone-boiling method, adding red-hot stones to skin containers to boil their food. By Gall's time, however, enough white traders had visited the Lakota camps to provide Indian women with more convenient metal kettles for the meals they prepared. But whether she used skin containers or kettles, Gall's mother had to be certain that her Little Cub Bear did not crawl too close to any of her hot cooking utensils.[2]

As was the case with most Sioux children, Gall was adored by his parents. Lakota mothers and fathers lavished love and attention on their children. Gall had at least one sibling, a brother named Lone Man, who was undoubtedly cherished as much by his parents as was Gall.[3] An example of their exceptional solicitude for children occurred when Gall's father gave him the name Red Walker, or Walks-in-Red-Clothing. This event was marked by a boyhood ceremony, several years after Gall had outgrown his infancy. At this celebration, the boy was dressed in vermilion garments with long trailing streamers. He was permitted to parade before invited guests, who would later receive generous gifts from Gall's proud father.[4]

Happily, Walks-with-Many-Names would have plenty of help in raising Gall and his brother because of the strong kinship that extended throughout Lakota society. It largely functioned in the *tiospaye*, the basic social unit of the Lakotas. The tiospaye was an extended family group, or lodge group, in which all members were related by blood, marriage, or declaration of kinship. Each of these vital social units was usually composed of at least ten or more bilaterally extended families, led by a headman whose leadership abilities were often crucial to all tiospaye members. In many ways, the powers exercised by these headmen constituted the most fundamental source of grassroots government for the Lakota people.

Because of the Lakotas' kinship system, the fatherless Gall would have many role models and teachers to help him meet the often rigorous challenges of growing up in the competitive Lakota society. Uncles, aunts, and grandparents would help raise almost any child with one parent or with no parents at all. In Gall's case, with his mother being the only surviving parent, most of those who gave him guidance were probably from the maternal side of his extended family.[5]

The closeness of tiospaye relationships can be demonstrated by Sitting Bull and his extended family. This future tribal leader enjoyed strong support, especially from his paternal relatives. Indeed, he addressed all his father's brothers and cousins as "father." Sitting Bull would become an important part of the fatherless Gall's support system.[6]

But for most of Gall's growing-up years, his mother would be the major provider. She, like most Lakota parents, would do all she could to help him achieve those four cardinal virtues of a Lakota warrior: bravery, fortitude, generosity, and wisdom.[7] These thoroughly admirable goals would be difficult for individuals in any society to achieve. Not everyone would be able to attain them, but their lofty nature could and did bring out the best in many Lakota men and women. Moreover, only two of them, bravery and fortitude, stressed the virtues necessary for survival in warfare. Generosity and wisdom, on the other hand, reflected such community values as concern and mutual care, important aspects of Lakota life that are often overlooked.

Of these cardinal virtues, bravery came to Gall most easily; this was often the first of the virtues to be demonstrated by Lakota youths. An early example of Gall's reckless courage occurred when he was only three. Gall and his mother were evidently on a buffalo hunt with a band of Blackfoot Lakotas, the Lakota tribe closest to the Hunkpapas. Gall's mother entrusted the care of her boy, who was called Shedding-His-Hair by most Hunkpapas at the time, to a reliable Eskimo dog. The band was apparently moving through the Powder River country, some distance from their usual hunting grounds. Walks-with-Many-Names and other women in the group were on a broad tableland, digging for *teepsinna*, an edible root popular with many Sioux.

The progress of this moving village had been slow and tranquil until an old jackrabbit bolted from a hiding place. Running at top speed, the frightened animal issued, in effect, a challenge to all the dogs. The chase was on as every dog, regardless of the infants they were hauling or the bundles they were carrying, began an intense pursuit of their zigzagging prey. The large, dependable Eskimo dog hauling little Gall, who was sitting in a basket secured to the travois, was in the forefront of the pursuit. Gall, showing no fear, held the dog's tail with one hand and a pole of the travois with the other. Finally, after the jackrabbit began to slow with exhaustion, the big dog leaped up and caught the elusive animal by the throat; the chase was over.

Walks-with-Many-Names tried to grab and embrace her little boy, but the excited Gall was only interested in his dog. "Mother, my dog is brave: he got the rabbit!" The Hunkpapa band's youngest hero, surrounded by relieved onlookers, fondled the triumphant Eskimo dog, oblivious to the potential danger this incident had posed. One old warrior allegedly remarked that, while incidents such as these may be mere accidents, they sometimes foretell the future. "I prophesize [*sic*] that he [Gall] will one day hold the attention of all the people with his doings."[8]

Gall's bravery and his skills were tested along with boys from other Lakota bands roaming the plains during the mid-nineteenth century. Childhood games, often vigorously competitive, were an important part of becoming a warrior. The goal was to make the boys physically and emotionally strong enough to become sturdy and resolute fighters. The games tended to focus on skills and fun during a child's earlier years. For example, spinning tops to see which boy could keep his going longer and stop on the agreed-upon spot first was popular with younger boys. The wind whirler was another favorite, particularly with Oglala boys. Using a blade of alder wood attached by a thong to a short handle, a young participant would whirl it in the wind to see if he could keep it going longer than his competitors.[9] Sitting Bull was especially fond of the hoop game, in which rival teams wielding sticks attempted to roll a hoop into the competing team's zone. Prizes were awarded to the winners, the tenacious Sitting Bull winning more than his share.[10]

Games that required team cooperation often created circumstances not unlike those encountered by warriors and were usually dominated by older boys. In such games, the participants were forced to work together closely if they expected to be victorious against their opponents. Snowballing would be in this category, given the long Dakota winters. Gall once engaged in a snowball fight that could have been a curtain-raiser for one of the battles against an enemy tribe he would one day fight. There were probably close to a hundred boys on each side, and according to the rules governing the game, every successful hit by a snowball meant that the receiver was officially dead; he was to remain at the spot where he was struck.

Gall's side was getting the worst of the fight, despite the fact that he was probably the strongest of the young Hunkpapas in his age group. His team was soon forced to retreat to a water hole and make a last stand; eventually, Gall was alone, dodging snowballs from eleven survivors on the other side. Suddenly a large gray wolf, which had sought refuge in the same washout where Gall had retreated, emerged to terrify Gall's once confident opponents; they thought Gall had somehow been transformed into a ferocious beast. Gall, exercising that initiative which would one day make him a war leader, took advantage of the panic that caused his rivals to flee. He ran from the dry water hole to a designated safety line that, according to the rules of the contest, made his team the winner.[11]

One sport that involved boys as young as three or four was horseback riding. Racing ponies was, thus, a popular game that could sometimes involve "a great drove of ponies running, every one with a little boy clinging to its back." Indeed, young Lakotas, whether they be Hunkpapas, Oglalas, or Miniconjous, usually had pet ponies. The two were often so close that the boy and the pony were almost like one. Learning to handle horses, however, was more than just a childhood activity. It was an essential skill for adulthood, because horses were vital in warfare among Plains tribes, often being the main object of raids by enemy tribes.

As Lakota boys approached their teens, organized games became more serious; the emphasis was definitely more on strength and courage rather than on fun and joy. One sport that prepared the tribe's older boys for combat was the throwing of javelins or spears. The object of the game was to see who could throw this potential weapon the farthest.[12] Gall, with his increasingly impressive physique, probably excelled in javelin contests as he did in so many others.

One highlight in Gall's preparation for adulthood occurred during a wrestling game called che-hoo-hoo. This contest involved Gall's band and a band of friendly Northern Cheyennes who were encamped nearby in the Dakota Badlands. Following the rules of the game, a number of young Hunkpapas (and possibly a few Blackfoot Lakotas) were pitted against an equal number of young Cheyennes in what would be a series of one-on-one contests. The mock battleground was a plateau between the two Indian camps. The game started when the participants from each camp were called together by a leader chosen for that purpose. Each boy was to line up and await the signal to attack his chosen opponent. The center of attention for the throng of excited spectators were the two Apollos of the contest: Gall, representing the Hunkpapas, and Roman Nose, representing the Cheyennes. Roman Nose, probably the famous warrior who became an uncompromising adversary of the U.S. Army, was considered the equal of Gall in both strength and bravery.

The competitors, as was the case in most contests involving tribal youngsters, had to follow strict rules. They could not strike with the hand or kick with the foot. They could not grab their opponent around the neck, nor pull him by the hair. They were allowed to break away and retreat a few yards to get a new start, and they could clinch a competitor to gain time. If a boy met an opponent who was clearly his superior, he could fall to the ground and escape rough handling. But to avoid the disgrace that would result from doing that, most young Hunkpapas and Cheyennes gave their full measure of effort before accepting defeat. Each individual match would end only when one of the boys was thrown to the ground and held there until counted out.

After intense struggling back and forth, amid the incessant cheers and groans from both Indian camps, all the boys but two emerged as either victorious or beaten. The two survivors were Gall and Roman Nose. Both were stripped down to breechcloth, "tugging like two young buffalo or elk . . . [and] writhing and twisting like serpents." Every so often one of them would be lifted off his feet by the other only to come down with his feet planted squarely on the ground. Thus, the fight continued with a ferocity reminiscent of two wild stallions during mating season. Finally, the husky Gall, either by force or through trickery, threw Roman Nose to the ground and held him there for a minute. The proud new champion promptly released his opponent, jumped up, and stood erectly, while the Hunkpapa camp wildly cheered his prowess. The Cheyenne camp took this defeat in good stride. Roman Nose's mother graciously threw an impressive buffalo robe over Gall's shoulders, while Walks-with-Many-Names returned the compliment by covering Roman Nose with a fine-looking blanket.[13]

Most available evidence points to Gall being truly a leader during his formative years. Like the great Oglala chief Red Cloud, who was also fatherless during much of his boyhood, Gall had to achieve recognition on his own; he did it by displaying exceptional enterprise and aggressiveness.[14] Yet both he and Red Cloud were exceptionally brave; both had supportive mothers; and, by tribal tradition, uncles, cousins, and other male kinfolk helped groom them for the life of a Lakota warrior. Moreover, Gall had the support of Sitting Bull, who took an increasing interest in his scrappy new protégé, who was nine years his junior.

Sitting Bull set high standards for the ambitious Gall. When Gall was only five, Sitting Bull won his first coup at the age of fourteen. Coups, which were acts of bravery such as touching or killing an opponent in combat, were coveted by all Lakota warriors. Sitting Bull won his first coup by hitting a Crow adversary in the head with his tomahawk and knocking him off his horse. Another Hunkpapa comrade finished off the unfortunate victim so that he, too, could earn a coup.[15]

Given Sitting Bull's young age, the celebration over his first coup was quite elaborate. There was a feast in his honor, and a white feather was placed in his hair as a symbol of early promise. Sitting Bull's father gave him his own name, taking the name of Jumping Bull for himself. The proud father had originally called his son Jumping Badger, even though most of Sitting Bull's peers called him Slow because of his careful, calculating ways.[16] Because the Hunkpapas were a small tribe, numbering in the hundreds rather than the thousands, Gall probably observed these rituals to honor Sitting Bull's courage; he may even have remembered them although he was only five.

As young Lakota boys approached their warrior years, tests of their bravery and fortitude became more rigorous. Some of the boys simply could not qualify. A few even became *winktes*, or male transvestites, doomed to spend their adult years at the outer edges of the camp circle, there to live with women and children who had no male champion to represent them.

Lakota girls in the encampment had challenges too. Their training was also important because as women they would be largely responsible for making the tribe's social system function as it should. They would do the work when the band had to move; they would butcher the buffalo carcasses after the kill; and they would acquire the skills of tanning, beadwork, quilting, and a host of other talents that were essential for the tribe's survival.

Their influence was everywhere. Some Lakota men even lived with their wives' folks when they got married, while others stayed close to their parents. Girls, like boys, learned about the plants, animals, and geography of their environment. In fact, women usually gathered the most beneficial plants growing on the plains, knowing which were good for food and which were good for medicine.[17] Perhaps even more important, women provided the support that tribes like the Hunkpapas needed to survive on the northern plains. Gall's mother, Walks-with-Many-Names, is a prime example of a woman who gave vital support to one of the most promising of the Hunkpapa warriors.

When a Lakota boy seemed ready to assume his role as a man, he was often sent on a trip to test his fortitude, another cardinal virtue of the Lakotas. These journeys were usually long and difficult. They customarily became vision quests, when a serious-minded young Lakota male would seek some noble mission for his life, a religious ritual considered sacred by all Lakota tribes. Given Gall's prominence in the leadership of the Hunkpapa tribe, he probably went on his own rigorous vision quest, although it never received the recognition that Crazy Horse's famous vision did.[18]

As a boy Gall did prove his remarkable fortitude once when he went scouting for game miles from his camp. It was midwinter, and he found himself right in the middle of a fierce three-day blizzard. The storm forced him to abandon his horse and dig a snow cave. There he persevered, enduring his hunger with characteristic self-discipline. He also suffered from extreme thirst and stiffness. The experience, in addition to demonstrating Gall's fortitude, also revealed the importance of the horse to all Sioux warriors, young or old. The Lakotas often searched for good grazing lands for their treasured horse herds. When the storm subsided, Gall saw his steadfast animal only a "stone[']s throw away." There was also a herd of buffalo nearby, allowing the young hunter to put an end to his gnawing hunger pangs.[19]

When Gall finally became a full-fledged warrior, he was confronted by numerous challenges. Horse-stealing raids and warfare waged against rival tribes were always there to test his bravery and fortitude. The Hunkpapa's major enemies at this time were probably the Crows, who for many years claimed the Powder River country as one of their main hunting grounds. But the Hunkpapas were determined to enlarge their territory to include the buffalo hunting grounds along the Powder. In September 1851, when Gall was only eleven years old, the United States government, in the first Treaty of Fort Laramie, tried to end Indian warfare. One of its major motivations was to protect the growing stream of white emigrants heading west on the Oregon Trail. A serious problem in achieving peace among these tribes, however, was the prolonged struggle over land between the Lakotas and the Crows.

Nevertheless, for eighteen days, federal officials feasted and parleyed with an impressive gathering of tribes at Horse Creek, thirty miles downriver from Fort Laramie. They gathered treaty signatures from such tribes as the Lakotas, Crows, Assiniboines, Cheyennes, Arapahoes, Arikaras, Mandans, and Gros Ventres. These Indians agreed to abstain from future hostilities and stay within their specific boundaries. The provisions of the treaty would hold until the conference ended. But upon adjournment, the Lakotas and Crows were again fighting one another with renewed vigor. The Hunkpapas were probably the most intransigent of all the Lakota tribes. When they heard about the treaty's provision that they avoid war with the Crows, they absolutely refused to abide by it.[20]

If coups could be won by fighting the Crows, they could also be won by fighting the Assiniboines. The rivalry between the Lakotas and the Assiniboines, who were also a Siouan people, went way back to their early days in Minnesota. There, the Assiniboines had allied with the Crees against the Yanktonais, because the Crees had gotten European guns first. At the time of Gall's birth, warfare between the Sioux tribes and the Assiniboines had been going on for almost a century. In fact, the Hunkpapas had fought these distant cousins on both sides of the Missouri River. When Gall reached his warrior years, the dividing line between the Hunkpapas and the Assiniboines was drawn along the Missouri, north and west of where the Yellowstone empties into it. Because this was good buffalo country, conflict was inevitable. Indeed, Gall could earn many coups stealing horses from or warring against the Hohes, or Fish Eaters, as the Lakotas commonly called the Assiniboines.[21]

Another tribe the Hunkpapas occasionally fought were the Bitterroot Salish. Members of this tribe were commonly known as Flatheads, because they had acquired slaves from tribes in the Pacific Northwest that had artificially deformed the foreheads of their infants. Although this tribe had originally roamed the western part of Montana, most of them by 1855 had been confined to a reservation just east of the Bitterroot Mountains, miles from those areas where the Hunkpapas made periodical hunting forays. One Salishan band, however, refused to be confined on any reservation. Band members often wandered east, where they sometimes clashed with Hunkpapa hunting bands. In fact, Sitting Bull was wounded twice in two separate skirmishes with Flathead war parties, thus receiving two red feathers, a badge of honor the Sioux awarded to warriors wounded in combat.[22]

Largely confined to traditional Hunkpapa and Blackfoot Lakota country, which extended along the Missouri from the Knife River in the north to the Grand River in the south, were the Mandan and Hidatsa tribes. These tribes, once formidable rivals of the Hunkpapas, lived in earth lodges along the banks of the Missouri like the Arikaras, where their accessibility to fur traders carrying European diseases upriver in search of pelts made them as vulnerable to smallpox as the Arikaras were. One of the worst of these smallpox epidemics plaguing these river tribes occurred in 1837, three years before Gall's birth.[23]

Although the Arikaras, before being decimated by smallpox, had been able to dominate the Lakotas for years, by Gall's time, relations between them and the Hunkpapas were still tense but not necessarily warlike. In fact, a degree of trade and social intercourse existed between the two tribes; there were even examples of intermarriage between tribal members.

The most famous result of intermarriage between the Hunkpapas and the Arikaras was Bloody Knife, who became one of Lieutenant Colonel George Armstrong Custer's favorite scouts. Bloody Knife was born in a Hunkpapa village around the year 1840 of a Lakota father and an Arikara mother. He was close to Gall's age and may have been born in Gall's camp. As one of four children, he showed as much potential for becoming a great warrior as any aspiring young Lakota male. But, probably because he was mixed-blood, he was not accepted by many of the boys in camp. There was a particularly strong animosity between him and Gall. The strapping young Gall, because of his exceptional strength, could dominate Bloody Knife, and along with some of the other boys, Gall picked on Bloody Knife, making his life miserable.

Bloody Knife endured the abuses of Gall and his friends for years, exercising a patience and fortitude that won him the admiration of many in the Hunkpapa camp. His possible blood relationship to Sitting Bull may have earned him additional sympathy. But with Gall becoming Sitting Bull's favorite protégé, these assertions of blood ties did Bloody Knife little good. His unhappy stay with the Hunkpapas ended when his mother decided to leave her husband and return to her Arikara kin in the early 1850s. Although Bloody Knife may have had misgivings about this departure—the lives of sixty-three Arikaras were claimed by small-pox in 1856—he must have felt a great relief to be among a people who could appreciate his exceptional talents. The bitter teenager would never forget his mistreatment by Gall, a resentment that did not bode well for the future of either boy.[24]

Although information about Gall's development as a warrior is scanty, one fact provides convincing evidence of his growing prominence. Sitting Bull was relying on him more and more as a trusted lieutenant, despite their nine-year age difference. It is well known that Sitting Bull received the traditional white feather for his first coup at age fourteen, but it is not certain at what age or under what circumstances Gall received his. Given Gall's later reputation as the Fighting Cock of the Sioux, he must have accumulated many white feathers. Sitting Bull's nephew One Bull credited Gall with twenty coups, which was probably a low estimate that did not count all of Gall's coups against his military foes. The U.S. Army's emphasis on discipline and group fighting did not always lend itself to the personal valor required to win a coup.

Moreover, Sitting Bull had at least a decade more of warfare against rival tribes than Gall had. Thus, he had greater opportunities for the hand-to-hand combat and bold horse stealing that traditionally qualified as legitimate coups. He is credited with winning anywhere from thirty to sixty-three coups.[25] Gall received at least one life-threatening wound, which would have entitled him to wear a red feather. Given the numerous battles he fought in, however, one suspects that he earned more than one feather of this color. It also seems probable that, because of his reckless ferocity, Gall was as much a terror in fighting the Crows and Assiniboines as he was in fighting the U.S. Army during his later years.

Warfare, however, was not the only facet of life to engross the energies of the Lakota people. They had to create other positions of responsibility and relevant institutions to govern the various elements of the Lakota community, including the community's social order. Operating on a higher level of tribal affairs than the tiospaye headman were civil societies such as the *naca ominica*, which comprised former headmen along with men who had gained renown as hunters, warriors, and shamans. These men were chosen for their wisdom in statecraft (wisdom, of course, being one of the four cardinal virtues of the Lakota people). Because most of them were well past their prime and had begun to develop a middle age spread, the *nacos* were often known by the less-than-flattering name Big Bellies. Nevertheless, these older leaders joined younger men, many of whom were known for their skills in warfare, as key members in the tribe's governing council.[26] Each Lakota tribe also had four shirt wearers. These men, held in exceptionally high esteem, were expected to help enforce tribal decisions and protect their tribe's most vulnerable members. A warrior chosen as a shirt wearer wore a colorful, distinctive shirt and enjoyed the enormous prestige that came from wearing it. The first four Lakota shirt wearers were chosen by the Hunkpapas in 1851, when Gall was only eleven. Their names were Four Horns, Red Horn, Loud-Voiced Hawk, and Running Antelope. Of the four, Sitting Bull's uncle Four Horns was probably the most able.[27]

Another important tribal leader was the medicine man; his advice and counsel was sought whenever an important tribal decision had to be made. The Lakotas were a spiritual people, and their medicine men, or shamans, some of whom were regarded as holy men, could be surprisingly influential. Indeed, they maintained the circle, or sacred hoop, which extended from the village circle outward. It included all the circular-shaped entities that surrounded it, including the sun and the moon above and the rocks and the boulders below. In the Lakota view, each circular-shaped lodge was located in the center of the universe. This centrality allowed the Lakotas, as creatures of the earth, to commune with the all-encompassing divine forces in their circle and in all other circles surrounding them. Lakotas, being true believers, also tended to view this circle as a symbol in which kinfolk and friends dwell on the inside of the circle while enemies and detractors remain on the outside.[28]

One of the key roles of the medicine man was to control the four cardinal directions of this sacred hoop for the good of his people. He would, through his religious rituals, influence the spiritual currents moving through the gates, or doors, of the surrounding hoop. The west door of the hoop was represented by the color black, the north door by the color red, the east door by the color yellow, and the south door by the color white. Tribal successes were often attributed to the medicine man's ability to control the spiritual forces emanating from these four directions, often starting with the west door, representing the blackness of night.[29] As a medicine man, Sitting Bull probably won as much renown for his ability to control these spiritual forces as he did being the leading warrior of his tribe.

Before Sitting Bull became a medicine man, however, he was made a Hunkpapa war chief in 1857. His selection was based on the coups he earned and the leadership skills he exhibited. Also instrumental in his elevation to chief was the campaigning of Sitting Bull's many admirers, including Gall, who was also attracting attention as a budding young warrior.[30] In time, Gall himself would become a war chief, or *blotahunka*. As he grew older, he would assume the role of a tiospaye headman. This role is commonly equated with that of an *itancan*, often referred to as a tribal peace chief, defined in the Lakota language as a master or a ruler. The role of this chief was to exercise his considerable authority in behalf of his followers to help them achieve their material and social needs. As a tiospaye headman, Gall often had the same objectives as those of an itancan, but he was inclined to lead by persuasion rather than through the exercise of power.

Assuming these dual tribal roles was not unusual among the Lakota tribes. Red Cloud did it, and so did Crazy Horse; Crazy Horse, regarded by many as the ultimate Lakota warrior, thrived as a blotahunka, but when he became an itancan after his surrender in 1877, he found that catering to federal authorities for his band's rations was a most distasteful duty.[31]

The tribal roles played by headmen, shirt wearers, war chiefs, peace chiefs, and medicine men were vital to the Hunkpapas as well as to the other Lakota tribes. These leaders were essential for the welfare, if not survival, of the individual bands that composed each tribe. Throughout much of the year, most Lakotas lived and hunted in bands or tiospayes; some even chose to roam and hunt together as members of one family. Only infrequently did all members of a tribe assemble in one place. One reason for avoiding large tribal gatherings involved the presence of pony herds; these animals could quickly devour the grass surrounding any large encampment.

Fundamental to the success of any Lakota tribe were the fraternal *akicita* societies. These exclusive fraternal organizations provided a social atmosphere for the most prominent warriors among the Lakota tribes. They focused on the battle deeds of their members, which they conscientiously validated for the rest of the tribe, and provided opportunities for feasting and dancing to solidify their unity and comradeship. The akicitas included various organizations with colorful names, such as the Crow Owners, Silent Eaters, Kit Foxes, and Badgers, to name a few.

Although society members rarely fought together in tribal skirmishes or horse-stealing expeditions, they would joyfully celebrate these activities as a group. One of their main functions was policing the major buffalo hunts, which usually occurred in the late summer or early fall after the June sun dance. Another of their important duties was to police or supervise tribal wars against traditional enemies. In addition to their social functions and those linked to hunting, they also policed those always vital challenges connected with warfare. Akicitas were sometimes granted extraordinary powers to prevent irresponsible individuals from undercutting the strategy of a tribe or band in time of war. For instance, if a warrior, reckless to distinguish himself, broke ranks and destroyed a carefully planned ambush against an enemy tribe, the akicitas could severely punish him, even putting him to death under rare circumstances.[32]

Another indication of Gall's growing reputation as a warrior was his membership in at least two of the tribe's secret akicita societies. It was most flattering when Gall, with Sitting Bull's sponsorship, was admitted to the prestigious Strong Heart Society. Sitting Bull had served this society as one of two exalted sash bearers. (Sash bearers carried into battle a picket pin and rope to stake themselves to the ground and fight until released by comrades or killed by enemies.) With only forty or fifty members, this society was an envied one and Gall's admission to it a real honor. Gall, along with Crow King, another Hunkpapa warrior who would win great renown, founded in cooperation with Sitting Bull an even more prestigious akicita society, called the Midnight Strong Heart Society. This group has been characterized by Sitting Bull's biographer Robert M. Utley as "an elite within an elite." The society became known for its night feasts, where members could relate stories to one another about their coups and other harrowing scrapes with danger.[33]

Gall may have also joined his brother Lone Man as a member of the secret Silent Eaters Society, founded in 1869. This society, also closely associated with Sitting Bull, not only believed in quiet meals without music or dancing, but worked assiduously in behalf of tribal welfare. Gall would later oppose the Silent Eaters when he and Sitting Bull were no longer close during the Hunkpapas' reservation years.[34]

Sitting Bull would not have placed his own prestige on the line to get Gall into these influential societies unless he was convinced of Gall's great potential. Gall, who regarded Sitting Bull as his mentor, would serve his illustrious war chief as a loyal lieutenant for a quarter of a century. Both men exuded physical strength; their bodies were compact and muscular. Although Gall was only five feet seven inches, three inches shorter than Sitting Bull, he looked larger and more formidable because of his massive chest and exceptionally powerful arms. Mounted on his horse, Gall could easily be mistaken as a six footer. When both men rode together on a mission of war, they would strip down to breechcloth and paint their bodies and the bodies of their horses. Both liked the color red. Sitting Bull would often use a swirl of red paint on his forehead, and Gall's preference for red was so great that he often used the names given him by his father when he was a boy: Walks-in-Red-Clothing or Red Walker.[35]

Yet each man had a distinctive personality. Gall was probably less reserved than Sitting Bull, but he had a mercurial temper that few were willing to provoke. Sitting Bull was a more intense and focused person. Gall was a more pragmatic individual; he would often chart his own course. When he acquired his own band in later years, he would sometimes engage in controversial trade with white traders or with members of rival tribes. In times of war, however, Gall would be Sitting Bull's trusted lieutenant, fighting with him or in coordination with him as an invaluable ally. Sitting Bull understood and tolerated Gall's independent ways, and their partnership would make the warlike Hunkpapas an even more formidable force in dealing with their enemies.

CHAPTER FOUR

The New Enemies

In 1862, when Gall was in his early twenties, a major Indian war occurred in southern Minnesota. Although it did not involve the Lakotas,
it did involve their eastern cousins, the Dakota tribes, which had chosen
to remain in their homes in the upper Midwest rather than join their
westward-bound Lakota and Nakota allies. The Dakotas' traditional rivals,
such as the Crees, Chippewas, and Assiniboines, were not involved in this
war. The new enemies of the Dakotas had not been present when
Minnesota had been the homeland for all the Sioux tribes.

The new menace to the Dakotas in 1862 was posed by white settlers
pushing westward in unprecedented numbers. Many of them were
German-speaking immigrants who, with Teutonic efficiency, were clearing the woodlands along the Minnesota River and replacing them with
well-tended farms. The result was the growing destruction of a once
favorite hunting ground for those Dakotas who had remained in
Minnesota. The war that erupted, the Minnesota Uprising, also called
Little Crow's War, was caused when four Sioux youths murdered five
white settlers on August 17. The episode was the result of a mindless dare
by one of the four, who had challenged a comrade to steal the eggs of a
white farm family. The event worsened an already bad situation largely
caused by a federal agent, Alexander Ramsey, and a leading Indian trader,
Henry H. Sibley. They, along with other traders and government agents,
had been cheating the Indians out of the compensation promised for the
sale of tribal lands to the federal government. To complicate matters even

more, desperately needed food rations had been held back from the Dakotas.

The enraged Dakotas, some near starvation, found a reluctant leader in Little Crow, chief of the Mdewakantons. Little Crow's resistance led to a bloodbath, including bold attacks on farm settlements, such as the Minnesota River town of New Ulm. The loss of life among the settlers, almost five hundred, was shocking. In the end, however, the uprising was brutally crushed, thirty-eight Dakota leaders were executed the day after Christmas, Little Crow was killed several months later, and some desperate Dakotas fled to the eastern plains of Dakota Territory; there, they told the Hunkpapas and other Lakota tribes of the white man's deceit.[1]

The irony of this Indian war was that whites had been living in peace with the Dakotas since the arrival of French traders in Minnesota during the 1650s. This good relationship continued with English and even American traders well into the nineteenth century. Although white traders, who often married Dakota women, could not obviously be accepted as kinfolk by blood, they could become a part of the Dakota tiospaye in a secondary arrangement called "social kinship," or "fictive kinship." Thus, those who married into Sioux families were fully accepted and were often addressed as "father" or "brother," a practice in kinship relations that continued right into the American period. This assimilation into Dakota society was most advantageous to whites, because they were greatly outnumbered until the nineteenth century.

When the numbers of white settlers increased significantly with the large migrations of Germans and Scandinavians moving into Dakota country, things began to change. Many of these new agrarian settlers had little need for the social kinship offered by the Dakotas. Eventually the Indians in Minnesota began to feel that their preferred way of life as hunters was being threatened. The attitude of some federal authorities in skimping on the annuities they had promised in exchange for Dakota hunting lands in the 1837 and 1851 treaties only worsened an already bad situation. Illustrative of the attitudes of some of the traders responsible for food distribution among the Dakotas was Andrew Myrick, who allegedly said of these Indians, "So far as I am concerned, if they are hungry, let them eat grass." Myrick eventually paid with his life for this remark, but this incident was just one of many that sparked the Minnesota Uprising of 1862.[2]

Prior to this tragic war in Minnesota, about the only whites in contact with such northern Lakota tribes as the Hunkpapas were frontier traders.

As was the case in Minnesota, many of them were French Canadian or English. By 1862, however, an increasing number of American traders had reached the Dakota plains. Most Plains tribes welcomed them because they could trade fur pelts and buffalo robes, so highly valued back East, for iron kettles, woven blankets, and muskets, which could make Indians more efficient hunters. Particularly important to Sioux women were cut glass beads, a significant improvement over the use of seeds for Indian beadwork. Lakota warriors like Gall delighted in decorating knife sheaths, musket handles, moccasins, tomahawk handles, arm bands, and other items of clothing with the glass beads acquired during this brisk new trade.[3]

The image of white traders and travelers was probably better among Hunkpapas, Blackfoot Lakotas, and the members of other northern tribes than it was among the Oglalas and Brulés, who lived closer to the Oregon Trail, which had been opened for overland travel as early as 1841. The wagon trains crossing the plains of present-day Nebraska and Wyoming would soon threaten the hunting grounds of the Oglala and Brulé tribes. This unwelcome traffic eventually resulted in violence. The Grattan Affair of 1854, caused by an unsuccessful military attack against a band of Brulés accused of killing a Mormon emigrant's cow, led to a major military expedition against them in 1855. Brigadier General William S. Harney's attack against a large encampment of Brulés on Blue Water Creek in western Nebraska took the lives of one hundred and thirty-six Indians.[4]

The isolation of the northern Lakota tribes had sheltered them from growing intrusions elsewhere, such as white settlements and military expeditions like Harney's. The arrival in Dakota Territory of eager Civil War volunteers from the Minnesota state militia during the summer of 1863, however, would dramatically change things. These men were commanded by Sibley, the state's first governor, who had been named a brigadier general by President Abraham Lincoln that year. General Sibley had already ended Little Crow's War by defeating the Dakota leader at Wood Lake on September 23, 1862.[5]

Despite their decisive victory over the Dakotas, political leaders in Minnesota were greatly alarmed over the potential of future Indian wars. Dakota refugees who had fled into eastern Dakota were spreading the message of white duplicity to their Lakota kin on the Great Plains. State officials feared that overland routes through the Dakota Territory to Montana, where promising gold strikes had occurred in 1862, could be

blocked by vengeful Lakota warriors. Even the expansion of the agricultural frontier into the northern plains seemed in jeopardy. The acting
governor of Dakota Territory, John M. Hutchison, warned that as many
as a fourth of the settlers pushing up the Missouri River into present-
day South Dakota had been forced to abandon their homesteads.

To cope with these concerns, General Sibley led an army northwest
from Minnesota in the summer of 1863. Another military force, under
the command of Brigadier General Alfred Sully, a seasoned West Pointer
with Civil War experience, moved up the Missouri to rendezvous with
Sibley. The two armies, comprising approximately five thousand blue-
coats, were encroaching on Hunkpapa and Blackfoot Lakota hunting
grounds. During the summer of 1863, following their sacred sun dance,
these two tribes were hunting buffalo east of the Missouri when they
became involved in Sibley's campaign against the Dakota refugees from
Minnesota. After a major battle with Sibley's men at Big Mound, near
the source of the James River, the Minnesota Sioux sought refuge with
the two Lakota tribes from the north. This action resulted in two decisive
clashes between all three tribes and Sibley: the Battle of Dead Buffalo
Lake on July 26 and the Battle of Stony Lake on July 28. In both engage-
ments, the Sioux were defeated. The effectiveness of General Sibley's
cavalry and his superior artillery proved decisive. Indeed, this lethal com-
bination sent the Indians back across the Missouri in full retreat.

Historian Robert M. Utley has speculated that Sitting Bull probably
fought at both the Dead Buffalo Lake and Stony Lake encounters. One of
Sitting Bull's hand-drawn autobiographical pictographs shows him attacking Sibley's mule team in a violent engagement at Dead Buffalo Lake. His
apparent motivation at this time was a desire to count coup on a stubborn
mule skinner armed with a blacksnake whip. If Sitting Bull was there, Gall,
his increasingly dependable war lieutenant, was probably there too.

In summer 1864, a large encampment of Hunkpapas, Blackfoot
Lakotas, Dakota refugees, Yanktonais, Sans Arcs, and Miniconjous gathered on the Knife River in the western part of Dakota Territory. These
tribes were beginning to feel the seriousness of the threat posed by the
armies sent from Minnesota.

The Lakotas had probably underestimated this danger until now. A few
of the Hunkpapas and Blackfoot Lakotas had even joined the Dakotas
when they had recrossed the Missouri River to hunt buffalo in late summer 1863. These tribesmen wanted to replenish their stock of winter

stores lost as a result of their defeats at Big Mound, Dead Buffalo Lake, and Stony Lake.

The Sioux knew that General Sully had only reached Fort Pierre in his long march up the Missouri and that General Sibley was returning to Minnesota.[6] They were confident that a drought that year would continue to slow the progress of Sully's army into Hunkpapa and Blackfoot Lakota country. As a consequence, they were surprised when Sully's troops attacked them at their encampment on Whitestone Hill on September 3, killing 100 Indians and capturing 156. Sibley's men also destroyed their tipis and needed food supplies. This defeat, which occurred about one hundred miles southeast of the present site of Bismarck, caused the Lakota survivors at Whitestone Hill to flee across the Missouri River. The embattled Dakotas from Minnesota were forced to seek the safest place they could find east of the Missouri.[7]

The humiliation at Whitestone Hill greatly angered the Lakota tribes west of the Missouri. They retaliated during late 1863 with raids on the stock herds at Fort Pierre, where most of Sully's men were spending the winter. They also attacked two trading posts on the upper Missouri: Fort Berthold, near the mouth of the Little Missouri, and Fort Union, near the juncture of the Yellowstone and the Missouri rivers. Fort Berthold was one of the trading posts Gall and his band often visited during the 1860s and 1870s. Historically, Fort Union catered to the Blackfoot tribe and the Lakota's longtime enemies the Assiniboines.[8]

Despite their defeats at the hands of these new enemies, the Lakotas still possessed feelings of disdain toward the blue-coated soldiers. These men did not fight as individuals for the honor and glory of combat, and the acquisition of coups was not part of their motivation. Instead, they fought as disciplined men who followed the strict orders of their superiors. Thus, the threats and challenges the Lakotas hurled at these invaders through white traders and those Indians friendly to them were laced with contempt.[9]

But the large 1864 Sioux gathering on the Knife River was apprehensive despite its confident boasts. They knew that Fort Sully, built by General Sully's men on the east side of the Missouri River below Fort Pierre, was a sure sign that the soldiers intended to stay. When Lakota scouts sighted the movement of three thousand soldiers under Sully's command marching up Cannonball River with a wagon train of argonauts bound for the Montana mines, the Indians camped along Knife

River moved north toward the Killdeer Mountains. There, on a low wooded range that extended northward to the Badlands along the Little Missouri, approximately fourteen hundred lodges of Lakota, Dakota, and Yanktonai Indians decided to make their stand. The steep ridges and buttes, divided by abrupt ravines and covered with tangled brush, made this location a natural fortress. A spring with clear water added to the craggy site's desirability. For years it had been a favorite hunting ground for the Hunkpapas and other Lakota tribes. Indeed, the Lakota word for the place meant "the place where they killed the deer."[10]

Sitting Bull, a mature war leader in his early thirties, was there, as was his uncle, the shirt wearer Chief Four Horns, and his nephew White Bull (only fourteen and fighting his first battle). Gall, now twenty-four, also participated in this first great battle against these new enemies.[11] As Sully's army got close enough to see their foes, the soldiers might have noticed Gall because of his massive arms and chest. Given their limited contacts with Lakota warriors, however, they probably would not have known him by name.

Although the southern approach to the wooded Killdeer Mountains presents a beautiful contrast to the miles upon miles of rolling prairie lands in western Dakota, Sully's five-mile march to reach the large Sioux village was a tense and uncomfortable one. Even though it was morning, the day would be hot and dry; it being July 28, the intense summer heat had already thinned the grass and muddied the water holes. Sully's slow march northward resulted in a war of nerves. On every hill along the valley at the south end of the village were clusters of mounted warriors. They looked especially fierce with their painted bodies and lethal weapons.[12]

The Hunkpapas and other Lakotas on Sully's left flank seemed completely confident, having dominated the other tribes in this region for years. On Sully's right flank stood a force of Dakotas and Yanktonais. They were fighting under a Dakota leader named Inkpaduta, or Scarlet Point, a seasoned veteran of Whitestone Hill and other battles with white soldiers. He had selected the defensible campsite at Killdeer, for many Lakota warriors at this battle had never fought soldiers before. His fighting reputation was based on two episodes in his life. In the winter of 1856–1857, prior to the Minnesota Uprising, he led a Dakota band in retaliation to an incident in which ten Indians were killed. On March 8, he led a band that killed thirty white settlers in what became known on the frontier as the Spirit Lake Massacre. At the Battle of Whitestone Hill, he had discovered an escape route for the women and children after the Sioux had been surrounded by Sibley's troops. He also protected the rear flank of the retreating Sioux from army skirmishers as the Indians crossed the Missouri after their defeat at Whitestone Hill. Sitting Bull and Gall could learn much about warfare against white soldiers and militiamen from this seasoned veteran. His composure also had a positive effect. The women, children, and old people from the Indian encampment appeared calm; many stood watching on a high hill, looking very much like spectators at a sporting event.[13]

But Sully's men, numbering about twenty-two hundred that day, were confident too. Finding the ground too difficult to negotiate, many of them dismounted to advance with the skirmishers in front, the horse holders behind, and the wagons and artillery to the rear. A Hunkpapa initiated the inevitable conflict: Lone Dog, whom the Hunkpapas believed had a charmed life, charged down a hill on his war horse. Knowing he was in rifle range of Sully's blue-coated skirmishers, he wanted to get close enough to test the resolve of the invaders. If they fired at him, that would be a signal for the Sioux to fire back. Swinging a large war club and shouting at the advancing skirmishers, Lone Dog became the target of three bullets, which dangerously whizzed past him, prompting him to make a hasty retreat. The battle had begun.[14]

The struggle moved northward along the five-mile route to the village. The Indians fought against these soldiers as they would against their tribal enemies. Most preferred individual combat, either on horseback alone or in small groups. They would charge Sully's men, shower them with arrows, and retreat when enemy bullets came too close.

Sometimes these mounted warriors would join in large groups to launch more coordinated attacks. In one case, a party of approximately one hundred warriors blundered into Sully's rear, where they were able to threaten the army's poorly guarded wagon train and some unattended horses. But the prompt arrival of Sully's artillery effectively scattered them.

As Sully's skirmishers neared the village, the complacency of the Sioux began to diminish. The women, assisted by their children and the older people, began to disassemble the tipis, preparing for a hasty retreat. Many warriors took cover in the thickets and ravines that characterized the Killdeer Mountains. The strategy of the Sioux had definitely shifted to a defensive mode.

Sensing an impending attack, the Dakotas and Yanktonais, under the leadership of Inkpaduta, comprising the Sioux's left flank, mounted a bold counterattack. A battalion of cavalrymen from Minnesota, having joined the skirmishers, responded by charging Inkpaduta's men with drawn sabers. Fighting on horseback with superior weaponry, they crossed a rock-filled ravine and charged up a hill. When the two sides met, there was fierce hand-to-hand combat. Inkpaduta's men gradually retreated for about a mile and a half until they reached the foot of a steep butte. At that point, the cavalrymen dismounted, drew their carbines, and began a volley of intense fire, eventually dispersing their stubborn foes. In the end, Inkpaduta lost twenty-seven warriors, while only two of Sully's men were killed. As testimony to Inkpaduta's qualities as a warrior, the forty-nine-year-old leader accounted, along with his men, for eight of the ten soldiers wounded during the Battle of Killdeer Mountain.[15]

In the meantime, General Sully's left flank clashed with the Lakotas, who were trying to prevent Sully's men from launching a circular movement toward their village. Sully responded with a devastating artillery barrage, which scattered the Indians and resulted in the largest number of casualties in the entire battle. To break the defenses around the village, shells were lobbed into the brush-covered ravines to rout those Lakotas seeking protection from the army's spreading carnage.

Sitting Bull, Gall, and their Hunkpapa warriors fought a good part of the day with these besieged defenders. They must have been keenly aware that their trade muskets and traditional weaponry were no match for Sully's heavy artillery and long-range rifles. This painful lesson was brought home to Sitting Bull when his uncle, the respected Four Horns, was hit in the back with a bullet. Sitting Bull promptly seized the bridle of his uncle's horse and, with his nephew White Bull, led him to a protective thicket where Sitting Bull treated his wound as best he could.[16] Gall, whose frustrations over the battle undoubtedly matched those of Sitting Bull, probably did not join this temporary withdrawal from the fray.

With the right flank of the Sioux defenders being largely pacified, Sibley's cannons bombarded the Indian camp, causing even more confusion. Terrified women gathered what they could for the retreat, while young boys drove the pony herds before them. "Children cried, the dogs were under everybody's feet, mules balked, and pack-horses took fright at the shell-fire or snorted at the drifting smoke behind them."[17]

When Sitting Bull, White Bull, and the ailing Four Horns returned to the battle, they saw that many of the tipis in their encampment had not been dragged to safety. They still stood loaded with next winter's vital supplies, including tons of dried meat and fruit, along with buffalo robes and elk and antelope hides. Bodies of dead comrades strewn around the campsite exceeded in number the women, children, and old people who could not escape.

Sully's troopers counted more than a hundred dead Indians, a high number for a culture that carried the wounded and the dead back to camp regardless of the danger. But the worse was yet to come. Before the soldiers left, they set fire to the tipis, destroying the food, the robes, and all the necessities that would help the Indians get through their next winter.[18] The carnage and loss of life was particularly difficult for Lakota leaders like Gall. In his early twenties at the time, Gall's sense of responsibility for his band, or tiospaye, must have been especially keen.

Sitting Bull and his two comrades followed the traces left by their retreating kin and, according to one Indian source, found most of them ten miles from the original battle site.[19] Although this large Sioux alliance had been defeated, tribal members had covered their retreat with all the skill of a savvy nomadic people. Their ability to lose themselves in the foothills west of the Killdeer Mountains helps explain the lack of an aggressive pursuit by Sully's victorious forces.

In less than a week, the Hunkpapas and their Lakota allies traveled approximately sixty miles, without the tipis and supplies needed for their sustenance. They crossed the Little Missouri River, establishing a camp on the western edge of the Badlands. Inkpaduta, for his part, took his Dakota and Yanktonai followers eastward. He, too, eluded General Sully's troops, who were particularly anxious to catch him, given his role at Whitestone Hill and in the Minnesota Uprising. In the wake of this Indian disaster at Killdeer Mountain, some of the Lakotas were even bitter toward Inkpaduta for involving them in the battle.[20]

Lakota scouts during the aftermath of the Killdeer fights carefully followed the activities of Sully's now elated command. When they ascertained that the soldiers were now heading up the Heart River toward the Yellowstone, one of the Lakota's finest buffalo ranges, they promptly communicated this news to their leaders. The Lakotas, in their new encampment at the edge of the Badlands, decided to pursue the soldiers. Emboldened by more Lakota tribesmen and friendly Northern Cheyennes from the Black Hills, they found and began to harass Sully's men. The difficult terrain, cut by steep gorges and ravines, was an even friendlier environment for the Indians' type of warfare than the terrain at Killdeer Mountain had been. Many of the soldiers were occupied blazing a trail through the almost impossible labyrinth of the Badlands, an area strangely beautiful in the spring but hot, dry, and dusty in early August.

For three days these Lakota warriors launched sporadic attacks on the long line of soldiers winding their way through the Badlands. The arduous trail they were blazing had to be wide enough for the army's supply train and the emigrant wagons of the Montana gold seekers under Sully's protection. This journey was much more of a nightmare for the soldiers than it was for their relentless adversaries. The Indians, counting on the element of surprise, usually attacked at dawn or at dusk. They hoped to stampede the army's livestock herd or kill the road builders in front of the column or the soldiers bringing up the rear. Indian sources for what would later be called the Battle of the Badlands believed that what the Lakotas put Sully's men through during these three days constituted at least a moral victory for the Sioux.

The army's superior firepower kept the Indians at bay and hampered the accuracy of the arrows they shot and bullets they fired. Sully's artillery claimed a host of lives, not unlike the casualties incurred at Killdeer Mountain. Sitting Bull was discouraged; he eventually persuaded his warriors to abandon the pursuit. The veteran war chief had concluded that his people needed more and better long-range weapons to deal with these new enemies. A buffalo hunt was also necessary to restore their diminishing food supply.

Sitting Bull and Gall, traveling with Four Horns's band, withdrew from this noisy and chaotic scene. By noon of August 9, Sully's exhausted troops finally reached more open country, thus leaving behind the dusty and forbidding Badlands. Once the soldiers had climbed out of the tortuous maze of gullies and ravines, the Lakotas gave up the pursuit. Their concerns also shifted. Aware that Sully's men were heading toward the Lakotas' newest campsite, the Lakotas decided to abandon it. Their evacuation happened so fast that when the soldiers reached the deserted encampment late that afternoon, the tribal campfires were still burning throughout much of the three-mile long village. As an indication of the haste of the Lakota flight, the bodies of many dead warriors had been left behind.[21]

The bitterness of the Lakotas over their defeats at the hands of Sully's intruders was illustrated two weeks later at the Battle of the Fisk Wagon Train. In late August, Sitting Bull, Gall, and other Hunkpapa warriors went on a buffalo hunt to restock their sagging meat supply. Along with Four Horns's band, they encountered an emigrant train from the East headed for the Montana mines, comprising of 100 wagons and carrying about 150 people. The Hunkpapas carefully tracked the wagon train, moving across a low divide between the Grand River on the east and the Little Missouri on the west. The large party was under the command of Captain James L. Fisk, who had received permission to open an overland route to the mines. Unfortunately for these hopeful settlers, they had reached the Missouri River after Sully's departure. But an army officer, left behind to build another fort, provided them with an escort of about fifty soldiers.

On September 2, 1864, while the wagon train was climbing a steep creek bank, one wagon turned over, and three emigrants and nine soldiers were left behind to repair it. Before the rest of the wagon train could cover even a mile, Sitting Bull and Gall led approximately a hundred warriors in an attack on those who had remained. When Sitting Bull was wounded in the left hip, Gall, along with other determined warriors, tried to finish the fight. Even though some fifty men from Fisk's wagon train returned to repel the attackers, the Hunkpapas accounted for the lives of six soldiers and two teamsters; three other men were reported missing. Sitting Bull and Gall, who was slowly developing into one of Sitting Bull's chief strategists, had learned another important lesson: surprise can be a key element in fighting a better armed enemy.[22]

The successes of Sully's forces significantly increased feelings of apprehension among the northern Lakotas. Although it stiffened the will of most of them, it created an attitude of despair and pacifism among a few. But this pacifism did not weaken Sitting Bull's or Gall's determination to drive these intruders from the hunting lands of their people. Especially disturbing to them were the forts and posts General Sibley had begun to establish after his victories at Killdeer Mountain and in the Badlands. For example, on August 18, 1864, after he reached the juncture of the Yellowstone and Missouri rivers, he assigned one company, the Thirtieth Wisconsin Infantry, to fortify John Jacob Astor's old trading post at Fort Union. He also fortified Fort Berthold in the more friendly Arikara country about a hundred miles southeast of Fort Union. Eventually, on June 15, 1866, the army would construct Fort Buford, two and one-half miles east of Fort Union, and, on June 14, 1867, Fort Stevenson on the Missouri, twelve miles downriver from Fort Berthold. Even more formidable was Fort Rice, built as early as July 7, 1864. It was located on the west bank of the Missouri River, near the mouth of the Cannonball.[23]

Sully's successful military excursions also resulted in a parley at Fort Sully on October 23, 1864. About two hundred wavering Hunkpapas and Blackfoot Lakotas conferred with Captain John H. Pell, Sully's adjutant general. These Lakotas were represented by Bear's Rib, the son of another Indian peacemaker with the same name, who had been killed by an embittered tribesman in 1862. Lacking his deceased father's forcefulness, Bear's Rib displayed a contriteness not shared by most Hunkpapas. He even apologized for the resistance his people had offered General Sully during his 1864 campaign.[24] But Sitting Bull, Gall, and the more adamant Hunkpapas were not as distressed with Bear's Rib's obvious appeasement as they were with the ambivalence of such leaders as Lone Horn, the Miniconjous' major chief, and Sitting Bull's uncle, Four Horns.

The most prominent of the fence straddlers, however, was Running Antelope, a Hunkpapa shirt wearer like Four Horns, whose autobiographical pictographs reveal his noteworthy skills as a warrior against his people's Arikara foes. The cleavage between Running Antelope and Sitting Bull, who was eleven years his junior, widened as the older warrior began to sound more like an accomodationist.[25]

General Sully's men were ready to exploit these divisions among the Hunkpapas and their allies. When Fort Rice replaced Fort Sully as the main army post in Dakota Territory, Charles A. R. Dimon, the young colonel in charge of the Fort Rice garrison, began to negotiate with Bear's Rib and the Yanktonai peace chief Two Bears. These two allegedly spoke for about 250 Hunkpapas, Blackfoot Lakotas, and Yanktonais. During their negotiations with Colonel Dimon, they set up their tipis on the narrow grassy flat bordering Fort Rice. There, the colonel had promised these Indians needed rations if they would help fend off any Indian attack on Fort Rice.[26]

This schism among the northern Lakotas only strengthened Sitting Bull's and Gall's resolve to drive these new intruders from their hunting lands, and explosive events to the south stiffened their determination. In November 1864 the Colorado militia, under the command of Colonel John M. Chivington, launched a surprise attack on Chief Black Kettle's band of Southern Cheyennes at Sand Creek, killing two hundred Indians, primarily women and children. The outrage caused by the Sand Creek Massacre led to an Indian war in Colorado Territory, which would spread northward to present-day Nebraska and Wyoming. Such southern Lakota tribes as the Brulés, and even the Oglalas, became involved. In a situation similar to the Minnesota Uprising of 1862, the news of this tragic event eventually reached the northern Lakota tribes.

The end of the Civil War further complicated the path of defiance that Lakota leaders like Sitting Bull and Gall had taken. After Appomatox, Union soldiers, whose terms of enlistment had not expired, were sent westward to deal with the Indian problem. Forces under the command of Brigadier General Patrick E. Connor, an officer who had been a successful Indian fighter in the far West, were dispatched in April to cope with the Sioux threat. By late summer, the three armies under Connor, utilizing Pawnee scouts, had failed to encounter any significant Lakota presence.[27]

General Sully also was sent back to Lakota country, traveling up the Missouri River to reinforce the military garrison at Fort Rice. When he arrived on July 13, he located his men on the east bank of the Missouri opposite Fort Rice. Knowing about the large Sioux encampment adjacent to the fort, Sully had himself ferried across the river to Fort Rice. Unfortunately, a young colonel at the fort, wedded to the rules of military correctness, ordered an artillery salute in his honor. The results were chaotic; the specter of Sand Creek had no doubt terrified many of these hang-around-the-fort Indian dwellers.[28] Indeed, 130 lodges of restless Lakotas, who were crossing the low hills adjacent to the Indian encampment toward Fort Rice, turned around in horror after the artillery salute and fled.

One of these newcomers who refused to join Fort Rice's makeshift Indian village because of this surprise military salute was Sitting Bull. The identity of this seasoned war chief was becoming known to the U.S. Army. In fact, General Sully was probably the first government representative to mention Sitting Bull by name, in a report he penned on August 8. In this document, he accused the Hunkpapa leader of traveling from one Lakota camp to another to undercut Sully's efforts to deal peaceably with the Indians seeking refuge at Fort Rice.[29] With Sitting Bull now known by name, it was just a matter of time before Gall and other Sitting Bull war lieutenants would be known by name too.

Sitting Bull followed up his campaign against Sully's peace efforts with an attack on Fort Rice on the morning of July 28. With three hundred followers, Sitting Bull and a party of warriors, splashed in red war paint, honed in on the herds of livestock grazing next to the fort, but the performance of his small war party was disappointing to Sitting Bull. After seizing two horses belonging to the post trader, they withdrew during the height of battle. The reasons for their retreat were understandable. The garrison at Fort Rice, after engaging in hand-to-hand combat, was able to drive the Sioux back with its superior small firearms. The fort's howitzers also effectively lobbed shells at the courageous but outgunned attackers. By noon, when all the Indians had withdrawn, one trooper was dead and four were severely wounded. Because of the ferocity of the Indians' charge, their casualties were undoubtedly higher.[30]

Although Sitting Bull did not achieve any glory in the Battle of Fort Rice, he did disrupt Sully's peace process. A large Lakota village west of Fort Berthold, for instance, interpreted the conflict at Fort Rice as an indication that Sully was no longer interested in peace. As a consequence, it struck camp and moved across the Badlands of the Little Missouri to the Powder River country. Here, to the Lakotas' surprise, they encountered two columns from Connor's frustrated summer expedition, commanded by Colonel Nelson Cole and Lieutenant Colonel Samuel Walker.

These two officers had combined their commands north of the Black Hills and now numbered about two thousand. Despite their numerical strength, Cole and Walker headed a surprisingly dejected fighting force. Undoubtedly, the men of both columns were demoralized by many years of Civil War service; in fact, Walker's men had already rebelled against being sent on this expedition. These tired campaigners had also spent a searingly hot and futile summer looking for Lakota bands in the Powder River country, and their rations were dwindling at an alarming rate.[31]

The two columns first encountered the Lakotas while moving down the Powder River toward the Yellowstone. They soon became victims of a concerted hit-and-run strategy involving approximately three hundred Hunkpapa, Blackfoot Lakota, Miniconjou, and Sans Arc warriors. These tribesmen managed to turn around the tired and discouraged columns of Cole and Walker and send them back upriver. Several army horses were also stolen during this conflict, and a few soldiers became casualties. But the worst setback for Cole and Walker was the storm that occurred on the night of September 2; it broke a severe drought that had long plagued the efforts of their combined column. The relentless wind-driven sleet and falling temperatures of this storm managed to kill 225 of the army's mules and forced its soldiers to abandon most of their supply wagons.[32]

In the aftermath of this storm, the Lakotas, with Gall actively involved, launched attacks from both sides of the Powder River valley. As was the case at Killdeer Mountain, the Badlands, and Fort Rice, the army's superior firepower made the difference. The besieged troops, using repeating Spencer carbines and artillery with great effectiveness, kept the Lakotas at bay. One company of charging cavalrymen, however, did lose four men when daring Lakota warriors infiltrated and broke up their attack. Sitting Bull participated in this Lakota counterattack, which was launched from the east side of the valley, but he did not prove to be a hero in this encounter either. A trio of warriors, including Bull Head, the warrior who thirty-four years later would be involved in the arrest and death of Sitting Bull, did more than the older leaders to blunt this cavalry charge.[33]

Eventually these elated bands of Lakota warriors, feeling victorious, abandoned their pursuit of the Cole-Walker column, but they sent couriers up the Powder River to warn such war leaders as Red Cloud of the Oglalas and Little Wolf of the Northern Cheyennes that a sizeable force was heading their way. The joint forces of Cole and Walker encountered a party of Sioux and Cheyenne Indians in an indecisive battle a day or two later. This battle was followed by another on September 8 with about two thousand Sioux, whose numerical strength was compromised by their usual lack of effective firearms. The Cole-Walker column finally reached a makeshift fort, built on the upper Powder River by General Connor's men in mid-August. Even though Connor and the troops under him had won little glory during the unproductive Powder River Expedition, the new post was named Fort Connor. On November 11, two months later, this minor travesty was corrected; it was renamed Fort Reno.[34]

With the retreat of the Cole-Walker column up the Powder River, the Hunkpapas were given a welcomed respite from their two-year struggle with these persistent blue-coated troops. Thus, the buffalo hunts, the religious ceremonies, and the horse-stealing expeditions that many of them felt were necessary for their survival could now be practiced without fear of danger. Indeed, whether or not the northern Lakota tribes realized it, they had prevented a possible link-up of the wandering armies of Connor and Sully.

The Hunkpapas, along with other northern Lakotas, could again exchange goods more freely with white traders and members of rival tribes. But there was a price to pay. Plains tribes were becoming increasingly dependent on manufactured goods from the East, ranging from glass beads and iron kettles to trade muskets. The infusion of more modern guns was especially welcomed, given the advantage of firepower enjoyed by both Sully and Connor's troops.

By 1865, the still young Gall had become the headman of a tiospaye comprising about a half-dozen lodges. There is some confusion over what this band was called. Sitting Bull's nephew and adopted son White Bull called it the Meat Necklace band. Another Sitting Bull nephew, One Bull, called it the Has Crow band. Because of Gall's growing reputation as a great war leader and a caring headman, the size and composition of his band may have changed during the years of crisis caused by the military threat to their secure hunting grounds. Because of the strongly independent nature of the Lakotas, many warriors who felt overlooked or underestimated would often leave the security of one band for another. Some would even try to organize their own band. Moreover, during times of stress, new people could be attracted to the band of an especially successful and persuasive headman like Gall. The Has Crow band, which may have been a different one or one reorganized from Gall's original band, had 150 members and was, according to One Bull, jointly led by another Hunkpapa headman named Bear Ghost.[35] During the mid-1860s Gall and his followers were particularly interested in trading with their old rivals, the Arikaras. In November or December 1865, a few months after the Cole-Walker column had been driven into Wyoming Territory, Gall's band set up camp south of Fort Berthold, near a village of Arikaras, Mandans, and Hidatsas.[36]

Unknown to Gall, an Indian standing in a nearby Arikara cornfield saw him and his band raising their tipis on a willow bar south of Fort Berthold. The keen observer was an old rival of Gall's, the half-Arikara, half-Hunkpapa Bloody Knife. His bitterness toward Gall went back to those days before his Arikara mother left Gall's Hunkpapa village to return to her people, when Gall and Sitting Bull had made Bloody Knife's life miserable. Moreover, in fall 1862, a war party led by Gall had encountered two of Bloody Knife's brothers in the Badlands and killed, scalped, and mutilated them after an especially bloody skirmish.[37]

Bloody Knife had ingratiated himself with the soldiers stationed at Fort Berthold, where the nomadic Hunkpapas, including Sitting Bull, were occasionally allowed to trade. These soldiers, a legacy of General Sully's 1864 invasion, had remained at the fort on a rotation basis to maintain peace in the area. Bloody Knife had become useful to Fort Berthold's small garrison of Galvanized Yankees, Confederates who preferred duty in the West during the Civil War to a Yankee prison camp. This able and intense Ree warrior had served as a reliable scout for General Sully. He also acted as a trusted messenger, or runner, to help the garrison communicate with other army units in this isolated territory still largely dominated by Lakota bands.

Shortly after Gall's arrival, Bloody Knife arranged a meeting with Captain Adams Bassett of Company C, Fourth U.S. Volunteer Infantry and convinced Bassett that Gall was not a friendly Indian eager for trade but a bloodthirsty warrior ready to make trouble. He insisted that the Hunkpapa warrior had already attacked and killed white men in remote places along the Missouri.[38]

Captain Bassett was convinced and ordered one of his lieutenants to lead a platoon to Gall's new encampment southeast of the fort. If Gall did not surrender at once, they were to kill him. That evening Bloody Knife led the soldiers to Gall's campsite, quietly surrounding the Hunkpapa leader's unguarded lodge. When Gall opened the flap of his tipi to leave, he saw, to his surprise, grim-faced soldiers waiting for him with Bloody Knife. He desperately tried to escape but never had a chance. During a violent struggle, the powerful Gall was bayoneted and knocked to the ground. His nearly helpless body was pierced by two more bayonet thrusts. With blood gushing from both his mouth and nostrils, the lieutenant in command declared him dead.

The vengeful Bloody Knife, however, was not satisfied. He thrust the barrel of his gun, loaded with buckshot, inches away from Gall's bloodied face. But just as he fired, the officer in charge struck the gun's barrel with either his arm or his leg and knocked it aside. The near-lethal shot dug a smoking hole in the ground alongside Gall's face.[39]

Bloody Knife was enraged by the officer's split-second intervention, and heated words were exchanged. But in the army, the man in charge almost always prevails; Gall's badly wounded body was left to die on the frozen ground near his tipi. Bloody Knife angrily returned to his village to enlist recruits to finish the job. Older tribesmen, however, predominated; most of the Arikaras did not want to antagonize the fort's military garrison.

Gall did not die, despite his severe wounds. Members of Gall's band bound his ugly wounds as best they could and promptly struck their tipis. Then they strapped Gall's body on a travois and made a hasty departure. During their fast trip to the main Hunkpapa camp, Gall's favorite wife placed him in the hands of an old woman with a reputation for treating serious gunshot wounds.[40] She began her vital resuscitation to save his life, while he was still being pulled along by the swift-moving travois. Gall's slow recovery was not only due to her patient care, but to his surprisingly strong constitution; few other men could have survived such devastating wounds.

The extent of Gall's injuries were revealed three years later, when he showed his deep scars to the famous Jesuit missionary Pierre-Jean DeSmet. They consisted of two nasty wounds in the body and one in the neck. Although Sitting Bull's warlike protégé would be out of action for months, these wounds did not dampen his fighting spirit. He told the black-robed priest that during the following year, seven white men had paid with their lives for this near-fatal attack.

Although Gall was still a young warrior in his mid-twenties, his reputation was spreading among the widely dispersed bands of Lakotas on the northern plains. One form of testimony involved the Sioux winter count. Winter counts, the closest thing to a written language for the Sioux and for other Plains tribes, were pictographs drawn on buffalo hides or deerskins. They pictured for each year one major event in the life of the Sioux people. The Cranbrook Dakota winter count identified that fateful winter of 1865 as the one in which "Chief Gall [Was] Stuck With Bayonet by Soldier."[41] His war deeds against the Sioux's new enemies had already won him wide recognition. Despite these serious wounds, Gall would continue his daring feats in the not-too-distant future.

CHAPTER FIVE

In Search of a Treaty

After the Civil War, the nation was able to turn its attention toward the western frontier with an intensity that had been largely absent for four years. Certainly gold was one of the great lures, especially in such territories of the Mountain West as Montana. There was also an expanding agricultural frontier to accelerate interest in the Great Plains. To the north, for instance, farmers were moving up the Missouri River and cultivating the virgin soil along its banks. From western Minnesota, other tillers of the soil were moving into the eastern part of Dakota Territory, once the major hunting ground of the embattled Lakotas. Movements were in motion that would eventually threaten Gall's world in profound ways.

Despite earlier military expeditions, such as those led by generals Connor and Sully, policy makers in Washington were leaning toward a peaceful solution to the West's growing Indian problem. The bloody aftermath of Sand Creek was one reason; the wars involving Cheyennes and Arapahoes in Colorado, Kansas, and Nebraska, which started in 1864, had also disrupted Colorado's Pikes Peak gold rush. The disappointing military excursions into Lakota country in the mid-1860s had proved onerous for a war-weary country that had paid much in life and treasure during the Civil War. Major General John Pope, who had been in charge of a major campaign against Plains tribes in 1865, deduced from his military reversals that the nation's frontier army should "return to a purely defensive arrangement for the security of the [West's] overland routes."[1]

With a focus on Pope's recommendation to switch federal Indian policy from a proactive to a reactive one, significant efforts were soon launched. From October 10 to 28, 1865, U.S. peace commissioners under Newton Edmunds, governor of Dakota Territory, who feared that a renewed Sioux war would discourage further settlement of his territory, negotiated with representatives from such northern Sioux tribes as the Hunkpapas, Blackfoot Lakotas, Sans Arcs, Miniconjous, Two Kettles, Lower Brulés, and Upper and Lower Yanktonais. Even a few Oglalas were involved in peace talks, despite their hunting grounds being many miles south and west. From these negotiations, peace treaties were concluded, most of which had similar verbiage. One provision did stand out in these new agreements. The federal government offered to provide annual annuities in return for Indian promises to withdraw from all existing and future white travel routes.[2] Not surprisingly, Sitting Bull, Gall, and most of the other prominent Hunkpapa warriors were not involved in these controversial treaty-making efforts. Indeed, during the previous month, they had helped to drive the Cole-Walker column from one of their favorite buffalo ranges.

Clearing travel routes from Indian interference was a companion strategy to providing defenses "for security of the overland routes." With defense in mind, Colonel Delos B. Sackett of the Inspector General's Department arrived at Fort Union on July 11, 1866. He concluded that this historic fur-trading post, abandoned by the American Fur Company in 1862, was not well situated to become a military fort; he suggested a new site three miles downriver. On the following day, Brevet Lieutenant Colonel William D. Rankin, commander of Company C, Thirteenth Infantry, arrived at Fort Union. Heeding Colonel Sackett's advice, he had a steamer carrying supplies for a military post dock some eight miles downriver, roughly in the same area that Sackett had recommended for a new fort, as had General Sully two years earlier.

On June 15 Rankin began building the fort at the confluence of the Missouri and Yellowstone rivers. It would be named after Major General John Buford, who had died during the Civil War. Although it could be argued that the fort was strictly a defensive military post guarding a possible route to the Montana gold fields, many northern Lakotas felt its construction was not in harmony with the treaties drawn up at Fort Rice. Because of their suspicions, Sitting Bull conducted raids against Fort Buford for four straight days, starting on December 20, 1866. On the morning of the fourth day, Lakota warriors even gained control of the fort's new icehouse and sawmill before Rankin's troops used their two twelve pounders to drive them out.[3] Six months later another proclaimed defensive post, Fort Stevenson, was established on June 14, 1866, on the left bank of the Missouri, twelve miles below Fort Berthold. Many northern Lakota warriors regarded this new post as a provocation too.[4] Given its nearness to Fort Berthold, where Gall and his band often traded and where he was almost fatally wounded, Gall must have been one of them.

Although a possible northern route through Dakota Territory to the Montana gold fields was of great interest to many settlers from the upper Missouri and Mississippi rivers, a new route was gaining favor with impatient gold seekers. It was inspired by John M. Bozeman, who blazed a new trail during the mid-1860s from the South Platte River, northward along Wyoming's Bighorn Mountains, to the Montana gold diggings. Responding to this gold fever, a presidential commission, headed by E. B. Taylor, arrived at Fort Laramie on May 30, 1866. Five days later, the commissioners began a persuasive effort to achieve a lasting peace among the southern Lakota tribes and their allies. Key to this peace offensive was a proposal to allow the federal government to "make and use through their country such roads as may be deemed necessary for public service and for emigrants to mining districts of the West."[5] Among the Indian participants was the Oglala war leader Red Cloud, who appeared to be open minded about these peace overtures, and the Brulé leader Spotted Tail, who was even more willing to cooperate.

The Fort Laramie peace conference went along smoothly until Colonel Henry B. Carrington arrived on June 13 from Fort Kearny on the Platte. He had orders to develop the Bozeman Trail into a major thoroughfare for the eager argonauts headed for Montana. His orders also included establishing forts along the trail to protect the anxious gold seekers. When Red Cloud learned that Carrington's orders were being implemented even before any final agreement had been reached between the government and the Indians, he bolted the conference. In anger, even the great peace chief Old-Man-Afraid-of-His-Horse went with him.

Red Cloud's abrupt departure did not deter Carrington's plans. He marched northward with a force of seven hundred men, building and garrisoning such "defensive" posts as Fort Reno, Fort Phil Kearny, and Fort C. F. Smith along the way.[6] But Red Cloud was unwilling to accept this encroachment on the rich hunting lands that the Lakotas had wrested from the Crows. For six months the Lakotas and the Northern Cheyennes waged guerrilla warfare against these three army posts. They also made travel on the Bozeman Trail almost impossible.

These attacks only strengthened the army's resolve to secure the trail as a major thoroughfare to the gold fields. Captain William Judd Fetterman, serving under Colonel Carrington at Fort Phil Kearny, retaliated against one Indian attack, an assault by Crazy Horse and other warriors on a wood-supply train on December 21, 1866, the day after Sitting Bull's initial assault on Fort Buford. But the daring captain was caught in a deadly ambush that cost him his life and the lives of his entire command. The army had to acknowledge the loss of approximately eighty men in what is now called the Fetterman Fight. Although for years this battle was dubbed the Fetterman Massacre, the Indians called it the Fight of One Hundred. They insisted that the lives of twenty soldiers were not counted as victims in this bloody ambush.[7]

By the year 1867, the war in the Powder River country, called Red Cloud's War by many, had largely eclipsed the efforts of Sitting Bull to force the closure of Fort Buford. Nevertheless, throughout most of 1867, Fort Buford was under a constant state of siege. Gall's involvement in this siege, if any, is difficult to ascertain. Surely his activities throughout much of 1866 were limited by his near-fatal wounds at the hands of Bloody Knife and his allies in December 1865. Yet some historians have placed him at the siege of Fort Buford and the Fetterman Fight at about the same time, and Gall insisted in later years that he had been a participant in Red Cloud's War.[8]

The problem in tracing Gall's movements at this time is the independence he had gained by his mid-twenties. Although one of Sitting Bull's chief war lieutenants, Gall was highly valued by the people of his band, who had spirited him away after his near-death encounter in 1865 near Fort Berthold. He was also more inclined than Sitting Bull to trade at the more friendly forts and agencies, especially when buffalo hunting on the open plains was difficult because of wintry weather or extended droughts. During the 1870s some of his contemporaries considered him to be as much an agency Indian as a hunter and a warrior. In good times, when game was plentiful, he preferred the plains, but in bad times, especially after most of the Lakotas had agreed to abide by the 1868 Treaty of Fort Laramie, he preferred the agency, where an issue of beef was readily available to him and his band members.[9] Add these factors to his exceptional physical prowess and it seems most probable that this sturdy warrior had recovered enough from his wounds to join Sitting Bull at the Fort Buford siege in 1867 after his reported participation in Red Cloud's War in December 1866.

The activities of the Hunkpapas continued to be overshadowed by the much larger conflict in the Powder River country. Indeed, the Fetterman Fight had aroused a great deal of ire against the Sioux throughout the nation. Calls for decisive action found the U.S. Army most receptive; the Civil War hero Lieutenant General William Tecumseh Sherman, now commander of the Military Division of the Mississippi, called for a major Indian campaign. He wanted to punish Red Cloud's followers "with vindictive earnestness, until at least ten Indians . . . [were] killed for each white life lost." In response to the disastrous defeat of Captain Fetterman and his command, Colonel Carrington was replaced as commander of the recently created Mountain District by Colonel Henry W. Wessells, who was already on his way to Fort Phil Kearny with fresh troops.

Members of Congress were also shocked by Fetterman's demise; in February 1867, Congress appointed a commission, which included generals J. B. Sanborn and Alfred Sully. Operating under the Department of the Interior, the Sanborn-Sully Commission, as it was called because of the prominence of these two men, visited Fort Laramie in a vain attempt to lure Red Cloud back to the fort for peace talks.[10]

Red Cloud and his coalition of tribes, however, refused to show any flexibility regarding the use of the Bozeman Trail. The Oglala chief also objected to the existence of the three forts built along this trail. On August 1, 1867, a band of five hundred Cheyennes and Arapahoes attacked a haying party three miles northeast of Fort C. F. Smith in what became known as the Hayfield Fight. One day later, a much larger party of Lakota warriors, led by Red Cloud, High Back Bone, and Crazy Horse, attacked a wood-cutting party five miles north of Fort Phil Kearny in what became known as the Wagon Box Fight. In both cases the Indian attackers were repulsed because the army had recently acquired the Model 1866 Springfield breechloader. This weapon gave the soldiers much more efficient firepower than the old muzzle loader had.[11] Although the army probably exaggerated the number of Indian casualties, they were considerably higher than what the Indians regarded as tolerable. Those at the Wagon Box Fight were especially high. The army's superior firepower became the decisive factor in this battle with the

Sioux just as it had at Killdeer Mountain, where Sitting Bull, Gall, and other tribesmen had found their trade muskets almost ineffective against the army's modern weaponry.

Ironically, one month before these two Indian setbacks, the U.S. Congress had decided to settle the Sioux question through peaceful rather than military means. Building a transcontinental railroad and reconstructing the vanquished South were considered to be more important national priorities than a major war against the Lakotas and their allies. Consequently, on July 20, 1867, Congress created the Indian Peace Commission. Although Red Cloud's stubborn resistance was the key reason for this legislation, the new commission was authorized not only to seek peace with the Sioux, but to negotiate with the other tribes throughout the Great Plains.

The Indian Peace Commission, which was headed by Senator John B. Henderson of Missouri, represented sharply opposing views on how to handle the Plains tribes. General Sherman, one of three army officers on the commission, led the hardliners, while Nathaniel G. Taylor, a large, bewigged man with contrary views, led the more flexible civilian members. One of Taylor's ardent supporters was Samuel T. Tappen, a former Colorado militiaman who had investigated the controversial Sand Creek Massacre. This divided, but resolute, peace commission traveled to the North Platte first to meet the Brulé leader Spotted Tail, who had already accepted the 1866 draft of the Fort Laramie Treaty, but it eventually reversed itself and decided to focus its initial efforts on the southern tribes instead. In mid-October 1867, the Indian Peace Commission negotiated treaties with such tribes as the Comanches, Southern Cheyennes, Arapahoes, Kiowas, and Kiowa Apaches. These patient negotiations occurred along Medicine Lodge Creek, some seventy miles south of Fort Larned, Kansas.[12]

Elated by its successes with the southern Plains tribes, the Indian Peace Commission moved north toward Fort Laramie, where it hoped to do as well with the northern tribes. But to their disappointment, when the commissioners arrived at the fort, only a few friendly Crows were there to greet them. Red Cloud, the obvious key to peace in the north, was not there. It was reported to the commission that he would not make peace until forts Phil Kearny and C. F. Smith were closed. Because of Washington's higher priorities, such as Southern Reconstruction and protection for the nation's transcontinentals, the federal government was ready to listen to Red Cloud's strong views. On March 2, 1868, General Ulysses S. Grant wrote Sherman, telling him to close these controversial forts along the Bozeman. On July 29 Fort C. F. Smith was abandoned, and on the following day Red Cloud and his warriors swept down from the nearby mountains and set fire to the fort. A few days later the detested Fort Phil Kearny, which also had been evacuated, was torched as well.

Two months before the destruction of these forts, some successes had been achieved by peace commission members J. B. Sanborn and retired General William S. Harney, who had stayed behind at Fort Laramie to negotiate some kind of peace treaty. They were able to reach favorable agreements with the Crows and with such strong Lakota allies as the Northern Cheyennes and Arapahoes. Moreover, on May 25 and 26, they even achieved an accommodation with a number of suspicious Oglalas, Miniconjous, and Yanktonais; indeed, these tribesmen were willing to put their mark on what would become the 1868 Treaty of Fort Laramie. When the two commissioners finally departed for the East, they left the treaty with the commandant at Fort Laramie. He was instructed to get the approval of the still absent Red Cloud whenever possible. On November 7, Red Cloud, during a visit to the fort, agreed to the treaty after a tumultuous three-day meeting.[13] Thus, the powerful Lakota chief, who had already made the federal government back down in a major Indian war, had now secured a favorable peace treaty for his people.

The treaty negotiated at Fort Laramie in 1868 met many of Red Cloud's insistent demands. It called for the closure of the Bozeman Trail and the forts built to protect it. It set aside an immense tract of land for the Sioux, extending from the Missouri River westward along the forty-sixth parallel to the Bighorn Mountains and southeastward to the Dakota-Nebraska border. The eastern portion, which included the western part of present-day South Dakota, including the Black Hills, was designated as a reservation for the Lakotas; indeed, this large tract of land would become known as the Great Sioux Reservation. Undoubtedly, this provision was the most traumatic for the Lakotas, because it would ultimately change the free and nomadic life of the seven Lakota tribes. Hunkpapa leaders such as Gall and Sitting Bull were particularly concerned about this treaty for that reason. This difficult transition for the Lakotas would be facilitated by the establishment of Indian agencies, the issuance of clothing and food rations for thirty years, and an educational system that would teach them farming rather than hunting as a way of life.

The western portion of this new Sioux domain, which included the Powder River country, was designated as unceded Indian territory. There, those Indians who insisted upon following the buffalo rather than living under a paternalistic system of government could continue their traditional way of life. But government negotiators were confident that the extinction of the buffalo would soon eliminate this issue altogether, and that all Lakotas would eventually live on the Great Sioux Reservation. Another favorable article in the treaty granted the southern Lakota tribes hunting rights along the Republican River and above the North Platte as "long as the buffalo may range thereon in such numbers as to justify the chase."

The two previous articles were particularly important to Red Cloud's Oglalas and Spotted Tail's Brulés. But to the northern Lakota tribes, such as the Hunkpapas, only the northern fringe of this vast unceded area set aside for the Sioux was regarded as an indisputable hunting ground. The unprotected buffalo ranges of eastern Montana, largely wrested from the Crows in recent years, and the buffalo ranges of western North Dakota were of much greater concern to these tribes. Sitting Bull's attacks on Fort Buford were just one indication of how important the upper Great Plains country was to the Hunkpapas and their northern allies.[14]

About the same time these vital negotiations at Fort Laramie were taking place, the federal government began a peace offensive at Fort Rice to win over the northern Lakotas. Officials in the Indian Office picked the widely admired Jesuit missionary Pierre-Jean DeSmet to be the chief negotiator. DeSmet, or Black Robe as he was known among the Sioux, had gained great respect for the righteousness of his faith and the sincere gentleness he had already shown the Indians.[15] Father DeSmet's dedication to peace among the whites and Indians was also well known.

The concept of peace, at least among the Lakotas, was not an unfamiliar one. It had been brought to them by White Buffalo Calf Woman, who according to the Lakota religion had appeared to the Sioux people dressed in white buckskins, enhancing an already radiant beauty. She presented herself to an Indian council at one of the Lakota villages, carrying a sacred bundle. This bundle contained a round stone and what would later be known as the sacred calf pipe. Carved on the bowl of this pipe was a buffalo calf, which stood for all four-legged creatures. The pipe's wooden stem represented all growing things. Those who smoked this sacred pipe, she proclaimed, could achieve a union with all people and with all things in the universe. Thus, better communications could be established with Wakan Tanka, the Great Mystery.

Although White Buffalo Calf Woman emphasized peace as Father DeSmet did, it was peace among all Lakotas, not necessarily among all their enemies. At the end of her meeting with this village council, she sank to the ground three times before disappearing. She arose the first time as a red and brown buffalo calf, the second time as a white buffalo calf, and the third time as a black buffalo. After assuming this last image and before she vanished, White Buffalo Calf Woman bowed in each of the four directions of the Lakota universe. From that day forward, this practice would become sacred to all Lakotas.

The emphasis on peace inspired by White Buffalo Calf Woman harmonized surprisingly well with DeSmet's message of peace. Indeed, when he finally encountered the northern Lakotas, his banner, with its image of the Virgin Mary circled by golden stars, sparked the same kind of feelings for peace that White Buffalo Calf Woman had communicated.[16] Father DeSmet launched his much-anticipated peace mission at Fort Rice, where in 1868, he met such friendly Lakota chiefs as Running Antelope, Two Bears, and Bear's Rib.[17]

Also present at the Fort Rice meeting was the trader Charles E. Galpin and his Sioux wife, Matilda or Eagle Woman; she being half Hunkpapa and half Two Kettle made Galpin an effective intermediary in dealing with the northern Lakota tribes.[18] In fact, during the previous year, Galpin and his wife had contacted many of the tribal leaders from the upper Missouri, paving the way for Father DeSmet's mission.

Upon the Jesuit missionary's arrival at Fort Rice, the peace chiefs gathered there warned him about the dangers he faced traveling into the Yellowstone country to deal with angry tribesmen. Nevertheless, when Father DeSmet organized his expedition for this purpose, Running Antelope, a Lakota shirt wearer, and Two Bears and Bear's Rib were among some eighty Lakotas and Yanktonais who accompanied him. Little Dog, Sitting Crow, Log, and Blue Thunder were also part of the group that accompanied DeSmet, who seemed oblivious to the hazards he might encounter. Galpin and his wife, of course, were present, too, their service as interpreters being essential.

Awaiting Father DeSmet's peace mission was a Hunkpapa village of about six hundred lodges, situated on the south bank of the Yellowstone River, several miles above the mouth of the Powder.[19] The village comprised several bands and included such war leaders as Sitting Bull and Gall. Sitting Bull's uncle, the shirt wearer Four Horns, along with the respected Black Moon, allegedly related to Gall, were present. Also at the village were leaders such as No Neck, Red Horn, and White Gut. DeSmet's entourage had good reason to be apprehensive as it approached this fateful rendezvous. Not all the Hunkpapa leaders respected or trusted Father DeSmet. White Gut, for instance, had threatened to kill the priest. He regarded DeSmet as just another white man who had come to cheat the Hunkpapas. Moreover, White Gut deeply resented Blue Thunder, who had been chosen to drive Father DeSmet's carriage; Blue Thunder, a Yanktonai warrior, had once served as an army scout against White Gut's people.[20]

Another source of uneasiness for Father DeSmet's entourage was Sitting Bull himself. He had recently returned from the northeast after leading widespread attacks on military posts not far from the Canadian border. He hit Fort Buford again in May 1868, and the results there were not pleasant to contemplate; two civilian laborers found in the fort's hay-field had been killed by twenty-seven barbed arrows embedded in their mutilated bodies. After this attack, Sitting Bull's war party headed down the Missouri toward Fort Stevenson. When his warriors found this fort too well garrisoned, they traveled eastward to Fort Totten, near Devils Lake, killing two mail riders encountered along the way.

But Sitting Bull did respect Father DeSmet as a man of peace. Thus, to guarantee the priest's security, Sitting Bull's uncle Four Horns dispatched twenty akicitas to accompany the four hundred warriors sent to greet DeSmet and escort him safely to the Hunkpapa village. Leading the procession, colorfully dressed and wearing war paint, were Sitting Bull, Gall, and the two most senior leaders from the Hunkpapa encampment, Four Horns and Black Moon. These four welcomed Father DeSmet with warm handshakes and rode closely alongside him all the way back to the village. Their conspicuous presence at DeSmet's side was a clear indication that the priest was under their protection. Gall's inclusion as one of these four guardians is a convincing sign of the growing prestige enjoyed by this young headman, who was two years shy of age thirty. In fact, when they reached the encampment, they put DeSmet's baggage into Sitting Bull's guarded tipi, where the courageous priest was to stay.

On the following day, June 20, 1868, a peace conference was held under a massive canopy made from ten tipis. Father DeSmet and the

Galpins sat in the center of this new conference site, under the banner of the Virgin Mary. Facing them were Four Horns and Black Moon, and opposite them sat Sitting Bull, Gane, No Neck, and White Gut. On the back fringe of this large gathering were the women, children, and old people. Watching over the entire scene were the alert akicitas.[21]

Four Horns convened the conference by lighting the peace pipe. He extended its bowl toward the earth and the sky and then toward the four sacred directions revealed by White Buffalo Calf Woman. Father DeSmet spoke first. He urged his listeners to come to Fort Rice and meet the Great Father's commissioners; these men had brought with them the 1868 Fort Laramie Treaty for the Lakotas to sign. He "beseeched" the Lakotas to bury their bitterness toward whites and "accept the hand of peace" extended to them. The priest also declared that he would leave his banner of the Virgin Mary with them as "a token of . . . [his] sincerity and good wisdom for the welfare of the Sioux Nation."[22]

Black Moon was the first of the Hunkpapa tribesmen to respond to Black Robe's sincere pleas for peace. He chided the whites for the herds of buffalo they had slaughtered, and condemned them for the detested forts they had built. An almost apologetic Sitting Bull spoke next, admitting that for four years he had led raids against white intruders. After his effort to conciliate Father DeSmet, he sat down only to rise again in a show of intense determination. The Hunkpapas had no intention of selling any of the hunting grounds used by them and their allies, he insisted. Moreover, all military forts in their northern territories must be abandoned.[23]

It was obvious that neither Sitting Bull nor Four Horns and Black Moon were ready to reach any meaningful accord over possible peace terms. A trip to Fort Rice by this trio was simply not a practical alternative. Largely out of respect for Father DeSmet, however, these leaders agreed to send a delegation of lesser chiefs, headed by Gall and Bull Owl, to meet the peace commissioners at Fort Rice.

On July 2 the much-anticipated meeting with the Indian Peace Commission convened at Fort Rice. Because the commission's members had divided up their responsibilities so that treaties with other Plains tribes could be negotiated at the same time, only three commissioners were present. One was Brigadier General Alfred H. Terry, commander of the Department of Dakota. Another was the retired General Harney. And the third was Sanborn, who, because of previous negotiations with the Lakotas, acted as spokesman for the three.

The conference, which was attended primarily by Hunkpapas, Blackfoot Lakotas, and Yanktonais, opened with a reading of the treaty. This was a wise procedure, because it gave Sanborn an opportunity to persuade the Lakotas to accept the Fort Laramie Treaty as many of their southern kinfolk had done. Sanborn warned the Indian delegates that their days of hunting were numbered; agriculture would now be their future. He also told them quite candidly that the forts and steamboats on the Missouri River would not be removed. They were necessary instruments for the army to protect all Indians from the continuing white invasion of their lands.[24]

The Indians that gathered at Fort Rice were not necessarily representative of those upper Missouri tribes most reluctant to give up their free and nomadic lifestyle. In truth, some, such as the Hunkpapa shirt wearer Running Antelope, were leaning toward peace in the hopes that a fair compromise could be achieved. Others were more inclined to make the transition from a buffalo hunter to a small farmer because of the subsidies promised in the new treaty. This was the stance taken by Bear's Rib the younger, who was no doubt influenced by his late father's long and amicable relationship with whites. Bear's Rib did not mince words in expressing his pro-treaty bias. "I want everything the whites have got, and, if I cannot get it, I will not stay here." It soon became obvious, however, that Bear's Rib's views were not that representative. In fact, of the twenty chiefs scheduled to speak in behalf of the Lakota and Yanktonai delegates, Bear's Rib was a lowly fourteenth in order of appearance.[25]

Gall was arguably the most important tribal representative at the Fort Rice conference; his selection as the first Indian speaker is persuasive testimony of that. His prominence was largely due to his effectiveness as a Hunkpapa war leader and his close relationship to Sitting Bull, who was starting to achieve the kind of prominence Red Cloud enjoyed in the south. Thus, Sitting Bull's choice of Gall to represent him gave this independent-minded war lieutenant new recognition. Gall's hostility to whites pleased hardliners at the conference. The near-fatal attack by soldiers at Fort Berthold in 1865 had aroused his intense ire; he had already taken seven white scalps in his quest for vengeance.[26] Yet Gall made many more trading visits to the forts and agencies in the region than Sitting Bull ever did. But some argued that Gall's more frequent contacts with whites better prepared him to negotiate with these potential adversaries on more even terms.[27]

In many ways Gall did not disappoint his supporters. His oration as the lead Indian speaker was the most dramatic event of this carefully orchestrated conference. The peace commissioners had expected him and the other delegates to sign the treaty with perhaps a few cursory remarks. Instead the muscular war chief, openly displaying the scars from his white-inflicted wounds for all to see, gave a forceful talk with little hint of compromise. "There is one thing I do not like. The whites ruin our country," he declared. "If we make peace, the military posts on the Missouri River must be removed and the steamboats stopped from coming here." He also underscored both his determination and independence. "You fought me and I had to fight back: I am a soldier. The annuities you speak of we don't want. Our intention is to take no present."

The young war chief, looking majestic and very much in his prime, also questioned the sincerity of the commissioner's pleas for peace. "If we make peace, you will not hold it. We told the good father [DeSmet] who has been to our camp that we did not like these things. I have been sent here by my people to see and hear what you have to say. My people told me to get powder and ball, and I want that." Gall also insisted that his people had been unfairly accused of causing much of the conflict. "We are blamed for many things. I have been stabbed. If you want to make peace with me, you must remove this post this year and stop the steamboats," he reiterated. The Hunkpapa war leader concluded his controversial remarks with a request for twenty kegs of powder. This request was accompanied by a threat to persuade all friendly Indians gathered at the fort and at the various Indian agencies to break all ties with their white friends.[28]

Emboldened by Gall's aggressive approach, Bull Owl, Gall's fellow Hunkpapa hardliner, also called for the removal of all forts and steamboats. He insisted that this was necessary "so that the buffalo will come back." Even the more accommodating Hunkpapa leader Running Antelope would not put his mark on the Fort Laramie Treaty without at least a minor qualification. After flattering the especially militant peace commissioner General Harney, he made one innocuous request: "We want Galpin to stay in this country and be our trader."[29]

Following the remarks of the twenty Indian speakers at the conference, Gall, despite his tough talk, put his favorable mark on the treaty. Moreover, at the conference he chose not use his more familiar name, Gall, or Pizi. Rather he chose the name he liked best: The-Man-That-Goes-in-the-

Middle. This designation would be translated today as "front and center," a position Gall greatly favored during the heat of battle.[30] Thus, five months before Red Cloud approved the Fort Laramie Treaty, Sitting Bull's reluctant war lieutenant had given his unexpected endorsement.[31]

Gall's surprise turnabout was the first of several controversial decisions subjecting him to the charge of opportunism. His later break with Sitting Bull and his close cooperation with reservation officials at Standing Rock during the late nineteenth century are other examples. But Gall's decision was not that unusual. He and the other Indian delegates at Fort Rice were feasted and given presents as an inducement to sign. Moreover, gift giving was a historically common federal practice for winning agreements from tribal leaders.

There is also the probability that he and the other Indian leaders did not fully understand the treaty's maze of complicated articles and provisions. Even a few federal officials were confused by some of them. The Fort Laramie Treaty served Red Cloud's people better than Gall's. The call for the removal of forts on the Bozeman Trail and the creation of an unceded Indian territory in eastern Wyoming was most welcomed by the Oglalas. The insistent demands of the Hunkpapas and their allies for the removal of forts along the Missouri River and the cessation of steamboat travel on it, however, were all but ignored. Yet Gall, who may have believed that the treaty did provide for the removal of Missouri forts, did agree to it.

Perhaps the best reason for Gall's turnabout was his lack of understanding regarding the nature and purpose of a treaty. Little did he know that by signing this document he had committed himself to many of its controversial provisions. Because the treaty allowed for railroad travel through Indian lands, for instance, the government could argue that it had the right to push a transcontinental railroad through the northern plains. If the Lakotas resisted, they, as treaty violators, could be punished.[32] Nor did Sitting Bull realize that he, too, was now committed by this treaty because of Gall's mark of acceptance. Yet Sitting Bull's response to the more incensed critics of Gall's action showed little alarm. Joking about his protégé's penchant to do anything for a "square meal," he defended Gall's willingness to accept presents customarily given to Indians by federal authorities during treaty negotiations.[33]

When Gall and his Indian delegation left Fort Rice, there were at least two opposing perceptions of what had been done at this brief conference. Certainly the peace commissioners must have felt that their search for a treaty had finally borne fruit. Those Indians closest to Sitting Bull, however, probably came to a far different conclusion. Putting their mark of acceptance on the treaty had little significance to them. It was just part of some strange ritual these impatient federal negotiators insisted they go through before they receive their coveted presents. Only the passage of time would make them realize how significant this treaty-making process could become.

CHAPTER SIX

Threats along the Yellowstone

The world Gall returned to after the Fort Rice conference was little changed. The Lakotas were still badly divided over what kind of accommodation they were willing to make with the advancing tide of white settlement, regardless of the new treaty. In time most members of the southern Lakota tribes, such as the Oglalas and the Brulés, would become treaty Indians; Red Cloud's tardy approval of the treaty document in early November 1868 would hasten this process.

But the tribes of the upper Missouri were much more divided. In essence, the seven Lakota tribes were faced with three choices: they could surrender and settle on the Great Sioux Reservation; they could follow the buffalo herds in the unceded Indian territory (spending the winter months eating beef rations on a reservation); or they could reject the first two options and live as far from the encroaching white settlements as possible. According to Robert M. Utley, about a third of the total Lakota population chose this latter option and became nontreaty Indians. Not surprisingly, the Hunkpapas had the largest number of such holdouts proportionately. Perhaps 50 percent or more of them chose to follow Sitting Bull, Gall, and other tribal leaders in their decision to go their own way.[1]

To underscore the independent course taken by most of his people, Sitting Bull, less than two months after Gall had signed the Fort Laramie Treaty, led some 150 warriors in a major attack on Fort Buford. His party ran off 250 beeves from the garrison's herd and killed or wounded six soldiers.[2] During the following year, 1869, Sitting Bull and his followers waged an almost continual guerrilla war against those manning Fort Buford. Department of Dakota commander Major General Winfield S. Hancock had to admit that this fort had become exceedingly "offensive to the hostile Sioux."[3] The tumultuous year ended with an attack by a band of Dakotas on a wagon train making its way from Fort Benton to Fort Buford. This Indian party was led by the resolute Inkpaduta, who had played such a major role in the Battle of Killdeer Mountain five years earlier.[4]

The impasse in Indian-white relations caused by these nontreaty Indians aroused great anxiety on both sides. The army, along with the federal authorities, began to label Lakota tribes, such as the Hunkpapas, Miniconjous, and Sans Arcs, as "northern Indians"; this term clearly implied that they were regarded as "wild" or "hostile" foes. The Sioux tribes from the upper Missouri remained fearful of such army encroachments as the forts built along the rivers and the increased military steamboat travel to connect them. This complaint had been raised often by Gall and the other Sioux delegates at the Fort Rice conference. There was also that long-range threat, still not fully appreciated by northern tribes, of the advancing agricultural frontier. It was gradually making its way up the Missouri River, north of Yankton, South Dakota.

The Lakotas faced another problem: there was a serious division within their own ranks. Hunkpapa hardliners, for instance, were keenly aware of the differing attitudes toward the reservation system embraced by such important tribal peacemakers as Bear's Rib and Running Antelope. A unity of purpose soon became the goal of many nontreaty Hunkpapas, who felt that the free and nomadic life they cherished was in grave danger.

One leader who felt especially strong about this issue was Sitting Bull's much-admired uncle Four Horns. The tall Hunkpapa chief was probably the only shirt wearer, among the tribe's four shirt wearers, who still had the prestige to unify most tribal members under one cause. The other three had failed to live up to the exalted status ordinarily enjoyed by a shirt wearer. Loud-Voiced Hawk had stabbed another Hunkpapa in a fight; Red Horn had stolen two wives from a fellow warrior; and Running Antelope, the shirt wearer most willing to cooperate with the federal government, had eloped with another man's wife.[5] Such misdeeds could not be easily overlooked if they involved a shirt wearer; even the illustrious Crazy Horse had lost his status as an Oglala shirt wearer for running off with another man's wife.[6]

But Four Horns was not a rash person; indeed, his leadership as a Hunkpapa chief, going back to 1851, had demonstrated his reassuring steadiness. Yet because of the deteriorating situation facing his tribe in the late 1860s, he was considering a revolutionary idea: one supreme chief to represent all those Lakotas and their allies committed to the traditional Plains Indian way of life. Endowing one leader with such power ran contrary to longstanding Sioux practice; when the federal government had suggested it at the 1851 Fort Laramie conference, along the North Platte, it had been roundly criticized and rejected.[7] But times were much more perilous now, and Four Horns felt he had the right man for such a responsibility in his nephew Sitting Bull.

Sitting Bull was thirty-eight years old when Four Horns began to agitate for the selection of a supreme chief. The shirt wearer's persuasive efforts reached their climax when five big Indian encampments gathered for a unity conference along Rosebud Creek, probably in 1869. These camps included such tribespeople as the Hunkpapas, Sans Arcs, Miniconjous, those Oglalas loyal to Crazy Horse, and some like-minded Northern Cheyennes and Arapahoes. Also represented, but in smaller numbers, were Blackfoot Lakotas (historically very close to the Hunkpapas), Two Kettles, and Yanktonais. A special lodge of tipi covers stretched on a large framework of poles, not unlike that constructed for the meeting with Father DeSmet, was to serve as the meeting place. The purpose of this rendezvous, if Four Horns had his way, was to make Sitting Bull the head chief of all nontreaty Indians.[8]

Although Sitting Bull was past his prime as a warrior, his persistent attacks on Fort Buford at the mouth of the Yellowstone had kept his name alive among the younger warriors. These free-spirited young men knew, almost instinctively, that Sitting Bull would be the most trustworthy one they could choose. He could best maintain the generations-old system that included counting coups, participating in hunting parties, and stealing Indian ponies from rival tribes. But older men, such as Four Horns and the other three Hunkpapa shirt wearers, spearheaded Sitting Bull's selection. Also participating were the war chiefs and warrior societies; all of them seemed to know what was at stake at this gathering on the banks of the Rosebud.

The most important phase of this conference was launched when the four Hunkpapa shirt wearers carried a buffalo robe to Sitting Bull's tipi. There the veteran warrior-chief was placed in the center of the robe,

each shirt wearer grabbing one of the four corners. They carried Sitting
Bull to a special lodge constructed for what would be the inaugural ceremony for the new supreme chief. Four Horns's nephew was given a
place of honor among the circle of Indian leaders that crowded into the
spacious lodge. A long pipe was lighted and extended downward toward
the earth and upward toward the sun and finally in the four traditional
directions. It was presented to Sitting Bull after every council member
had taken a puff and offered a prayer to Wakan Tanka.[9]

After this initial ceremony, a number of speeches were made amid the
rendering of songs familiar to most present. Four Horns, who acted as
the master of ceremonies, praised Sitting Bull's bravery in battle, pledging
in behalf of all conference participants total cooperation with the new
leader. "When you say, 'fight,' we shall fight: when you say 'make peace,'
we shall make peace."[10]

In another strategic stroke, the circle of chiefs, warriors, and other
tribal leaders made Crazy Horse second in command. As this group was
acting in complete defiance of the treaty Indians, such as the Oglala chief
Red Cloud and the Brulé chief Spotted Tail (who was Crazy Horse's
uncle), this elevation of Crazy Horse might attract a number of southern Lakotas to the cause. Moreover, Crazy Horse, who was Sitting Bull's
junior by seven years, was as committed to this bold course as any of the
participants, including Sitting Bull himself.

When the ceremony ended, Sitting Bull was presented with a flintlock
and a bow with ten arrows. He also received an impressive war bonnet,
with ermine pendants and a swagger crown with black and white eagle
plumes, which were matched by a trailing double tail of eagle feathers long
enough to drag on the ground. This elaborate headgear was in sharp contrast to the two modest eagle feathers Sitting Bull had been wearing, one
of which was red to represent the battle wounds that now caused the veteran warrior to limp. Certainly as important as any of the gifts he received
was a handsome white horse. Gall, who with Crow King had been made
a war chief prior to the ceremony, and Running Antelope lifted the newly
inaugurated chief into his saddle as part of the gathering's overall pomp. A
long parade through the nontreaty camps ended the ceremonies. At the
head of the column were Sitting Bull and his intimates. Behind them,
dressed in their finest regalia, were numbers of still important warrior societies such as the Crow Diviners, Fox Soldiers, Badgers, and Mandans. Of
course, the Strong Hearts, through which Sitting Bull and Gall had worked
together in such intimacy, were also present.[11]

The importance of this Rosebud meeting would be difficult to over-estimate. It meant that the Lakotas and their allies would strongly contest the presence of all white intruders on the northern plains. It was, in many ways, a precursor to the fateful Battle of the Little Bighorn, which occurred seven years later. The meeting's leaders, particularly Sitting Bull, Crazy Horse, and Gall, to name only three, would play key roles in the demise of Custer's column along the banks of the Greasy Grass.[12]

Furthermore, the participants were part of an exclusively Indian effort; unlike the peace negotiations that led to the Treaty of Fort Laramie, whites were not involved. Indeed, the army and the settlers could be viewed as the targets of this bold move toward self-determination. Perhaps of equal importance was the momentum they had generated, involving not only important minorities from the independent northern Lakotas, but also enough Yanktonais, Northern Cheyennes, and Arapahoes to act as a magnet. The effort could even attract treaty Indians from the agencies, particularly during the warmer months when the unceded Indian terri-tory of Wyoming and the buffalo ranges of Montana were at their best.

During the months that followed the dramatic rejection of the Fort Laramie Treaty by these nontreaty Indians, there was little response from the federal government to their defiance. News of the 1869 rendezvous on the Rosebud was almost totally eclipsed by the joining of the Union Pacific and the Central Pacific at Promontory Summit, Utah, on May 10 of that same year. The nation was also focused on the settlement of newly opened lands in the central plains and in the Rockies. Ranches and farms were being developed in the Platte corridor of Nebraska, which had been admitted to statehood in 1867. Kansas was even further along in the development of an agricultural frontier.

The inroads of cultivation in the Dakota Territory were much smaller. Nevertheless, farmers from Minnesota and Iowa, along with those mov-ing up the Missouri from northeastern Nebraska, were pushing into the territory. This movement foretold problems for the Lakotas, who were still hunting on the vast landscapes of the upper Missouri. Gold seekers continued to persevere in Colorado Territory, despite some disappoint-ments, and the meeting at Promontory Summit, which connected California to the rest of the nation by rail, would open new routes to gold and silver camps throughout the West.

The two southern Lakota tribes, the Oglalas and the Brulés, were in the pathway of this expanding area of settlement. Indeed, the effects of this settlement had not made their transition to treaty Indians a smooth one. In 1873, Red Cloud's Oglalas from the Sod Agency, established in 1871 along the North Platte near the Nebraska–Wyoming border, were compelled to move to the northwestern corner of Nebraska.

The new Red Cloud Agency, situated just west of Spotted Tail's Brulé agency, was much more successful because of its greater isolation from white settlers. Indeed, many Lakotas, including members from the more suspicious tribes of the north, such as the Hunkpapas, Miniconjous, and Sans Arcs, would often visit the Red Cloud Agency, where they would camp and partake of the beef rations in what was almost an ideal atmosphere.[13] The agency's closeness to the Black Hills, the sacred Paha Sapa of the Lakotas, made their extended stays particularly attractive. This relaxed situation continued for several years until it was finally disrupted by the strains that ultimately led to the Battle of the Little Bighorn.

Gall was more inclined than Sitting Bull to go to one of these agencies on the Great Sioux Reservation for trade. He, too, would partake in a beef ration if one were available. Sitting Bull and Crazy Horse, on the other hand, avoided such visits with surprising consistency. But there were other differences between Sitting Bull and his loyal protégé. Gall was more approachable than the often reserved Sitting Bull. By nature a rather talkative person, the powerfully built war chief, with his intense eyes and broad nose, was usually more open to casual conversation. To cross Gall, however, could be perilous. He could turn his gregarious personality into an intimidating one almost instantaneously.

Standing Rock Indian agent James McLaughlin, who became very close to Gall after the Hunkpapas surrendered, characterized Gall as a "man of great force of character, quick to resent insult and ready to acknowledge his own mistakes." But this flattering assessment was not shared by some of those who knew Gall. Pragmatic or opportunistic actions like signing the Treaty of Fort Laramie after severely condemning it made some tribal members seriously question his sincerity.[14]

The early 1870s were quiet enough to allow the nontreaty Lakotas of the upper Missouri to revert to their old ways. Skirmishes with traditional rivals, particularly the Crow and the Bitterroot Salish, also known as the Flatheads, became more commonplace.[15] Sitting Bull, often assisted by his loyal war lieutenant Gall, would forcefully discourage white encroachments on Lakota lands whenever such intrusions seemed too blatant. The strategy of this resistance, however, was primarily defensive; unlike the more cooperative attitude of their Lakota kin on the Great Sioux Reservation, they just wanted to be left alone.[16] Gall probably had more wanderlust than Sitting Bull, who was hampered in his travels by the new responsibilities he had assumed as supreme chief of the nontreaty bands of the north. Gall, often clad in his favorite color red, kept up his guerilla tactics against such familiar Missouri tribes as the Arikaras, Mandans, and Hidatsas, whom he would happily trade with at other times.

One fairly successful governmental tack in dealing with the Lakotas at this time was to feed them during times of scarcity. Such a procedure, federal authorities argued, could win the good will of the Indians and further divide the more accommodating Sioux from Sitting Bull's "troublemakers." In Montana, at the Milk River Agency north of the Missouri, old adversaries of the Lakotas, such as the River Crows, Assiniboines, and Gros Ventres of the prairie, were fed, and when approximately six thousand Yanktonais and Dakotas arrived in spring 1871, they, too, were given rations. This generous feeding was done even though the Dakotas, being refugees of the Minnesota Uprising of 1862, were regarded as dangerous "hostiles." The results were so impressive that a number of Lakota bands began taking advantage of this welcomed food program.

The new program impressed even some of the more intransigent nontreaty Lakotas, who also took advantage of the government's studied generosity. Jasper A. Vaill, the Indian superintendent in Montana, saw an opportunity to soften the attitude of those Indians toward talk of a proposed northern transcontinental railroad through Indian lands. He gained governmental permission to invite Sitting Bull to the Milk River Agency for peace talks, which occurred in November 1871 at Fort Peck, near the junction of the Milk and Missouri rivers. Although Sitting Bull and Black Moon had agreed to parley with Vaill, Sitting Bull soon lost interest, and Black Moon only reiterated Sitting Bull's tough peace terms. The two chiefs, at the head of seven hundred lodges, spent the winter of 1871–1872 at Fort Peck, hoping to avoid a harsh and hungry Montana winter.

During that same period, Gall and Sitting Bull's uncle Four Horns, also motivated by hunger, spent six months on government beef rations at the Grand River Agency before returning to their familiar buffalo ranges. Grand River was one of the agencies established by the Fort Laramie Treaty as part of the Great Sioux Reservation. In April 1868 its headquarters were located where the Grand River joins the Missouri near present-day Mobridge, South Dakota. The new agency spanned the Dakota plains from the Grand River northward to the Cannonball. It was designated as an Indian reserve for the Hunkpapas, Blackfoot Lakotas, and the Upper and Lower Yanktonais. Gall had already spent one previous winter there, switching lifestyles from free hunter on the plains to agency Indian when times were bad and food was in short supply.[17]

Events were transpiring in the East, however, that would shatter the relative tranquility of these suspicious "northern Indians." Agitation regarding a transcontinental rail route, which would ultimately connect Duluth at the west end of Lake Superior with Portland on the Pacific Coast, was gaining momentum. Of course, such a railroad would mean laying tracks through the treasured hunting lands of many of these non-treaty Lakotas.

But the idea for such a rail line was not new. As early as 1859, Captain William F. Reynolds had led a survey, at the behest of the secretary of war, through the Yellowstone valley. He had claimed that the area had "peculiar facilities for a railroad." Even during the Civil War, the federal government supported the construction of transcontinental railroads. In 1862, Congress chartered the Union Pacific and the Central Pacific. This action was followed by a charter granted to the Northern Pacific Railroad on July 2, 1864, to bridge the Pacific Northwest with the rest of the country.

Although Congress provided generous grants of land—twenty sections per mile for the states involved and forty for the territories—the mileage loans received by the Union Pacific and the Central Pacific to start up their projects were not made available to the Northern Pacific.[18] The railroad's directors turned to the banking house of Jay Cooke and Company in 1869. When Cooke, the financial angel for the Union cause during the Civil War, agreed to help raise money for the struggling railroad, things began to happen. In 1870 the first tracks were laid, and in two years Cooke's company had sold thirty million dollars worth of bonds for the Northern Pacific.[19]

Soon representatives from the mining areas of western Montana got involved. On February 4, 1873, Samuel T. Hauser of Helena's First National Bank wrote Jay Cooke and Company, boasting of the "gold fields now being worked in the Yellowstone." He also offered Cooke a few hundred pounds of Montana gold dust to display at the Vienna World Exposition, along with grain samples to highlight the territory's agricultural potential. During that same year some thirty buildings were constructed along the east bank of the Missouri, composing the new town of Edwinton, named in honor of Edwin F. Johnson, chief engineer of the Northern Pacific. The important new railhead was later moved a mile to the east and renamed Bismarck. Naming it after the famous prince premier of the German empire was a not-so-subtle effort to attract German capital. The new town would be the main jumping-off place for railroad construction in the vast trans-Missouri area so important to such nomadic tribes as the powerful Lakotas.[20]

Surveying a route along the Yellowstone River valley was the next logical step. A surveying party under the direction of a former Confederate general, Thomas L. Rosser, left Fort Rice on September 9, 1871, and traveled six hundred miles through Yellowstone country in search of the best railroad route it could find before returning to the fort on October 16. Because the U.S. Army knew that this vast region was one of the last hunting grounds of the nontreaty Lakotas, it dispatched an escort force under Major J. N. G. Whistler to provide military protection for Rosser's men. On November 2, another expedition, led by the Northern Pacific's chief engineer, W. Milnor Roberts, under the protection of Major Eugene M. Baker, left Fort Ellis, heading eastward to survey the Yellowstone from the west end.[21] Significantly enough, the nontreaty Lakotas, while no doubt aware of the Northern Pacific's expeditions along the Elk River (as they called the Yellowstone), made no attempt to interfere.

In spring 1872, however, the Sans Arc leader Spotted Eagle visited the Cheyenne River Agency with 150 lodges of his followers. A confidant of Sitting Bull, the tall young chief minced no words regarding his anger over the 1871 expeditions through the Yellowstone country. He told Colonel David S. Stanley that the Sioux had not given their consent to this intrusion. Moreover, if it led to the building of a railroad, they would tear up the tracks and kill the builders.[22]

This threat had little impact on the federal government and the backers of the Northern Pacific. On July 19, 1872, six hundred men, under the command of Colonel Stanley himself, left Fort Rice for the Yellowstone country with General Rosser's latest crew of surveyors. About the same time, another group of surveyors, again under the protection of Major Baker, left Fort Ellis, near the town of Bozeman. The presence of these two surveying groups and their military escorts revealed just how determined the supporters of this railroad project were.[23] Their unwelcomed incursion also provided a major challenge for the new alliance of nontreaty Indians under Sitting Bull.

At the time, many of the northern Lakotas, along with their Cheyenne and Arapaho allies, were focusing on a war with the Crows. In summer 1872, about two thousand of them had gathered at the big bend of the Powder River, approximately 125 miles above its mouth. There, after the traditional sun dance, the encampment's tribal leaders decided to launch an expedition against their Crow rivals. Included among them was Spotted Eagle, who had returned from the Grand River Agency five months earlier, after warning Colonel Stanley of the dire consequences of building a railroad through Sioux hunting lands. These combined tribes, now numbering about a thousand, crossed into some of the traditional Crow hunting grounds in the Yellowstone valley. The progress of their invasion was slowed, however, when advance scouts spotted Major Baker's force of about five hundred men guarding a party of twenty engineers employed by the Northern Pacific.[24]

This chance encounter forced the Lakotas and their allies to decide whether they should continue their Crow invasion or attack Major Baker's men and the survey party these men were guarding. The major's bivouac, which was established on August 12, 1872, was on the north bank of the Yellowstone River near present-day Billings. It was near the mouth of Arrow Creek, now known as Pryor Creek; therefore, the skirmish that ensued has been called the Battle of Arrow Creek by some historians and the Baker Battle or Baker's Battle on the Yellowstone by others.[25] The major's men were encamped at a strategic site, protected by an arc of stunted trees and brush encircling an old riverbed behind them. While the Indian expedition's leaders were debating whether to continue their Crow expedition or attack the engineering party, younger hotheads made the decision for them. During the night of August 13, they evaded the akicitas and charged through the survey party's sleeping camp, stampeding army livestock in the process.

On the following day, a large Indian force under Sitting Bull and Crazy Horse, responding to this night raid, crossed the river to take a position on the bluffs above Major Baker's well-fortified riverbed site. Some warriors fired at the soldiers and terrified engineers below, while others raced back and forth on horseback to intimidate them. A number of these mounted warriors performed their daring deeds perilously close to the ragged arc of brush and timber that constituted Major Baker's defenses.

But the most memorable part of the battle occurred when Sitting Bull sauntered down from the high promontory where he and Crazy Horse had been directing the battle. After the veteran war chief reached the

open country below, he sat down within firing distance of Baker's soldiers. In this tenuous position, he calmly lit his pipe and passed it along
to the four warriors he had beckoned to accompany him. His comrades,
who could not duplicate Sitting Bull's serenity, sat alongside their leader,
watching the bullets kick up dust around them. After each man had taken
his puff, Sitting Bull, wearing only two simple feathers and carrying his
bow, quiver of arrows, and gun, carefully cleaned the bowl of his pipe. He
then got up and slowly led his anxious comrades back to the main Indian
lines. There, with a new authority bestowed by his incredible courage,
the supreme leader of the nontreaty Indians announced to his warriors
that the battle was over.[26]

Sitting Bull's decision may have been motivated more by his warriors'
dwindling supply of ammunition than for any other reason. Many of his
followers, who would be involved in the Battle of the Little Bighorn four
years later, were now equipped with rifles. Some of these rifles, such as
the Henry repeating carbines, were far superior to the trade muskets the
warriors had used at the Battle of Killdeer Mountain. When Sitting Bull's
attacking warriors got close enough to Major Baker's soldiers, they poured
what limited ammunition they had into Baker's besieged camp.[27]

But the accuracy of the combatants on both sides was highly ques-
tionable. Casualties on Baker's side were limited to one dead soldier, two
wounded ones, and one mortally wounded civilian. On Sitting Bull's side
were two dead Indians and a half-dozen wounded ones. The Baker party
did provoke great bitterness among the Lakotas when four of the major's
men tossed the dead body of a popular Hunkpapa warrior named Plenty
Lice into a campfire.

Sitting Bull and Crazy Horse's warriors may not have crushed Major
Baker's men in this encounter, which was more of a skirmish than a battle,
but the conflict was probably one of the curtain-raisers of the Great Sioux
War. One result of this attack, which may have involved as many as a thousand warriors, was the insistence of the survey leader, J. A. Haydon, and his
edgy colleagues to return to Fort Ellis. Their refusal to continue survey
work down the Yellowstone River, in fact, caused the survey expedition to
redirect its efforts forty miles northward to the Musselshell River, regarded
as an optional route for the proposed transcontinental railroad, before
returning to Fort Ellis.[28]

The brief siege of this embattled survey party had barely ended when
Sitting Bull encountered a messenger from Gall. According to this excited
courier, Sitting Bull's chief lieutenant, heading a party of twenty or thirty

Hunkpapa warriors, had discovered Colonel Stanley's force from Fort Rice. The colonel was escorting the other 1872 Northern Pacific survey party, which had hoped to rendezvous with those surveyors under Major Baker's protection. Two days later, on August 16, Gall's determined war party took cover in the woods just east of Stanley's camp on O'Fallon Creek. The long-distance communication between Gall and Sitting Bull is a good example of how these two leaders could coordinate their efforts; O'Fallon Creek was more than 160 miles east of the Baker battlefield.[29]

Shortly before dawn, approximately twenty of Gall's warriors, uttering shrill war cries and wildly firing their rifles, caused Stanley's men to scramble out of their bedrolls and take defensive positions. The surprise attack failed to stampede the army's stock, which was corralled inside by the colonel's wagons and tents, but it did manage to penetrate this large and unprepared military encampment before being forced to turn back.

With Colonel Stanley's Northern Pacific engineers showing the same signs of nervousness that their counterparts under Baker had a couple of days earlier, Stanley decided to move his camp. The party's soldiers and engineers traveled down O'Fallon Creek and up the Yellowstone. There, at the mouth of the Powder River, the surveyors erected the first mound for their rail survey back toward the Missouri.[30] Near this point, one foolish engineer, searching for agates in the nearby hills, was almost captured by Gall's alert warriors before a last-minute rescue saved his life.

The near seizure of this lucky straggler was yet another demonstration of how dangerous the Sioux and their allies could be. The army could never relax its vigil. The Stanley party stayed on the move after another brisk exchange of fire, retreating to the west bank of the Powder River, only to be followed by Gall and his warriors.

At this new site, the tenacious Gall decided on another tack in his strategy of continued harassment. He walked down to the riverbed, placed his rifle on the ground, and announced his intention to speak to the leader of these trespassers. Colonel Stanley, his bearded and heavily garbed appearance in sharp contrast to Gall's, laid his pistol down and walked to the bank opposite the defiant chief. He asked Gall to meet him on a sandbar in the middle of the river, but the war chief, equally wary, refused. Instead Gall, standing ramrod straight, tauntingly challenged the colonel's presence on Sioux lands, warning him that he could bring many more bands of warriors to this fight. With Gall's men lurking in the woods behind their leader, Stanley broke off the talk and turned around to leave. This movement triggered an almost immediate exchange of fire, with Stanley's men hitting two of Gall's men with their much better-aimed bullets.[31]

Sitting Bull arrived soon after this encounter with a much larger party of warriors. Although the stocky leader's force was not up to full strength, it, along with Gall's Hunkpapas, was ready for action. Gall's war party, presumably made up of loyal band members and perhaps a few allies, was proving to be crucial to the joint battle strategies of the two war chiefs. Both bands followed Stanley's party back to O'Fallon Creek, where on August 22 another major skirmish involving about two hundred warriors occurred. In an effort to shake off these persistent marauders, Colonel Stanley sent two companies to drive Sitting Bull and his men off the bluffs west of his position. Although only one warrior was killed in this action, Sitting Bull, screaming from a high vantage point behind a rock, insisted that more warriors would come and destroy all those who dared to intrude on these Indian lands.

While Stanley's soldiers were attacking Sitting Bull's skirmishers on the bluff, Gall's Hunkpapas were attacking the colonel's men from the rear. Stanley, who had Gatling guns with him, promptly turned these guns on Gall's warriors and easily drove them back. A writer from the *Sioux City Daily Journal* was impressed by this successful counterattack. "If Mr. Big Gaul [*sic*] ever again attacks any party crossing the plains, he will, in my opinion, first look sharply to see if they got any Gatlins with them."[32]

The actions that ensued during the days after this encounter at O'Fallon Creek were largely confined to a cautious pursuit of Stanley's men down the Yellowstone. Gall's warriors continued to follow them through the Missouri River Badlands and down the Heart River toward Fort Rice. Their tactics were to keep Stanley's force under constant surveillance and pick off stragglers whenever the opportunity occurred. On September 30, Rosser told Stanley that, with few signs of Indians in the area, Stanley could send part of his force back to Fort Rice. Two days later, Stanley dispatched Major R. E. A. Crofton and three companies of the Seventeenth Infantry east toward the fort. Little did he know that Gall and about a hundred Hunkpapa warriors were tracking them. On October 3, the next day, these warriors caught one of Crofton's officers, Lieutenant Eban Crosby, hunting many miles away from Crofton's campsite, twenty miles east of Stanley's. Crosby was killed and scalped, and Gall rode to Crofton's camp on October 4 to display Crosby's scalp on a pole.

On the following day, Gall and his warriors killed Lieutenant Louis Dent Adair and Stanley's mulatto cook, Stephen Harris; they, too, were hunting too far from camp. Adair's death would have an impact on the entire nation, because he was the cousin of President Grant's wife, Julia Dent Grant. Shortly thereafter, Gall would sear his memory in the minds of Major Crofton's soldiers for years to come when he dangled the scalps of at least two of these unfortunate victims from a hillock near Fort Rice.

Gall's flamboyance and Lieutenant Adair's death would cause a reaction that neither Gall nor Sitting Bull could have anticipated. Grant's son, Frederick Dent Grant, also an army officer, bitter over the death of his relative, asked to go on a Northern Pacific survey expedition planned for the following year. Lieutenant General Philip H. Sheridan, no doubt aware of the implications of Adair's death, ordered fifteen hundred soldiers to protect the 1873 survey party. President Grant himself began to have a change of heart regarding his handling of the Indian problem in the West. Believing that the Creator did not place "different races of man on this earth with the view of having the stronger exert all his energies in exterminating the weaker," Grant's policies after his reelection in 1872 would demonstrate a much more hardline approach toward the Lakotas and their allies.[33] Evidently, Gall's ambushes had been too successful.

The 1872 survey was largely a failure. Its disappointment was not due to any decisive defeat of the survey parties headed by Baker and Stanley; the soldiers under the command of both officers were able to account for more casualties than their Indian foes. The soldiers' disciplined fighting style and their more successful use of long-range rifles made the difference. Nevertheless, the determination of nontreaty Indian leaders like Sitting Bull, Crazy Horse, and Gall had made the challenges of building a northern transcontinental route through the still pristine buffalo grounds of the Sioux and Cheyennes that much more difficult. Moreover, there was general disappointment among Northern Pacific engineers from both survey parties; the 1872 survey had as an objective to cut an angle off the 1871 survey, which they felt was located "too far . . . north." Unfortunately, this new route also proved "impractical."[34]

Notwithstanding these discouragements, railroad builders and federal officials were undeterred; bridging the Pacific Northwest with the rest of the nation was considered vital to the future growth of the entire country. With this lofty goal in mind, General Sheridan, recalling how valuable Lieutenant Colonel George Armstrong Custer had been under his command during the Civil War and at Battle of the Washita, transferred the "boy general" from the Department of the South to the Department of Dakota.

Custer arrived in Yankton, the capital of Dakota Territory, on April 13. The Yellowstone Expedition of 1873 was to be commanded by Colonel Stanley, who, like Custer, had been a brevet major general during the Civil War. It was now greatly strengthened by ten of the twelve companies of Custer's Seventh Cavalry. Thomas L. Rosser, who had been in charge of Northern Pacific engineers in the two previous surveys, was destined to play a key role in this one, dealing with the sometimes flawed personalities of both Stanley and Custer.

Rosser, a Custer classmate at West Point who had fought against Custer during the Civil War, knew how willful his old rival could be. He was also aware of Stanley's drinking problem and warned him that Custer would take over the expedition's leadership if the colonel did not bring this destructive habit under control. His advice to Stanley proved prophetic. Although Colonel Stanley was in overall command of the Twenty-second Infantry and the ten companies of Custer's Seventh Cavalry when his forces left Fort Rice on June 20, 1873, his frequent bouts with the bottle eventually allowed Custer to act with almost complete independence.[35]

During the first six weeks of the new survey, the soldiers of the 1873 expedition encountered no groups or parties of nontreaty Indians during their long trek into the Yellowstone country. Traveling up the Yellowstone River, near the mouth of the Powder, some of the expedition's pickets on August 2, revealing nervousness shared by many of their fellow soldiers, fired at eight suspicious Indians.

One particularly apprehensive member of the expedition was Gall's mortal enemy, Bloody Knife, who was now serving as one of Custer's scouts. As this latest expedition came within twenty-five miles of Rosebud Creek, Bloody Knife warned his leader, whom the Indians called Long Hair because of his lengthy reddish gold locks, that they were approaching one of the favorite summer encampments of northern Lakotas.[36] The wily Arikara scout, who had already noticed signs of a Sioux presence, proved correct; there was a village of Hunkpapas and Miniconjous located right in the path of Colonel Stanley's main forces.

On August 4, Custer, who had hoped to talk peace with these nontreaty Indians, was fired upon by a half-dozen warriors intent on stampeding his horses. What they succeeded in doing, however, was to draw Custer and an advance party under his command into hot pursuit. Custer began the chase, even though he probably knew that these attackers were part of a decoy force setting him up for a classic Sioux ambush. After about a two-mile pursuit, Custer was forced to retreat by some three hundred warriors who came charging out of the nearby timber; at this point in the conflict, Custer's men were probably outnumbered five to one. Custer's sole refuge from total destruction was a triangle-shaped skirmish line, formed under his command by such favorite officers as his brother, Lieutenant Tom Custer. This skirmish line, which surrounded Custer's army horses and their horse holders, began a slow retreat. The soldiers fired at their tenacious enemies as their hastily organized skirmish triangle gradually moved toward a protected wooded area.

After an exchange of gunfire, which took most of the afternoon, the warriors, undoubtedly including the omnipresent Gall, set afire the grassy area that separated them from their enemies, but there was not enough wind to drive the flames into Custer's new defensive position. Later that day, a large army relief column charged into the smoky fray, and the warriors had to make a fast retreat. In response to this welcomed development, Custer and his men, quickly mounting their horses, joined in an intense chase after them. The fleeing Lakotas, however, knowing the terrain much better, could not be caught.[37]

This particular Lakota offense, more ambitious than any of those in 1872, resulted in few losses for the Seventh Cavalry; one soldier was shot in the arm, and two horses were wounded. But two prominent civilians and one soldier, who had separated from Custer's modest force of eighty or ninety, were killed. They were Augustus Baliran, a well-known sutler from Fort Rice; John Honsinger, the regimental veterinarian; and an army private named John H. Bell.

The death of the two civilians especially outraged Custer and his brother. The best evidence of responsibility implicated Rain-in-the-Face, the Hunkpapa warrior immortalized by Henry Wadsworth Longfellow in his poem "The Revenge of Rain-in-the-Face." The consensus among Seventh Cavalry members was that this man headed the guilty party of warriors, which led to Rain-in-the-Face's arrest by Tom Custer sixteen months later at Standing Rock. Indian losses in this battle were not great, but their casualties were higher than those inflicted on the soldiers; an estimated ten warriors were killed that day.[38]

Four days after the August 4 encounter, Custer's men made an especially disturbing discovery. A village site revealed that there were more
Indian adversaries than the army had estimated. Bloody Knife, after a
careful search, concluded that there may have been as many as five hundred lodges in this recently vacated village. Such a large encampment
could have provided a pool of warriors numbering about a thousand. An
alarmed Custer easily gained Stanley's permission for a night pursuit of
these Indians, who had evidently abandoned their camp in great haste.
But Custer's thirty-six-hour pursuit failed to catch his highly mobile
adversaries in time; the Indians had already crossed the Yellowstone on
horseback or in bull boats. Custer, after he had reached the river on
August 10, was determined to catch these resourceful Lakota tribesmen.
He recruited Bloody Knife to stretch the hides from two beeves over a
frame of willows to make bull boats for his troopers.[39]

But a concerted effort on August 11 to carry the battle across the river
by bull boats or other conveyances largely failed; Custer's troopers simply
could not match their Indian foes in every aspect of wilderness warfare.
In the meantime, warriors on the other side of the Yellowstone, fighting
under Sitting Bull, solicited crucial help. A significant number of Oglalas,
Miniconjous, Sans Arcs, and Cheyennes from a nearby encampment on
the lower Bighorn readily responded to Sitting Bull's urgent pleas.[40]

Custer met the frustrations of his unsuccessful river crossing with a
plan to post sharpshooters to fire at their adversaries across the river, warriors using the protection of the cottonwoods that lined the opposite
bank. The Indians were also being supported by cheering women, children, and old people, watching from the bluffs. One Seventh Cavalry
marksman, Private John H. Tuttle, using a Springfield breechloader given
to Custer by the Springfield Company, killed three Indians before he was
fatally hit by a Indian marksman.[41]

As was the case in most battles and skirmishes with the Lakotas since
Baker's Battle on the Yellowstone, these Lakota and Cheyenne warriors
were surprisingly well armed with Henry and Winchester repeating
rifles.[42] After this exchange of gunfire, the resourceful Sioux and Cheyenne defenders decided to take the fight to Custer by recrossing the river.
Gall was to play a prominent role in this attack, given at least nominal
direction of two of the three groups of warriors who had assembled on
Custer's side of the river. Custer's flanks were well covered; it was in the
center of his line where the fighting for the Battle of the Yellowstone

proved most fierce. The Indians attacked Long Hair's center in two waves with about one hundred warriors in each. The tide of battle turned, however, when troopers from the Seventh Cavalry under Lieutenant Tom Custer and Captain Owen Hale charged down a steep ravine to meet these screaming attackers.[43]

Samuel J. Barrows, a New York *Tribune* correspondent who later became a congressman, observed the cavalry charge. He likened it to a "whirlwind," claiming it caused many Indians "to jump off their horses and flee." He also noted that "one conspicuous Indian in a red blanket, supposed to be Gall, an important chief, had his pony shot dead under him. [But he] leaped on a fresh horse and got away."[44] This reference to Gall's role in the battle should cause no surprise. His new prominence as a Lakota war leader went back to his angry oration at Fort Rice in 1868, when he not only denounced the 1868 Fort Laramie Treaty but bared his muscular torso to show the deep scars inflicted upon him by soldiers.[45]

Custer, who had his eleventh horse shot from under him during this battle, aggressively continued the fight, as did Gall. Moreover, Custer wore a red shirt, making him as conspicuous a target as Gall was. New York *Tribune* correspondent Barrows begged Custer, for his own safety, not to fight in that brightly colored shirt. Custer did not heed this advice and switch to buckskins until his wife, Libbie, pressured him to do so.[46]

Gall's reputation was greatly enhanced by his participation in the 1872 and 1873 Yellowstone encounters. Indeed, the involvement of Gall and his band in the death of one of the First Lady's cousins had led to a much larger and more energized military escort for the 1873 survey party. It had also brought the best known Indian fighter in the army, the indomitable Custer, into direct conflict with Gall for the first time. Gall truly became a national figure during the Yellowstone campaigns, eclipsing in recognition even his forceful oration at the Fort Rice meeting. His powerful gesture of defiance, when he waved the scalps taken by members of his war party near Fort Rice in 1872, had probably convinced more people back East of just how determined the nontreaty Lakotas on the Montana buffalo ranges were to maintain their generations-old way of life. It also symbolized the cultural differences in this bitter conflict. Although federal officials and army personnel, along with many journalists, would demonize Gall for his fierce style of warfare, nontreaty Lakotas, and even many of those who had already located on the agencies that composed the Great Sioux Reservation, saw things quite differently. Gall was regarded as a patriot chief not only by the members of his loyal band, who seemed willing to follow him anywhere, but by many other representatives of this powerful Lakota confederation, which had dominated the plains for so many years.

This last major encounter with the Indians on August 11 ended with Custer pursuing the Lakotas and their Cheyenne allies for eight miles after repulsing their attack. Colonel Stanley and his infantry, who arrived near the end of the battle, utilized the army's effective Rodman guns to drive the Indian sharpshooters from the woods across the river. A number of Hunkpapas on the shell rock above, including the cheering noncombatants, were forced to plunge sixty to eighty feet into the water below as a result of Stanley's barrage.[47]

The Battle of the Yellowstone, while fought with enormous intensity, did not exact the number of casualties usually expected when more than a thousand participants are involved. Custer lost only one man, while three were wounded. Custer's officers, on the other hand, placed Indian losses at forty for both the August 4 and 11 battles; a figure of thirty for the August 11 encounter would probably be close, although the time-honored Sioux practice of carrying off their wounded and dead makes any accurate count difficult.

In fact, these same officers estimated that 800 to 1,200 Lakotas and Cheyennes were involved in the Battle of the Yellowstone. Colonel Stanley thought these figures were too high, believing only 500 Indians opposed Custer's 450 cavalrymen.[48] Notwithstanding these disagreements, Lieutenant Colonel Custer's handling of these intransigent nontreaty Indians in 1873 brought him great national acclaim and enhanced his reputation as a peerless Indian fighter.

Custer returned to the banks of the Missouri near Bismarck in September, greatly buoyed by his successes against the Lakotas and the Cheyennes. When he arrived, there was a new and impressive post for him and his men, appropriately called Fort Abraham Lincoln. The cautious Stanley finally reached this new fort later that month and eventually returned to his home post, Fort Sully, where he was able to avoid being completely overshadowed by Custer.[49]

But upon their arrival at Fort Abraham Lincoln, both Custer and Stanley heard some news that would significantly undercut their military achievements during the Yellowstone campaign. A national panic had resulted from the failure of the banking house Jay Cooke and Company.

The firm had closed its doors on September 18 due to gross mismanagement and financial problems. This collapse not only doomed many of the country's businesses, but ended any possibility of laying tracks west of the Missouri for years to come.[50] The railroad's surveyors were deeply disappointed because the route they had surveyed in 1873, when connected with the one in 1871, would have shortened the route to the Pacific considerably.[51]

Although the importance of Lieutenant Colonel Custer's military exploits in Montana Territory had been somewhat deflated by the Panic of 1873, Sitting Bull, Crazy Horse, Gall, and other leaders of the 1869 alliance of nontreaty Indians could take heart in this development. Indeed, there would be no major effort to lay tracks for a northern transcontinental line through this last great Sioux hunting ground for six years. When the time did come for a resumption of railroad building through this pristine wilderness, however, the power of the northern Lakota tribes and their Cheyenne allies would be broken by the Battle of the Little Bighorn and its bleak aftermath.

CHAPTER SEVEN

The Path to War

Nine months after Custer and his Seventh Cavalry returned from the Yellowstone country, they were off on another expedition to Sioux country. On July 2, 1874, the irrepressible Custer left Fort Abraham Lincoln and headed toward the Black Hills. The pretext for this newest expedition was to reconnoiter the mountainous region straddling the South Dakota–Wyoming border for the location of a new army post. This post was to be close enough to the Red Cloud and Spotted Tail agencies to keep a better watch over the treaty Indians, but it would ultimately affect such nontreaty Indians as Sitting Bull, Gall, and Crazy Horse. A more important reason for Custer's latest foray into Indian country, however, was to investigate the persistent rumors that there was gold under the dark stands of lodgepole pine covering these hills.[1]

The major problem confronting this decision to send Custer into the Black Hills was the federal government's decision in the Fort Laramie Treaty to include the hills in the Great Sioux Reservation. Indeed, the claims of the treaty Sioux to the Black Hills were significantly stronger than the claims of Gall and his nontreaty kin to the Yellowstone country; the boundaries for the "unceded Indian territory" west of the Great Sioux Reservation were not nearly as precise in the case of Montana Territory as they were for the Black Hills.[2] But there was now a new dimension in the complicated relations between the Sioux and the federal government. The gold fever that had swept the West during the past quarter century was now sweeping through the farm communities of the upper Great Plains, where the effects of the Panic of 1873 had made the lure of a new gold strike irresistible.

Custer's 1874 Black Hills Expedition would prove to be the major catalyst for a gold rush to the Paha Sapa.[3] The enterprising Custer had brought along journalists who in their press releases could assure would-be gold seekers that there were promising signs of gold in the Black Hills. Such favorable reports put both the federal government and the U.S. Army on the spot. Episcopal bishop William Hare, member of a commission established to deal with the Sioux, warned of dire consequences. In a letter to President Grant on June 9, 1874, almost a month before Custer's departure from Fort Abraham Lincoln, Hare insisted that such an expedition would violate the country's national honor. The bishop was among a number of prominent people in and out of government who proclaimed their opposition to any gold rush that would violate the terms of the Fort Laramie Treaty.

These critics were bolstered by a report from Custer's chief geologist, Professor Newton H. Winchell. Winchell, supported by President Grant's son Colonel Frederick Dent Grant, found little evidence of gold during the Custer probe into the Black Hills. President Grant was impressed by these developments. In September 1874, he announced his intention to keep all argonauts and other white intruders out of this disputed area.

The exciting prospects of a gold strike could not be easily stemmed, however, given the depressing nature of the nation's economy during the mid-1870s. Custer's glowing reports regarding the potential for mineral wealth in the Black Hills were soon widely dispersed, especially after he and his thousand-man force returned to Fort Abraham Lincoln on August 30. They were buttressed in 1875 by Professor Walter P. Jenny of the New York School of Mines. Jenny, at the request of the Office of Indian Affairs, methodically explored the Black Hills for evidence of the coveted yellow metal. His report, while not as exuberant as Custer's, confirmed that these sacred Sioux hills did hold deposits of gold. Yet, even as this debate wore on, gold seekers were drifting into the Black Hills; they faced little interference from the officers and men posted around the disputed hills to prevent this from happening. Soon there were approximately twelve thousand miners in the area, notwithstanding the treaty violations of these incursions and the obvious outrage felt by the Lakotas and their Cheyenne allies. These argonauts were wildly optimistic about the future. As late as June 1876, one of them insisted there was still "plenty of gold" in the Black Hills. "The quartz rock is as rich as any I ever saw, and you know it will last."[4]

The response of the Lakota tribes to this crisis, however, was not as decisive as it should have been. The nontreaty Lakotas, headed by such leaders as Sitting Bull, Crazy Horse, and Gall, were cautious in their opposition. Their policy of reacting to the provocations of the U.S. Army and outside intruders through defensive rather than offensive means seemed to prevail in this case as it had in others. Moreover, they did not feel as directly affected by the threat to the Black Hills as they had felt when the army sent expeditions into their hunting grounds in the Yellowstone country.

The more southerly Lakota tribes, such as the Oglala and Brulé, on the other hand, had an immediate stake in the outcome of this dispute. The Red Cloud Agency was only about thirty miles from the southern flank of the Black Hills. In fact, these low mountains, blanketed by dark stands of timber, could be seen from certain locations in the northern part of Red Cloud's agency, especially on clear days. Also, just to the north and east of the Black Hills, stood that great mountain holy to both the Sioux and the Cheyennes, Bear Butte, situated approximately ten miles from present-day Sturgis, South Dakota.[5]

But surprisingly, the nontreaty Indians at about the time of Custer's 1874 expedition were much more engrossed in fighting traditional warfare against such old enemies as the Crows. This classic brand of Indian combat, involving coups, horse stealing, and other acts of personal courage, was the kind of warfare that Sitting Bull's followers preferred; much of their culture was built upon it, and they had done it for generations.

One of the points of contention between the Crows and the Lakotas, even before the threat of railroad building in the Yellowstone country, was the Crow Agency along the Bighorn River. As warring parties from both sides conducted raids against one another, casualties among both Lakotas and Crows grew. Because several white traders and trappers lived with the Crows, whites inevitably became involved; some even lost their lives in the process. Lakota raids went beyond the Crow reservation, spilling into the Gallatin Valley, near the farming settlement of Bozeman; the motivation of these Lakota raiders, mostly young warriors defying their tribal elders, was to drive off farm stock. Nevertheless, some settlers also paid with their lives as a result.

The territorial governor of Montana, Benjamin F. Potts, managed to heighten the tensions caused by these raids through his protests to

Washington during the years 1874 and 1875. He demanded prompt action against Sitting Bull and "his band of murdering robbers." Having very little patience, the volatile governor encouraged a military expedition made up of like-minded territorial citizens from Bozeman, calling themselves The Boys. They entered Sioux country, ostensibly to find gold but actually to avenge Montanans for those Sioux forays conducted against them. The group, comprising 150 men who knew the dangers of frontier life, was heavily armed with repeating rifles and cannons. They also had a brass howitzer with ammunition supplied from the territorial arsenal by Governor Potts. They fought three battles with the Sioux during April 1874, inflicting rather heavy casualties before returning to Bozeman.

Another attention-getting intrusion into Sioux country was led by Fellows D. Pease, a former Crow Indian agent. Also originating in Bozeman, the daring band of forty-five under Pease's leadership built a fort in 1875 on the north bank of the Yellowstone, close to a site where Custer had fought his nontreaty foes in 1873. Pease naively believed that this new fort could serve as a friendly neutral ground where Lakotas and Crows could settle their differences, but the construction of the fort had the opposite effect. The insistence of its occupants to fly the American flag in the heart of Sioux country became a constant irritant to Sitting Bull's followers. Indeed, they besieged the fort for months. Pease's noble but foolish experiment ultimately cost the lives of six of his men and the wounding of eight others. Eventually only a small remnant of the fort's original force remained to maintain this dangerous outpost.

Although the northern Lakota tribes were more focused on their traditional enemies at this time, they had not forgotten the ominous threat posed by the influx of settlers and gold seekers. Nor were they apt to forget the well-trained and well-armed soldiers who often accompanied settlers. The Yellowstone expeditions, the territorial army known as The Boys, the stubborn defenders of Pease's fort, and the recent trespasses into the Black Hills were all not-so-gentle reminders of the determination of the Lakotas' new foes.

Moreover, the Lakotas could not ignore the lessons of recent history. Since the Battle of Killdeer Mountain in 1864, they had been gradually arming themselves with some of the devastating weapons that made their white opponents so effective. Prior to Killdeer Mountain, they had been content to trade for old muskets, along with powder and ball, all of which were lacking in accuracy. Now, in the 1870s, they were trading for weapons which fired metallic cartridges, preferring, whenever possible, Henry and Winchester repeating rifles.

Such weaponry was sometimes hard to come by, especially at military posts and Indian agencies. Traders could lose their licenses for selling to non-treaty Indians and other potential "troublemakers." There were, however, better places for the illicit arms trade to occur, such as trading posts along the Missouri and Milk rivers, where unsupervised traders operated, and towns such as Fort Benton and Helena, where traveling merchants were willing to overlook trade restrictions. And, of course, there were always traders throughout the West who would sell arms to "friendly" Indians, knowing full well that the guns would end up in the wrong hands.[6]

The appearance of repeating rifles and other coveted armaments was evident at the Baker Battle and at other battles and skirmishes in the Yellowstone country.[7] Yet their use by the Lakotas would have been more effective if the warriors had not been so wedded to the old concepts of warfare, including their stress on individual combat and coup taking over the cooperative strategy of their army foes. Ammunition was also a problem. Because the supply was unreliable, warriors had to save their cartridges and reload with already expended ones. Nevertheless, as time passed, more and more Lakota war chiefs and their warriors would utilize these precious new weapons. They could be used along with the bows and arrows, knives, and lances that made up their old arsenal. Gall, for instance, treasured his 1876 Winchester rifle when he acquired it, jealously regarding it as one of his most prized possessions.[8]

The nontreaty Sioux, living in the unceded Indian territory guaranteed to them in the Fort Laramie Treaty, were often joined by their tribal brothers from the Great Sioux Reservation. In the late spring, Lakota warriors from such agencies as Red Cloud, Grand River, and Cheyenne River would move west or northwest to spend their summers hunting in the vast spaces of the Powder River country or on the buffalo ranges along the Yellowstone. Then, sometime during the fall, when game was becoming scarce, they would return to their agencies, where they would live off government beef rations during the harsh winters that customarily plagued the northern plains. This yearly migration proved frustrating to the federally appointed Indian agents whose responsibility it was to distribute limited food allotments to all their charges.

To complicate matters even more, nontreaty Indians would often join their reservation kin during these annual trips back to the agency. This move would allow them to share in government rations during the difficult winter months. In the early and mid-1870s, Gall often returned to the Grand River Agency, which in 1873 became the Standing Rock Agency. The headquarters for this newly created Indian reserve was Fort Yates, located on the Missouri River, midway between the Grand and Cannonball rivers, about forty-five miles north of the old agency headquarters by land and about seventy-five miles by water, using the Missouri River. The old location had been more subject to flooding, and the new one would provide the agency's residents, the Hunkpapas, Blackfoot Lakotas, and Yanktonais, with more agricultural lands. In April 1875, three months prior to Custer's Black Hills Expedition, Gall and two other Sioux leaders, Hawk and Little Wound, arrived at Standing Rock with fifty lodges of hungry, almost destitute followers. Gall, no doubt influenced by his band's elders and concerned about the entire band's welfare, even agreed to stay at the agency. Moreover, at almost the same time, such members of Sitting Bull's band as Little Knife, Slave, and Red Horn sought food rations from the officials at Fort Yates while encamping along the Grand River.[9]

But not all nontreaty Indians would make these periodical visits to the agencies on the Great Sioux Reservation. Sitting Bull and Crazy Horse tended to avoid such trips altogether. Gall, on the other hand, not only returned to his agency but continued to visit certain forts and trading posts, such as Fort Berthold, where he had almost forfeited his life in 1865 as a result of Bloody Knife's thirst for vengeance.[10] Although the Hunkpapa war leader was one of Sitting Bull's major lieutenants in warfare, Gall was pragmatic, and he and his band would customarily go wherever they pleased.

The mass invasion of the Black Hills by gold seekers, however, exacerbated all previous tensions between the federal government and the Lakotas. Curiously, during this increasingly serious crisis, Red Cloud, the chief Indian architect of the 1868 Fort Laramie Treaty, was absorbed with other problems. Consequently, he did not protest Custer's 1874 expedition to the Black Hills with his customary vigor. In fact, the chief leader of the Oglalas was involved in a bitter two-year dispute with John J. Saville, the Indian agent at the Red Cloud Agency. Red Cloud had accused Saville of short-changing Red Cloud's people in the quality and quantity of food rations distributed at the agency. These charges ultimately led to a three-month investigation of Saville's management of affairs at the Red Cloud Agency.[11] The result was a long, detailed report, which, although absolving Saville of fraudulent conduct, greatly weakened his authority.[12] Despite the furor generated by this feud, which had already gained national attention, it could not distract Red Cloud from the Black Hills issue indefinitely.

Indeed, it was a federal initiative that forced him to face this contentious issue sooner than expected. A special commission, headed by Senator William B. Allison of Iowa, was sent to the Great Sioux Reservation in September 1875 to negotiate the purchase of the apparently gold-rich Black Hills. The Allison Commission met at a site between the Red Cloud and Spotted Tail agencies in northwestern Nebraska. Aside from the commissioners' determination to buy the Black Hills from the Lakotas, they were divided over how much they should offer. Three commissioners thought that the Sioux's annual appropriation of $1.75 million for a stated period would be enough; others were prepared to be more generous.

Senator Allison, who had underestimated the great value the Sioux placed on their sacred Paha Sapa, even suggested a plan for the federal government to lease the Black Hills "for a fair and just price" and return them to the Sioux when the gold deposits were exhausted. Equally outrageous was Allison's proposal to buy the unceded Indian land east of the Bighorns from the Lakotas because it did "not seem to be a great value or use" to them.

Red Cloud matched Senator Allison's proposals with one as outrageous: the Sioux would give up the Black Hills, but the price for their agreement would be seven generations of governmental care and support. This support would include Texas steers as the Sioux's major food staple and "six yoke of working cattle" for each of Red Cloud's followers. When the more amenable Lakota leader Spotted Tail, chief of the Brulés, agreed with Red Cloud's demands, the Allison Commission realized that successful negotiations at this time were impossible. In fact, when the frustrated members of the commission returned to Washington, they strongly suggested that the federal government should offer the Sioux a "fair equivalent" for the acquisition of the Black Hills on a take-it-or-leave-it basis.[13]

Attendance at this ill-fated conference was impressive, although estimates of its number vary. Some observers claimed that as many as twenty thousand Indians were present, but Allison insisted there were only five thousand. Although his estimate was probably too low, the other one was probably too high. Ten thousand would be a more realistic figure. One disturbing element regarding those in attendance was the small number of nontreaty Indians present; only four hundred or so were there to speak for those Indians who insisted on remaining free to pursue their old ways. Sitting Bull did not attend; nor is there evidence that Gall did. Crazy Horse also refused to participate, even though Red Cloud, his fellow Oglala leader, had sent couriers to persuade as many Lakotas to come as possible.

Little Big Man, a shirt wearer in Crazy Horse's camp, made the meeting, but he proved to be an exceptionally divisive representative for the nontreaty Sioux warriors. The erratic shirt wearer almost broke up one of the conference's two major meetings; he led a mock charge of warriors toward the shocked members of the Allison Commission, screaming that he would shoot anyone who agreed to sell the Black Hills.[14]

The failure of the Allison Commission occurred at the wrong time for the Grant administration, which was already torn by political scandals on top of recurring charges of corruption. President Grant could ill afford to appease the Lakotas and their allies. Fifteen thousand miners were now involved, including a growing number of gold seekers who were slipping past army sentries stationed around the Black Hills to prevent such illegal migration. Grant and his embroiled administration were truly in a bind. The treaty rights of the Sioux clearly gave them title to the Black Hills. Yet to buck the popular will, so strong in the West, by blocking a gold rush after two years of economic depression was politically risky. One tack the federal government increasingly used was to blame the Indians for their alleged treaty violations. Attacks on Montanans on the upper Yellowstone and attacks on friendly Crows and Arapahoes, which often jeopardized the lives of white traders, were used as ploys to keep nontreaty Indians on the defensive.

On November 3 a fateful meeting was held at the White House (or Executive Mansion as it was then called), involving high civilian officials and senior generals; the president was also at this secret session, called to find some solution to the Sioux problem. Two major decisions were made at this meeting: one was to continue the government's prohibition against mining in the Black Hills, but not to enforce it. Actual possession of the Black Hills by miners and settlers, it was argued, would thwart the power of independent bands such as those of Sitting Bull, Crazy Horse, and Gall. The other decision was even more provocative: northern nontreaty bands should be forced to abandon their unceded Indian lands and settle on one of the agencies on the Great Sioux Reservation.[15]

Later that month a strong rationale for what Grant and his advisers had decided to do was provided by the return of U.S. Indian inspector Erwin C. Watkins from a trip to the upper Missouri country. The inspector had been dispatched by the Indian Office, largely at the behest of the military, to investigate these northern bands and report on their conduct. In a November 9, 1875, report, Watkins was critical of the nontreaty bands who still wandered freely throughout the plains of Montana and Wyoming in search of buffalo. He insisted that these "untamable hostile" Indians were continuing to make war against the friendly tribes of the region. Moreover, they were undercutting the government's humane policy of civilizing the Lakotas, "the *only* policy worthy [of] an enlightened Christian nation."

Watkins strongly advocated a winter campaign against the nontreaty bands, whose disdain toward authority, in his opinion, distressed even their own tribespeople living on the reservation. Indeed, there was absolutely no doubt in his mind that the government should send troops against them "in the winter, the sooner the better, and *whip* them into subjection."[16]

Although Inspector Watkins's sentiments matched the mood of Grant's inner circle, Washington balked at launching a winter campaign against Sitting Bull and his nontreaty allies without some kind of warning or ultimatum. Secretary of the Interior Zachariah Chandler provided such a notice. He directed his Indian Affairs Commission to notify the independent Indian bands that they must move to the Great Sioux Reservation before January 31, 1876. If they "neglect or refuse" to do so, "they will be reported to the War Department as hostile Indians, and ... military force will be sent to compel them to obey."[17]

Couriers were sent to the various Sioux and Cheyenne encampments during the exceptionally severe winter of 1875–1876. Sitting Bull and his Hunkpapas, huddled around their campfires on the Yellowstone, were found and warned, as were the Miniconjous, Sans Arcs, and Northern Cheyennes encamped farther west on the Tongue. (Eventually most of these nontreaty warriors and their bands would move to campsites on the Powder River.)

The response of these Indians was one of surprise and disbelief. Some thought it was an invitation rather than an ultimatum; it was similar in tone to an invitation they had received four months prior to their meeting with the Allison Commission. Others understood the seriousness of this communication, but having a different concept of time, decided to wait; they wanted winter conditions to improve before taking any action. Few probably understood the dire consequences of ignoring the federal government's warning that troops would be dispatched after January 31 to force them to become reservation Indians. As a result of these misunderstandings and misconceptions, there was virtually no movement on the part of the nontreaty bands to comply with the government's tough ultimatum.

Gall's response to this ultimatum was typical. On December 28, 1875, Captain J. S. Poland, who was in charge of the military units at Standing Rock, was told by John Grass, the leading Blackfoot Lakota at the agency, that Gall had left Standing Rock to join Sitting Bull. He had taken with him the majority of the eighteen to twenty lodges that composed his band; because of the severity of the winter of 1875–1876, some of Gall's older band members had probably decided to stay at the agency. Gall and his followers had also traded their agency rations for metal cartridges acquired from J. W. Casselbury, who held a government license to trade with Standing Rock's Indian residents. Thus, it was evident that Gall intended to play a vital role with those Lakotas willing to fight the impending threat to their traditional way of life.[18]

The failure of these maverick Lakotas to heed the warning contained in the January 31 ultimatum resulted in the military taking over the Sioux problem. General Philip Sheridan, who usually agreed with the hardline tactics of his friend and superior General Sherman, began planning a winter campaign against the nontreaty bands. His strategy depended on the element of surprise, which had been one of Sheridan's contributions to Indian warfare on the Great Plains; the army's successes against southern Plains tribes, as represented by the Washita campaign, had brought both Sheridan and Custer widespread recognition.

Sheridan's new campaign called for an ambitious three-pronged movement into Sioux country. General Terry would lead his troops, including the twelve companies of Custer's Seventh Cavalry, westward from Fort Abraham Lincoln. Brigadier General George Crook, recently transferred from the Southwest, where he had campaigned successfully against the Apaches, would move his forces northward from Fort Fetterman in eastern Wyoming. And Colonel John Gibbon would march eastward from Fort Ellis, three miles west of Bozeman in southern Montana.[19] The extent of the geographical area being invaded was staggering, but the severity of the winter of 1875–1876 would ultimately thwart the kind of major winter campaign Sheridan had wanted. Indeed, Terry did not leave Fort Abraham Lincoln until May 17, and Crook was unable to launch a truly major offensive effort until May 29.

Yet Crook, whose personal relations with Sheridan were not that good, decided to heed his superior's wishes for a winter campaign. He left Fort Fetterman on March 1, 1876, with eight hundred men. Although spring was only three weeks away, the weather Crook's men encountered on their trek up the old Bozeman Trail could not have been worse. The temperature was forty to fifty degrees below zero, snow was on the ground, and driving blizzards hampered their movements well into the middle of this stormy month.

When the general's scouts spotted an Indian encampment on the Powder River, however, the shivering expedition was ready for action. Crook ordered Colonel Joseph J. Reynolds to take six companies of cavalry and attack the Indian camp. Approaching from the west, Colonel Reynolds' troopers arrived at the village early on the morning of March 17. The maneuver caught the Indians by surprise; many of them had fastened their tipis the night before to keep out the bitter cold. When Reynolds attacked them, the villagers were forced to cut their way out of the camp's tipis before fleeing to the bluffs on the west side of camp.

The soldiers quickly torched about half the tipis and all the possessions within them. To the dismay of the troopers, though, the village's occupants, primarily Northern Cheyennes along with smaller numbers of Miniconjous and Oglalas, quickly recovered. Soon they were firing down at the flaming camp below from secure positions on the adjacent bluffs.

To avoid heavy casualties, a retreat was ordered shortly after the noon hour, and the opportunistic cavalrymen left the smoldering village and crossed the difficult snow-covered landscape, hoping to reach Crook's main force as soon as possible. To the relief of the Cheyennes and Lakotas, their casualties were surprisingly light. One Cheyenne and one Lakota were killed, while several others were wounded. Reynolds, on the other hand, lost four men on top of six who were wounded.

The biggest disappointment for the approximately 735 Indians in the encampment, however, was the loss of half the village's pony herd. That night a group of warriors, following the retreating column under Reynolds' command, found the captured ponies, which were unguarded, and brought nearly all of them back to camp.

The army had largely botched this potentially victorious encounter, called the Battle of the Powder River, and disgust for this failed effort in Sheridan's much-anticipated winter campaign came down on the shoulders of the aging Colonel Reynolds. He had not shone on that fateful day. The disgraced colonel was later court-martialed for his timid performance and retired from the army.[20]

One belief that General Crook nurtured after this debacle was that his expedition had reached and badly damaged the encampment of Crazy Horse. One incident provided the basis for this apparently spurious claim. During the battle, scouts for the Reynolds column had discovered an elderly and disabled woman during their search of the largely devastated camp. She told them that the leaders of her village were Crazy Horse and his unpredictable ally Little Big Man. A month later, on April 19, a group of Lakota mixed-bloods arrived at the Cheyenne River Agency and insisted that Crazy Horse was nowhere near the encampment during Reynolds' attack. Moreover, the army's target during the Battle of the Powder River was primarily a Cheyenne rather than an Oglala village. For many years this claim was denied by Crook and his officers, who insisted, despite subsequent developments, that they had attacked and partially destroyed the indestructible Crazy Horse's village.[21]

The victims of the March 17 attack, many without proper clothing or adequate food, migrated northward to the village where Crazy Horse and his closest allies were actually staying. Unfortunately, this camp, on the Little Powder, was not large enough to accommodate the dispossessed refugees. Crazy Horse's followers, along with their new guests, were compelled to travel sixty miles northward to a much larger Hunkpapa encampment, near the Chalk Bluffs between the Powder and Little Missouri rivers. This village comprised about a hundred lodges, not only of Sitting Bull's Hunkpapas but also of Miniconjous. Not all of them were present; some, perhaps like Gall and his band, who had left Standing Rock in December 1875, were trading for goods at Fort Berthold, while others were on separate missions. Those remaining in the encampment, however, which had now swelled to 235 lodges, generously fed the new arrivals. They provided them with plenty of meat, cooked in boiling kettles, which had been set up even before the guests had reached camp. The gratitude of these desperately cold and hungry people was poignantly stated by the Northern Cheyenne leader Wooden Leg: "Oh, what good hearts they had."[22]

The controversial mid–March attack on the unsuspecting Powder River village was the first major military strike launched directly against the Lakotas and Cheyennes since the ratification of the Treaty of Fort Laramie in 1868. In 1871 soldiers had intruded on the buffalo ranges along the Yellowstone, a bountiful wilderness area in Montana that nontreaty bands regarded as unceded Indian territory and, thus, guaranteed to the Sioux by article 16 of the treaty. But the army's mission was simply to survey the area for a potential railroad route as permitted by article 11.[23]

Crook's March expedition, however, was clearly an assault on Indian people, which even put the lives of women, children, and elderly at risk. This kind of action justified war, notwithstanding the reactive position taken by Sitting Bull's and Crazy Horse's nontreaty bands when they had organized in 1869. Feeling the dangers that were apparently not conveyed in the January 31 ultimatum, they began to draw together as one enormous village. The camps that composed it were located as close together as grass for the growing pony herds would permit.

The number of nontreaty Indians who rarely, if ever, went to an agency was not very large. Indeed, around thirty-four hundred would be the maximum. Of these, only about a third were able-bodied warriors who could resist the new pressures being applied by the United States government. Not surprisingly, the Hunkpapas were the most numerous of these independent tribespeople. Of the 500 lodges occupied by nontreaty Indians, Sitting Bull and Gall's people accounted for 154 of them.

The Hunkpapas exceeded even the Cheyennes in the number of nontreaty lodges; there were only about one hundred Northern Cheyenne lodges. Crazy Horse's Oglalas comprised seventy lodges, and the Miniconjous and Sans Arcs had fifty-five lodges apiece. Far fewer Brulé, Two Kettle, and Blackfoot Lakota tribe members had chosen to live off the reservation, although because of their close alliance with the Hunkpapas, many Blackfoot Lakotas tended to camp near the more militant Hunkpapa bands. One especially strident eastern Sioux war chief was Inkpaduta, who had a number of Dakotas and Yanktonais willing to follow his leadership.[24]

Gall, unlike some of his Hunkpapa comrades, tended to move back and forth from his band's encampments in the wilderness to the Standing Rock Agency assigned to his people. After his pledge to stay at the agency in April 1875, he temporarily left Standing Rock to spend at least part of the summer with Sitting Bull in the Black Hills. In fact, when Sitting Bull was accused of an attack on a party of whites in Deadwood Gulch, Gall, who had been with him, testified to Standing Rock's agent in September 1887 that this charge was false. Because Gall's reputation for honesty had become solid during his first years as a full-time reservation Indian, the agent, Major James McLaughlin, believed him and informed the commissioner of Indian Affairs that the accusation could not be substantiated.[25]

In the meantime, the growing Indian village, rapidly reaching the size of all the nontreaty bands that were once spread throughout the northern plains, was on the move. In late spring 1876, it crossed the Powder and Tongue rivers, reaching Rosebud Creek in late May. The sprawling Indian encampment usually had to move every two to five days because of pony herd overgrazing and the need to cut substantial numbers of nearby trees and shrubs for firewood.

The Northern Cheyenne warriors took the lead in the frequent tribal migrations to the new campsites. These trusty allies of the Sioux, who also felt their territory was being invaded, would determine the route to be taken before each move and would choose the village's next destination site.[26] The Hunkpapas had an equally important responsibility. As the last band in the long trek of migrating tribespeople, it was their function to keep a wary eye on the countryside behind them, knowing full well that a Cheyenne-Sioux encampment on the Powder River had been struck in March without warning. Between these two tribal groups were bands of Oglalas, Miniconjous, and Sans Arcs, each large enough to have its own tribal circle, as well as smaller numbers of Blackfoot Lakotas, Brulés, Yanktonais, Dakotas, and even Arapahoes, who customarily camped near one of the larger tribal circles.

Old-timers have described in graphic terms the village's last migration to the Little Bighorn River, or the Greasy Grass, as the Lakotas called it. "That straggling column was half a mile wide (each band and family traveling by itself), and it was so long that the Cheyennes in the lead would have their tents pitched and supper over before the Hunkpapas in the rear reached the camp-ground." There was frenzied activity of an exceptional nature caused by the "travois and pack-animals, the bunches of loose horses, people mounted and on foot [and] the dogs—it was like a lot of ants running over the prairie."[27]

While camped along the Rosebud, Sitting Bull began to have inspiring visions that caught the attention of this mobile coalition of nontreaty bands. The coalition's supreme chief had made his reputation as a warrior, but having reached the age of forty-five, he was now regarded as lame by many warriors because of a decided limp. But the once respected war chief had already begun to use his skills as a medicine man to make up for the loss of his former vigor, even though Sitting Bull would never become a medicine man known for his powers to conjure and administer healing herbs for his people. "He was not classed as a doctor." Rather, he became the kind of medicine man, or holy man, who exercised "supernatural power" through "dreams and visions" that inspired his Lakota followers. He was, to use the words of one Hunkpapa admirer, "a man medicine seemed to surround."[28] His first vision during this crucial time for his nontreaty bands occurred when he climbed to the top of a butte to communicate with Wakan Tanka, the Great Spirit or Great Mystery of the Lakota people.

During the first week of June, Sitting Bull, honoring a pledge he had made to the Great Spirit during an earlier prayer, decided to organize a sun dance. His Hunkpapas were encamped on the east side of Rosebud Creek. Their Cheyenne allies were on a bench on the other side of the creek where, as the village's trail-blazing band, they had located the current campsite. All the bands in this great migration had arrived at this location on or about June 4. The site selected for the sun dance was about a quarter-mile north of the Hunkpapas' circle and several miles from a familiar landmark, the Deer Medicine Rocks.[29] The dance was solely for the Hunkpapas, although Indians from the other tribal circles came as observers because of Sitting Bull's prominence. Gall was probably there, although the pertinent sources do not mention him in connection with the dance or the Battle of the Rosebud, which followed two weeks later.

Lakota sun dances usually lasted twelve days and were always preceded by the customary search for the tallest and straightest cottonwood tree by Indian women selected on the basis of the respect they enjoyed in the tribe. After this tree was cut and its branches removed, it would serve as a pole around which the dancers could circle again and again. Those warriors willing to make the greatest, most painful sacrifice for their tribe's welfare in this sacred ceremony of tribal renewal were tied to this sturdy pole, connected by rawhide lines attached to skewers that pierced their skin. Once securely connected in this agonizing manner, the warriors would circle the pole, eyes lifted toward the sun, dancing until the skin covering their breasts was torn, causing them to fall to the ground exhausted. Sitting Bull, probably because of his age and physical condition, was not put through the entire ordeal, but, without being tied to the sun dance pole, he had small bits of flesh removed from his body, fifty from his right arm and fifty from his left.[30]

Sitting Bull's vision after the dance made a huge impact on all the bands gathered along the Rosebud. As related to the Hunkpapa chief Black Moon, the weakened Sitting Bull, covered with fresh cuts and old scars, testified that he "had seen right below the sun [and] where he looked [were] many soldiers and horses all with heads down and some Indians with [their] heads down." They were falling upside down into the Indian camp.[31] Because all the soldiers were falling in this fashion but only *some* of the Indians were, this vision foretold a great Indian victory. Many Lakotas now believed that these blue-coated soldiers, who had already attacked one Indian encampment, would be soundly defeated if they attacked another.

Sitting Bull's optimistic interpretation would soon be tested. This shortened version of the Hunkpapa sun dance ended on June 8, and the large and mobile village moved after only four days of celebration. On June 16, after camping at three intermediate sites, it arrived on the upper fork of Reno Creek, where the various bands began to form their tribal circles. But that evening, as the women were putting up the village's tipis and organizing for the first night, a party of Cheyennes, headed by a warrior named Little Hawk, came dashing into camp to report the presence of a large army the party had sighted the day before.

The response of the older leaders, including Sitting Bull and Crazy Horse, was to stand pat and to fight only if the soldiers attacked them. The young warriors of the village, however, had different ideas. They began to arm and paint themselves for combat in defiance of the established policy of their elders not to provoke hostilities. Indeed, warriors from every tribal circle, numbering about five hundred, left that night at the behest of Little Hawk and his followers. They headed some twenty-one miles southeast toward the Rosebud, where Crook and almost a thousand officers and men were camped. The surprise act of defiance worked; both Sitting Bull and Crazy Horse followed these aroused young men when the sun rose on June 17.

The initial contact with Crook's command occurred that morning when the first of the hastily assembled bands of Lakota and Cheyenne warriors encountered approximately 160 Crow and Shoshone army scouts. At the time of this first clash, an almost nonchalant Crook, probably dressed in his casual pith helmet and canvas suit, was playing a game of whist with his officers. An exceptionally savage battle followed this first attack; it would spread for five miles throughout the canyons and plateaus along the Rosebud, characterized by attacks and counterattacks that consumed six hours of intense fighting.

During much of the battle, Crook's men were in one of the canyons, straddling both sides of the creek, while the Lakotas and Cheyennes had taken strategic positions around them. Outmanned by Crook's Second and Third cavalries and five companies of his infantry, the Indians took advantage of their control of the heights, firing down at their more exposed enemies. Efforts to dislodge them from their positions on the adjacent plateaus brought mixed results. Lieutenant Colonel William B. Royall's Third Cavalry tried to do it but was forced to withdraw with thirteen dead and twenty-one wounded.[32] The Lakotas and Cheyennes were no doubt inflamed by the bitter memories of the surprise attack on their people in March.

During the afternoon of that bloody day, the Lakotas and Cheyennes broke off the engagement. They, too, suffered heavy casualties according to Indian standards. Crook initially had no idea of the extent of their losses, but thirteen Lakota bodies were found near his lines. Crazy Horse, who eventually got deeply involved in the battle, estimated that as many as thirty-nine Indians were killed and sixty-three wounded.[33] It is difficult to determine how many Hunkpapas fought at the Rosebud. Sitting Bull was there, but because of his age and the mutilation of his body at the sun dance, his efforts were confined to encouraging those warriors who did participate.[34]

The Lakotas and the Cheyennes felt they had won a strategic victory; they had never fought with such ferocity. Much of the press agreed, feeling that General Crook had received a decided setback. The *Bismarck Daily Tribune* asserted that Crook, in trying "to play a lone hand" without General Terry's men, who were within a short distance of him, had gotten "the worst of it." The journal acknowledged that Crook's men put the Indians "to flight," but, unfortunately, failed to follow them.[35] The nontreaty bands at the village also sensed the importance of this battle; a major celebration occurred, but only after they had prudently moved to their next campsite on the Little Bighorn. Sitting Bull's vision had been at least partly fulfilled at the Rosebud.

Gall's whereabouts during these tumultuous events surrounding the Rosebud have been a source of confusion. He claimed to have fought with Crazy Horse at the battle. Because of his prowess as a warrior, historians have generally assumed he was there; indeed, a few have even believed that he was one of the leaders. General Crook's great respect for Gall's fighting abilities was another reason for this widespread assumption. He thought Gall was the equal of Crazy Horse if not superior to him when it came to warfare. With the possible exception of the Battle of Slim Buttes, fought four months later, Crook's only military encounter with Gall was at the Rosebud. Thus, one might conceivably conclude that Crook's evaluation was based on Gall's performance there.[36] But, interestingly enough, Neil Mangum, who published a book-length account of the battle in 1987, found no evidence of Gall's participation. Nor was any such evidence uncovered by Jerome A. Green, the author of a number of published studies on Lakota and Cheyenne warfare against the army.[37]

If Gall was not on the battlefield, then where was he? There are several possibilities. Being highly independent and having his own band, he may have been one of the nontreaty Indians exchanging goods at Fort Berthold or at some other trading post at this time. This particular argument, however, ignores the existence of that strong bond between him and Sitting Bull. Moreover, in such a time of danger, it seems unlikely that Gall would not want to be with his old mentor, participating in the strategic and tactical decisions necessary to protect their unified and defiant nontreaty village.

Another reason for Gall's possible absence at the Rosebud may have been his active participation in the sun dance. This early June dance, which preceded Sitting Bull's extraordinary vision, was strictly a Hunkpapa affair. The importance of this ceremony to the welfare and security of the Hunkpapas made some kind of involvement on Gall's part essential. Being younger than Sitting Bull and believing in his mentor's visions, he could have been one of the dancers with skewers cut into the skin around his breasts. This most demanding aspect of the ritual would have been difficult for a younger warrior, but given Gall's old wounds, the seasoned thirty-six-year-old war chief may have been particularly drained by this physically painful experience. In truth, scholars familiar with the sun dance, which was practiced by other Plains tribes but often under different names, have recognized what the rigors of this most sacred Sioux ceremony can do to even the most able-bodied warrior; indeed, the Lakota sun dance could take about four days to prepare for and another four days to recover from.[38]

A more convincing reason for Gall's omission from the battle accounts may be his late arrival at the Rosebud. Perhaps angered when his tribe's younger warriors defied Sitting Bull and Crazy Horse by following Little Hawk to the Rosebud, Gall, weakened by his participation in the sun dance, could have hesitated too long. As a result, Crazy Horse became the major Lakota leader in this fateful encounter. Apparently, Gall, who customarily acted as Sitting Bull's right hand man during previous battles, acquiesced to his mentor's decision to leave with Crazy Horse in their ride to the Rosebud. One suspects that he may have known that his long-time friend and comrade planned to inspire the Lakota and Cheyenne warriors only by his presence not by his prowess.

Gall, having arrived too late to see action, might have decided to hold his band in reserve in case Crazy Horse's warriors got into trouble. Historian J. W. Vaughn concluded that Gall and Crow King, another Hunkpapa war chief who would later distinguish himself at the Little Bighorn, were both absent from the bloody fray.[39] Given the geographical enormity of this battlefield, these two warriors and their followers could have been nearby, ready to fight if the battle shifted their way. In earlier conflicts, fighting under Sitting Bull, Gall had pursued separate but coordinated strategies, such as his determined confrontation with Colonel David S. Stanley's large expedition from Fort Rice while Sitting Bull, totally unaware of Stanley's presence, was engaged in the Baker Battle many miles away.

Despite the confusion over Gall's whereabouts during the Battle of the Rosebud, Sitting Bull's war lieutenant was destined to play an important role eight days later at the Battle of the Little Bighorn. In the meantime, the strong and independent-minded Gall continued to cooperate, no doubt on his own terms, with the various and diverse tribal members now united and living in one enormous village. And, recognizing that there was great strength in numbers, he gladly joined the coalition's other warriors in their six-day victory celebration after they had reached the Little Bighorn.

CHAPTER EIGHT

The Little Bighorn

The victory celebration along the Little Bighorn was a jubilant affair. Although their successes at the Battle of the Rosebud could not be characterized as a decisive victory, the Lakotas and the Cheyennes had given a good account of themselves. Their feelings of optimism were buoyed by the arrival of a large number of agency Indians. This influx of newcomers more than doubled the size of their village. One estimate placed its numbers at seven thousand, an increase of about four thousand newcomers in only six days. From these numbers, historians have calculated that eight hundred to as many as three or four thousand warriors could have been drawn to resist the arrival of any more soldiers.[1] As Crook's bruised army was now moving southward, increasing its distance from the mammoth encampment, these villagers, bolstered by their growing numbers, had reason to feel confident.

Their exaltation was tempered by the fact that the large pony herds brought into the valley of the Little Bighorn were consuming the grass around the village at an alarming rate. Also, the game animals in the area were being driven away. The council of chiefs at the sprawling camp, in response to these problems, was considering a southward move along the Little Bighorn toward the Bighorn Mountains. When scouts from the village reported large antelope herds to the northeast of the encampment, however, the bands decided to move northward from their current site near the junction of Reno Creek and the Little Bighorn.[2] Traveling eight miles down the Greasy Grass, they found a good stretch of land along the river's twisting course. The villagers made this short trip on June 24, employing the same procedures they had used during the past three months: Cheyennes in the lead, and Hunkpapas bringing up the rear.

When the Cheyennes discovered a good site with nutritious grass and nearby trees, they established the first camp. The other tribes of this growing alliance located their camps along the west bank of the Little Bighorn for one and a half to perhaps three miles south of the Cheyenne encampment.[3] Just upriver from the Cheyennes, for instance, was the small tribal circle of the Brulés. Behind the Brulés was a much larger circle of Crazy Horse's Oglalas. Next to these two tribal circles were the encampments of the Sans Arcs and Miniconjous, both of which were located along the banks of the Little Bighorn above the Oglala and Brulé camps. Above the Miniconjous and bordered on the south by two large loops of the winding river was the tribal circle of the Hunkpapas. Next to it was a small circle of Blackfoot Lakotas, who had traditionally lived and hunted with the Hunkpapas.

By late June, the size of the village had increased even more; the Cheyenne leader Wooden Leg placed the figure as high as twelve thousand, even exceeding an exaggerated estimate by the *New York Times*.[4] In truth, the number of Indians occupying the string of encampments along the Greasy Grass probably numbered only about half that figure. Although this concentration of warriors and their families was one of the largest ever to assemble on the western plains, the Indian village at Killdeer Mountain was even larger. When Custer's troopers and Indian scouts first saw the village, they were deceived about its dimensions. In their minds they had merged the recently vacated village site with the new one established eight miles downriver on June 24. Thus, some of them concluded that the encampment was as long as ten miles and a half a mile wide.

Whether Custer misgauged the size of the village is unclear, but his future actions that day reveal a confidence not entirely justified by the circumstances. On the other hand, when Major Marcus A. Reno surveyed the village before his attack on the Hunkpapa and Blackfoot Lakota camps, an unencumbered view of these southernmost tribal circles was blocked by the hills and bluffs south of both camps. Thus, he may not have understood the magnitude of the mission Custer had given him.

The day of the attack on the Hunkpapas and Blackfoot Lakotas, which opened the Battle of the Little Bighorn, was a quiet one. It was a Sunday

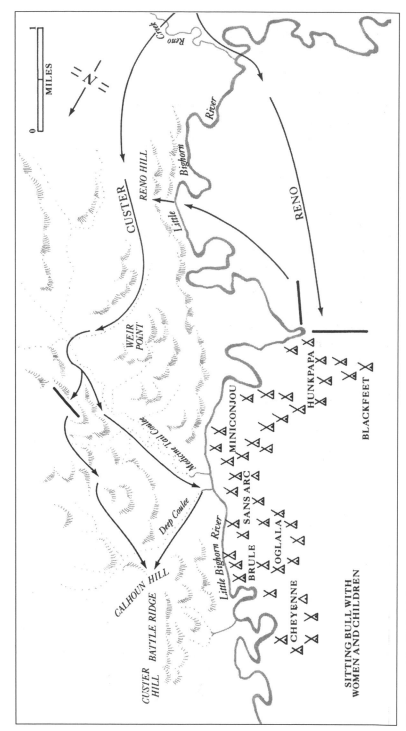

The Battle of the Little Bighorn, June 25, 1876. Courtesy of Robert M. Utley.

during an increasingly hot June day. That afternoon some of the Hunkpapa warriors had headed north to the benchlands above the village to tend their horses. Most of the villagers were probably resting after the eight-mile journey to their new encampment. Gall, for his part, was sitting in his lodge, probably attending to those daily tasks for which even famous warriors were responsible.[5]

Although the trip the day before was not a long one, the job of pulling down the tipis and loading them on travois was tedious. Setting up a new camp shortly thereafter was equally tedious. As was the case throughout the tribes' long migration, any new site would be their home for only as long as the prairie grass could accommodate their pony herds. When this grass was exhausted, they would have to start the process all over again, which was a challenge for all tribal members but particularly for the women, who assumed most of the responsibilities.

Had these nontreaty bands not been attacked on June 25, some of the tribal circles would have probably held councils that evening. The usual procedure for these council meetings was to have leaders from each of the circles meet on a rotating basis at one of the tribal sites. Frequent meetings of the warrior societies also provided a system of communications for the far-flung village. Not all the village residents, however, had access to these tribal conferences. According to the Cheyenne warrior Wooden Leg, there were not enough Brulés to justify an active council; he discounts the idea embraced by some historians that the Brulés had their own separate tribal circle.

A scattering of Indians, not necessarily a part of any of the established circles, lived as guests in the lodges of friendly tribespeople. For instance, six Arapaho warriors stayed with the Northern Cheyenne war chief Two Moon and eight Southern Cheyenne warriors, along with six women and a few children, stayed in Wooden Leg's spacious lodge. Some of the Brulé warriors lived with the Blackfoot Lakotas, while others lived with the Oglalas. Even members of the Assiniboine tribe, longtime enemies of the Hunkpapas, were in the village when Custer attacked.

In addition to the main tribal circles, which were arranged in the customary manner, with the entrance on the east side facing the morning sun, there were makeshift lodgings outside these circles. Some of them were dome-shaped willow dwellings, while others were constructed with branches and covered with robes. These temporary abodes, which had to be abandoned, with a new one constructed, after every move, were primarily for younger single men or older couples who had joined this surprisingly diverse village community.[6]

But the bustling activity that usually characterized this village with its conglomerate of tribal allegiances and its diversity of dwellings was not that evident on June 25, 1876. A relaxed Gall was apparently not concerned about any imminent danger as he went about his business at the Hunkpapa camp. Indeed, the threat of a major assault on the village seemed somewhat remote. Crook and his weakened force were far enough south not to be a major concern. Gall had heard from some of the Indian scouts searching for buffalo that soldiers were seen camping east of the divide separating the Little Bighorn and Rosebud rivers. But apparently this news did not greatly alarm him.[7]

The problem was the vagueness of these reports; they knew that soldiers were around, but where? Years later Gall would sum up the almost fatalistic mood of that day: "Some of our men that were out scouting the country . . . reported to the camp that they had seen great clouds of dust, and knew it must be soldiers on horses, and heavy wagons: and we were on that account . . . expecting them."[8] But he could not have known that troopers of the Seventh Cavalry, under the command of a far more determined officer than General Crook, were rapidly making their way toward his village.

That determined commander, of course, was Lieutenant Colonel George Armstrong Custer, whom the Lakotas had faced during the Yellowstone Expedition of 1873. Having displeased President Grant at secretary of war Belknap's impeachment trial with testimony that brought into question the integrity of Grant's brother, Custer was not put in command of the large military force that left Fort Abraham Lincoln on May 17.[9] Instead Brigadier General Alfred H. Terry was in charge of the Dakota Column, which comprised twelve companies of the Seventh Cavalry, two of the Seventeenth Infantry, and one of the Sixth Infantry. There were also forty Indian scouts (some were Crows transferred from Gibbon's command to Custer and the others were Arikara), a Gatling gun detachment from the Twentieth Infantry, and, perhaps as a show of confidence, the smart-looking band of the Seventh Cavalry.

The plan was for Terry's one-thousand-man force to rendezvous with the Montana Column under Colonel John Gibbon at that point where the Yellowstone River meets the Rosebud. Gibbon's column had four companies from the Second Cavalry and several more from the Seventh

Infantry. After the two forces met on June 21, Terry called a conference of all the military commanders on the *Far West*, a supply boat that could navigate the Yellowstone. His major objective was to cut off any escape route to the south for those bands still in defiance of the federal government.[10]

The main flaw in Terry's strategy was the role planned for General Crook. Crook's force, the third column in this three-pincer movement, which had originally been conceived by General Sheridan for his ill-fated winter campaign, could not fulfill its role. The general the Indians called Three Stars had been checked at the Rosebud on June 17 and could not prevent any Indian retreat southward.[11]

Unaware of Crook's setback, Terry ordered Gibbon to follow the Yellowstone River to its junction with the Bighorn River, advancing southward along that tributary. Terry ordered Custer and his Seventh Cavalry to move up the Rosebud, believing that an Indian trail picked up earlier by Gibbon's scouts would eventually lead to the Little Bighorn. There, the campaign leaders believed that the elusive nontreaty village was located. But Custer was also directed to move toward the headwaters of the Tongue River first, before heading west toward the Little Bighorn. The delay caused by this more circuitous route would give Gibbon's force, largely hampered by its slow-moving infantry units, time to rendezvous with Custer's more mobile cavalry on June 26. On that day they would either attack the Indian village or prevent its panicked occupants from escaping southward toward the Bighorn Mountains.[12]

General Terry made one mistake in the orders he gave to Custer: he told his strong-willed subordinate to use his own discretion in following these directions. Custer, who had already refused Terry's offer to take the Gatling gun detachment with him for fear of losing time, decided to move toward the Little Bighorn as fast as possible. His scouts, including six Crow scouts who had been with Gibbon, had looked for Indian tracks and village sites as Custer's fast-moving cavalry companies traveled up the Rosebud. On the morning of June 24, the third day of this much-anticipated Indian campaign, Custer's men discovered the abandoned sun dance lodge, where Sitting Bull had seen soldiers falling upside down into the village.

On the same day, Custer's troopers also viewed a dramatic change in the condition of the trail: it was much larger, and the horse droppings were noticeably fresher. The original trail, now crisscrossed by an array of tracks caused by the influx of agency Indians making their way to the insurgent village, turned westward toward the Little Bighorn. This was encouraging to Custer because this was where the army expected the nontreaty Indians to be. Instead of being alarmed by these signs, Custer ordered an all-out night march. He had hoped to reach the valley of the Little Bighorn in time for his men to rest on June 25 and then, on the following day, surprise the village with a typically bold and devastating Custer charge.

The dauntless cavalry leader, considered by many to be the best Indian fighter in the West, first viewed the huge Indian encampment from a high point in the Wolf Mountains east of the Little Bighorn. His Crow scouts pointed to the haze of the campfires some fifteen miles away and the barely visible pony herds on the benchland to the west of the village. Although Custer could not make out what they saw, he trusted the instincts and skills of these scouts. What did disturb him, however, were the parties of Indians he sighted in the hills around him. Convinced that the presence of his forces had already been detected, Custer decided to attack on the afternoon of June 25, despite the fatigue his men must have felt from their night march. [13]

As the twelve companies of the Seventh Cavalry descended into the valley of the Little Bighorn, their leader, more concerned about preventing an Indian escape than meeting with resistance, decided to divide his command. Captain Frederick W. Benteen and the approximately 125 men of companies D, H, and K were to cut off all possible Indian escape routes to the south and west. Captain Thomas McDougall was given command of Company B. His men were to supervise the movements of Custer's pack train, which carried vital supplies such as extra ammunition. Given the nature of its assignment, McDougall's column, which numbered about 130 men including civilians, was a slow one. Because of the cumbersome pace of the pack mules, it tended to lag behind the rest of Custer's troopers. The main body of this confident attack force was under the command of Custer and his most senior officer, Major Marcus A. Reno. Reno was assigned to lead the 130 men from companies A, G, and M, while Custer would assume responsibility for the 210 men of companies E, F, C, I, and L.

Traveling on opposite sides of what would be called Reno Creek, Custer and Reno followed this small tributary of the Little Bighorn downstream for about nine miles. Their first major contact with the enemy occurred when they sighted forty Lakotas fleeing before them, presumably toward the village. Custer ordered Reno to pursue these Indians in preparation for an attack on their encampment.[14] Major Reno was promised support for this mission, which was replete with such unknowns as the size of the village and the level of its preparedness. Knowing that Captain Benteen and his men were many miles away, Reno must have assumed that this support would come from Custer, but the energetic Custer was already moving down the east bank of the Little Bighorn with his five companies, by far the largest force of his now fractured command.[15]

Reno's forces, alone but reassured of the necessary backup, quickly reached the Little Bighorn, ready for action. They crossed the river at about 2:30 P.M. Companies A and M formed the first line, while Company G was held in reserve. Preceding the troopers across the river were Crow and Arikara scouts, including Gall's mortal enemy Bloody Knife. He was usually at Custer's side but was given to Reno for the first assault on this village.

Reno's men had to ride almost three miles before they reached the first tipis of the unsuspecting encampment. Counting on the element of surprise, Major Reno's cavalrymen and scouts did very well at first. But as the minutes passed, it began to appear that Reno's luck that day would not be much better than Custer's. Although the westernmost of the two tribal circles at the southern edge of this village belonged to the Blackfoot Lakotas, the easternmost, which was closer to the river, belonged to the Hunkpapas. They were probably the toughest of all the Lakota bands present that day, having guarded the rear of this highly mobile village for the past three months; this assignment had become an especially important one since the federal government's January 31 ultimatum.[16]

As soon as the troopers and scouts under Reno's command got within seventy yards of the nearest tipis, they began to fire into the Hunkpapa and Blackfoot Lakota tribal circles. In the case of the Blackfoot encampment, which was on a benchland somewhat lower than that occupied by the Hunkpapas, most of the bullets hit only the tops of the tipis. But the more exposed Hunkpapas made easier targets, and the women, children, and old persons, as well as the warriors, became unsuspecting victims of this attack.

The assault, which gave the entire village no more than a half-hour to respond, had an element of surprise reminiscent of the attack on the Powder River village in March. Crow King, who would distinguish himself that day, later described the chaotic scene that followed. The shriek of a Hunkpapa woman shot in the shoulder while standing near him was his first indication of trouble. Other Hunkpapas around him were wounded or killed that afternoon, including Knife Chief, the aging camp crier for Sitting Bull's band, who was badly wounded by a bullet that went through his body and broke both arms.[17]

Probably the most vulnerable victims were those outside the camp when Reno's assault began, including several boys playing in the woods just south of the village. These terrified youngsters shouted the first warnings of danger as they ran back to the Blackfoot Lakota camp. The women, children, and old people who tried to flee as a result of their alarm soon found their lives in danger too. Two weeks later, the July 7, 1876, edition of the *Bismarck Tribune* reported that ten women were found slain in a nearby ravine below the camp, "evidently by Ree or Crow scouts." In later reports, the composition of these dead noncombatants was changed from ten women to six women and four children.[18]

Gall first became aware of this attack when he heard the shouts of those boys fleeing back to camp.[19] The loud reports from the army's Springfield single-shot breechloading rifles, relentlessly strafing the tipis in the Hunkpapa encampment, startled him into immediate action. During the first lull in the gunfire, he no doubt made a futile search for his family. Perhaps believing they had joined the panicky rush of families northward for refuge in one of the tribal circles downstream, he turned to ideas of revenge and retaliation. He wanted to punish these attackers, whether they be Crook's men or troopers from other army units.

His first major problem was that his horses were grazing on the benchlands north of the Hunkpapa circle. Wanting to put his skills as a warrior to their most effective use, he promptly left camp and headed toward the large pony herds that had been so necessary to the mobility of all the tribal circles. While rounding up his horses just beyond the Northern Cheyenne camp, he could hear an increasing volume of noise from gunfire and whoops of fear and anger reverberating all along the Greasy Grass.

For a time he might have felt that he had completely missed the action he craved. As he headed back south with his horses, however, he had time to plan what his role would be in this deadly crisis. Hoping to cut off any escape route across the Little Bighorn for these attackers, he began circling outside the lower end of the battling village.[20] Working out offensive strategies such as this was not new to Gall; as the head of his band, he often acted independently or in close concert with Sitting Bull.

In the meantime, Major Reno was becoming gravely concerned about the tenuous position of his troopers. After much of the dust had settled that dry June day, he saw, to his horror, masses of Indians heading toward him and his troopers. He dispatched an urgent message to Custer reporting his dilemma, halted his advance on the Hunkpapa and Blackfoot Lakota camps, and formed a defensive line, but his three companies were able to hold this first position for only fifteen or twenty minutes.

Indeed, the momentum of this ferocious counterattack was too much; Reno had to retreat again to a grove of trees, his back now along the river. Bloody Knife and two other Arikara scouts joined Reno after gathering as many Indian ponies as they could. They justified their action by insisting that they, like Custer, believed that taking horses was as necessary in humbling these Indian foes as taking their lives. Reno could only hold his new position for about a half-hour; Indians were infiltrating this new location by using the wooded cover along the river to conceal their advances.

One incident that significantly demoralized Reno was the death of Gall's nemesis Bloody Knife. He was hit in the head by a volley of gunfire, which scattered his blood and brains all over Reno's face. At that point, the major ordered another retreat, this one back across the Little Bighorn.[21]

Upon reaching the Hunkpapa camp, Gall saw fighting almost everywhere. Crazy Horse and Crow King were there, providing the decisive leadership expected of these two warriors. At this juncture of the conflict, Gall's participation is somewhat mired in controversy. Some historians have insisted that Gall led the final attack against Reno, which drove the harried officer across the river and onto that hilltop now called Reno Hill. Here, he and his men were able to hold out for two days.

Gall, however, never claimed a major role in the decisive fight that drove Reno's men out of the valley.[22] Gall's major contribution at this stage of the battle was probably to use his leadership abilities and charisma to inspire other Lakota warriors to engage in a full-fledged charge through the timber to avenge the women and children killed that day, but whatever his true role in this bloody counterattack, its results were devastating for the luckless Reno. His men were shot or pulled off their horses; in fact, these terrified animals had great difficulty crossing the Greasy Grass and climbing up its slippery banks to escape the swarms of charging warriors. Thirty-five men lost their lives in that river crossing and an indeterminate number were killed in the valley below.[23]

Gall was deeply angered by the participation of Arikara and Crow warriors in the battle. One suspects that his thoughts flashed back to his long and bitter feud with Bloody Knife, who was probably dead by now, but he was also determined that his people should root out all the soldiers under Reno's command, many of whom were now on foot or hiding in the brush. Most of the Indian scouts had already fled this chaotic scene on horseback. Before Gall could fully participate in this last decisive charge, however, he heard the voice of an Indian woman screaming "Dacia! Dacia!" ("Here they are!"). This shrill reference to the troopers under Custer's command, who had been sighted across the river, was followed by Gall's encounter with one of his trusted warriors, Iron Cedar.

Iron Cedar had just returned from the high bluffs east of the Little Bighorn, where he saw even more U.S. cavalrymen heading north to threaten Hunkpapa allies downstream.[24] Although the welfare and whereabouts of his family remained unknown, Gall felt a responsibility toward this coalition of nontreaty Indians and Sitting Bull; he did not intend to let his old mentor down now. Gall crossed the Greasy Grass with Iron Cedar, perhaps hoping to do for the other tribal circles what he had done so often for his own people.

Gall's role in this new phase of the Little Bighorn would become noteworthy because of several circumstances. First, with the annihilation of all the troopers under Custer's command, information about what actually happened on the east bank of the Little Bighorn would have to be drawn primarily from Indian sources. Later archaeological evidence, much of it uncovered in the charred grass on the east bank, the result of a prairie fire in 1983, would provide some new and significant evidence about the battle.[25] But the testimony of military participants in this final stage of the country's most famous Indian battle was lost in what is still called by many Custer's Last Stand.

The last trooper to see Custer and his men alive was the bugler, an Italian immigrant named Giovanni Martini, or John Martin, as his fellow soldiers called him. He was given a final note for Captain Benteen, which became so memorable because of its dramatic tone of urgency: "Benteen, Come on. Big Village. Be Quick. Bring Packs. W. W. Cooke. P. bring pacs [sic]."[26] Although this note was hastily scribbled by Custer's adjutant, William W. Cooke, it certainly reflected Custer's concern that he was on the verge of a most important battle.

After the departure of trumpeter Martin, the destruction of Custer's five companies occurred. The only firsthand observers of Custer's stunning defeat, aside from the victorious Lakotas and Cheyennes, were the Crow scouts that Custer had released just prior to the battle. They watched part of the bloody struggle from a slope overlooking Medicine Tail Coulee from the south. Unfortunately, their reports were rather garbled and confused, as critics believe the recollections of the Lakota and Cheyenne warriors were regarding that fateful day.[27]

Gall became the first major Indian participant at the Little Bighorn to give his version of the battle. More important, his rendition was believed by many heretofore dubious people, including a number of prominent army officers. Gall's initial opportunity to present his views occurred on June 25, 1886, when he was invited to attend the ten-year commemoration of this controversial battle. He had been induced to be there by his persuasive Indian agent at Standing Rock, Major James McLaughlin. During the reunion, he became part of a group carefully going over the scene of the battle to determine its course. This party numbered among its members Captain Benteen, now a colonel, and First Lieutenant Edward S. Godfrey, who had fought under Reno.

They were listening to a translator whose interpretations of the conflict greatly angered the mercurial Gall. He communicated his disgust to Godfrey, whom he induced to leave the group so that he could give him his own recollections of what actually happened. The two former enemies rode together to Calhoun's Hill, where they had a good view of most of the sprawling battlefield. Showing a keen intensity, Gall used sign language, interspersed with English and Lakota words. He tried to show Godfrey where Custer's forces had traveled as they headed north toward their tragic fate. He opened his fingers and used them to show Custer's subsequent movements. Following these careful explanations, he asked the inquisitive officer, who had been especially active at the Reno fight, to dismount. With both of them on the ground, Gall bodily turned Godfrey from one direction to another toward such battle sites as Custer Hill, giving his account of the fighting that had ensued at each of them.[28]

The most important aspect of Gall and Godfrey's friendly encounter was that it was the first time the insights of a major Indian participant were widely believed and incorporated into the battle's description. Indeed, for many years Gall's observations were part of the standard interpretation of the Battle of the Little Bighorn. Their meeting was, in many ways, just a simple case of one prominent Indian warrior convincing a prominent army officer of what actually occurred along the Greasy Grass that hot June day.

Later, some of Gall's critics would question the role of Agent McLaughlin's Sioux wife, who, along with another interpreter from Standing Rock, translated Gall's remarks into English. McLaughlin's strong bias against Sitting Bull, and his successful efforts to turn Gall, Crow King, and other Hunkpapa warriors against their old chief, made the contributions of these two translators controversial to many. But the prior testimony of Pretty White Buffalo, a respected Lakota woman who with her husband Spotted Horn Bull also observed the battle, did not conflict significantly with Gall's version.[29] Moreover, Gall did not denigrate the efforts of Custer's ill-fated troopers; if anything, he concluded that they had died bravely. This rather benign perspective made Gall's interpretations much more palatable to the supporters of earlier army accounts.

Years later, Walter S. Campbell, who published his biography of Sitting Bull under the name of Stanley Vestal, conducted a series of interviews with Indian survivors of the Little Bighorn. Despite their criticisms of Gall's interpretations, Campbell did not harshly condemn the Hunkpapa war leader. In fact, he questioned the complaints of both military and Indian survivors who believed that Gall had padded his role in the battle to make himself look good. Campbell also felt that some of the army officers who listened to Gall were unaware that it was "bad form for a warrior to discuss the exploits of other men." In fact, in Campbell's opinion, if any other warrior had been asked to speak as Gall did, "his name would now adorn the history books as the great Indian leader on that fatal day."

Campbell concluded that "Gall was a man of action, merely." Indeed, he denied that warriors like Gall or Crazy Horse were the great generals who decided the fate of all the participants that day. In a defensive fight like that at the Little Bighorn, "there could be no commander, no director: every man fought for and by himself, or with a small group of friends." Even though only one of five of Campbell's Indian informants knew Gall was there, Campbell was convinced that the Hunkpapa warrior, along with Crazy Horse, Crow King, and others, were as brave as lions. The complete surprise of Custer's attack, however, prevented any well-thought-through strategy from being implemented. "When they saw the enemy, they charged, that was the whole of their strategy." To be fair to Gall, in his remarks at the 1886 reunion, he did not boast of being the great strategist at the battle, but in the years that followed, many of his supporters would claim that he was.[30]

One of Gall's observations that won wide acceptance among Little Bighorn historians was his assertion that Custer never got across the Greasy Grass to attack the village. When Gall and Iron Cedar reached the other side of the river, Gall was as alarmed as Iron Cedar to see several companies of mounted troopers riding behind the bluffs, approximately two miles east of the string of tribal circles along the river. He was certain they were not General Crook's men because there were not as many white horses as Crook had had at the Rosebud.

At first Gall was uncertain whether they intended to attack the village; they were not heading toward it. Rather, these blue-coated troopers were moving in a northwesterly direction. Gall's doubts were promptly removed, however, when the cavalrymen descended a coulee approaching the east bank of the Greasy Grass. Looking across the river, the man who appeared to be their leader rode with his orderly some three or four hundred yards ahead of them. Using his binoculars, he was apparently pondering their next move.

Gall and Iron Cedar, who had been joined by several other warriors, watched the movements of this column intently from a nearby vantage point. The cautious troopers were perhaps only six hundred yards away from Gall's party when they filed down the ravine into the valley below.[31] Although Gall had faced Custer during the 1873 Yellowstone Expedition, he evidently did not recognize that the officer with the binoculars was probably Custer. One problem might have been the way Custer looked that day. He had cut the long golden locks that had made him such a conspicuous figure, and he had shed his familiar buckskin jacket, wearing a dark blue shirt instead. He did, however, wear his buckskin pants, encased in his boots, and a broad-brimmed hat to protect his sunburned features.[32]

The commander of this force must have seen Gall's party because he and his warriors were in full sight, but at this point, the hesitant officer had become wary, waiting for the rest of his command to join him. Gall, who had scouted in this fashion for Sitting Bull many times, became convinced later that this was the closest Custer' troops ever got to the river during the battle. Many historians would embrace this belief in the years that followed.[33]

Whatever war plans were brewing among these unexpected cavalry-men, located so far from Reno's besieged troopers, the men were still an undefeated force. Moreover, they continued moving toward those Indian encampments downstream. "I saw what was going on and left the hill, Reno Hill," Gall later observed. (Actually Gall was on a northern slope of those bluffs that stretched beyond Reno Hill.)[34] In response to this troop movement, Gall hurriedly crossed back over the bluffs separating Medicine Tail Coulee from the Little Bighorn to inform his fellow tribespeople of this new threat.

Although he still had not gotten into the thick of battle, the Lakota leader had hoped to warn others of this new menace, just as he had warned Sitting Bull about Colonel David S. Stanley's presence at the Yellowstone in 1872. Such a deed would not bring him the same satis-faction he would have received if he had led the charge against the troopers sighted near Medicine Tail Coulee. Nor would it match the glory that would have been his if he had taken some coups in the process. Nevertheless, many of his peers would recognize him for yet another important contribution as one of the most effective war strategists for his people. Such a distinction, however, was not to be his that day. The word had already been spread, as Gall soon witnessed; when he reached the Greasy Grass, he saw scores of warriors heading north from the Reno fight in much the same way as they had headed south when his Hunk-papa circle had been hit by the Seventh Cavalry's first attack.[35]

Relieved that this newest arrival of troopers had not surprised his Indian allies at the north end of the village, Gall had time to reflect on his next move. His mind was no doubt still focused on the whereabouts of his family. He evidently concluded that they must be among those vil-lagers who had evacuated the Hunkpapa camp and headed north.[36]

Hoping to find his family among the harried refugees who had scram-bled northward to avoid destruction, Gall reached an area where a number of them had gathered for safety. Although he did not find his kinfolk there, he did encounter Sitting Bull and his nephew One Bull. They were offer-ing protection to many of these terrified women and children. One young warrior who saw Gall there was a twenty-year-old Lakota named White-Hair-on-Face. He had given his horse to his mother-in-law and two little girls so that they could escape the carnage of the Reno attack. While guarding them on foot, with only bow and arrows for protection, the young Indian observed that both Gall and One Bull were on horseback.

Moreover, White-Hair-on-Face heard Sitting Bull cautioning his warriors not to take things from their enemies. Sitting Bull had already given this advice to many Lakotas since his vision at the Rosebud of mounted soldiers falling upside down into camp.[37] The old chief had argued persuasively that such acts would not help his people and might bring serious retribution in the future. His warning at this time provides additional proof that the leadership of the nontreaty Indians was still hopeful of fighting a defensive rather than offensive war against white intruders, even at this late date.

Following his fruitless search among these refugees, Gall concluded that there was only one feasible alternative left in the search for his family: he must return to his lodge in the now devastated Hunkpapa camp. Riding southward as fast as he could, he reached the largely abandoned tipis of his once active tribal circle. A search of his lodge revealed no clues that they had returned after he had left an hour and a half earlier to get his grazing horses. He expanded his search efforts to the timber south of camp, where Reno's men had sought refuge for a short time during their retreat toward the river. There he discovered five members of his family, dead victims of Reno's surprise attack.[38]

George Herendeen, one of Custer's white scouts, who found the bodies of six slain Indian women in a ravine located in this area, insisted that none of his men were involved in these deaths. He claimed that Reno's Arikara scouts were the perpetrators. According to later reports, the bodies of four children were found near these women, making it possible that members of the Gall family were among the fatalities.[39]

A perusal of tribal records and pertinent interviews dealing with Gall's life have not revealed the names of any of his slain family members; unfortunately, their identities have been lost to history. Gall was, like many Sioux warriors, a polygamist with a large family. During his 1886 conversations with Godfrey and other army veterans of the Little Bighorn, he revealed that two of his wives and three of his children were killed as a result of Reno's raid. It was a terrible loss but not a total one, for he may have had as many as three wives and five children at the time of the battle.

According to an 1885 census of Hunkpapa Indians at Standing Rock, Gall had one wife, two daughters, and a mother-in-law living with him that year. One of the women was White Lightning, the mother of one of Gall's two slain wives, who would have been forty-five years old at the time of her daughter's death. Another was his wife, Stand-in-Center, who was fifty-one in 1885. The two daughters were Brown Woman, who was twenty-two, and Red Horse, who was fifteen. These four would have been alive in 1876 and would, in all probability, have been with Gall at the Little Bighorn.[40]

A particularly bitter factor in the deaths of most of Gall's family in 1876 was the involvement of Gall's old nemesis Bloody Knife. Little Sioux, one of the Arikara warrior scouts who preceded Reno's crossing of the Greasy Grass, claimed in a later interview that he and three other Arikara scouts saw three women and two children running as fast as they could toward the river. He fired twice at them, and then he and his comrades rode through the timber toward the river, where they killed all of them.[41] Whether or not any of these victims were members of the Gall family cannot be proven with certainty, but Bloody Knife's involvement in this phase of the battle seems unquestionable. As Custer's chief Indian scout, he was probably at the head of this scouting party, searching for ponies and not being averse to killing Lakota families in the process.

Obviously Gall was grief stricken when he saw the dead bodies of these family members. The Little Bighorn would mean glory for many of his comrades, but it would be an almost unbearable personal tragedy for him. He no doubt pondered the irony of this tragic development. He was one of the fiercest of the Lakota warriors, and yet he could not protect his own family. Of particular surprise to him was the fact that Reno's troopers, as well as those hated Arikara scouts, got close enough to kill the most defenseless members of the Hunkpapa camp.

Had the distraught war leader made this discovery upon his first return to camp, he would have vigorously pursued Reno's troopers to their final defensive position on the hilltop east of the Little Bighorn. Revenge would have been his overwhelming emotion. When he finally did recover from his crippling anguish, startled by the sound of increasing gunfire to the north, his mood was dominated by a thirst for vengeance. "It made my heart bad," he later remarked. "After that I killed all my enemies with the hatchet."[42] With his immobilizing trance broken, Gall mounted his steed and headed north to that river crossing where he had tried to warn tribespeople of the presence of fresh troops on the east bank of the Greasy Grass.

The resolute war chief arrived at Medicine Tail Coulee sometime before five o'clock. One of those who observed his approach was Pretty White Buffalo, the astute Lakota woman who would give her testimony about the battle even before Gall did. Obviously not knowing about Gall's disastrous loss, she assumed that he, too, had been delayed by the pursuit of Reno's men across the river. Indeed, she would testify later that Crazy Horse and Crow King had preceded Gall in crossing the Greasy Grass. Thus, the battle had already been forcefully brought to the troopers under Custer's direct command.

Gall promptly organized the milling warriors and Indian women who had gathered at the river crossing. The scene was a frenetic one. Women were bringing ponies in from the benchland to the west, where these animals, so vital as war horses, had been calmly grazing. Warriors were there, too, some of whom had been participants in the Reno fight and others who had not yet committed themselves to battle. They needed to be reassured by the charismatic Gall. Gall complied, urging them to follow him across the river, where they could frighten and stampede the army's horses, which could be seen on the bluffs across the river being held by desperate blue-coated soldiers.

After he forded the river, Gall realized that not only were the warriors with him but many of the Cheyenne women were as well. They were determined to grab as many loose horses as they could and bring them back across the river as coveted prizes of war. Gall's hastily organized party, after it had gathered on the other side of the Greasy Grass, found that it had reached the spot where Gall had first sighted that solitary officer with binoculars, probably Custer himself.[43]

But Custer's troopers had made some significant advances since Gall and Iron Cedar had observed their activities on the east bank. After leaving Reno, the still confident leader of the Seventh Cavalry divided his five companies into two wings. The left wing, comprising companies E and F, was commanded by Captain George W. Yates. The right wing, comprising companies C, L, and I, was commanded by Captain Myles W. Keogh. Yates's left wing, which was probably accompanied by Custer, headed toward Medicine Tail Coulee to ford the river, while Keogh's right wing moved northward along the ridges parallel to the Greasy Grass. Captain Keogh eventually deployed Company L, under First Lieutenant James Calhoun, along what today is called Calhoun Hill. When the companies under Yates and Custer encountered resistance at the Medicine Tail Coulee ford, they moved northward in search of another crossing.[44] Apparently Gall was at least partly right in his conclusion that Custer's men never made a major successful thrust across the Greasy Grass.

According to Richard A. Fox, Jr., however, Custer and his officers were confident of victory throughout most of the battle. Their main objective was to attack the women, children, and old ones fleeing northward to escape the fate suffered by those unfortunate noncombatants at the Hunkpapa and Blackfoot Lakota camps. If the troopers could overtake these terrified refugees, this would draw the Indians out of those encampments that made up the village downstream. Moreover, it has been argued that in the early phases of the battle, Custer felt that he could relieve Reno by such a move. His strategy would enable Reno to resume his sputtering offense and ultimately bolster Custer's position.[45]

Custer also wanted to hasten the arrival of Captain Benteen's three companies, along with the slow-moving pack train escorted by Captain McDougall and Company B; the message carried by trumpeter Martin to Benteen reflected the desperate need for reinforcements that had become obvious when Custer and his men had ascended those bluffs high enough to get a panoramic view of the enemy's enormous village.[46] Although Benteen hastened his troops, he failed to quicken his movements enough to make a difference. In fact, when Benteen encountered Major Reno's routed troopers on his way northward, he joined the despairing officer, who claimed that he had already lost half his men and much of his ammunition.

Consequently, the forces under Custer would remain divided throughout the rest of the battle, resulting in disaster. Benteen's men, for their part, spent two days with Reno, fending off constant Indian attacks. One effort by Captain Thomas B. Weir and the mounted troopers of Company D to aid Custer fizzled out when Weir viewed from a hill, now called Weir Point, a massive force of Indians galloping toward them. Weir was forced to retreat. His return to the position held by Reno and Benteen meant that seven companies of the Seventh Cavalry would be separated from the five commanded by Custer.[47] The result was the loss of 210 men under Custer and more than 50 killed and 60 wounded under the command of his subordinants.[48]

In the meantime, Lakota and Cheyenne warriors in increasing numbers were crossing the Little Bighorn and attacking Custer's troopers on the bluffs above. If Custer survived the attack on Yates's forces at Medicine Tail Coulee, he would have been with these troopers as they headed north to eventually make their stand on Custer Hill.[49] Custer Hill was at the north end of Battle Ridge (or Custer Ridge), a steep slope a half-mile long, which was connected to Calhoun Hill to the south. The last phases of the

Battle of the Little Bighorn would occur here. The ubiquitous Crazy Horse would play a prominent role in this phase of the battle as he had in the counterattack against Reno, but claims that he had led a large Indian force that crossed the river well below the village and swept southward to attack troopers all along Battle Ridge have been disputed.[50]

Crazy Horse's legendary sweep to the north also contradicts Pretty White Buffalo's testimony. She claimed that Crazy Horse, along with Crow King, forded the Greasy Grass at a point opposite Medicine Tail Coulee, but this crossing was considerably upriver from Crazy Horse's northern thrust. The Lakota woman's testimony and those of other Indian participants at the battle have even challenged Gall's role, too. The popular consensus that Gall, who crossed the river after Crazy Horse and Crow King, was the bellwether at the Little Bighorn is apparently not justified by the facts. He participated in the mass assault across the river that ultimately crushed Custer, but he did not lead it.

Gall was, however, involved in the last stage of the Custer fight. Wielding a hatchet, by his own testimony, the broad-shouldered Hunkpapa war chief, filled with a vengeance that bordered on rage, led a resolute charge of warriors against the dismounted troopers under Captain Keogh on a slope north of Deep Coulee. Despite a heavy volley of fire by his men, Keogh's troopers were forced by this charge to move northward and join Yates's troopers after a half-hour of vicious fighting.

Perhaps Gall's major contribution in the charge was his effective exhortation of these determined warriors to stampede the horses. The success of this tactic proved decisive. With one of every four troopers at the besieged site assigned to keep the army's horses from fleeing, concentrated Indian fire on the horse holders eventually caused the stampede. "We tried to kill the holders," Gall claimed, "and then by waving blankets and shouting we scared the horses down that coulee where the Cheyenne women caught them."[51] When most of the animals fled, the cavalrymen were forced to fight on foot, without a reserve supply of ammunition to hold back the charging warriors. "After this the soldiers threw aside their guns and fought with little guns [pistols]," Gall later boasted.[52] When all resistance had failed, the soldiers retreated up Custer Hill, also overlooking Deep Coulee, where they joined Yates's troopers still struggling to turn the tide.

In response to the collapse of Keogh's right wing, Yates's men were forced to withdraw to Custer Hill in the vain hope that they could hold the high ground, but they, along with a few survivors from Keogh's command, were soon surrounded by hordes of angry warriors. Even during this deteriorating phase of the battle, most of the soldiers showed admirable courage, as Gall and Sitting Bull would later acknowledge.[53] Members of Yates's Company E, for instance, charged down a hill toward the Greasy Grass only to be cut down, their dead bodies scattered on the ground below. According to a disputed account by Charles Kuhlman, one of the battle's early historians, four or five of these desperate men ran right into Gall's arms. There Gall released much of his pent-up ferocity by promptly killing them.[54] Eventually many of the remaining troopers on Custer Hill were ready to make the Last Stand of legend and history. They shot their horses for breastworks and prepared for a fight to the death.

But time was running out for Custer's troopers as emboldened tribesmen soon overran this position, too. Gall, despite the controversy over his role during the earlier phases of the battle, was apparently one of the more intense participants, charging across Custer Hill on horseback at the close of the battle. Later, after the arrival of Terry and Gibbon's forces, forty-two bodies would be found at this site.

Custer, who either rode or was carried there, was the most prominent of the victims. His body, in fact, was one of the few not desecrated by the gleeful warriors or the women from the village. Another victim whose body was not desecrated was Mark Kellogg, a special correspondent for the *Bismarck Tribune*. As reported by the *Tribune*, his body "alone remained unstripped of its clothing, and was not mutilated." The newspaper, facetiously but with respect, speculated that Kellogg may have been spared because he was merely a "humble shover of the lead pencil."[55]

Actually the practice of mutilating enemy bodies after a battle was often based on the belief that if an enemy was not crippled or disabled in some way, he might be able to retaliate against you in the hereafter. One suspects, however, that the desecration at the Little Bighorn, which largely involved Indian women, was motivated as much by revenge as it was by religious conviction. One example of the revenge motive involved a group of poorly armed young Lakota and Cheyenne warriors, now called the Suicide Boys. Knowing that the U.S. Army troopers were probably close by, they made a suicide pact the night before the battle. It was implemented by a desperate attack on Custer's men just below Last Stand, or Custer, Hill, and it left all of them dead or dying by the end of the fray.

But the most significant loss by far was incurred by the five companies under Lieutenant Colonel Custer. Among the most prominent of these victims, besides Custer himself, were his brothers Tom and Boston, his nephew Harry A. "Autie" Reed, and such Custer confidants as Captain Yates and Lieutenant Cooke.[56]

This traditional account of the Custer fight has been challenged by Richard A. Fox, Jr., and Douglas Scott, who examined the trail of spent bullets and cartridge cases throughout the battlefield after the 1983 fire finally exposed them. As a result of this investigation, they not only found that the Indians had repeating rifles to use against the troopers' single-shot Springfield rifles, but concluded that there was no heroic Last Stand. Rather, there was a sudden and unexpected collapse of Custer's troopers, causing many of them to run for their lives. A number of Keogh's men who had faced the vengeful Gall, for example, fled toward Custer Hill in complete panic, but fewer than 20 percent of them made it. Moreover, Custer's alleged stand, in which Gall was an active participant, was not the last gasp of these five ill-fated companies that followed Custer down the Little Bighorn early that afternoon. Indeed, the last phase of the battle occurred at Deep Ravine, where twenty-eight men, including army scout Mitch Bouyer, were killed in their attempt to escape Custer's fate.[57]

As persuasive as Fox and Scott's findings are, there were many other reasons for Custer's demise. His division of troopers was certainly one of them; near the end, he had more troopers on Reno Hill than he had under his own command. But there was plenty of blame to go around. Reno's timidity could have prevented Custer's scattered companies from rendezvousing in time to stave off their ultimate disaster. Benteen could have moved his troopers faster when he received that urgent message begging him to come quick and bring packs.

These explanations for Custer's defeat, however, do not take into account the ferocity of the Indians that day. The angry hordes of warriors, enjoying a significant numerical advantage, did not flee as Custer had thought they would. Although they did not stand up and face Custer's superior long-range firepower, they did utilize the cover provided by the broken country bordering the Greasy Grass; it allowed them to creep up on the Seventh Cavalry's harried troopers with considerable stealth. When they got close enough, these warriors employed, with deadly effectiveness, their rifles, trade muskets, bows and arrows, and even their hatchets, if we are to believe Gall's account. Their motivation was obvious: these Lakota and Cheyenne warriors were defending their women and children from the devastating surprise attack that had been launched earlier that day.

Gall's role at the Little Bighorn has been disputed for many years. One reason for this controversy was his early rendition of the battle's major events, as the first major Indian figure to give his interpretation of the conflict. His remarks stirred many emotions; some Lakota participants in the battle felt Gall took too much credit for the victory. The interpreter Willis Rowland, for instance, insisted that he could not find one Indian who "saw Gall at the battle or did not smile at the claim that he directed it."[58] White Bull, one of Sitting Bull's nephews, accused Gall of just being "a good advertiser," a remark he made after Gall broke with Sitting Bull during their Canadian exile.[59] Obviously such a comment could reflect White Bull's bias toward his uncle after this break.

Interestingly enough, the claims of these men regarding Gall's alleged self-promotion were seriously questioned, if not contradicted, by Walter Campbell, who interviewed many of these Indian critics, including White Bull.[60] During Gall's reservation years, such supporters as Indian agent James McLaughlin and photographer David F. Barry insisted that Gall was the key Indian figure at the Little Bighorn. He was, in their opinion, the wise and clever strategist for most of the Lakotas and Cheyennes during this bloody contest.[61] Standard histories of the battle during much of the twentieth century largely accepted this interpretation; Gall was, indeed, the most decisive personality at the Little Bighorn. But in 1997 Gregory F. Michno persuasively challenged the extent of Gall's participation.

Gall's role at the Little Bighorn was not entirely hampered by the tragic loss of his family and his futile scouting mission with Iron Cedar on the east bank of the Greasy Grass. His participation in the Reno fight was cut short, and his participation in the final assault on Custer's five companies was tardy, but his courage and craftiness as a warrior were not compromised, nor was his role in the final attack on Keogh's and Yates's troopers negated; his tactic of stampeding the horses by shooting the Seventh's vulnerable horse holders proved to be his most important contribution in the Indian victory at the Little Bighorn.

Because Gall remained Sitting Bull's chief lieutenant after the Custer fight, clearly he was feted after the battle, as were such war leaders as Crazy Horse, Crow King, White Bull, Hump, and the Cheyenne leader Two Moon, who played such a key role in the last stages of the fight.

Even Rain-in-the-Face was recognized, despite his failure to make good on his vow to kill Custer or Custer's brother Tom.[62] One savvy frontiersman claimed that Gall did not participate in the scalp dance that followed because of his grief over the loss of five family members. His gloomy mood was lightened, however, when he was shown the severed head of Bloody Knife: "Now that my vilest enemy is dead, I can join you in the dance."[63]

But there was little time for the dancing and the unfortunate desecration of bodies that followed the battle. The long blue-coated columns under Terry and Gibbon were soon sighted coming from the north. In fact, the troopers under Reno and Benteen, besieged on Reno Hill for two days, undoubtedly wondered why the victorious Indians were igniting huge prairie fires to obscure their movements. Their question was soon answered when they saw a long procession of Indians leaving the village around 7:00 P.M. on June 26, followed by the arrival of Terry's men the next morning. The warriors on horseback, women and children on foot, and travois carrying all their belongings wound their way across the broad benchlands southwest of the now quiet battlefield, heading toward the Bighorn Mountains.[64] Little did they know how bleak their future would be.

This photograph, taken by David F. Barry at Fort Buford after Gall's surrender in 1881, is probably the first photograph of Gall. George Armstrong Custer's wife, Libbie, even regarded him as a "fine ... specimen of a warrior." Courtesy of the State Historical Society of North Dakota, 0123-08.

This oil painting of Gall by E. A. Burbank, which hangs in the Hubbell Trading Post in Ganado, Arizona, reveals his proud and handsome features as a reservation leader before his new lifestyle at Standing Rock caused him to gain more weight than was healthy for him. Courtesy of Hubbell Trading Post National Historic Site, HUTR 6059.

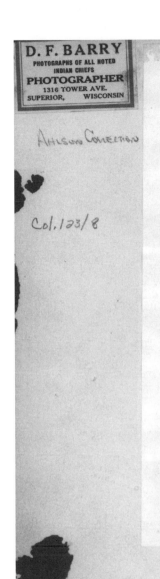

Chief Gall

Photo From Life by

David F. Barry

Photographer of

NOTED INDIANS

Superior, Wisconsin

CHIEF GALL.

THE Photograph of Chief Gall, with his head and body unadorned by savage finery of any kind with the Buffalo robes thrown back, baring his magnificent Torso, is one of the most striking of all Indian pictures, and it is a speaking likeness, too, looking just as if he had stepped forth to address his people.

GENL. CHAS. KING.

Mr. Barry:

Painful as it is for me to look upon a pictured face of an Indian, I never dreamed in all my life, there could be so fine a specimen of a warrior, in all the tribes as Chief Gall.

MRS. ELIZABETH B. CUSTER.

The Monarch Chief, with the Daniel Webster face, of all the North American Indians.

D. F. BARRY.

The greatest and the strongest Indian face I have ever seen.

TRENTANOVA.
The Sculptor of Florence, Italy.

Gall died in Dec. 1894, at Standing Rock Agency, North Dakota.
Gall was the Master Mind and the leader of the Indians in the Custer fight.

David F. Barry's advertisements for his photography business relied largely on his many photos of Gall. He once wrote a friend that Gall's face had been a "money maker" for him. Courtesy of the State Historical Society of North Dakota, 0123-08.

Gall's widowed mother, Walks-with-Many-Names, shown on the left, raised Gall after his father's death. Courtesy of the State Historical Society of North Dakota, A0108.

Brigadier General Alfred Sully led the force that defeated Gall and Sitting Bull at the Battle of Killdeer Mountain in July 1864. This battle was one of Gall's first encounters with federal troops. Courtesy of the State Historical Society of North Dakota, 0123-29.

An armed and determined-looking Gall appears ready for battle in this May 1881 photograph taken at Fort Buford, even though the Indian wars involving his people are largely in the past. Courtesy of the State Historical Society of North Dakota, 0022-H-0090.

The site of the Battle of Killdeer Mountain as it appears today. Except for the road, a monument, and two gravestones, it has changed very little since 1864. Courtesy of Gregory F. Michno.

Lieutenant Colonel George Armstrong Custer, his officers, and their wives pose in front of the Custer home at Fort Abraham Lincoln in 1873. Custer is standing in the second row, left side, between Second Lieutenant George D. Wallace and Custer's wife, Elizabeth B. "Libbie" Custer. Courtesy of the State Historical Society of North Dakota, 0022-H-0034.

Red Cloud played a major role in eliminating the forts along the Bozeman Trail, in the aftermath of the Red Cloud War of 1866–1867. The Oglala Sioux leader was also a key figure in bringing about the 1868 Treaty of Fort Laramie. Courtesy of the U.S. Military Academy Library.

Arikara scout Bloody Knife, kneeling at Custer's right over a grizzly bear they and their two companions had killed during Custer's 1874 Black Hills Expedition, was Gall's sworn enemy until the scout's death at the Little Bighorn in 1876. Courtesy of the State Historical Society of North Dakota, 0026-1-065.

This pictographic account of the Battle of the Little Bighorn by Kicking Bear omits Gall from the four Indian leaders standing in the center: Sitting Bull, Crazy Horse, Rain-in-the-Face, and Kicking Bear himself. Kicking Bear resented Gall's close cooperation with such federal officials at Standing Rock as Major James McLaughlin. Courtesy of the Autry National Center, Southwest Museum, Los Angeles, photo 1026.G.1.

Brigadier General Edward S. Godfrey, to whom Gall gave his version of the Battle of the Little Bighorn during the ten-year reunion of participants along the Little Bighorn River in 1886, had been a young lieutenant under Major Marcus A. Reno during that fateful encounter. Courtesy of the Montana Historical Society, Helena.

Brigadier General George Crook, one of the major figures in the Great Sioux War despite his less-than-successful encounter with Lakota and Cheyenne warriors at the Battle of the Rosebud, poses in his campaign attire, including the general's familiar pith helmet. From John Gregory Bourke's *On the Border with Crook*, frontispiece; courtesy of the State Historical Society of North Dakota, 978 B667.

CHAPTER NINE

The Zealous Pursuit

In their retreat from the Little Bighorn, the victorious Lakotas and their Cheyenne allies were faced with a host of problems. The most obvious was the arrival of the fresh troops from the north under Terry's command, but this military threat would not become truly serious for several months. Although the people back East were shocked and angered by Custer's humiliating demise, they would have to wait for the army to retaliate. Indeed, it would take time for General Sheridan to implement his plans for "total war" against this triumphant alliance of nontreaty Indians and their new agency allies. The most immediate problem facing such Lakota leaders as Sitting Bull, Crazy Horse, and Gall, however, was how to feed the Indians in this giant village. The search for buffalo became their top priority. The encampment's warriors would have to hunt and kill as many of these shaggy beasts as possible to stockpile enough meat to feed everyone.

Following the buffalo eventually took them eastward to the Rosebud. From this creek, where they had earlier fought Crook to a standstill, they continued their mass migration to the Tongue River. At their camp on the Tongue, the warrior-hunters of this increasingly unwieldy alliance broke into two large parties to search for buffalo, one going upstream and the other going downstream. When the hunt was completed, they moved eastward to rendezvous on the Powder River some twenty miles from its mouth.[1]

At their Powder River encampment, the villagers decided, after several days of debate and discussion, to disband. The problems involved in feeding such a large number of people was the main issue, but a decline in morale was another. Many warriors wanted to return to their agencies, where the supply of government meat rations was much more dependable. Resentment over the disciplining, or soldiering, of the village's warriors by the akicitas also created discontent. Sitting Bull could identify with this kind of frustration, because he had been an akicita at least twice during his long career as a warrior.[2]

After their decision to separate was made, several Little Bighorn veterans followed Crazy Horse up the Little Missouri toward the Black Hills, where they could hunt in smaller, more scattered parties, not driving away game as they had before. Another segment of warriors from this once grand encampment followed Sitting Bull. These warriors and their families included most of the Hunkpapas, along with a large number of Miniconjous and Sans Arcs. They traveled down the Little Missouri to Killdeer Mountain, where a dozen years earlier, many of them, including Gall and Sitting Bull, had first fought the blue-coated adversaries who had changed their lives so dramatically.

Although most of the nontreaty Indians and their recent allies were now in western Dakota, the forces of Crook and Terry were many miles away in Montana. On August 10, 1876, the men under both these commanders gathered on the Rosebud. They numbered more than four thousand soldiers, Indian scouts, and civilian employees. The decision of the two commanders to follow the trail of these migrating Indians east to the Tongue and Powder rivers would ultimately lead to frustration. The constant rain and mud generated by the weather had lowered their morale significantly. Prickly relations between the two generals only exacerbated the situation.[3]

On August 26 General Crook departed without even informing Terry of his decision. Moving eastward toward the badlands of the Little Missouri, he turned sharply southward in the direction of the Black Hills, traveling through country that is still remote and sparsely populated. His troops were hungry and dispirited as they slogged through the rain-soaked terrain of this wilderness region.

On September 8 a party under one of Crook's subordinates, Captain Anson Mills, who had been sent to the Black Hills to buy provisions for Crook's weary soldiers, encountered an encampment of Lakotas. It was near Slim Buttes, a rugged geological extension of the Black Hills. The village, as it turned out, was just one of a number of Indian camps in the area. Crazy Horse's Oglalas were there, as were White Eagle's Sans Arcs. There were also Miniconjous and some Hunkpapas in the region; indeed, about this time, Sitting Bull, along with Black Moon, Four Horns, Gall, and No Neck, had come down from Killdeer Mountain to camp in the vicinity.

The village Captain Mills reached was a Miniconjou one, comprising about thirty-seven lodges. Mills attacked it before daybreak on September 9, catching the Indians by surprise. In desperation, the Miniconjous broke out of their tipis, tightly fastened to make them as rainproof as possible, and scrambled toward a cluster of defensible bluffs to the south.[4] From their new positions, the warriors had recovered enough to pour gunfire on the soldiers below. Their firepower became increasingly effective as more and more Lakota warriors arrived from the nearby camps. The aging Sitting Bull, for instance, along with a number of Hunkpapa warriors, possibly including Gall, eventually joined the fray.

Crook arrived on the scene just before noon, and Captain Mills's 150-man force was enlarged to more than two thousand. After a blistering exchange of gunfire, which lasted throughout the day, the soldiers found various Seventh Cavalry possessions in the village, such as Company I's guidon. Inflamed by this discovery, they burned the encampment's lodges in revenge. Because the Lakota tribespeople in the Slim Buttes region had been as plagued by scarce provisions as had Crook's soldiers, they never forgave Captain Mills for starting the fires; he would be known to them thereafter as Jirug Narya, or Burns Lodges.[5]

After hours of fighting, Crook withdrew early the next morning. The growing numbers of vengeful Indians pursued him for a day before giving up the chase. Crook's forces, exhausted by the four hundred miles they had traveled since leaving Terry, headed toward the Black Hills. They hoped to acquire food supplies from the mining camps that had been proliferating there for two years, despite provisions in the Fort Laramie Treaty that forbade such inroads.

Crook declared the Battle of Slim Buttes a victory just as he had the Battle of the Rosebud six weeks earlier. It is true that his men destroyed the enemy's badly needed provisions by burning the Miniconjous' tipis; these lodges were so cleverly nestled in a wooded depression that their presence was all but concealed. Crook's men also boasted that they had killed, among the many adversaries they fought that day, American Horse, an uncle of the famous Oglala warrior of the same name. But this

American Horse was only a minor war chief.[6] If Gall had been at the battle, his participation did not attract much notice. Although Crook's attack was undoubtedly very effective, its overall result was to strengthen the resolve of many Lakotas not to surrender. There was also a degree of irony about this battle; it was fought on the western edge of the Great Sioux Reservation, which by treaty had been granted to the Lakotas.

During the following month, General Crook was sent to Camp Robinson, adjacent to the Red Cloud Agency in Nebraska, to disarm all the Lakota warriors and take their mounts away from them. This drastic move was part of General Sheridan's plan to crack down on the Sioux in retaliation for their bloody resistance at the Little Bighorn. In implementing Sheridan's new policy, Crook was acting in tandem with General Terry, who was doing the same thing at the Standing Rock and Cheyenne River agencies in the Dakotas.

Prior to disarming and dismounting all the Lakotas, the federal government had set into motion steps to acquire the gold-rich Black Hills. In mid-September, a panel headed by George W. Manypenny, a former commissioner of Indian affairs, won an agreement from such Oglala leaders as Red Cloud. These chiefs were to cede both the Black Hills and the unceded Indian territory west of the hills. Flushed with this success, the Manypenny Commission won agreements at such Lakota agencies as Standing Rock and Cheyenne River, where many of the treaty Indians had been located following the ratification of the Fort Laramie Treaty. Manypenny succeeded where Senator Allison and his commission had failed a year earlier because he was able to ignore article 12 of the treaty requiring the approval of three-fourths of all adult Indian males for any such measures of this importance.[7] Even the ordinarily obstinate Red Cloud finally realized the futility of fighting the loss of the Sioux's beloved Paha Sapa in light of the great anger in the East over Custer's defeat.

In implementing many of these new policies, Crook had the services of Colonel Ranald S. Mackenzie, who had earned much prestige in fighting the Comanches and Kiowas in the Southwest. An able but sometimes erratic officer who eventually retired because of mental problems, Mackenzie had been given command of Camp Robinson. Under Crook's orders the decisive Mackenzie took eight companies to Chadron Creek, east of the Red Cloud Agency, to disarm and dismount two Oglala encampments: one under Red Cloud and the other under Red Leaf. At dawn, on October 22, Mackenzie surrounded the two unsuspecting camps and disarmed both chiefs and their followers. He also allowed the Pawnee scouts under him to collect 722 ponies, giving each of them a mount apiece and selling the rest to the citizens of Cheyenne.

The only disappointment Mackenzie and his men faced in this hasty expedition was that the armaments these reservation Indians were suspected of having consisted of only a few old guns and pistols, plus a meager supply of ammunition, which largely undermined the justification for this seizure. Following this raid, all able-bodied Indians, including Red Leaf and the fifty-five-year-old Red Cloud, were forced to march thirty miles back to the Red Cloud Agency. Shortly after reaching the agency's stockade, Crook stripped Red Cloud of all his leadership authority and replaced him with Spotted Tail, a Brulé chief who was often at odds with Red Cloud.[8]

In September, soon after Crook parted ways with Terry to seek out recalcitrant Lakota warriors near the Black Hills, General Terry left for Fort Abraham Lincoln in Dakota Territory, while Colonel Gibbon left for Fort Shaw in northwestern Montana. In accordance with Sheridan's orders, Terry left Colonel Nelson A. Miles and the Fifth Infantry to winter in the Yellowstone country. Miles, a highly competent but vain officer, would become a most worthy adversary for Sitting Bull, Gall, and the other tenacious nontreaty Indians.

Miles established his headquarters on the Tongue River where it empties into the Yellowstone. Located downriver some 110 miles was the Glendive Cantonment, where the bulk of Miles's needed supplies were kept.[9] These two posts were part of a long defensive line established to contain such nontreaty Lakotas as the Hunkpapas south of the Yellowstone, but coordination among the military posts along this lifeline, which extended east to Fort Buford at the Yellowstone-Missouri junction, could be imperiled; the currents of the Yellowstone were sometime too shallow for steamboat travel. This made transportation between Miles's Tongue River post and the Glendive Cantonment particularly difficult at times.

Miles, relying on information provided by spies at the Indian agencies, was convinced that the bands following Sitting Bull were well below this new defensive line. Consequently, he was greatly surprised on October 10 when twenty or thirty Hunkpapa warriors attacked him and his military escort as they traveled from Glendive to his Tongue River outpost. It was now obvious that the nontreaty Hunkpapas, Miniconjous, and Sans Arcs, including such leaders as Sitting Bull, Gall, Pretty Bear, Red

Skirt, Bull Eagle, and No Neck, had left their encampments in the Black Hills area and breached the army's defenses along the Yellowstone. An even more serious threat to Miles's command was an assault made the following day on a military train of ninety-four wagons carrying supplies to the colonel's Tongue River cantonment. This raid, in which Lakota warriors ran off forty-seven mules, was so successful that the wagon train had to return to its starting point at Glendive.[10]

Because the dreary cluster of huts that made up Miles's Tongue River post badly needed these supplies, another wagon train with a military escort, comprising 11 officers and 185 infantrymen under the command of Lieutenant Colonel Ellwell Otis, left Glendive on October 14 to make another try at provisioning the Tongue River outpost. About fifteen miles west of Glendive, Otis's wagon train was attacked by a sizeable force of warriors at Spring Creek. Although hundreds were involved in the running skirmish that ensued, including Gall, casualties were low. Sitting Bull did, however, lose the support of his nephew White Bull, who was badly wounded when a bullet shattered his left arm.[11]

Sitting Bull faced other problems besides the loss of White Bull. Although Gall, no doubt still smoldering over the loss of most of his family, was determined to resist, many warriors were tired of fighting and wanted to negotiate. These warriors were encouraged by the arrival of two Indian couriers from Standing Rock, Bear's Face and Long Feather, with a message from Lieutenant Colonel William Carlin, the agency's commanding officer, urging all Sioux to surrender. But a parley with Otis on October 16 to discuss the question of peace did not bear fruitful results.[12]

A few days later, Colonel Miles, understandably concerned by the delay of Otis's wagon train, arrived with a formidable force of 449 men, the core of what would become known as the Yellowstone Command. After a successful rendezvous with Otis, the aggressive colonel moved his men northward to a broken upland region of ridges and ravines north of the Yellowstone; it was here that he believed his Lakota adversaries had retreated. He got within a few miles of the Lakota camp on Cedar Creek before he was approached by Bear's Face and Long Feather. The result was a subsequent encounter on October 20 between Colonel Miles and Sitting Bull, the first meeting Sitting Bull had with a major representative of the federal government.

Miles impressed these Indian negotiators with his attire. To cope with the cold weather, he wore a fur cap and a long overcoat made of bear fur;

indeed, he would be known to the Lakotas thereafter as Bear Coat. Sitting Bull, also feeling the cold of an otherwise sunny day, was wrapped in a buffalo robe; it covered his leggings and breechcloth but not his moccasined feet. He was accompanied by his injured nephew White Bull, the Sans Arc Fire-What-Man, the Brulé High Bear, and the Hunkpapa Jumping Bear.[13] Although Gall was not part of this inner circle, which represented the major nontreaty tribes still at war, he was probably among that group of warriors sent to back them up.

A good deal of time was consumed in arranging the preliminaries for this conference. The language barrier had been the initial impediment to progress, but this problem was solved when the presence of John Bruguier was discovered. Bruguier was a mixed-blood who had acted as an interpreter at Standing Rock. He had arrived at Sitting Bull's camp sometime before the Battle of Slim Buttes, looking like an overdressed cowboy; because of the large chaps he wore, the Lakotas began calling him Big Leggings. Bruguier had won Sitting Bull's confidence, and he probably saw in his role as conference translator a real opportunity to win Miles's friendship. Bruguier needed the support of an influential personage like Colonel Miles to beat a murder charge against him resulting from a drunken brawl that had occurred at Standing Rock in December.[14]

Because of Bruguier's skills as an interpreter, a good dialogue between Miles and Sitting Bull was possible. During this tense meeting, which lasted the entire afternoon, Miles criticized Sitting Bull for stealing mules from the army's wagon train on October 11, while Sitting Bull accused Miles of driving away all the buffalo herds in the region. The two men were poles apart throughout this intense meeting. Miles insisted on unconditional surrender on Sitting Bull's part and Sitting Bull insisted on a complete withdrawal from the Yellowstone country on Miles's part. Because of this stalemate, a frustrated Miles finally broke off the meeting. He suggested, however, that they meet the next day and try again.[15]

The second meeting on October 21 was equally tumultuous. On this occasion the Lakota delegation was much larger. Sitting Bull's still militant lieutenant Gall was there, as was Black Eagle, Bull Eagle, Standing Bear, Small Bear, Pretty Bear, Red Skirt, John Sans Arc, Yellow Eagle, and Rising Sun. Bull Eagle and Red Skirt were prepared to yield to Miles's demand at the meeting and had made their intentions clear enough to disturb Sitting Bull greatly.[16] Sitting Bull repeated many of the same arguments he had made the previous day, but this time the intransigent

Hunkpapa leader was not as articulate. His distress over the more conciliatory attitude of his Miniconjou and Sans Arc allies had robbed him of
some of his bluster.

Colonel Miles's shrewd moves to placate these wavering allies had
undermined Sitting Bull's confidence even more. The result was a dangerous escalation of anger, not only among the divided Indian delegation
but among Miles and his officers as well. Bear's Face, who along with
Long Feather had initiated these peace talks, claimed that at one of these
meetings, Bruguier did not even translate some of Colonel Miles's more
intemperate remarks for fear of an ugly outburst of violence in which
many of the negotiators would have been killed.[17] This second and final
meeting finally adjourned amid bitter recriminations.

In the early afternoon, shortly after the conference's angry dissolution,
Bear Coat and his large force of infantrymen began advancing toward
Sitting Bull's camp, located along Cedar Creek about five miles away. The
colonel's warlike movements should not have caused any surprise. He had
warned Sitting Bull during their last meeting that if the Lakota leader
did not surrender unconditionally, Miles would attack. In fact, Sitting
Bull's people were well prepared for such a contingency. The women and
children of the village had struck their tipis and made ready for flight
even before Sitting Bull's second conference with the resolute colonel
had begun.

Miles's Fifth Infantry, fully arrayed, marched slowly toward the defiant
Lakotas in what would later be known as the Battle of Cedar Creek. The
colonel's adversaries occupied a maze of ridges in this largely broken landscape. Colonel Miles suspected that Sitting Bull's warriors were hoping to
lure his men into a trap and create another Little Bighorn.[18] To prevent
such a scenario, Miles ordered his men to fan out and fight as skirmishers,
compelling the Lakotas to fall back slowly in a series of maneuvers that historian Paul L. Hedren has compared to a "giant chess game."[19]

Both sides were hesitant to fire the first shot, but when the Indians set
a large grass fire to cover the retreat of their women and children, an
explosion of gunfire began that lasted most of the afternoon of October
21. Because of the pressure Miles brought to bear, the Lakota warriors
eventually gave way, retreating for eighteen miles with the tenacious Bear
Coat in hot pursuit. Despite the large numbers involved in this battle,
casualties were low on both sides, just as they had been at Spring Creek;
five Indians were killed, and only two soldiers were wounded.[20]

With more Seventh Cavalry relics found in Sitting Bull's captured Lakota village, Miles was motivated to continue his zealous pursuit of these stubborn nontreaty Indians. Their new whereabouts in this wilderness country were finally discovered by the famous scout Yellowstone Kelly. They were now located many miles northeast of Cedar Creek on the Yellowstone River, just opposite the mouth of Cabin Creek. When Miles reached this site, he communicated with the Indians across the river, asking them for another parley. His strategy was to play on the fears and apprehensions of those more conciliatory tribesmen whom he had met during his earlier conferences with Sitting Bull.

On October 25, the leaders of these suspicious Lakotas crossed the Yellowstone to discuss Miles's peace terms. Most of them were flexible, except for Gall, who was clearly opposed to any surrender. During their meeting, Colonel Miles discovered the reason for this more cooperative attitude: Sitting Bull and thirty lodges of Hunkpapas had left the group during its retreat down Bad Route Creek. They were now heading north toward the Missouri in search of better hunting.

Sitting Bull's departure had embittered such influential tribesmen as the Miniconjou warrior Red Skirt. The shrewd Bear Coat was able to arrange a follow-up meeting with some of these unhappy Indians the next day. At that gathering, some two thousand Miniconjous, Sans Arcs, and Hunkpapas agreed to leave on October 27 for the Cheyenne River Agency to live in peace. Moreover, five of their leaders, including Red Skirt, agreed to go to St. Paul, Minnesota, as guarantors of this pledge. Only about 10 to 15 percent of these tribal members reached the Cheyenne River Agency by mid-November. Red Skirt evidently had a change of heart; he jumped the boat carrying the hostages to St. Paul. Yet the philosophical Miles considered the agreement the "beginning of the end" for all recalcitrant Lakota bands.[21]

By the end of October, Sitting Bull was encamped on the Big Dry about twenty-five miles south of Fort Peck. The resourceful chief and medicine man made promising contacts with the leaders of a nearby 125-lodge Hunkpapa encampment along the Missouri. These leaders, who included Crow, Little Knife, and Long Dog, had agreed to negotiate peace terms with Thomas J. Mitchell, the agent at Fort Peck, in exchange for badly needed food. Mitchell's terms were basically Bear Coat's: all Indians who surrendered were to be disarmed and dismounted. Before any agreement could be finalized, however, a convoy of supply boats for Colonel

Miles arrived from Fort Buford with 140 soldiers under the command of Colonel William B. Hazen. This new influx of soldiers shattered any possible accord with the army and, on November 1, the skeptical Hunkpapas struck their tipis and joined Sitting Bull on the Big Dry.

Sitting Bull's determination to continue his resistance did not abate. Gall, invaluable to Sitting Bull despite an occasional tendency to go it alone, eventually joined his mentor. His arrival, along with that of Pretty Bear and other hardline chiefs, brought the number of Sitting Bull loyalists to about four hundred.

Two weeks later Colonel Miles arrived at Fort Peck, promptly dispatching his troops down the Big Dry in search of Sitting Bull. But Sitting Bull, Gall, and their stubborn followers had moved east to Red Water, one of the many tributaries of the Missouri. There, Sitting Bull received a runner from Crazy Horse's encampment, asking for more ammunition so that the nontreaty mavericks to the south could continue their resistance.

By early December Sitting Bull was able to acquire fifty boxes of needed ammunition for Crazy Horse from the Slotas, or Métis, from Canada, a ubiquitous group of French mixed-bloods.[22] But his efforts to get these boxes to Crazy Horse's camp, located where the Tongue River leaves the Bighorn Mountains, was complicated by the ever-present threat posed by Miles. General Crook had largely ended his campaign against the nontreaty bands in the south after Colonel Mackenzie had successfully attacked Dull Knife and Wild Hog's Northern Cheyenne village on the Red Fork of the Powder on November 25, 1876. Miles, however, decided to keep his men in the field all winter rather than wait for late spring as Crook had done.[23]

Indeed, Bear Coat kept hounding Sitting Bull and his allies, despite the severe weather so common at the end of the year. No doubt his persistence was forcing Sitting Bull to acknowledge grudgingly that Miles's Tongue River outpost was becoming as permanent a fixture in Montana's buffalo country as Fort Buford had become a decade earlier. Miles's unwavering determination to make life impossible, even during the harshest weather, was demonstrated by his month-long pursuit of Sitting Bull's band in the area around Fort Peck. On December 7, for instance, three infantry companies led by First Lieutenant Frank D. Baldwin struck Sitting Bull, Gall, and their followers as they tried to cross the Missouri River opposite the mouth of Bark Creek.[24] This effort, an episode in what historians have called the Fort Peck Expedition, was part of Colonel Miles's grand strategy to fulfill Sheridan's ongoing desire to launch aggressive winter campaigns. Although the Lakotas eluded Baldwin and suffered no casualties, this incident heightened Sitting Bull's concern and apprehension over Bear Coat's unremitting threat.

After some dogged maneuvering, Baldwin discovered the old chief's village on Ash Creek, only seven miles from the site where the Battle of Cedar Creek had been fought less than a month earlier. On December 18, Baldwin's men attacked the village, forcing its inhabitants to flee. His use of a makeshift Howitzer, which he had assembled earlier, was responsible for part of his success; the weapon badly rattled the already exhausted Lakota warriors. After seizing the encampment, Miles's able lieutenant destroyed 122 tipis, which the Indians had been forced to abandon in the haste of their retreat. Gall, who fled westward with two other chiefs, claimed a lack of sufficient ammunition was the cause of this defeat. Ironically, though, Sitting Bull was able to escape with those fifty boxes of ammunition destined for Crazy Horse.[25]

It took Sitting Bull about a month of difficult travel to reach Crazy Horse's camp along Prairie Dog Creek, close to where the Tongue River flows out of the Bighorns. It is not certain whether Gall accompanied him or whether he and Sitting Bull had to scatter in different directions when their village was captured. The once supreme leader of all the non-treaty bands had only a hundred Hunkpapa lodges under him when he arrived at Crazy Horse's encampment on January 15, 1877. To his disappointment, Sitting Bull found Crazy Horse's village to be crowded with discouraged hunting bands, including Cheyenne refugees from Mackenzie's successful November 25 attack on Dull Knife's camp. The uneasy collection of Lakota and Cheyenne warriors who greeted him was sharply divided over the question of war or peace. The Miniconjous and Sans Arcs were ready to surrender, while the Oglalas and Cheyennes were determined to resist.[26]

One reason for this sharp schism, aside from the lack of food and other needed supplies, was the military setback that had occurred in the Wolf Mountains on January 8. This encounter, considered the last major battle of the Great Sioux War, again involved the peripatetic Colonel Miles. He and his force of seven companies from the Fifth and Twenty-second infantries had left their Tongue River outpost, traveling upriver to the Wolf Mountains in southeastern Montana where Crazy Horse had been at the time.

Crazy Horse, in an increasingly rare opportunity to demonstrate his prowess, tried, without success, to lure Miles's infantry forces into an ambush. When that strategy failed, both sides fired copious amounts of ammunition at each other; the Indians managed on this occasion to shatter the belief that, even when they were well armed with repeating rifles, they were chronically short of ammunition.[27] But because of the notoriously bad weather, the two opposing forces, maneuvering near a cone-shaped landmark called Battle Butte, suffered few casualties. A blizzard finally ended this futile conflict about midday; the scrappy Oglala and Cheyenne warriors reluctantly felt compelled to withdraw from the battle.[28]

A couple of weeks after the arrival of Sitting Bull's band at Crazy Horse's encampment, the bands decided to separate. The Miniconjous and the Sans Arcs struggled eastward, many of them reaching the Cheyenne River Agency to surrender. The Oglalas and Cheyennes, who had played the most prominent role at the Wolf Mountain Battle, crossed these same mountains to hunt buffalo in the valley of the Little Bighorn.

During spring 1877 both Spotted Tail and Red Cloud began their efforts to persuade Crazy Horse's followers to make peace by going to the Oglala agency at Red Cloud. On May 6, a long procession of 899 people, led by Crazy Horse and Red Cloud, arrived at the agency, ending most of the opposition to Miles's determination to crush all Indian resistance.[29] But the last gasp of their cause occurred on May 7, four months after the Wolf Mountain Battle. The Miniconjou leader Lame Deer, who had vowed never to surrender, was defeated and killed, along with thirteen of his followers, only thirty miles from the site of the Little Bighorn.[30]

Long before the collapse of Lakota and Cheyenne resistance in the south, however, Colonel Miles had successfully divided the nontreaty bands, separating the northern ones from the southern ones. When Sitting Bull returned north with his dispirited followers, he was aware of a strong sentiment among his people to seek refuge in Canada. Two leaders he greatly respected, his uncle Four Horns and the veteran Hunkpapa leader Black Moon, clearly preferred such an option. To them, exile in Grandmother's land was better than being at the mercy of the Great White Father in Washington.[31]

As early as December 1876, Black Moon, with fifty-two Hunkpapa lodges, settled with refugees from other Lakota tribes at Wood Mountain, north of the border. Three thousand Lakotas had now taken the *chanku wakan,* or sacred road, to the vast prairie lands of Canada in the hopes of finding a better life. In March 1877, Four Horns, leading another band about the size of Black Moon's, joined this northward migration.

Sitting Bull, following his arrival from Crazy Horse's camp in April, convened a council at Beaver Creek, sixty miles northwest of Fort Peck. He wanted to discuss with his warriors the possibility of moving to Canada. No Neck, who had accompanied him to Crazy Horse's village in January, was there, as was Spotted Eagle, who had broken with most of his Sans Arc tribe over the issue of surrender. Sitting Bull announced at this meeting that he intended to take his band northward to explore the possibilities of a Canadian exile. On April 16, he reached a Slota trading camp on the Milk River, eventually crossing the Canadian border during the first week in May.[32]

Gall, who had his own band, was probably not at the Beaver Creek council, but he, too, would decide for Canada, along with such warriors as Rain-in-the-Face, Bear King, Charging Thunder, and Bone Club.[33] Even the sixty-two-year-old Dakota warrior Inkpaduta, who had played such a vital role at the Battle of Killdeer Mountain, made the trip, only to die during the four-year Canadian exile with these still proud and hopeful people.[34] The nontreaty bands of the Lakotas were ready for a new life in a land where there would be no blue-coated adversaries to pursue them with the zeal that had marked the difficult months since their victory at the Little Bighorn.

CHAPTER TEN

The Canadian Exile

In early May, Sitting Bull, at the head of 135 Canadian-bound lodges, traveled along the White Mud River, a tributary of the Milk River familiar to the Sioux in northern Montana. The White Mud, also called Frenchman's Creek, flowed through the Canadian prairie lands that constituted much of the province of Saskatchewan. The river started on Saskatchewan's western boundary, in the Cypress Hills, which bordered an enormous grassland that would become the new home of the Lakotas for the next four years. This grassy region stretched from the Cypress Hills eastward along the U.S. border, for approximately 180 miles, to Wood Mountain. At this partially timbered escarpment, Four Horns and Black Moon had already established their Wood Mountain encampment.

The entire region must have appeared to Sitting Bull's and Gall's bands as the promised land. Buffalo still roamed its greening plains in greater numbers than in the United States.[1] Moreover, the great spaces of this new land were comparable to the Lakotas' traditional hunting lands in Montana and the Dakotas. Many northern Lakotas knew this to be true because of previous forays into southern Canada in search of buffalo.

At the end of their sixty-mile journey, Sitting Bull's followers encamped near the Pinto Horse Butte, a geological extension of Wood Mountain, which was located east of the new site. Shortly after their arrival, they encountered a man who would have a great influence over all the Lakotas during their Canadian exile: Major James M. Walsh, an inspector in the Northwest Mounted Police and commander at Fort Walsh in the Cypress

Hills. This handsome, well-built man, with a regal moustache, arrived at Sitting Bull's new camp with six other horsemen, most of whom wore the white helmets and red tunics of the Mounted Police. Walsh, a forceful, self-confident man, had, without hesitation, led his men past the suspicious Indian pickets guarding Sitting Bull's village. Although the Canadian tribes in this area called him White Forehead, perhaps because of his white helmet, the Lakotas promptly dubbed him Long Lance, a name probably inspired by the lances tipped with red-and-white pennons that Walsh and his men carried.[2]

The exceptional confidence that Walsh showed was rather remarkable, considering the warlike reputation the Sioux had gained because of their decisive victory at the Little Bighorn. Nor did the newness and limited experience of the Northwest Mounted Police deter the major's attitude of self-reliance. The Mounted Police were only three years old at the time, being formed seven years after the eastern Canadian provinces had been confederated as a dominion of the British Empire. Only in 1869, the year that Sitting Bull had become the supreme chief of all the non-treaty bands, did these eastern provinces organize western Canada into provinces such as Saskatchewan.

Prior to this date, the Hudson's Bay Company governed this vast land of prairies and mountains west of Hudson Bay. The political vacuum caused by the termination of this company's governing authority made the Northwest Mounted Police a necessary force for law and order in the region. The activities of the ubiquitous American whiskey peddlers in the Saskatchewan area alone would have necessitated some kind of intervention to keep the peace among such Canadian tribes as the Crees, Blackfeet, Piegans, Bloods, Assiniboines, Sarsi, and Salteaux, not to mention such mixed-bloods as the Slotas. The arrival of the Sioux in 1877 would undoubtedly complicate the challenges faced by this recently formed police force.

At this first meeting with Sitting Bull, Major Walsh laid down the law to the chief's weary and bedraggled Lakota tribespeople. He told them that they were now in the land of the Great White Mother, a term the Mounted Police favored over Grandmother's Land when dealing with Canadian tribes. The Lakotas would have to obey the queen's laws, he said, but in return they would receive the queen's protection, a guarantee enjoyed by all Canada's inhabitants, regardless of color.

He warned the Lakotas against any return to the United States to steal property or hunt buffalo; any serious violation of this kind could mean a loss of the Lakotas' Canadian asylum. Because the Indians in Canada had long crisscrossed the border in search of buffalo on both sides of the international boundary, this ultimatum would one day be difficult to obey, but during late spring 1877, buffalo were plentiful in Canada, and this decree posed no immediate problem.

Sitting Bull's encampment near Pinto Horse Butte consisted of only 135 lodges, so Gall and his band may not have been with them, but Major Walsh would have probably communicated with Sitting Bull's longtime lieutenant during the spring or summer of 1877; Walsh had already delivered his message regarding strict obedience to the queen's law to the camps of Four Horns and Black Moon before his encounter with Sitting Bull.[3] Presumably, sometime during these first few months, Gall would have received the major's characteristically strong ultimatum and would have received it as favorably as Sitting Bull had.[4] The two Hunkpapa leaders were still close, Gall having served Sitting Bull without serious deviation for years. In Canada, however, Sitting Bull would rely more on his nephew One Bull to carry out his wishes for the Hunkpapas and their allies. Spotted Eagle, who had broken with many of his Sans Arc tribesman, also seemed to enjoy more stature among the nontreaty bands than Gall did during these early days in Canada.

One incident that particularly impressed Sitting Bull in his first meeting with the Northwest Mounted Police was Walsh's forceful handling of a surly Assiniboine warrior named White Dog. As Sitting Bull's meeting with the Mounted Police was about to end, White Dog and two of his companions entered the village with five horses, three of which Walsh's men recognized as being stolen. The major promptly challenged White Dog. The Assiniboine made an open appeal to the members of Sitting Bull's band, who, like the Assiniboines, believed that horse stealing was just a part of life, but the willful major dragged a set of large irons toward the recalcitrant warrior. White Dog, fearing jail time, backed down, and the surprised onlookers from the Lakota camp became convinced that Major Walsh would always mean what he said.[5]

As Sitting Bull and other Lakota leaders interacted even more with these red-coated law enforcers, their respect for them grew. The Mounted Police were usually fair in their judgments; indeed, some of them, including Walsh, honestly believed that the Lakotas had been badly treated below the Canadian border. But the migration of so many bands of American Indians into this still largely undeveloped part of Canada posed an enormous challenge to the recently organized Mounted Police. By spring 1878, the number of nontreaty bands in Canada reached about eight hundred lodges, bringing the total population of Lakotas in Saskatchewan to approximately five thousand, a number that exceeded by about 50 percent the population of those independent bands gathered on the northern plains before the Little Bighorn.[6]

The influx of tribes from the United States increased after Crazy Horse was fatally shot while being arrested on September 5, 1877.[7] Responding to Congress's decree to move the Sioux from the Red Cloud and Spotted Tail agencies in Nebraska east to a new reservation on the banks of the Missouri, Red Cloud led eight thousand Lakotas, most of whom were Oglalas, eastward during fall 1877.[8] About a fourth of the Lakotas involved in this version of the infamous Trail of Tears were from the northern plains; a number of them separated from this great migration to make their way to Canada.

Indeed, by spring 1878, some 240 lodges, allegedly part of Crazy Horse's old nontreaty band, arrived in Canada. Their leaders included Crazy Horse's uncle Little Hawk and Fools Heart, the son of the martyred Miniconjou warrior Lame Deer. Another Oglala arrival, Big Road, who was threatened by his own people if he did not move to Canada, later became a major Sioux leader north of the border. Many of the Oglalas insisted that Crazy Horse had remarked before his death that he would eventually join his followers in Grandmother's Land.[9]

The arrival of American Indians to the grasslands of southern Saskatchewan undoubtedly disturbed the Canadian tribes. Such long-time enemies of the Lakotas as the Crees, Blackfeet, Piegans, and Bloods were especially suspicious, but as long as the bison herds were plentiful, there would be no major conflict; the Northwest Mounted Police would see to that. A more immediate problem was the attitude of the United States government. Bear Coat Miles, whose men were building new posts, such as Fort Keogh and Fort Custer, on the Lakotas' old buffalo grounds, was itching to cross the Canadian border and deliver a final blow to all Sioux resistance.

General Sherman did not mind having the Sioux in their new homes north of the United States if the Canadian government would create reservations for them and feed them; such a commitment would relieve the U.S. federal government of any future responsibility. But the Canadian government, acting through the Mounted Police, was not going to accept the Lakotas as reservation Indians; it was only willing to offer them a haven in southern Canada as long as they obeyed the queen's law. The British government, which acted in Ottawa's behalf, would have preferred having these Indians return to their agencies in America, but it did not want them to be dismounted and disarmed; this was London's position as it was argued in Washington.[10]

The international implications of this latest chapter in the all-consuming Sioux question were made evident by General Terry's mission to Canada in late October 1877. Terry met with Sitting Bull and other Lakota leaders at Fort Walsh in a tense conference made possible only by the presence of the Northwest Mounted Police; these Canadian constables insisted on as much civility from the Indians as possible. Terry, a more patient and gentle man than Colonel Miles when it came to dealing with the Lakotas, opened the conference with a call for peace. He promised the Indians that the United States government would receive them in a hospitable manner and refrain from punishing them. The Lakotas would have to surrender their guns and ponies, but these possessions would be sold and the money spent on livestock to start them off on a new life. Sitting Bull was adamantly opposed to any such arrangement and said so forcefully: "The country we came from belonged to us; you took it away from us; we will live here."[11] The conference, which was almost chaotic at times, ended in failure.

One embarrassing incident that cast a shadow over these proceedings was caused by the seventeen hundred-mile journey of Chief Joseph and his Nez Percé followers. They were fleeing from a federal Indian policy that would have placed them on an Idaho reservation. Colonel Miles was able to intercept Joseph's eight hundred Nez Percé Indians in early October at Bear Paw Mountain, only forty miles south of the tribe's hoped-for Canadian sanctuary. Messengers had kept the Lakotas informed of Chief Joseph's progress, even though the Nez Percés were allies of the Sioux's Crow adversaries. The Lakotas identified with what the Nez Percés were going through.[12]

One Nez Percé leader, White Bird, did manage to cross the international boundary a couple of weeks before the October 17 meeting with General Terry convened. Ninety adults and their children were with him, many of whom had been wounded during their escape from Miles's tenacious pursuers. Eventually some forty five Nez Percé lodges under White Bird would join the Lakotas in their Canadian asylum.[13]

Despite the international tensions that marked the early months of the Lakotas' move to Canada, life in the new land was not much different from what it had been south of the border. The great grasslands were much like those in northern Montana and the Dakota Territory. Buffalo herds were still plentiful; the ceremonies tied to the hunting of these beasts could be celebrated as they had been for decades. In summer 1877, for instance, a big sun dance was held on a slope of Wood Mountain.[14] There was even a promising trade outlet: a friendly French Canadian named Jean Louis Legaré established a post at Wood Mountain for trade with the Lakotas. Except for the sanctions against tribal warfare and horse stealing, the old way of life was still largely intact.

There was, of course, some restlessness, particularly among younger warriors embittered by the unhappy circumstances of their exile. Being separated from friends and family made it difficult for most members of these nontreaty bands; Sitting Bull, for instance, sorely missed the support of White Bull, who was now living on the Cheyenne River Agency, having been too badly wounded at Spring Creek to accompany him to Canada.

Because of these symptoms of discontent, the Lakota leadership felt it necessary to maintain a tight grip on tribal activities that might defy the queen's law or involve possible defections to the United States. This policy of enforcing certain strict standards of behavior was called "soldiering" by the Sioux. It became particularly important as the Canadian buffalo herds began to dwindle in 1878. This development, which increased the rivalry among all Canadian tribes over their diminishing food supply, tempted many Lakota warriors to cross the border in search of buffalo. Sitting Bull, who was determined to maintain his good relations with Major Walsh and other Mounted Policemen, largely used One Bull, his favorite Miniconjou nephew now that White Bull was gone, to oversee this soldiering.[15]

In disciplining his independent-minded warriors, Sitting Bull risked both his popularity and his moral authority over them. Individual war chiefs like Gall could be especially sensitive to intervention of this kind, even though they reflected Sitting Bull's honest convictions. One example of the dilemma that this policy could cause involved Gray Eagle, the young brother of two of Sitting Bull's wives. Gray Eagle allegedly stole the horses of a French citizen and kept them hobbled in a hidden place. One account claims this theft was part of a successful effort involving others to abscond with 150 horses that belonged to the Slotas. The Mounted Police, who suspected that Gray Eagle was part of this unsavory conspiracy, which was in clear violation of the queen's law, went to

Sitting Bull for help. The old chief, no doubt coping with pressure from his wives to be merciful, ordered Gray Eagle to return the horses. He also asked for permission to punish Gray Eagle and the others involved.

Sitting Bull's brother-in-law and his partners in this misdeed were ordered to ride over a nearby hill, where the *akicitas* in charge of soldiering could fire shots over their heads. Gray Eagle claimed that he was given an especially spirited horse, and that if he had fallen off this mount, the Canadian police could, by agreement, shoot him. Gray Eagle, an excellent rider, stayed on his horse, as Sitting Bull thought he would. His punishment was completed by being tied to a tree, where he was to fast for the entire day.

His three fellow malefactors, according to other sources, were tied to the ground for a week before a tribal reconciliation ceremony brought this entire incident to a close.[16] But Gray Eagle never fully reconciled with Sitting Bull as a result of this brutal soldiering; indeed, when the Hunkpapas were sent to Standing Rock in the early 1880s, Gray Eagle became a member of the police force that would be responsible for Sitting Bull's arrest and death thirteen years later.

Sitting Bull probably could have maintained this tight discipline indefinitely if it had not been for the increasing scarcity of buffalo. The mild climate of late spring and summer 1877 had been extremely beneficial to the Lakotas. The winter of 1877–1878 was also uncommonly mild, allowing large herds to graze on the land from the Cypress Hills to Wood Mountain. Although many buffalo had remained on these grasslands, some began to scatter and travel in small groups during the summer. More ominous were the large numbers of bison who drifted across the border into the United States. When these animals left Canada, scores of them were felled by rapacious Montana hide hunters. Within three or four years, the Canadian herds would be driven to near extinction.

The tragic fate of the buffalo was complicated by the needs of rival Canadian tribes. The moderate winter of 1877–1878, for instance, caused huge prairie fires northwest of the Cypress Hills, where the Blackfeet, the major Indian tribe in this part of Canada, had hunted for years. Forced to search for the indispensable bison herds on the western edge of the new Sioux hunting grounds, these Indians, longtime rivals of the Lakotas, began to resent the recent Lakota intrusion into Canada.

Sitting Bull was keenly aware of the potential dangers of this kind of situation; earlier, in summer 1877, he had made peace with the most powerful leader of the Blackfeet, Crow Foot. It had worked surprisingly well for a time, but as the number of bison herds began to diminish, serious differences between these two tribes started to simmer.[17]

The Canadian government, recognizing the alarming problems caused by the declining herds, concluded a series of treaties with the Blackfeet and other Canadian tribes. In these new treaties, the tribes of western Canada were given reservations. More important, they were promised yearly annuities to avoid the potential for starvation if the buffalo herds continued their steady decline. But Canadian authorities would not even consider giving the Lakotas a reservation or even feeding them, as the U.S. federal government would if they returned to the United States.

The most formidable adversaries of these nontreaty bands, generals Sherman, Sheridan, and Terry, were frankly relieved to have the Lakotas living outside the country's boundaries. Colonel Miles, however, was eager to cross the international border and end the Lakota threat once and for all. Like many of those in the government or with the national press, men who had built up Sitting Bull's fearsome reputation through published interviews with him, Miles believed that Sitting Bull had become an evil magnet.[18] He could and would draw troublesome Indians northward to increase his numbers and spark mischief among them south of the border. Because of Miles's hawkish views, he was commanded by his more cautious superiors to stay south of the Missouri River.

But early in 1878, the Lakotas, along with other tribes from Canada, began to straddle the international boundary; they often encamped north of the border and hunted buffalo south of it. Most of them probably did not realize that the vast grasslands between the Missouri River and the Canadian border had been recently set aside by the U.S. federal government as reservation lands for such tribes as the Assiniboines, River Crows, and Gros Ventres. Moreover, the federal government had reserved a broad stretch of territory south of the Missouri for the ordinarily peaceful Yanktonais. These tribes had been fed and managed from Fort Peck until a devastating flood in March 1877 destroyed the fort. The agent at Fort Peck now fed the Yanktonais at a new agency on the Poplar River, where it joined the Missouri at Wolf Point. This agent had often complained to higher authorities about the amount of rations received by the Yanktonais that ended up in the hands of their Hunkpapa relatives.[19] Indeed, most of the Indian agents along the Missouri were becoming as impatient as Colonel Miles with the controversial practices of such tribes as the Yanktonais.

As starvation became an increasing reality along the Canadian border in 1879, more nontreaty Lakota bands began to cross the boundary in search of buffalo. Gall and his band were among them. Sitting Bull's long-time lieutenant, who continued to trade with treaty Indians and friendly whites during the most stressful of times, had even developed friendships with certain agency workers; the close relations he enjoyed with the agency employees at Poplar River, where he would surrender in 1881, indicated the probability of earlier contacts with them. His connections to people like Edwin H. "Fish" Allison, the scout, interpreter, and live-stock raiser who in 1880 was employed by the Circle F Ranch in Montana's Sun River range, could hardly be considered natural friend-ships in this part of the West.[20]

But Gall seemed to be undergoing some kind of change. He tended to maintain a rather low profile during his people's Canadian exile, allowing One Bull and White Eagle to act as Sitting Bull's major spokesmen.[21] Moreover, Gall's border crossings in search of the diminishing buffalo herds apparently caused no major incident, but other crossings, particularly those by younger, more reckless warriors, often resulted in serious incidents, such as livestock thefts or attacks on whites who attempted to resist these thefts.

Ironically, the incident that finally brought Colonel Miles back into the lives of these nontreaty exiles involved Sitting Bull. In early June 1879, Sitting Bull joined a Sioux hunting party in the vicinity of the Milk River, south of the Canadian border. His warriors, feeling the des-perate effects of the hunger that afflicted them and their families, discovered a sizable herd of bison. The intense hunting efforts that fol-lowed this discovery soon accounted for many welcomed buffalo carcasses. During that same month, Indian incursions all along the bor-der had provided a strong rationale to unleash the determined colonel, who had been agitating for months to put an end to Sioux defiance.

Responding to General Terry's order on June 5 to drive the Lakotas back across the international boundary, Miles headed north from the now ruined and abandoned Fort Peck with seven hundred infantry, cavalry, and artillery, along with a number of Crow, Assiniboine, and Cheyenne scouts. On July 17, Miles's men found the hunting party Sitting Bull had joined; many of them were women and children butchering the carcasses of the recently killed buffalo.

An attack by two mounted companies under the command of Lieutenant William P. Clarke drove these surprised Indians back. The decisiveness of the assault could have been disastrous if some sixty warriors who had left the hunt had not returned to reverse the tide of battle. In the end, however, the hungry Lakota warriors and their families had to retreat when Miles arrived with his main force and turned those feared howitzers on them. Even though Sioux casualties were light, Miles was able to boast of his great victory on the Milk River; after all, Sitting Bull, whose name had become a household word in America, was there.[22]

After the Battle of Milk River, there was great apprehension among the Lakotas about whether Miles's forces would cross the Canadian border and attack all the Lakota encampments on the Saskatchewan grasslands. The Canadians were apprehensive, too, and Major Walsh visited Colonel Miles's camp twice in July. During the second meeting, on July 28, 1879, Walsh brought along a Hunkpapa warrior named Long Dog, who had become very popular with officers of the Northwest Mounted Police; he had also attracted the attention of the American journalists covering this major international news story. When Miles candidly asked this colorful and quotable Hunkpapa war chief on which side of the Canadian border he and his people intended to live, the Indian's reply was equally candid: we want to stay in Canada.[23] Bear Coat Miles accepted this answer, perhaps with some relief, and, declaring victory, withdrew his troops to the south.

Major Walsh, despite some differences with Sitting Bull, remained the supreme Hunkpapa chief's champion, but the Canadian government was becoming disenchanted with the colorful major and his outspoken views. Ottawa no longer wanted the Lakotas to remain in Canada, nor was it willing to feed them and give them a reservation. In essence, it had decided that the only solution to the stalemate between the United States and the Dominion of Canada was to let starvation take its course. This cruel solution would ultimately drive the Lakotas back across the border, where they could join their families and relatives on the Great Sioux Reservation. In spring 1880, the authorities in Ottawa decided that, after Major Walsh completed his scheduled July leave in the East, he would be reassigned to Fort Qu'Appelle, some 140 miles northeast of Wood Mountain, far enough to limit significantly his contacts with Sitting Bull.[24]

Walsh, probably the only white man Sitting Bull ever fully trusted, felt a genuine concern over the fate of this strong-willed leader and his people. In fact, in his efforts to reassure them, he built up hopes that could never be fulfilled. He promised the chiefs of Sitting Bull's perplexed non-treaty bands that he would ask the Canadian government to permit him to visit Washington and ask the American president to designate a reservation for such especially cooperative Indians as Big Road, Little Hawk, and their Oglala tribespeople. Walsh, who had become quite controversial in Canada as the Lakotas' main spokesman, would also work to have a reservation created for the Oglalas on the Tongue River or, if that effort failed, have them share with the Yanktonais the relatively new Indian agency on Montana's Poplar River.

If Walsh were successful in achieving these objectives, however, Sitting Bull and Spotted Eagle would be required to surrender. If he failed, he would lobby his government for a long-sought reservation in Canada for Sitting Bull's Hunkpapas and Spotted Eagle's Sans Arcs.[25] Sitting Bull had great hopes for Walsh's dubious mission, refusing to surrender or return to the United States until he had personally consulted with this trusted officer of the Canadian Mounted Police.

In the meantime, Walsh's replacement, inspector Lief N. F. Crozier, took command of Walsh's old post at Wood Mountain on July 13, 1880. The new commander, who was soon promoted to the rank of major, had a much different attitude toward the Lakotas' Canadian exile than did his predecessor. Lacking Walsh's charisma, Crozier refused to acknowledge Sitting Bull's special status as the leader of those Lakotas still struggling to survive on Saskatchewan's no longer game-rich grasslands. In his new role Crozier tended to address the Lakotas as a large tribal group rather than simply as Sitting Bull's people.[26] Moreover, he pressed the Lakotas to surrender and return to the United States much more fervently than Walsh ever did.

Major Crozier's efforts were soon rewarded. Within a week of assuming his new assignment, he successfully persuaded White Eagle of the utter futility of staying in Canada. The popular young Sans Arc leader, who had supported Sitting Bull for three years, had been encamped with his people on the banks of the Red Water, between the Yellowstone and Missouri rivers. He was later joined there by Rain-in-the-Face's small band, bringing the number of lodges under White Eagle's leadership to approximately eighty. On October 31, 1880, these two chiefs surrendered all their guns and ponies to one of Colonel Miles's officers from Fort Keogh.

Bear Coat Miles had already enjoyed considerable success in luring such nontreaty veterans to Fort Keogh as the Miniconjou leader Hump and such Northern Cheyenne leaders as Two Moon, Dull Knife, and Little Wolf. With the arrival of the Oglala chief Big Road, the army could count 1,510 Lakotas and Cheyennes peacefully encamped near the fort by the end of the year.[27]

Even Sitting Bull had been forced to think about the painful issue of surrender.[28] He had already sent One Bull to Fort Buford to discuss peace terms in May 1880. Colonel William B. Hazen, then in command at Buford, told Sitting Bull's nephew and emissary that the government had not changed its terms: the Sioux would have to be dismounted and disarmed as part of the peace process. Because of the government's continued insistence on these harsh terms, Sitting Bull would remain ambivalent on the subject of surrender for another fourteen months.

Because of Sitting Bull's stubbornness, Gall, who had his own band to care for, began to challenge the leadership of his old mentor. He probably had decided that his duties as a tiospaye headman were more pressing than those of a blotahunka, or war chief, given the hunger and destitution of his band as well as the other bands. This change of attitude probably started rather early during the Lakotas' Canadian exile. Gall had not been very active in the politics of his people since arriving in Grandmother's Land. Like Sitting Bull, he respected the queen's law, but this respect did not prevent him from crossing the border to hunt buffalo, especially when the once large Canadian herds began to decline.[29] One suspects, though, that the forty-year-old warrior, a seasoned veteran of many hunts, was much more discreet than many of the younger warriors in his infractions of the queen's law.

That Gall had begun to see the futility of staying in Canada became especially obvious during the summer of 1880. On August 1, Gall, while engaged in one of those forbidden hunts south of the border, encountered his old friend Edwin H. "Fish" Allison at the confluence of the Milk River and Frenchman's Creek. Fish was acting as a scout and interpreter for two Montana ranchers, who were driving a herd of twelve hundred cattle from the Sun Range in Montana to the railhead at Bismarck.[30] He nervously told Gall and the large hunting party he headed that these beeves were bound for Canada; they "belonged to the Queen of England" and were part of the food provisions destined for Canada's Mounted Police. To Fish's relief, Gall accepted this story, even if he did not fully believe it. The two promptly engaged in a friendly conversation made possible by Fish's able command of the Lakota language. The shrewd scout and interpreter invited Gall and his perpetually hungry Lakota companions to share in a grand steak feast that evening.

The remarks exchanged between these two men inevitably touched upon the subject of surrender. Fish suggested to Gall that if he could arrange a conference with Sitting Bull for him, this could hasten the process of surrender. In fact, such a visit might even end the painful cycle of hunger for Gall's people. Gall was reticent about making any promises, but he did seem rather interested in Fish's proposal to visit Sitting Bull. In fact, he told Fish that Sitting Bull and his band were currently encamped at Ruined Timber, a cluster of forested hills located twenty miles north of Wood Mountain.

Seeing an opportunity to make a name for himself, Allison told Major David Brotherton, the new commandant at Fort Buford, about his meeting with Gall when he arrived at the fort with his herd of cattle. Brotherton quickly grasped the importance of Allison's proposal for a visit to Sitting Bull's camp; he even hired Allison as an army scout and made the fort's military stores available for the success of his mission. Several days later, Allison reached the principal Lakota encampment at Ruined Timber, where Gall warmly greeted him. Although he was there for three days, the ambitious peacemaker was unable to schedule a visit with Sitting Bull. He did, however, arrange to meet Gall again in twenty-two days, at a point on the Missouri River where they could discuss workable terms for a possible surrender.[31]

Upon Allison's return to Fort Buford, he met an unhappy, if not testy, Major Brotherton; the major had been reprimanded by General Terry for authorizing Allison's mission. But when Terry heard about the arrangement to meet Gall again to discuss peace terms, he, too, became one of Allison's avid supporters. On October 25, Allison and an enlisted soldier named Day, who was sent along to assist him, met a messenger sent by Gall. This courier directed Allison and his new companion to another Lakota camp near the juncture of Frenchman's Creek and the Milk River, about fifty miles south of the Canadian border, where Allison finally got his long-sought meeting with Sitting Bull. After a cordial but not particularly fruitful encounter with the Hunkpapa leader, Allison again contacted Gall. The veteran war chief, still vigorous and formidable looking despite his age, informed Allison that he fully intended to arrange a surrender involving everyone in the Lakota camp, including Sitting Bull.

It was obvious to Allison that there was a serious political crisis brewing among these now destitute Lakota exiles. Sitting Bull, in his opinion, was out of touch with reality, while Gall was obviously adamant about ending the days of near starvation for his people. But Gall insisted on caution. He wanted to give his old mentor another opportunity to visit Major Walsh, whom most of the Lakotas still believed would return to Fort Walsh at the end of his leave. He also proposed another rendezvous with Allison at Wood Mountain after Sitting Bull and Walsh had conferred. Allison insisted that, as a token of good faith, Gall should send twenty families to Fort Buford to reassure the army of his good intentions.[32]

Gall, whom Allison now believed was in charge of the daily activities of Sitting Bull's camp, agreed to send the twenty families to Fort Buford. Indeed, on Allison's way back to the fort, he encountered these families waiting for him near Montana's Poplar River. But Gall's plans could not be kept a secret indefinitely. An enraged Sitting Bull heard about them and heaped bitter criticism on his old friend. Gall exploded, telling the astounded members of the divided Lakota camp that he was now their leader; he even insisted that they break with Sitting Bull and follow him to Fort Buford.[33]

Some historians feel that the extent of this quarrel, which eventually resulted in the unraveling of an old friendship, has been greatly exaggerated. Campbell insisted that the question of surrender was actually debated in a series of councils. According to this version, Gall was far too forthright a person to undercut his mentor in such an underhanded way. Indeed, Old Bull and One Bull have testified that in meetings involving Crow King, No Neck, Big Road, Turning Bear, He Dog, Fool Bull, Fools Heart, and Gall, it was decided that all of them should "go in and surrender." Sitting Bull's alleged response was that they should go in and do just that, adding, "I am coming too," but the old chief's desire to visit Major Walsh first would delay this pledge to return. Notwithstanding Campbell's decidedly different account of Sitting Bull and Gall's break, these two men would never be as close after this incident.[34]

The sharp differences sparked by this event were probably due to the buildup of tensions caused by Sitting Bull's continued intransigence in the face of his peoples' deteriorating circumstances. The quarrel also brought out the basic personality differences between Sitting Bull and Gall. Sitting Bull would cling to causes he believed in with a steely determination. Gall was a pragmatist, often willing to change his position on issues according to new or different circumstances. On the issue of surrender, most of the remaining Lakota refugees in Canada were in agreement with Gall. When he left for the United States, most of the remaining Lakota exiles followed him.

The exact numbers who joined Gall, however, have been a subject of dispute. Utley claims that twenty-three lodges departed with him, followed by fifteen lodges under Jumping Bull, Sitting Bull's adopted brother.[35] Allison, whose numbers seem somewhat exaggerated, insisted that as many as three hundred lodges left with Sitting Bull's once indispensable lieutenant; in fact, Allison estimated that by February 10, 1881, six hundred Lakota lodges had moved south to Fort Buford.[36] If his estimates are correct, as many as a one-half to two-thirds of the Lakota refugees left Canada as a result of Sitting Bull and Gall's break. Indeed, the rupture left a grim but still stubborn Sitting Bull with only two hundred loyal followers to carry on in his defense.[37]

The course that each of these once close friends took did not result in an entirely satisfactory outcome for either man. Gall balked at surrendering when he and his followers reached the Poplar River Agency. A misguided army officer, Major Guido Ilges, possessed with unclear instructions from his superiors, provoked Gall and a totally indiscreet warrior chief named Crow to resist Ilges's demand that Gall's people go immediately to Fort Buford. Gall was particularly unhappy over the prospect of a long march by his weakened followers through the deep snow and cold temperatures. Gall's ugly mood when he and the other Lakota refugees finally reached Fort Buford on January 9, 1881, was not improved by the anger Allison expressed over Major Ilges's harsh treatment of Gall and his adherents.

Events following Sitting Bull's clash with Gall did not find Sitting Bull in much better circumstances. Canadian authorities, including such officers of the Northwest Mounted Police as Major Crozier, Lieutenant Colonel Acheson G. "Big Bull" Irvine, and inspector Alexander Macdonell, along with Indian commissioner Edgar Dewdney, continued to pressure him on the issue of surrender.[30] They warned Sitting Bull repeatedly that the Canadian government would never give him and his followers a reservation in Canada. Nor would Sitting Bull's faction, a remnant of the once large Indian coalition he led, ever get their desperately needed food rations. Sitting Bull, aware of the increasingly dim prospects for his cause, changed his mind on the question of surrender a number of times. He would, for instance, promise an officer of the Mounted Police on one occasion that he was going to surrender, only to retract this pledge with what Canadian authorities felt was a weak excuse.

Sitting Bull continued to insist on seeing his old friend Major Walsh before making any commitment to return to the United States. In late April, with thirty-eight lodges, the frustrated Hunkpapa leader even traveled to Fort Qu'Appelle, where Walsh was to be transferred after completing his eastern leave, but the sympathetic Walsh never came; the minister of Indians for the Canadian government would not permit him to return for another meeting with Sitting Bull.

The discouraged but stubborn Indian leader finally succumbed to the persuasiveness of Jean Louis Legaré, the French Canadian trader at Wood Mountain, who had befriended the Lakotas soon after their arrival in Saskatchewan in 1877. Legaré, who in early 1880 had moved his trading post to a wooded area on the plains east of Wood Mountain called Willow Bunch, was willing to feed Sitting Bull and his still loyal followers. His kindness toward them ultimately convinced Sitting Bull to surrender. Eventually, after several false starts, Legaré led a wagon train carrying forty families, including Sitting Bull's, to Fort Buford.

The surrender party arrived at the fort on July 19, 1881. Sitting Bull was riding on a gaunt pony; his uncle Four Horns was the most prominent Lakota leader with him. The families in this long trek rode in distinctive two-wheeled carts that Legaré had used for trade; they had traveled in a long line behind Sitting Bull and fourteen mounted warriors as they had made their slow trip to Fort Buford. According to the regular post returns from Fort Buford, Sitting Bull came "with 184 Sioux Indians . . . (44 men, the remainder women and children) conducted by Mr. Lagare from Woody [sic] Mountain."[39]

Sitting Bull looked positively destitute, wearing a dirty calico shirt and covering his waist with an equally dirty blanket. Because of an eye infection, he had tied a handkerchief around his head, which partially covered his eyes.[40] On the following morning, he surrendered to Major Brotherton. According to an old, now disputed, tradition, he gave his five-year-old child Crow Foot his rifle; it was to be turned over to Brotherton as a gesture that Sitting Bull was indeed the last warrior to surrender to the United States government.[41]

Two months before Sitting Bull's surrender on May 26, Gall, Black Moon, Crow King, Fools Heart, Long Dog and other noted Lakota leaders, along with a large group of Lakotas, were put on a steamer traveling down the Missouri River. Three days later, this group of 1,149 Lakotas reached the military post at Standing Rock, called Fort Yates after Captain George Yates, the cavalry officer who had died with Custer at the Little Bighorn.[42] On June 15, seven weeks later, five steamers from Fort Keogh carried 1,700 more Lakotas downriver to Fort Yates, including such prominent warrior chiefs as Spotted Eagle, Rain-in-the-Face, and Big Road.[43] Assurances had been given to Sitting Bull that he, too, would soon be with his old comrades at Standing Rock. But these assurances, like so many others, would never be fully honored.

CHAPTER ELEVEN

Standing Rock

On May 29, 1881, when Gall arrived at Standing Rock, the Sioux inhabitants lived almost exclusively along the Missouri River. The headquarters, Fort Yates, was situated on the banks of the Missouri, next to a stone formation called Standing Rock, which resembled a woman with a child on her back.[1] Some twenty miles upriver from the fort was the Cannonball River, the upper boundary of the agency, where some fifteen hundred Yanktonais lived. Most of them were clustered at the mouth of the Cannonball or the mouth of Porcupine Creek, just above Fort Yates. South of the fort, and primarily along the Missouri, lived approximately seven hundred Blackfoot Lakotas and fifteen hundred Hunkpapas. These Hunkpapas included many of the warriors, such as Gall, who had recently surrendered at Fort Buford.[2]

During the next four years, the number of Indians at Standing Rock would grow by more than 700, raising the total Indian population to 4,427. This figure is probably accurate because it is based on the number of Indians who applied for rations during July 1885.[3] Indeed, no Lakota or Yanktonai could afford to pass up these rations because during the early 1880s, farming at Standing Rock was developing at a glacial pace; this was particularly true during Gall's first couple of years at the agency. Thus, rations, such as beef, biscuits, flour, hard bread, coffee, sugar, rice, baking powder, soap, and hides, were absolutely essential to all Standing Rock Indians.[4]

Three and a half months after Gall's arrival at Standing Rock, the agency's new administrator, Major James McLaughlin, stepped off a riverboat called the *Sherman*. This same steamer was carrying Sitting Bull to Fort Randall, despite Major Brotherton's assurances that the old chief could join his people at Standing Rock. Little did Gall know that this new Indian agent would make him quite famous during the remainder of his life. McLaughlin was not an army man—the title "major" was an honorary one given to some Indian agents at this time.[5] His experiences, rather, involved working with Sioux reservation Indians and administering many of the new activities that filled their badly disrupted lives.

McLaughlin had been an Indian agent at the Sioux agency at Devils Lake for a decade. His tenure there had been marked by a competence and honesty not too common for Indian agents during the late nineteenth century. He truly liked most of his Sioux charges, and when he published a book thirty years later about his experiences with them, he titled it *My Friend the Indian*. Unfortunately, his attitude toward the recently vanquished Sioux was strongly paternalistic, a trait that, when blended with his authoritarian personality, would bring him into bitter conflict with the more strong-willed reservation Indians. A short man, just over five feet six, he exuded a most formidable presence. His erect posture, jet black hair, well-trimmed goatee, and riveting eyes commanded immediate respect. As he grew older, his hair turned iron gray and finally snow white; in fact, as the years passed, more and more of the Lakotas and Yanktonais at Standing Rock called him White Hair.[6]

When McLaughlin began his work as Indian agent at Standing Rock, he faced fewer significant obstacles than his predecessors had on the Great Sioux Reservation. The 1868 Treaty of Fort Laramie had provided the Lakotas with an immense amount of room to continue their nomadic lifestyle. The unceded Indian territory west of the Black Hills gave the nontreaty bands an opportunity to continue their beloved horse and buffalo culture for another decade. Reservation Indians, for their part, would often go to these unceded lands to hunt buffalo during the spring and return to their agencies in the autumn when the snow began to fall; there they could live off government beef rations during the wintry months.

With this independence, Indian leaders were in a better position to defy an agent if they felt he was acting in an authoritarian way. At the Spotted Tail Agency, where most of the Brulés were, this problem of Indian mobility was not so vexing because Spotted Tail was a reasonable and flexible leader. At the Red Cloud Agency, located west of Spotted Tail's agency in northwestern Nebraska, Red Cloud, who had more to

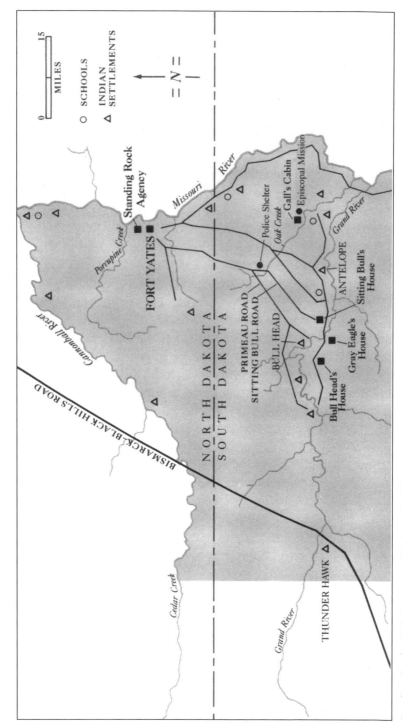

Standing Rock, 1890. Courtesy of Robert M. Utley.

do with the favorable Fort Laramie Treaty than any other Indian leader, could be most difficult, as illustrated by his long feud with Agent Saville during the early 1870s.[7]

After the Great Sioux War, the Indian agents had more leverage in dealing with those chiefs and headmen who still exercised some power and authority over their followers. Because of the ultimate defeat of the Lakota tribes in this last great struggle, the Sioux lost the unceded territory that had given them so much freedom. Moreover, the size of their immense reservation was significantly reduced by the loss of the Black Hills.

Reservation Indians were now largely confined to their agencies, while nontreaty Indians were forced to either flee to Canada or return to their previously assigned agencies. These new circumstances provided the Indian agents at Pine Ridge, where the Oglalas had been forced to move in 1879, more power over their Oglala charges than any of the earlier agents had ever had. Thus, when the strong-willed Valentine T. McGillycuddy, the Camp Robinson post surgeon who had treated Crazy Horse's fatal bayonet wounds, arrived at Pine Ridge on March 10, 1879, he could deal with the frequently obstinate Red Cloud much more effectively than his predecessors could. In fact, these two extraordinarily determined men clashed frequently during McGillycuddy's tumultuous seven-year tenure at Pine Ridge.[8]

McLaughlin had some important advantages over McGillycuddy when he assumed the top federal post at Standing Rock. His experiences at the Devils Lake Agency had taught him how to play Indian factions against each other to achieve political and economic goals. His wife, Mary Louise, was an important asset. Having Indian blood—she was part Mdewakanton Sioux—she understood the thinking of her husband's charges and could act as an interpreter or mediator in the disputes he had with certain Standing Rock Indians.[9] Her skills were especially necessary after Sitting Bull was transferred from Fort Randall to Standing Rock in 1883. As a Roman Catholic, McLaughlin also had the Church behind him. Particularly helpful in this regard was the Bureau of Catholic Indian Missions, which unlike many Protestant missionary organizations believed that Indians should be allowed to be Indians, at least in cultural matters.[10]

McLaughlin was aided in his endeavors by an increasingly popular attitude toward Indians that was sweeping the country during the 1880s. It could be summed up by the word "assimilation," the idea that Native Americans should be absorbed into the mainstream of the nation's culture by being transformed from nomadic hunters into small farmers. Also, fully assimilated Indians should have their own plot of land, free from tribal control. Indeed, if these goals could be achieved, reservations would no longer be necessary. As Senator Henry L. Dawes of Massachusetts, the leading governmental exponent of assimilation, put it in 1887, reservations would some day "pass like snow in the springtime, and we will never know when they go; we will only know they are gone."[11]

This new assimilation movement, which had its roots in the early nineteenth century, was formally launched in 1883 at a posh resort on the shores of Lake Mohonk in New York's Catskill Mountains. Gathering into their fold earlier ideas regarding assimilation, these eastern reformers who attended the Lake Mohonk conference were anxious to absorb the Lakotas and other western tribes into the country's culture as rapidly as possible. They wanted to Americanize the Indians as the country had Americanized many of the immigrant groups that had reached the nation's shores in such large numbers in the 1870s and 1880s. They were also determined to inculcate Christian values, which in 1883 meant Protestant values. In short, these earnest reformers wanted to create a class of industrious farmers or grazers imbued with the work ethic, or the Protestant ethic as it was often called at the time. Thus, reservation Indians would be wards of the state no longer but rather a class of productive people who could be responsible for themselves.

Among the more prominent leaders of the assimilation movement were the twin brothers Albert K. and Alfred Smiley. These two owned the Lake Mohonk resort hotel where the nation's leading reformers gathered every autumn to discuss the best ways to civilize the recently vanquished western tribes. The two Quaker brothers were true believers. They were representative of the well-to-do and well-educated people who attended the Mohonk meetings. At the 1889 conference, for instance, former president Rutherford B. Hayes, like most of the other delegates, did not mind the ban on alcoholic beverages imposed by the Smileys; during his presidency, Hayes and his wife, Lemonade Lucy, did not serve liquor at White House functions.

Several prominent groups and personalities grew out of the Mohonk movement. Probably the most effective organization to emerge was the Indian Rights Association, founded by a wealthy Philadelphian named Herbert Welsh. In 1882, Welsh, the nephew of the first chairman of the Board of Indian Commissioners, had toured the Great Sioux Reservation with a friend during McLaughlin's second year at Standing Rock. This visit had an enormous impact on him, and in December of that year, he and thirty like-minded people organized the Indian Rights Association in the parlor of Welsh's home. In their goal to civilize and assimilate the Indians, they made this organization the leading one of its kind. Branches of the Indian Rights Association were founded throughout the country; lobbyists for the organization were busy in Washington; lectures became an integral part of its mission; and publications provided a wealth of information about the Indian's difficult plight during this time of change.

Another reformer who personified the Mohonk movement was the Baptist minister Thomas Jefferson Morgan, who became commissioner of Indian Affairs in 1889; he was especially strong on the education of Indians as the best way to transform them into civilized yeomen farmers.[12] His ideas would be tested, if not challenged, when the Ghost Dance swept through the unhappy Sioux agencies in 1890.

Not all reform groups who focused on the Indian question were assimilationist in their views. The Bureau of Catholic Indian Missions was more inclined to give Indians a greater role in determining their future, but the most forthright organization in this regard was the National Indian Defense Association, founded in 1885. Headed by the tenacious Thomas A. Bland, this group vigorously fought for the Indian's right to act and be like an Indian. Bland edited the *Council Fire*, which repeatedly attacked the federal government's paternalistic Indian policy. Indeed, the determined Bland was physically removed from the Pine Ridge Agency in 1884 by the dictatorial McGillycuddy's Indian police when he attempted to visit the agent's bitter nemesis, Red Cloud; the angry Bland would later pepper the pages of the *Council Fire* with criticism of this incident and other high-handed ones committed by the more zealous apostles of assimilation.[13]

The National Indian Defense Association (NIDA) was active on most of the Lakota agencies scattered throughout the Great Sioux Reservation, including the one at Standing Rock, but it had about as much influence on the thinking of McLaughlin as it had on McGillycuddy. Major McLaughlin sincerely believed that civilizing the Indians could not be achieved without assimilation, and that, as he put it in a letter written in April 1889, the "Indians must either fall in with the march of civilization and progress or be crushed by the passage of the multitude."[14] Standing Rock's energetic agent also believed that the agricultural life was one of the key factors in transforming his charges into law-abiding, God-fearing farmers.

His approach was similar to that of the even more authoritarian McGillycuddy, who was determined to make farmers out of the strong-willed Oglala tribespeople at Pine Ridge. In McGillycuddy's first meeting with Red Cloud and the other agency chiefs, he displayed a new map of Pine Ridge, which included the many fertile valleys that characterized the rolling landscape of this recently created agency. McGillycuddy insisted that the dubious, if not sullen, Red Cloud should go out with his followers and cultivate these valleys as independent farmers rather than cluster idly around McGillycuddy's agency headquarters.[15]

McLaughlin faced a similar problem at Standing Rock. Almost all of its inhabitants were located along the Missouri River. Many lived near Fort Yates, where McLaughlin managed agency affairs, while others cultivated garden plots on the rich bottomlands near the mouth of the Cannonball River and along Porcupine Creek. These relatively new initiates to agriculture were cultivating less than fifteen hundred acres of crops such as potatoes, pumpkins, melons, turnips, squash, and oats, grown to feed the limited number of livestock animals.

Reservation Indians, like the nontreaty Hunkpapas who arrived at Standing Rock in 1881, had very few horses. These animals, once so useful in warfare, had been taken from them by the army in 1876 and in 1881 as part of the process to end the Sioux threat once and for all. To complicate the economic growth at Standing Rock even more, only a small number of the agency's residents owned beef cattle or oxen. Moreover, Hunkpapas like Gall, who had just reached the agency, had little experience in farming and even less inclination to try it.

Like McGillycuddy, Agent McLaughlin looked to those river valleys that had never been put to the plow. He wanted to cultivate the virgin soil along the banks of Oak Creek or the Grand River, south and west of Fort Yates. Utilizing the talents of George Faribault, who had been one of his most valuable assistants at the Devils Lake Agency, McLaughlin enticed many Hunkpapas to move into these undeveloped valleys and began farming. Cooperation was good in the beginning because the Indians really had no other choice. Such leaders as Gall, John Grass, and even the maverick Rain-in-the-Face were soon observed hoeing potatoes or making hay near their new valley homes, some of which were miles from Fort Yates. Agricultural progress was slow, particularly in the beginning, but by 1891, Major McLaughlin could report to his superiors that five thousand acres were under cultivation.[16]

Gall, who became a cooperative Indian despite the bitterness he felt at the time of his surrender, would become one of McLaughlin's model farmers. Eventually cultivating land near a small but comfortable cabin he occupied in the mid-1880s in the Oak Creek valley, he demonstrated a considerable diligence for a man who had little, if any, experience in farming. But Gall's unusual perseverance as a tiller of the soil should not come as a complete surprise. McLaughlin, in his 1882 report, declared that the recently arrived Hunkpapas, "late hostiles" as he called them, were superior to the old agency Indians in such categories as industry, uprightness, truth, and honor.[17]

Gall became a key figure in McLaughlin's program to divide the Standing Rock Agency into approximately twenty farming districts, each to be headed by a district farmer, or "boss farmer." The position of assistant farmer was also created to provide the necessary backup. The Native American farmers would closely cooperate with Faribault, who served as head farmer throughout most of the 1880s. Gall started as an assistant farmer on May 15, 1883, at a salary of $10 a month. On September 4 of that same year, he became a district farmer for the fiscal year 1883–1884. The verbiage for the latter appointment approval letter indicated that district farmers would be paid $120 a year.[18] The compensation was not startling, but the value of United States currency was much greater during the late nineteenth century.

Gall continued to serve as a district farmer with only one interruption until 1891, when he resigned to accept an appointment as one of three native judges on the court of Indian offenses.[19] After serving in that capacity for one year, he was again made a district farmer in 1890, a position he held until his discharge on December 31, 1892.[20] Gall, getting on in years, probably vacated this position because of failing health. Congressional appropriation cuts resulting from the Panic of 1893 could also have been a factor.

Other Standing Rock Indians besides Gall were willing to cooperate with McLaughlin and participate in his reform programs. Their attitude increased the growingly sharp differences between them and those Indians who resisted many of McLaughlin's changes. Many federal authorities like to call their more cooperative Indian charges progressives and their less cooperative ones traditionalists. Some scholars have characterized those agency Indians more amenable to the changes imposed on them by the reservation system as opportunists, people who were willing to do anything to gain the favor of reservation authorities. Because of Gall's change of heart after his surrender in 1881, he was often put into this dubious category by his critics. In truth, Gall was one of those Hunkpapas who, accepting the realities of the situation, consented to those changes that he believed would be best for all his people. Like the Blackfoot Lakota leader John Grass, Gall would attempt to strike a balance between the Lakotas' old way of life and the inevitable modifications that now threatened their traditional lifestyle. Ethnohistorians and anthropologists have preferred to call Lakota leaders such as Gall and Grass culture brokers or cultural mediators, those who were trying to bridge the gap between reservation Indians and federal officials such as McLaughlin.[21]

Deep differences between many Lakotas were revealed after their reluctant surrender at Fort Buford and other army posts along the Canadian border. One controversial figure among the Hunkpapas was the former tribal shirt wearer Running Antelope, an early peacemaker among his people who was one of the agency Indians who did not fight against the army during the Great Sioux War nor participate in the long Canadian exile.

Sitting Bull, who once held Running Antelope in high esteem because of his effectiveness in intertribal conflicts, eventually changed his attitude toward him. He came to regard Running Antelope as a fool because of his close cooperation with the tribe's white adversaries. When Sitting Bull came to Bismarck, following his surrender at Fort Buford and prior to his exile at Fort Randall, he refused to acknowledge Running Antelope's warm greetings and sincere efforts to help him adjust to reservation life. This slight no doubt hurt the older man, who had become one of McLaughlin's more cooperative allies, but Running Antelope continued to represent the more positive attitude of the progressive faction of Standing Rock's Indian population. In fact, he served as one of Major McLaughlin's district farmers throughout most of the 1880s.[22]

The most able of the cooperative Indians at Standing Rock, however, was the Blackfoot Lakota leader John Grass. Grass, too, had been a warrior who gained renown as a fighter in intertribal warfare, yet he had rarely fought against the whites, making it easier for him to cooperate with McLaughlin and his staff. Josephine Waggoner, a mixed-blood who was married to J. F. Waggoner, an army private who later was employed as a carpenter at Standing Rock, regarded John Grass as the best Indian orator she had ever heard.[23]

The handsome Blackfoot Lakota chief, who was somewhat sensitive because of his thinning hair—unusual for an Indian—also had a fine mind.[24] His intellect won him the respect of McLaughlin and most of the progressive-minded Indians at Standing Rock. A number of the more traditional Indians at the agency, however, were suspicious of and resentful toward the articulate Grass. Sitting Bull's nephew White Bull, while admitting that John Grass was a good speaker, felt he was not a "thinker or smart man." He could "always say yes [to the government] but never no," White Bull argued.[25]

Like Gall, Grass was district farmer. He served in that capacity from 1887 to 1889, resigning in 1889 when he and Gall became judges on the court of Indian offenses.[26] Although White Bull may have regarded Grass as a "yes man," Grass was in many ways an original thinker. For instance, he became a friendly critic of McLaughlin's tenacious efforts to promote farming in every valley or portion of arable land on the Standing Rock Agency.

Grass sincerely believed that much of the agency's acreage was too arid for successful farming, which would soon be borne out by subsequent facts and statistics. Despite McLaughlin's unceasing pressure on the Standing Rock Indians to farm, only 50 families, about 1 in 20 of the 3,755 Indians living at the agency, put in a wheat crop in the spring of 1882. Indeed, the largest farm on the agency was only five acres.[27]

John Grass believed that the solution to many of the economic woes faced by Standing Rock's often demoralized inhabitants lay in stock raising. Raising beef cattle and "fine blooded horses" could endure and survive the uncertain rain patterns in much of the Dakota country. A dubious McLaughlin, who saw the yeoman farmer as the absolute symbol of assimilation, finally came around to Grass's viewpoint, largely because of Grass's persuasiveness.

Many of the Hunkpapas, Blackfoot Lakotas, and Yanktonais became stock grazers. Eventually dipping tanks would be built to protect the growing herds of cattle from the danger of ticks, and vaccines were soon adopted to prevent cattle diseases. In time herds of cattle were even shipped to Chicago to provide money for the more industrious Indians, who were indeed becoming participants in the nation's capitalist economy. Moreover, agriculture was not entirely ignored by this somewhat overdue shift to stock grazing: little ponies were bred as "fine horses strong enough to plow fields or do any kind of work."[28]

Much of the harmony that McLaughlin enjoyed during his first two years as Indian agent at Standing Rock was ended by the arrival of Sitting Bull, who had been released from Fort Randall in 1883 and transferred to Standing Rock. The veteran chief was probably aware by now that the old nomadic life of his people was no longer possible. Earlier hopes that he might be put on a reservation along the Little Missouri, or at some other location where buffalo could still be hunted, were largely dashed.

Ironically, during Sitting Bull's stay at Fort Randall, McLaughlin had sanctioned two buffalo hunts for his Standing Rock charges: one in June 1882, in which five thousand buffalo were killed, and the other in the fall of that year, in which two thousand were killed. Given how rapidly these monarchs of the plains were disappearing, the hunts seem most foolhardy in retrospect.[29]

In the June 1882 hunt, Gall and Grass showed that they had not abandoned their old and familiar lifestyle. Almost all factions at Standing Rock came together for this one great event, headed by White Antelope. When the enormous hunting party reached a point about fifty miles west of Fort Yates, the leaders of the party of about eight hundred held a strategy conference. At the gathering, Gall demonstrated his skill as an experienced buffalo hunter. He provided a vivid picture of the geographical landmarks where the large herd was grazing while his comrades listened with rapt attention. According to McLaughlin's daughter-in-law, Annie Goodreau McLaughlin, Gall looked like the great warrior of old. "His shirt was opened to the waist in the summer sun and sweat streamed across his barrel chest as he raised his voice in description of the land to the west." During this successful hunt Gall also proved that he could be a mediator among his people as well as a cultural mediator between whites and Indians. When two large groups of Indians became involved in a fight in which guns were displayed, Gall intervened, seized the guns, and refused to return them until the two parties reconciled.[30]

Fortunately for the absent Sitting Bull, who found the twenty long months at Fort Randall almost unendurable, he was treated well by the fort's commandant, Colonel George S. Andrews. Andrews thought it was cruel to keep Sitting Bull and his pitiful followers apart from their kinfolk at Standing Rock. On December 20, 1882, the cautious secretary of war Robert F. Lincoln, son of the martyred president, finally endorsed efforts to transfer Sitting Bull to Standing Rock.[31]

When Sitting Bull arrived at Fort Yates on May 10, 1883, he was most anxious to talk to McLaughlin. When the two met the next day, he told McLaughlin that the president of the United States had written and told him that he would be the "big chief of the agency." McLaughlin denied that Sitting Bull had ever received such a letter. (It is possible, of course, that someone just told Sitting Bull that he had.) Greatly exasperated, McLaughlin told Sitting Bull that he would be treated just like any other Indian at Standing Rock; he would not be given any special privileges.[32]

McLaughlin's dislike of this Lakota chief, whose name had become widely known throughout much of the country, was almost instantaneous. The bearded Indian agent developed a habit of pushing his hat to the back of his head whenever he met anyone who displeased him. One suspects that McLaughlin's hat was far back on his head during much of this first meeting with Sitting Bull. He was especially irritated by Sitting Bull's announced intention not to plant a crop this year because he felt mid-May was too late for any success. Even though the bewildered Lakota leader promised McLaughlin that he would look around so that he could learn how to plant next year's crop, McLaughlin had already developed a distrust of Sitting Bull. To him the crafty chief was a dangerous threat to his program of civilizing the Indians at Standing Rock by making them diligent farmers or grazers.

McLaughlin followed up this first meeting with Sitting Bull by arranging to have twelve acres plowed for the chief and his extended family; he also expected them to begin their planting immediately. The crestfallen Hunkpapa leader was soon out in the field hoeing his acres, as Gall and Crow King had done during the previous two years.[33] Despite this act of cooperation on Sitting Bull's part, the damage to any future good relations between him and McLaughlin had already been done.

McLaughlin reported to his superiors three months later that Sitting Bull was a man of "mediocre ability." His intellect was decidedly inferior to other Indian leaders at Standing Rock. Moreover, the Hunkpapa chief, in his opinion, was "pompous, vain and boastful and ... [considered] himself a very important personage."[34] This negative attitude toward Sitting Bull never wavered.

When McLaughlin published his book *My Friend the Indian* in 1910, twenty years after Sitting Bull's death, he was still critical of this proud and willful adversary. Devoting much of his book to the Great Sioux War, particularly the Battle of the Little Bighorn, he described Sitting Bull as being a "crafty, avaricious, mendacious, and ambitious" war leader, who possessed "all of the faults of an Indian and none of the nobler attributes." As for his characterization of Sitting Bull's eight years as a reservation Indian under his supervision, McLaughlin was equally critical.

"Sitting Bull always exerted a vicious influence over . . . [the reservation's] unreconstructed element, and remained opposed to the white man's influence to the last."[35]

The aging chief, who had already dealt with such eminent persons as Miles (now a general in the U.S. Army) and Major Walsh, was not prepared for McLaughlin's unwavering disrespect. Because his past experiences had trained him to pick up on various nuances in white behavior, the agent's condescending tone of voice and inflexible behavior toward him must have been particularly insulting.

Sitting Bull should have had some inkling that McLaughlin would be a difficult man. In 1882 the willful agent arbitrarily eliminated the sun dance from the sacred rituals allowed at Standing Rock.[36] His plans to civilize and transform Indian life were already being forcefully implemented at the agency before the two met in 1883. And McLaughlin was certainly shrewd enough to anticipate that a man as stubborn as Sitting Bull could be a major obstacle to his plans for change and reform at Standing Rock.

McLaughlin's strategy for coping with Sitting Bull's obstructionism was to organize a faction of more flexible Indians at Standing Rock to act as a counterpoise to those Indians drawn to Sitting Bull's traditional views. The shrewd agent had been quite successful in playing Indian factions against each during his tenure at Devils Lake. Possible leaders for such a faction of supportive Indians at Standing Rock included Gall and Crow King, both Hunkpapas, and John Grass, the Blackfoot Lakota chief. The process of winning the confidence of such potential leaders as these three took several years.[37]

John Grass, who could speak English, was the most able and probably the most willing of McLaughlin's choices to get involved in what could become a bitter reservation fight. Because Grass had never fought against the army, however, if selected as one of the leaders, he might be perceived as a McLaughlin puppet.[38] Crow King, one of the truly genuine heroes at the Little Bighorn, would have been a more popular choice. Unfortunately for McLaughlin's plans, Crow King died in 1884. The Catholic burial of Crow King at the agency, which by 1872 was designated as part of the Roman Catholic Church's conversion mission among the Sioux, indicated how acceptable Crow King would have been to a staunch Roman Catholic like McLaughlin.[39]

Gall's background and availability eventually made him the logical top choice for this new pro-McLaughlin faction. As the Fighting Cock of the Sioux, he, like Crow King, had played an important role at the Little Bighorn. His imposing physique and dark good looks impressed whites and Indians alike, and his flamboyance during the Yellowstone campaign negated the impression that he could become a mere puppet of Standing Rock's agent. After all, this was the fierce Lakota warrior who had thrown off his robe and bared his army-inflicted battle scars at the Treaty of Fort Laramie conference at Fort Rice.

In the opinion of many, Gall seemed to be the kind of progressive-minded Indian who could stand up to the intransigent Sitting Bull. Moreover, his cooperative attitude toward McLaughlin had been evident soon after he arrived at Standing Rock. The once great warrior was indeed a hard-working, uncomplaining farmer, a man who could provide an example of what McLaughlin thought a civilized Indian should be like.

McLaughlin was willing to reward both Gall and Grass for their important roles in the agency's newly organized reform faction. Grass, it would turn out, would wield more power than Gall, but Gall would receive more kudos for what he did. As time went by, however, some regarded Gall as an opportunist because of his alliance with McLaughlin. They saw his appointments as district farmer and judge of the court of Indian offenses as being part of a cynical quid pro quo. Such a conclusion is not entirely fair; Gall worked hard and conscientiously as a district farmer and a judge for the Indians at Standing Rock. Apparently he believed that the economic betterment of his band depended on its members becoming good farmers. Understanding the new legal system under which they would live also became a top priority for him. Loyalty, whether to McLaughlin or Sitting Bull, was another trait consistent with Gall's character. He had indeed proven himself to be one of Sitting Bull's most faithful lieutenants. Although the two men had not been close since their break in Canada, Gall had served Sitting Bull loyally up to that time.

Indeed, Campbell, who largely used the testimony of Sitting Bull's two favorite nephews White Bull and One Bull for his biography of their uncle, insisted that Gall had been "straight as a string" as far as serving his mentor prior to their Canadian schism.[40] There is even evidence that Gall tried to mend their frayed relationship. When Sitting Bull made a brief visit to Standing Rock in 1881, prior to being sent to Fort Randall, Gall, Crow King, and other longtime followers of the old chief invited him to their camp. There they counseled and feasted him in what was to all intents and purposes a warm reunion.[41]

Throughout his life Gall had been an independent and ambitious man; he and his band had often hunted, traded, and even made war on their own. He may have tired of living in Sitting Bull's shadow, but it was Sitting Bull's stubborn unwillingness to surrender that had shaken his influence over such Lakota warriors as Gall; they honestly believed that their followers were slowly starving in the Lakotas' once secure Canadian sanctuary. Gall, who like most great warriors loved the adulation he received for his brave deeds, undoubtedly saw the opportunities that could be his as McLaughlin's favorite Indian. Given his once staunch loyalty to Sitting Bull and his continuing loyalty to the causes of his people, he was probably more of a pragmatist than an opportunist. Utley has concluded that Gall was a "shrewd pragmatist."[42] Perhaps a better term for Gall would be "realist," because he comprehended more than most the lack of options open to his people.

The changes in Gall's daily routine offers further proof of the sincerity behind his swift adjustment to reservation life. He was a good farmer. Working hard all day, he would enjoy with satisfaction his evenings of relaxation. Indeed, he would smoke contentedly in his cabin overlooking the cultivated acreage that absorbed his energies during the day. Gall was also receptive to other agency pressures urging him to follow the white man's ways. He was amenable to the call for Christian conversion as one of the crucial keys to the attainment of civilization, as interpreted by McLaughlin and other whites.[43] In fact, both the Catholic clergy and the Episcopal clergy worked with considerable energy to convert Gall and Sitting Bull.

The Catholic Church was active in the Grand River valley, west of Oak Creek where Gall and his family ultimately settled, but Catholic missionaries, such as Bishop Martin Marty, had to compete with Congregational ones, such as Mary C. Collins, in their efforts to Christianize Sitting Bull. Even though Sitting Bull often wore the wooden cross given to him by Father DeSmet, he ultimately rejected bids for conversion by both religious denominations. In fact, this leader, who had envisioned soldiers falling upside down into the Lakota camp at the Rosebud, remained an influential religious force in his own right.[44]

The Episcopal Church enjoyed much greater success with Gall than did the Catholic Church. Episcopal bishop William H. Hare, of the church's Niobrara Mission of the Dakotas, started his conversion efforts at Sitting Bull's camp first because the old chief was better known than

Gall. Sensing the intense competition coming from Catholic and Congregational missionaries, however, he decided to focus his attention on such chiefs and headmen as Gall and the Blackfoot Lakota leader Mad Bear. With this in mind, the bishop established the St. Elizabeth Episcopal Mission on Oak Creek in the southeastern corner of Standing Rock. On February 11, 1886, Gall and John Grass moved their bands to the Oak Creek area to farm so that their children could be educated at St. Elizabeth's. Later in the year, Episcopalian missionaries had started a day school there in response to Gall and Grass's persuasive efforts.

Gall soon became intimately involved in the activities of this Episcopal mission, despite McLaughlin's strong commitment to the Catholic Church. A couple of Gall's daughters were converted to Christianity, but Gall, no doubt still loyal to many of his old beliefs, decided to wait.[45]

Education had been another key facet in the Mohonk movement's quest to "civilize" the Indians. By 1878 the federal government was operating day schools and boarding schools on reservations throughout the country; there was almost a dual system of education for the Indians at this time, with the government operating one system and the churches operating the other. In his Niobrara Mission, Bishop Hare encouraged the establishment of small boarding schools at such mission stations as St. Elizabeth.

Gall would sometimes visit St. Elizabeth's school. He also attended church services with his daughters, tending to sit in the back as sort of a halfway conversion. St. Elizabeth's mission drew impressive numbers of people, particularly during Christmastime. Hunkpapas and Blackfoot Lakotas would camp outside in wall tents surrounding the mission during the entire Christmas season.[46]

At St. Elizabeth's school, Gall apparently did not encounter many of those educational practices that turned Red Cloud and Spotted Tail against such off-reservation boarding schools as the Carlisle Indian Training School in Pennsylvania, where they were shocked to see Sioux youngsters dressed in military blue uniforms with hair closely trimmed.[47] Not surprisingly for the time, English was the only language allowed at any Indian school expecting financial support from the federal government, but the regimentation of Indian students that had shocked Red Cloud and Spotted Tail was not as noticeable at St. Elizabeth's.[48]

Indeed, the Episcopal Church was quite successful in training Indians to become catechists, or "helpers." The Reverend Philip J. Deloria, grandfather to Indian writer Vine Deloria, Jr., is a good example of a Sioux

Indian trained for an important role in the Episcopal clergy. According to Vine Deloria, his able and devout grandfather had worked diligently to convert Gall, but the aging chief had remained reluctant, determined to stay loyal to the old Lakota ways. Finally, because of his fondness for Deloria, Gall was baptized an Episcopalian on July 4, 1892. By Christmas of that year, he was ready to take his first communion. He fasted the entire day before attending the Christmas Eve mass. Because the weather was bitingly cold, Gall, one of the leading headmen in the Oak Creek area, was given a seat of honor near the church's solitary stove. He was also the first to be offered communion. When he emptied the entire chalice of wine, however, there was some understandable consternation among the other parishioners. The wine ultimately took its toll, and a rather exhilarated Gall said to Deloria, "now I see why you wanted me to become a Christian. I feel so nice and warm and happy. Why didn't you tell me that Christians did this every Sunday. . . . I would have joined your church years ago." The fact that Deloria established the school at St. Elizabeth's in 1886, as well as ran the mission, demonstrates that religion and education were rarely far apart in the country's efforts to make Indians more like whites.[49]

Gall also participated in the legal system imposed on the Indians at Standing Rock. His one-term appointment as a judge on the court of Indian offenses in 1889 gave him an opportunity to render justice to a divided reservation, where the differences between the various factions were sometimes bitter.[50] Gall proved to be a fair and compassionate judge, whose decisions on this three-man panel were sometimes overruled by McLaughlin. His efforts to moderate the ruling that card playing by Indian women on ration day was an act of misconduct is an example of Gall's efforts to minimize any undue interference in his people's social culture.[51] Ration day at Standing Rock was a big social event that occurred once every two weeks. All the agency's Indians were required to gather at Fort Yates to select and butcher enough beef rations to last them for two weeks; card playing was considered a necessary diversion for these women, liberated from their arduous household and agricultural duties during this time.

Gall's independence on the court evidently did not alienate the important white personages involved in agency life. The noted photographer David F. Barry, who also enjoyed good relations with McLaughlin and his staff, praised Gall's tenure on the court of Indian offenses. "There is no justice in any court of the United States that could give you the limit with more solemn dignity than Chief Gall." In 1890 Gall, along with his two fellow jurists, John Grass and Standing Soldier, tried ninety-one criminal cases. Many of them dealt with crimes that were common among white people, such as family disturbances, assault, alleged rape, and larceny, to crimes that could involve a clash of cultural values, such as desertion on the part of a wife or husband, adultery, and a married husband taking a second wife.[52]

Gall was a picture of great dignity while serving on the court. Barry, who had taken Gall's first photograph a decade earlier, dubbed him "The Monarch Chief with the Daniel Webster Face" because of his strong good looks.[53] When the new judge assumed his responsibilities, he wore a dark blue business suit that stretched over his increasingly corpulent frame; Gall's weight had varied from 250 to 280 pounds during the late eighties and early nineties. Indeed, this once hyperactive and powerful warrior may have vacated his treasured role as district farmer two years before his death in 1894 because of obesity and health problems resulting from old war wounds.[54]

Gall's desire to live the white man's way apparently extended to a diet far different from the buffalo-based one of his warrior years. He liked rich food. When he visited Washington in fall 1888 with a large Indian delegation to discuss the possible implementation of the Dawes Act on the Great Sioux Reservation, he was taken to an elegant restaurant by Captain Edward S. Godfrey, who had served under Reno at the Little Bighorn. Gall's appetite for food never available during his warrior years was most evident at this meal. "The big Sioux mogul took to oysters in the shell like a Norfolk oyster man."[55]

Another area where Gall immersed himself in the culture of his Indian agent involved Sioux marital practices. Tribal warriors, particularly chiefs and headmen who could afford it, were by custom polygamists. This practice had nothing to do with their religion; if a married man wanted another wife, there was nothing in the Lakota code of conduct that prevented him from taking one. In fact, it was McLaughlin's understanding that if a Sioux male married the eldest sister in a family, he had the right to marry her younger sisters or arrange their marriages with other men when they reached the right age.[56]

Sitting Bull may have had as many as nine wives, and in 1885 Gall lived with one wife, Stand-in-Center, and White Lightning, the mother of one of his two wives killed at the Battle of the Little Bighorn. According to Episcopal church records, on November 12, 1894, he married a fourth wife, Martina Blue Earth, a few weeks before his death. Thus, Gall had at least four wives during his lifetime.[57]

McLaughlin greatly disapproved of polygamy, but even with his strong Christian convictions against plural marriage, he did not attempt to illegalize the practice outright; he feared the turmoil it might create among his more traditional charges at Standing Rock. He did, however, reward those Indians who were willing to abandon their polygamous practices. When the Blackfoot Lakota chief Mad Bear chose to be married to only one of his two wives after being converted to Christianity, McLaughlin would later show his genuine appreciation. When two of Mad Bear's daughters died from an epidemic sweeping Standing Rock, McLaughlin ordered and paid for marble headstones for their graves.[58]

In 1885, Gall became personally involved in the polygamy issue at the same time McLaughlin was building up Gall's image at Sitting Bull's expense. Gall's wife Stand-in-Center at fifty-one was six years his senior. He apparently had gotten along well with her until he fell in love with another woman whom he wanted as a second wife, even though she lived in the lodge of another man.

One morning he came to Major McLaughlin's agency office for a private interview with the agent, who had become in many ways his new mentor. After receiving McLaughlin's assurances that during the past four years, Gall had conscientiously followed "in the footsteps of the white man," Gall asked for McLaughlin's advice on this touchy new marital matter. Baring his soul like a son would for a father, he revealed his dilemma as persuasively as he could. "My heart is good, but it is sad, for I am in love." But McLaughlin was unbending. "I told him that one of the important things in the turning of the Indian into a white man was the taking of a single wife; how the white man had become great by making marriage a solemn thing to which only two people could become parties."

Gall apparently did not take McLaughlin's advice, which was given in a diplomatic manner. In fact, the Indian agent never heard anymore about Gall's decision to take another wife.[59] About ten years later, on November 12, 1894, Gall married Martina Blue Earth less than a month before his death. She had been the wife of Iron Cloud, one of Gall's comrades killed in battle. Gall and Martina raised at least one child, suggesting that his

Lakota marriage to her probably occurred earlier under the traditional marital customs of his people.

Two of the Hunkpapa chief's other daughters lived with him in 1885, Brown Woman and Red Horse. One of them had a daughter who was given the Anglo-American name Jenny Gall. Jenny's daughter was Lavora Jones, a third cousin of Vernon Iron Cloud, one of the great-grandsons of Gall and Martina.

Gall's baptism two years and four months before his death on December 5, 1894, probably prompted his decision in November to marry Martina in the church. He was motivated by his strong desire as a Christian convert to go to heaven. Martina may have been the same woman with whom Gall had fallen in love in 1885. Regardless, it seems evident that Gall ultimately rejected McLaughlin's advice. Stand-in-Center was continually listed as his sole wife in the censuses taken at Standing Rock from 1885 to 1894.[60]

Gall's cooperative attitude only made Standing Rock's ambitious Indian agent more determined to enhance Gall's reputation as what a civilized Indian should be like. From the beginning his strategy had been to denigrate Sitting Bull's reputation and elevate Gall's, but to McLaughlin's great consternation, Sitting Bull remained the best-known Plains Indian in the West. People visiting the Great Sioux Reservation ordinarily wanted to see Sitting Bull; he was the local celebrity among all the Lakotas. When Buffalo Bill Cody asked Sitting Bull to appear in his Wild West show in 1885, an unhappy McLaughlin resisted. Reluctant to offend the famous ex-army scout and showman, however, the willful agent finally relented.

For four months Sitting Bull was one of the stars of the Wild West show. He also got along well with many members of Buffalo Bill's cast of entertainers; he was the one who dubbed Annie Oakley, whom he admired because of her marksmanship, Little Sure Shot.[61] Having learned to write his name, the Indian most associated with the Little Bighorn was overwhelmed by autograph seekers as he traveled with Buffalo Bill from city to city. His fame had obviously eclipsed all others at Standing Rock, and McLaughlin knew it.

The flustered agent tried to offset Sitting Bull's popularity by pushing Gall as the real hero of the Lakotas. He sent his favorite Indian to the New Orleans Exposition in 1885, after denying Sitting Bull the same opportunity; he would go to great lengths to prevent Sitting Bull from achieving any public acclaim. He also allowed Gall to attend the tenth anniversary of the Battle of the Little Bighorn in 1886, no doubt to counteract the public's close identification of Sitting Bull with this greatest of Indian victories during the late nineteenth century.[62]

Gall benefited from being at the Little Bighorn. At the reunion, he gave, in a most straightforward manner, his version of the battle. It seemed to be an honest account, but, in typical Indian fashion, it did focus sharply on his own role. His confident manner during a tour of the battlefield impressed such observers as Edward S. Godfrey, the army officer who wrote his own account of the battle (one significantly influenced by Gall's version), and David F. Barry, who also gave a pro-Gall account of the battle.[63] The blunt candor of this dignified Indian leader, much praised by McLaughlin, was noticed and admired by others who attended this reunion.

But Gall could not always control his temper. One person who felt his fury was the Crow scout Curly, whose view of the battle was obviously not favorable to Gall's. Gall accused Curly, who had survived the Little Bighorn, of being a coward. "You . . . ran away before the battle began; if you hadn't you would not be here today." A stunned and intimidated Curly made no reply.[64]

For many years after the 1886 Little Bighorn reunion, McLaughlin, along with many colleagues and friends at Standing Rock, praised Gall as the most noble of the Lakota warriors. The determined agent, plainly on a mission, insisted that Gall was the real Indian hero at the Little Bighorn. He was the man who thwarted Reno's attack and later led the assault on Custer's ill-fated troopers. "It was Gall's knowledge of men and military affairs," McLaughlin asserted, "that led the Indians to leave Reno undisturbed while crushing Custer."

Although Gall, Crow King, and Crazy Horse had "plainly outgeneraled the commanders of the three columns sent against them, Gall was the greatest of the three war chiefs." Moreover, both Gall and Crow King had "nothing but contempt for Sitting Bull."[65] Gall, in a most unfair remark, once accused his old mentor of cowardice at the Little Bighorn; this remark is perhaps the most convincing example of McLaughlin's powerful influence over him.[66] Usher L. Burdick of the prominent North Dakota political family also claimed that Gall had "only contempt for the great Medicine Man." Gall, in Burdick's opinion, "showed intelligence far in excess of any of his contemporaries, and his face showed traces of a strong determined character, honest to complete frankness and far seeing almost to the point of prophesy."[67]

Barry was another Gall admirer. Although he did not denigrate Sitting Bull as McLaughlin and Burdick did, he did praise the fighting qualities of McLaughlin's favorite Indian. "Look well at the strong powerful face of Chief Gall and you will not wonder why the Custer fight lasted only thirty-five minutes."[68] This praise of Gall, however, was not confined to just friends and coworkers of McLaughlin at Standing Rock. For instance, in 1890, Gall was lauded as the foremost leader of all the Sioux in the popular national journal *Harper's Weekly*.[69]

The often extravagant promotion of Gall continued for many years, but ultimately Sitting Bull would prevail as the best known of all the Lakota leaders. His name recognition even exceeded that of Red Cloud, who probably exercised power longer and more effectively than any other Lakota leader. Today Sitting Bull's most prominent challenger in this category would be Crazy Horse, whose reputation as the greatest of the Lakota warriors has soared as a result of the Native American movement that emerged during the late twentieth century. Gall's fame, which was extolled with such energy during the four decades following the Little Bighorn, would gradually diminish during subsequent years.

An example of Gall's decline in the public memory is found in a letter received by Standing Rock superintendent Eugene D. Mossman on January 19, 1932, thirty-eight years after Gall's death. Sent by an Oregon attorney who visited Standing Rock in 1928, the writer wanted to know more about Gall. "There is considerable written of Sitting Bull, Crow King, Crazy Horse and some other chiefs but I have found mostly silence on Gall and in what there is written he seems to be given credit for being quite unusually capable."[70]

Mossman, in his response, gave the official line on Gall developed at Standing Rock since the 1880s: Gall not only was "the greatest Sioux general" but was also a most constructive member of the Indians at Standing Rock. While Sitting Bull, who was held in contempt by "the better class of Indians," was a destructive rather than constructive person. Mossman enthusiastically recommended McLaughlin's book *My Friend the Indian* for more information about Gall.[71]

By the early 1930s Mossman's hardline views regarding Sitting Bull were being challenged. Russell Reid, superintendent of the State Historical Society of North Dakota, wrote Mossman on July 20, 1931, disagreeing with Mossman's bitter criticisms of Sitting Bull and extolling the old chief's "strong character." In his opinion, Sitting Bull was "a good

Indian and always loyal to his people." Reid further urged the biased Indian superintendent to read Stanley Vestal's new biography of Sitting Bull, one of the first accounts published since the Little Bighorn to give Sitting Bull's side of the story.[72]

Gall's historical image today is still affected by the controversy over McLaughlin's concept of a good Indian, as envisioned by the proponents of the Mohonk movement. Although a number of Lakota leaders, such as Spotted Tail, Young-Man-Afraid-of-His-Horse, George Sword, Crow King, and Rain-in-the-Face, were clearly identified as members of the cooperative factions at their agencies, Gall undoubtedly received the most criticism for his progressive stance.[73] Traditional Lakota leaders were critical of his break with Sitting Bull, his version of the Battle of the Little Bighorn (especially as it was embroidered by his white friends), and his later resistance to the Ghost Dance, a movement that all Lakota leaders would have to face in 1890. Indeed, because of the controversy over his lifestyle and the choices he made during the 1880s and early 1890s, Gall was omitted from Kicking Bear's pictographic version of the Battle of the Little Bighorn. This panoramic visual interpretation of the battle pictured Sitting Bull, Crazy Horse, Rain-in-the-Face, and Kicking Bear himself as the most important Sioux leaders at the battle.[74]

Yet Gall did play his new role as a cooperative Indian with a certain degree of integrity. He was a good district farmer and a conscientious judge while serving on the court of Indian offenses. He continued to advance the needs of his band and honestly believed that cooperation was the best way to address the social and economic concerns of the Standing Rock Indians. He made a sincere effort to reconcile the cultural differences between the federal authorities and his people, albeit receiving in the process advantageous benefits from McLaughlin and his allies. But soon Gall and those Lakotas who thought like him, along with their critical rivals from Sitting Bull's camp, would have to confront a common threat. This new danger came in the form of the Sioux bill of 1889, and it threatened to reduce drastically the size of the Great Sioux Reservation.

CHAPTER TWELVE

The Sioux Bills

In November 1882 a commission authorized by Congress visited the Standing Rock Agency, headed by the former governor of Dakota Territory Newton Edmunds, who in 1865 had traveled up the Missouri to negotiate peace treaties with friendly Lakota tribespeople. His treaties were meaningless, however, because they did not involve those Indian leaders who had been staunchly resisting encroachments on their lands during the previous three years.[1] The motives of the 1882 commission clearly reflected the attitude of the white settlers who had participated in that big land rush the Great Dakota Boom. These farmers, who had been encouraged by the Sioux cession of the Black Hills in 1876, began to swell in numbers by 1878. In essence, the Edmunds Commission was anxious to satisfy the cravings for land of most of the white settlers, numbering about 117,000 people in 1880, not including the 17,000 prospectors scrambling for gold in the Black Hills.

The commission's goal was to divide the Great Sioux Reservation into six separate ones. Thus, the Standing Rock, Cheyenne River, Pine Ridge, Rosebud, Lower Brulé, and Crow Creek agencies would each be given reservation status. The plan would guarantee for each major tribe exclusive ownership of its new reservation, uncomplicated by the old concept of common ownership by all Sioux people. Not clearly articulated, however, was the commission's primary motive for advancing this proposal: it wanted to open up for white settlement those lands not allotted to individual Indians. The ramifications of this proposal were enormous; the area available to whites under this proposal would be almost half the size of the Great Sioux Reservation.[2]

The Edmunds Commission managed upon its arrival to spread panic and confusion among most of the Standing Rock Indians. Persuaded that this new proposal would ultimately benefit his charges, McLaughlin lobbied for it. Among the Indians he approached were the suspicious Hunkpapas, who were probably more dubious about the plan than most Standing Rock residents. The agent was supported by the clergy of the Roman Catholic Church, which had strongly backed McLaughlin as one of their most devout and able members. Indeed, the crusading Catholic bishop Martin Marty clearly communicated to all agency Indians his belief that to oppose the commission's plan would displease God.[3] Those Sioux leaders whom McLaughlin had started grooming for leadership at the agency, John Grass, Gall, Mad Bear, and Big Head, appeared ready to accept this deceptive reorganization plan. In fact, Gall and Grass signed the agreement on November 30, 1882.[4]

Despite the ready acceptance of the Edmunds plan by the more prominent Lakota leaders at Standing Rock, there was still considerable tension throughout the Great Sioux Reservation. One cause for the anxiety involved a Yanktonai named Brave Bear, who had returned from Canada with Sitting Bull. In 1874 Brave Bear had been accused of murdering members of a mixed-blood Chippewa family near the town of St. Joe in Pembina County, in the northeastern corner of present-day North Dakota. He was confined in the Pembina County jail but managed to escape in late 1878. Major McLaughlin, then acting as the agent at the Devils Lake Agency, at first believed that Brave Bear had fled to Canada, but later concluded that he was heading for the now-abandoned Red Cloud or Spotted Tail agencies by way of Standing Rock. On May 21, 1879, Brave Bear was implicated in another crime; with a party of other maverick Indians, he had attempted to steal the horses of a settler named John Manning.

When he was finally apprehended, the controversial Brave Bear was tried for murder in January 1882. It was not for the murder of the Chippewa family, however, but for an 1879 killing of an ex-soldier named Joseph Johnson, who had befriended him. He was found guilty, and his execution was scheduled for March 9, but it was postponed to May 18 and later to July 20. Because of the strong emotions on both sides, the Dakota Territory Supreme Court got involved and an appeal was even made to President Chester A. Arthur for a stay of execution. Working to get Brave Bear's sentence commuted to imprisonment, Bishop Marty solicited the help of McLaughlin, who by now was the Indian agent at Standing Rock; both men felt that Brave Bear's exposure to Catholicism had been too brief to affect his sense of right and wrong. Moreover, his crimes unhappily reflected the old racial and tribal hostilities still existing throughout the territory.

An attempt was even made to have the Edmunds Commission join in their appeal, arguing that Brave Bear's execution would only infuriate the Sioux and cripple the work of the commission in its efforts to get the Standing Rock Indians to agree to its proposals. Notwithstanding these efforts, Brave Bear was hanged on November 15, 1882. The prolonged nature of this crisis and the belief of many Lakotas that Brave Bear's execution was in violation of Sitting Bull's terms of surrender (and their own sovereign rights) poisoned the political atmosphere to the decided disadvantage of the Edmunds Commission.[5]

The Brave Bear incident was only one problem faced by the frustrated commission. Edmunds and his fellow commissioners, Peter C. Shannon and James H. Teller, had overlooked one important fact. Any land cession by the Lakotas had to be ratified by three-quarters of all adult Lakota males, according to the 1868 Treaty of Fort Laramie. Although Edmunds would argue the three-quarters provision had been ignored when the Black Hills were wrested from the Lakotas six years earlier, the United States Senate, largely influenced by Senator Henry L. Dawes, refused to ratify the Edmunds agreement because it was signed by only a few tribal leaders. Instead the senators sent a select committee to the reservation under the chairmanship of Senator Dawes, who had become the leading congressional proponent for those reforms advanced by the Mohonk movement. At an August 1883 hearing at Standing Rock, the senator and his colleagues listened patiently to such leaders as Gall, Grass, and Running Antelope, who were starting to have second thoughts about the Edmunds proposal. Sitting Bull was there, too; as a staunch opponent, he managed to alienate most members of this influential Senate committee.[6]

Senator Dawes may have been instrumental in thwarting the plans of the Edmunds Commission to partition and allot land on the Great Sioux Reservation, but he remained dedicated to the concept of land allotment. Because of his strong conviction on this score, he pushed through Congress what became known as the Dawes General Allotment Act, which was signed into law by President Grover Cleveland on February 8, 1887. Although allotment, or severalty, bills affecting the Indians had been debated in Congress during the 1870s, it was the agitation of reformers of the Mohonk stripe that gave the Dawes plan its momentum. The senator's bill not only got through the friendly Senate but even made it through the more reluctant House.

This new piece of legislation called for the allotment of tribal reservation lands in which each family head would receive 160 acres, each single adult male, 80 acres, and each minor, 40 acres. The allotted acreage would be doubled for grazing lands, and those lands not allotted could be opened up to white settlement. The title to each land allotment, moreover, would be held by the government for twenty-five years to protect new Indian landowners from covetous white speculators. Also, to deal with Indian resistance, the federal government could select individual plots of land for reluctant or uncooperative tribal members after a lapse of four years. This rather punitive provision, however, was balanced by another that granted U.S. citizenship to those Indians who voluntarily took their allotments.

Most Indian reform organizations were enthusiastic over the passage of the Dawes Act. The Washington lobbyist for Herbert Welsh's Indian Rights Association, Charles C. Painter, likened this new legislation to the Magna Carta, the Declaration of Independence, and the Emancipation Proclamation as far as its impact on the Indians was concerned.[7] But the National Indian Defense Association, apprehensive over the provision of the Dawes Act that would open up surplus reservation land for white homesteaders, opposed the measure. Its attorney, Judge A. J. Willard, prepared a persuasive legal brief in 1886 outlining the group's objections; his arguments probably forced Congress to postpone passage of the Dawes bill from the forty-ninth session to the fiftieth.[8] NIDA's skepticism over opening these surplus lands was not baseless; from 1887 to 1934, such unallotted lands, coupled with those acres sold by Indian owners after the twenty-five-year protection period, reduced the total acreage of all Indian lands from 138 million to 55 million.[9]

An especially important step for the Dawes Act would be its application to the Great Sioux Reservation. There, would-be white landowners and speculators were salivating over the prospect of acquiring those undivided lands not allotted to Indians. The lure of such an immense tract of land, amounting to more than 9 million acres and almost equaling in size the six current Lakota agencies, was irresistible.

These land-hungry settlers were joined by statehood boosters in Dakota Territory, who also saw increased opportunities in the land expansion that the Dawes Act could provide. In fact, the proposed division of the sprawling territory into two states, North Dakota and South Dakota, had made the partition of the Great Sioux Reservation particularly important to South Dakotans. The boundaries of the existing reservation had separated the eastern part of this proposed new state from the Black Hills ever since the Sioux had been forced to cede these hills in 1876.[10] In many ways, the same pressures that had inspired the proposals of the Edmunds Commission to partition the reservation in 1882 were again at work in 1888.

The result of all these frenzied activities was the Sioux bill of 1888, a measure that not only called for the partition of the Great Sioux Reservation, but guaranteed a payment of fifty cents an acre to the Sioux for those surplus lands not allotted. Thus, an enormous part of the old reservation would be restored to the public domain and opened to white homesteaders. Moreover, the Sioux bill reversed one of the procedures specified in the Dawes Act: it allowed negotiations for surplus lands to start even before surveys were run and allotments were made. The Lakotas would be given clear title to their lands under this measure. Also, proceeds from the sale of surplus land to white settlers would be put into a permanent Sioux fund, whose interest at five percent would be spent on an Indian educational program.

To sweeten this new legislation, or land grab, as many detractors would eventually call it, the Sioux would receive twenty-five thousand cows and one thousand bulls. Also, each family head or single adult would receive farming tools, a two-year supply of seeds to cultivate five acres, two oxen, a pair of milk cows, and twenty dollars in cash. In accordance with the 1868 Treaty of Fort Laramie, however, this bill would not take effect until three-fourths of all adult males on the reservation agreed to its provisions.[11]

The last requirement, which Senator Dawes insisted on, entailed some adroit persuasion on the part of the federal government. To obtain the necessary signatures of approval for the bill, a three-man commission was appointed, headed by Captain Richard H. Pratt, founder and superintendent of the renowned Carlisle Indian Training School. The choice of this tall army officer seemed a wise one until his doctrinaire and unbending personality surfaced during the bill's hearings. As far as the other two commissioners were concerned, Reverend William J. Cleveland, a cousin of President Cleveland, probably carried more weight than Judge John V. Wright of Tennessee, who gained the dubious distinction of provoking the Sioux almost as much as Captain Pratt did.

The effort to sell this new plan, which would significantly shrink the size of the reservation, would not be as easy in 1888 as the similar effort had been in 1882. The Pratt Commission decided to go to Standing Rock first, because six years earlier 143 of the agency's residents, including Gall and John Grass, had given their approval to the Edmunds plan.[12] In contrast to this support, only 119 Pine Ridge Sioux and 37 Rosebud Sioux agreed to the less controversial 1882 proposal. Even before the commission's arrival, delegations from all the agencies met at the Rosebud Agency, home of the Brulés, where they decided to resist the Sioux bill and, thus, protect the reservation's current boundaries.

On July 23, 1888, the Pratt Commission opened its hearings on the Sioux bill at Standing Rock before more than seven hundred rather glum-looking Sioux, including thirty-four suspicious chiefs. The *Bismarck Weekly Tribune* claimed that nearly all five thousand Indians at the agency had already encamped within two miles of Fort Yates, distrustful and "loaded with oratorical fire." Gall, described by the newspapers as the "handsomest and most commanding Indian of the tribe," urged his admirers to listen to the commissioners but to be wary. When he had been the chief Hunkpapa representative at the 1868 Fort Rice conference, the whites had made great promises to the Lakota people regarding the merits of the Treaty of Fort Laramie, promises that were never fulfilled. The commissioners, sensing this hostility, were probably bolstered somewhat by McLaughlin's glowing introduction. "This Commission is composed of gentlemen who are all known men of respectability in their own homes, each bearing a national reputation and they are not strangers to this country."[13]

McLaughlin was evidently trying to put the best face on a bad situation; the agent did not feel that this bill was a fair one, but as a federal employee, he could not express his true feelings. President Cleveland's secretary of the Interior, William F. Vilas, had written McLaughlin July 9, soliciting his support for the Sioux bill of 1888 while stressing the importance of winning the consent of at least three-fourths of the adult males at Standing Rock. The aging Running Antelope, who had already been displaced by Gall as McLaughlin's favorite Indian, also tried to sooth the mood of his people. "I want you all, young men particularly, . . . to listen attentively and quietly to what they have to say."[14]

Gall, still enjoying McLaughlin's adulation, was particularly outspoken during this meeting with the commission. When Judge Wright belittled him for saying that the "Great Father was guilty of lying and stealing," Gall responded with obvious anger. "You speak to us just the same as children. You might as well come out and say—Gall, you are a bad man, and Mad Bear you are a bad man, and John Grass you are a bad man, and Big Head you are a bad man."[15]

Captain Pratt, throughout these meetings, was a man of exceptional persistence. Day after day, for almost a month, he pressured the Indians to accept the Sioux bill. His determination even irked the publisher of the *Bismarck Daily Tribune*. The July 29, 1888, edition condemned this noted founder of the Carlisle School for displaying the "arrogant dictation of an army martinet and the disgusting pedantry of an Indian school pedagogue." The journal even got to the core of the dispute, claiming that the Indians could lose 11 million acres of land "they thought was theirs" but would have to concede was now "the property of Mr. Pratt." Although the *Tribune* often revealed a paternalistic attitude toward the "dusky Sioux" at Standing Rock, it's publisher particularly resented Captain Pratt's efforts to censor the commission's proceedings so that the newspaper could not publish them with accuracy. Although Pratt never relented, his claims that this bill would give the Lakotas five times more financial remuneration than the Edmunds plan ever would have were either refuted or ignored. Many of the Sioux insisted that they did not have more land than they actually needed. Others thought that it was most unfair that the government was only offering the Sioux fifty cents an acre for their surplus land when an acre on the public domain sold for $1.25.[16]

After weeks of debate, the Hunkpapas and the Yanktonais were becoming increasingly impatient with these lengthy proceedings. Gall complained bitterly that the hearings were taking him and other Indians away from their "fields of oats, wheat and pumpkins and potatoes." As a result, these crops were being devoured by insect pests and devastated by dry weather. On August 21, the last day of the hearings, Gall urged his compatriots to leave the meeting at once and return to their farms. "We have spoken to you pleasantly," he reminded the commission, "and we have got much to do, and we are going home today."[17] Sitting Bull, who was unalterably opposed to the Sioux bill, must have been delighted with his once close friend that day. But McLaughlin's influence over Gall was still paramount; he ordered Gall and his followers to stay, thus allowing the Reverend Cleveland to adjourn this final meeting in a face-saving way.

In the end the Pratt Commission had little to show for its efforts. During the hearings, it had given the Standing Rock Indians two sets of ballots. One set, in which the ballots were black, would be signed by those who approved the Sioux bill, while the other set, in which the ballots were red, would be signed by those who opposed the Sioux bill. As it turned out, only twenty-two Standing Rock residents put their mark on the black ballot, while all the others refused to place their mark on either ballot.

There is evidence that great pressure was placed on Hunkpapa and Blackfoot Lakota tribespeople not to mark the black ballots in favor of the controversial Sioux bill of 1888. White Bull told the Pratt Commission of the intimidation that he and other dissenters felt because they agreed with the provisions of the 1888 Sioux bill. John Grass, who spoke English and often acted as a spokesman for Gall and other like-minded Indians at Standing Rock, insisted that those people who wanted to sign the Pratt agreement could do it without fear of retaliation, but if they did, they would be considered white people and would be "taken off to the East" by their new white friends. White Bull, whose politics were now much different from those of Gall and Sitting Bull, remained steadfast in his determination, declaring that he would put his trust in the American people and the Great Father. In the end, only five Hunkpapas and eight Blackfoot Lakotas approved of the Sioux bill.

Acknowledging their defeat, the frustrated commissioners sailed down the Missouri to the Lower Brulé Agency, where 244 Sioux favored the bill, and later to the Crow Creek Agency, where the 120 favorable signatures were negated by the 282 Indians who refused to commit themselves either way. Convinced that they would get nothing close to a three-quarters majority, the commissioners ultimately went home and prepared a stinging report against the Lakotas. It concluded that the federal government should put the 1888 Sioux bill into effect without Indian consent.[18]

But insiders in Washington realized that this course would not be acceptable to many Indian sympathizers from the East. The NIDA would find such an action outrageous. Even proponents of the Mohonk movement, such as Senator Dawes, could hardly remain credible if they allowed the federal government to ignore article 12 of the Fort Laramie Treaty; to defy this provision would be highly controversial.

Some compromise was needed, and a trip to Washington by Sioux leaders seemed to be a good way of reaching it. The result was a large delegation of more than sixty chiefs, representing all six agencies. Those chosen for the long railroad journey to Washington, which Sioux leaders always seemed to enjoy, arrived in the capital on October 12, 1888.[19] For the most part, these leaders were "progressive" in their views and included men like Gall and John Grass from Standing Rock and American Horse and George Sword from Pine Ridge. Two curious aspects about this mission, which was carefully supervised by the alert agents and interpreters who accompanied it, was the inclusion of Sitting Bull in the Standing Rock delegation and the omission of Red Cloud from the Pine Ridge delegation; Red Cloud's absence was probably due to Captain Pratt's strategy of going over the heads of particularly effective leaders to reach the rank and file.[20]

As was the case in most of the earlier Indian delegations, these chiefs were made to feel welcome. They were entertained by visits to landmark sites like the Smithsonian Institution and the National Zoo. Their lodgings at the Belvedere Hotel provided them with heretofore unrealized luxury. Gall, described as "a big, stout, bully fellow," proved popular with many of the curious onlookers they encountered; indeed, it was during this trip that his old rival from the Little Bighorn, Captain Edward S. Godfrey, treated him to an oyster dinner at one of the capital's upscale restaurants.

But much more important was the meeting between these Sioux leaders and Secretary Vilas. In this encounter, the old Sioux complaint that fifty cents an acre for their surplus lands was grossly unfair was met by Vilas's enticing counteroffer of a dollar an acre. At this point, Sitting Bull got involved in the bargaining; he raised the ante to $1.25 an acre, the going price for the sale of land on the public domain. When forty-seven of the chiefs supported Sitting Bull's proposal, it looked like an unbridgeable chasm now separated the Department of the Interior from these independent-minded representatives of the Great Sioux Reservation. Most of the Indian delegates were happy with this hardline position, because they did not want to lose any more land. What they did not realize was that government negotiators regarded Sitting Bull's counterproposal as a breach in the Sioux ranks; these Sioux leaders were now willing to negotiate some kind of compromise.[21]

Although the 1888 Washington visit resulted in a stalemate, Secretary Vilas's opposition to the $1.25 per acre provision became meaningless when President Benjamin Harrison's newly appointed secretary of the Interior, John W. Noble, and most Republicans, proved to be more determined than the Democrats to break up the Great Sioux Reservation. The admission of North Dakota, South Dakota, Washington, and Montana under the Springer omnibus bill, which passed in February 1889, greatly strengthened the GOP's congressional delegation.[22] When the two Republican-leaning Dakota states were officially granted their new status in November 1889, this two-state area on the high plains would have four senators and two congressmen rather than just two nonvoting territorial delegates. This new political strength would put even more pressure on the Sioux to open up their surplus lands for homesteading.

Supporters of a new Sioux bill managed to push through Congress the Sioux bill of 1889. Although this measure included some compromises, it had more clout behind it than the unsuccessful Sioux bill of 1888. On the assumption that white settlers would claim the best lands first, Congress in 1889 agreed to pay the Sioux $1.25 per acre for all land homesteaded by whites during the first three years, $0.75 per acre for land sold during the next two years, and $0.50 per acre thereafter for all lands that remained unsold. Other provisions in the 1889 measure included 320 rather than 160 acres for family heads, plus many of the benefits that were promised in the 1888 Sioux bill. To buttress the federal government's legal position, the process of land allotments could not begin until a three-fourths majority of adult males on the Sioux reservation approved the new bill.[23]

A new Sioux commission was established to win Indian approval for the 1889 bill. Two of its members, Charles Foster, former governor of Ohio, and William Warner, a prominent Senator from Missouri and commander of the Grand Army of the Republic, knew little about the Lakotas. But the third member, General George Crook, knew a great deal about these willful tribespeople whom he had faced during the Great Sioux War. Thus, it was only logical that this veteran army officer, now a major general, should be the leader of the 1889 Sioux commission. In fact, the new commission became known as the Crook Commission.

To show that the federal government really meant business, the Crook Commission was given a special railroad car, which left Chicago on May 28 for the Great Sioux Reservation. The commissioners were given twenty-five thousand dollars for expenses, which was a large sum of money in 1889. These funds were to be used for generous feasts, which the commissioners hoped would make the Sioux more receptive to the new bill's proposed compromises. Commission members also decided to be more relaxed and less tenacious than the doctrinaire Pratt and his two colleagues had been. These new tactics would be important, because throughout the Great Sioux Reservation, Indian leaders had decided to oppose the new bill and have only Indian agents present the case to all the others.

Rosebud was the first agency the commission visited, where it was able to breach the wall of opposition because of the continuing lack of leadership caused by Spotted Tail's death in 1883. By using the support of mixed-bloods and white men married to Indian women, the commission was able to employ Pratt's strategy of going over the heads of Indian chiefs to reach the desired consensus. The Crook Commission acquired the necessary three-quarters vote at all the agencies except Pine Ridge prior to their visit to Standing Rock. At Pine Ridge, the opposition of Red Cloud and his allies prevailed in a surprisingly stiff ratification fight. Not only did Red Cloud oppose this Sioux bill, but a number of usually cooperative Oglala leaders like Young-Man-Afraid-of-His-Horse and Little Wound resisted the persuasive blandishments of the Crook Commission. Opposition was also encountered at the Cheyenne River Reservation, where an effort to prevent people from signing the rolls in favor of the 1889 measure was successfully resisted by a majority of the Indian police and some well-to-do mixed-bloods allegedly from other agencies.[24]

Standing Rock, the last Sioux agency visited by the Crook Commission, was considered by many to be the most uncompromising of the six. Gall, John Grass, Mad Bear, and Big Head were prepared to speak out against the second Sioux bill as strongly as they had the first. There would, however, be one significant change. Major McLaughlin had switched positions on this controversial issue, evidently feeling that the Sioux could not get anything better from the federal government and, if they continued their resistance, might even do worse.

For three days in late July, John Grass, Gall, Mad Bear, and Big Head criticized the 1889 bill, with Grass demonstrating particular eloquence. But on the night of the third day, McLaughlin slipped away from a grand reception his wife was giving for the commissioners. Accompanied by his translator, Louis Primeau, he secretly met with Grass at a vacant building near the home of Grass's brother-in-law Nick Cadotte. McLaughlin persuaded Grass to reverse his old position on the Sioux bills or risk having the federal government impose a far less desirable piece of legislation on him and his people. He urged Grass to push for new federal concessions first and then, as gracefully as possible, make that difficult transition to support the new Sioux bill.

After convincing Grass of the wisdom of this new approach, McLaughlin asked him to explain it to Gall. But Grass, who feared Gall's volatile temper, absolutely refused to lobby Gall in behalf of the bill; he was probably the one who had convinced Gall of the validity of their original position in the first place. The resolute McLaughlin, not undaunted by Grass's apprehensiveness, approached Gall, Mad Bear, and Big Head, convincing all three of the correctness of this new position.[25]

The result of McLaughlin's persuasiveness was a convincing speech in favor of the 1889 Sioux measure by Grass; the talented Indian leader argued "with the facility of a statesman." His oration was followed by shorter, but nonetheless influential, talks in support of the bill by Gall, Mad Bear, and Big Head. The initial opposition of the Hunkpapas and Yanktonais at Standing Rock had been decisively blunted. Undecided agency Indians, fearing to be left out of the sweetened provisions in what would become the Sioux Act of 1889, lined up, ready to sign. The plan was to have Grass be the first signer, followed by Mad Bear, Gall, and Big Head, but, according to McLaughlin, Gall, fearing bodily harm by Sitting Bull's angry Hunkpapas, hesitated long enough for Yanktonai chief Big Head to step in and win the "coveted distinction" of being the third signer. In fact, in the official roster of those Indians affixing their mark to the bill, Gall was number 416 of 803 signers.[26]

Sitting Bull's growing displeasure toward his former war lieutenant must have exploded into rage; there were two efforts by twenty of his followers to disrupt the voting altogether. But these attempts were broken up by McLaughlin's Indian police, under the command of Lieutenant Bull Head. McLaughlin also gained the cooperation of the agency's Lower Yanktonais under the leadership of Chief Two Bears. Indeed, Two Bears placed the members of his band in a semicircle around the speaker's platform to protect the proponents of this latest Sioux bill.[27] A disappointed Sitting Bull left the scene in bitterness: "There are no Indians left but me." The commissioners were elated. A jubilant General Crook chortled that Sitting Bull had been "flattened out" and his "wind bag punctured."[28] Their efforts resulted in 803 favorable votes for the bill at Standing Rock; the

Sioux Act of 1889 was now law, the Crook Commission having garnered 5,678 eligible voters.

The defeat of Sitting Bull and the more traditional faction at Standing Rock could not have been more complete. Not only did a son and stepson of the old chief agree to ratify the new law, but his nephew and once most intimate supporter, White Bull, did too.[29] The leaders of the so-called progressive faction, however, would receive the most blame when conditions at the six new reservations began to deteriorate during the following months.

Shortly after the ratification fight, McLaughlin selected Gall, Grass, Mad Bear, Big Head, and Two Bears to visit Washington as part of another Sioux delegation. The trip was scheduled for December 1889, and its purpose was to discuss with the secretary of the Interior the concessions that the Crook Commission was willing to make if the new Sioux measure were to be approved. But the selection of Gall and the others for this coveted journey to Washington was regarded by many as a payoff for going along with the government's plan.[30] Such a conclusion is difficult to accept as a sole motive on Gall's part. His attentiveness to the needs of his band were almost always uppermost in his mind. Even though Secretary Noble agreed to such concessions as employing more Indians at the new reservations, removing the ban on "innocent dances," building new grist mills, and providing for more equality between mixed-bloods and full-bloods, only Congress could make the really important changes.

It was Congress alone that could make available the interest on the reservation's $3 million permanent fund and apportion that interest among all six reservations according to population. Congressional powers could also accomplish other things important to the Sioux. It could compensate the Standing Rock and Cheyenne River Indians for the ponies seized by the army in 1876. More important, it could restore the unpopular $100,000 cut in the beef allowance, which had been made prior to the ratification fight but had nothing to do with the negotiations over the new Sioux act.

Hope remained surprisingly high among Indian leaders during the winter months following the ratification of the Sioux Act. Of course, most of the Indians did not fully appreciate the difference between what the Crook Commission could recommend and what the Congress and the secretary of the Interior would be willing to do. As it turned out, Secretary Noble agreed with most of the Crook Commission's promises, but it ordinarily takes Congress much longer to reach decisions of this gravity.

The biggest shock of all, however, came with President Harrison's acceptance on February 10, 1890, of the land agreement reached in the 1889 Sioux Act. With almost no warning, he acted on this controversial provision before the promises made to the already suspicious Sioux Indians could be carried out. In fact, prior to Harrison's action, no surveys had been made to define the boundaries of the new reservations, and no provisions had been made for those Indians living on the ceded tribal lands to take allotments there.

Harrison's action had an enormous impact. Feelings of anger and betrayal were felt by most Sioux, whether they be reformist or traditional in their views. Their deepening resentment was compounded by the severe winter of 1889–1890. This frigid season, along with the hot and dry summer that followed, resulted in a series of crop failures. The subsequent decline in agricultural production, when compounded by the cut in the beef allowance, pushed many Lakota families toward starvation.

A great deal of sickness was associated with the growing food shortage. Measles, influenza, and whooping cough epidemics spread throughout the six new reservations, sometimes causing death. Although these devastating conditions resulted in fewer settlers homesteading the newly opened lands in North Dakota and South Dakota, most Indians derived little satisfaction from this development; they feared that any delay in such sales would ultimately result in land going for $0.50 to $0.75 an acre rather than a $1.25, the guaranteed price during the first three years of the Sioux Act.[31]

Federal authorities could take pride in the results of their negotiations with Indians over the land cessions required by the Sioux Act. They had opened up large tracts of land that were once part of the Great Sioux Reservation, adroitly outmaneuvering Indian leaders such as Gall and John Grass to achieve their objectives. But they would eventually have to face a backlog of resentment.

CHAPTER THIRTEEN

The Death of Sitting Bull

During those dreary months following the ratification of the Sioux Act, a new crisis erupted that further divided the Lakotas from their white adversaries. A new religion was making its way to the six recently created reservations scattered throughout the Dakota plains. The source of this fresh new faith, gripping many of the Indian tribes in the West, was a Paiute shaman from Nevada named Wovoka. This Indian visionary, who had been adopted by a white family and given the name Jack Wilson, had learned about Christianity through reading his adoptive family's Bible. On January 1, 1889, during an eclipse of the sun, the fever-stricken Wovoka, lying sick in a brush lodge, had a vision that he ascended to heaven. There, he saw not only God but many Indians living happily in a celestial world most reminiscent of the old Indian way of life. As a result of this vision, he soon became the messiah to many Indian tribes, preaching an electrifying new faith that combined the teachings of Christ with the traditional beliefs of the Indian people.

In Wovoka's revelation, the earthly world was to be regenerated. Ancestors would return, and wild game, including the vanishing buffalo, would be restored. White people, who had subjugated the once dominant Indian tribes, would be pushed back across the ocean from where they came. To hasten this coveted process, a mournful circle dance was stressed to achieve Wovoka's ultimate vision. Because this dance could bring back the dead, it was performed over and over again. Nervous whites living on or near the affected reservations would later call it the Ghost Dance.[1]

After emissaries from the Plains tribes visited the charismatic Indian prophet, they spread his teachings eastward. The Lakotas initially learned about Wovoka's new religion from the Crows, Shoshones, or Arapahoes. In her diary, Elaine Goodale, the supervisor of education in the Dakotas, mentioned that as early as July 1889, an Indian testified that Christ had appeared before the Crows and proclaimed himself the same savior who came to earth before only to be killed by the whites.

The two most important Lakota emissaries to visit Wovoka were Kicking Bear and Short Bull; these men were able warriors who had become influential medicine men. Their efforts to win converts to the Ghost Dance religion in 1890 were especially effective at Pine Ridge and Rosebud, the southernmost of the six new reservations. Because the Sioux were more warlike than most western tribes, their adaptation of Wovoka's Ghost Dance was especially frightening to those whites living in Nebraska and the two fledgling Dakota states. The Ghost Dance shirt worn by many of the Lakota dancers was particularly menacing; the Lakotas believed that this shirt made them impervious to bullets.[2]

To many people in Sioux country, especially Daniel F. Royer, the Indian agent at Pine Ridge, the Ghost Dance was a war dance. This was an incorrect perception because there were women participants and women were never involved in war dances. Royer, who lacked the effectiveness of McLaughlin, tried to persuade the Lakota leaders at Pine Ridge to abandon the Ghost Dance. His efforts, however, were met with only ridicule and defiance; indeed, some of the Indians gave him the nickname Young-Man-Afraid-of-Indians, even though he was well past his prime. President Harrison in November 1890 dispatched Brigadier General John R. Brooke to Pine Ridge with five companies of infantry and three companies of cavalry.

This move was probably overkill, because no more than a third of all the Lakotas throughout these new reservations were practicing believers.[3] Troops were also sent to Rosebud, while members of the Nebraska National Guard were ordered to patrol the state's common border with the reservation at Pine Ridge. When Colonel Miles, now a major general, was given the command to deal with this imminent crisis, the Ghost Dance became a national news story; journalists and photographers arrived in large numbers from the East to cover the disturbing event and its potentially dire consequences.

Many Lakota leaders were unconvinced by Wovoka's comforting religious teachings, despite their miserable conditions of life and their feelings of betrayal over the Sioux Act. At Pine Ridge the influential American Horse and Young-Man-Afraid-of-His-Horse were quite dubious. Red Cloud, who often tried to straddle the progressive and traditional camps in his political and social views, was willing to let this religious phenomenon play itself out, despite his conversion to Catholicism. When the situation became serious enough to bring the U.S. Army into the picture, however, he began to have second thoughts.[4]

In those Lakota reservations to the north, Gall, greatly influenced by the Episcopal Church although not yet a member, was skeptical. John Grass, an Episcopalian who later converted to Roman Catholicism, was also distrustful. But Sitting Bull was the major concern of the federal and military authorities at Standing Rock. The old chief once admitted that he preferred the White Gowns, the Episcopal priests, to the Black Gowns, the Catholic priests, but never joined either church. Even though he sometimes responded to Christian evangelists like the Congregational missionary Mary C. Collins, who befriended him but could never convert him, he remained an unknown factor in this growing crisis.[5]

The tardy arrival of the Ghost Dance at Standing Rock on October 9, 1890, occurred because Sitting Bull sent a small party of his men to the Cheyenne River Reservation to invite Kicking Bear for a visit.[6] When Kicking Bear arrived with six helpers, he demonstrated his eloquence in sermons more militant, and perhaps more vivid, than Wovoka's. Kicking Bear insisted that this new messiah would cover the ground with a layer of soil from which nutritious grass and running water could flourish and herds of buffalo and ponies could wander about in abundance. Moreover, when this cataclysmic event was completed, all the white people would be buried under the thickness of this new grass cover.

The people who had gathered to hear Kicking Bear on October 13 were entranced, as were members of the Indian police sent by McLaughlin to eject Kicking Bear from Standing Rock. So powerful were Kicking Bear's words that Captain Crazy Walking, who headed this police detachment, lost his nerve. In effect, he asked rather than ordered Kicking Bear to leave. The understandably angry McLaughlin responded to this timidity by instructing one of Crazy Walking's subordinates, Lieutenant Chatka, and another policeman to escort Kicking Bear and his acolytes out of Standing Rock two days later.[7]

Sitting Bull's attitude during this emotionally charged episode is a puzzling one. He had moved his people from their cluster of cabins in the

Grand River valley to an encampment of tipis, located on some level ground north of his band's compound. There, the Ghost Dancers would begin early in the morning, after they had purified themselves in nearby sweat lodges, and dance throughout most of the day. When Sitting Bull was visited by Robert Higheagle, an astute observer of Hunkpapa life at this time, the aging chief, almost sixty, insisted that he was not a Ghost Dancer. He was an adviser to his people, as far as this new faith was concerned, not a convert. He wore no Ghost Dance shirt, taking a stance similar to Red Cloud's that his people had at least a right to learn about Wovoka's religion.[8]

What concerned McLaughlin and other officials the most was the invitation Sitting Bull had received from both Kicking Bear and Short Bull to join the more zealous Ghost Dancers at the Stronghold. The Stronghold was a large and defensible plateau located in the northwest corner of Pine Ridge, where many of the Ghost Dancers had gathered. When conditions to the south worsened in mid-November because of the arrival of troops at Pine Ridge and Rosebud, the attitudes of both McLaughlin and Sitting Bull toward the Ghost Dance hardened. Of course, McLaughlin's opposition had been evident from the start, but Sitting Bull had to ponder this invitation, knowing the serious ramifications that could result from his acceptance.

When Sitting Bull's headmen from the Grand River valley decided in council that he should go to Pine Ridge and learn more about this new religion, they must have been aware of the possible consequences. On December 12, when McLaughlin received a message from Sitting Bull informing him of his intention to go to Pine Ridge, McLaughlin was ready for decisive action. His resolve was strengthened by a letter from John N. Carignan, a teacher at the Grand River Day School. The concerned Carignan claimed that Sitting Bull had indeed received word from that "Pine Ridge outfit, asking him to come over there as God was to appear to them."[9]

For McLaughlin the tensions at Standing Rock created by the Ghost Dance represented the greatest challenge to his authority and leadership. Now widely regarded as the best Indian agent among the Lakotas, he felt confident that he could handle his Indian charges without taking drastic measures.[10] Earlier he had suggested to the Office of Indian Affairs that he could inform those followers of Sitting Bull who opposed the Ghost Dance that they could come to the reservation's headquarters and be counted; the chief's followers who declined this invitation would have their rations with-held.[11] Before the office could respond to McLaughlin's plan, conditions had reached a stage where more extreme measures were needed.

McLaughlin's Indian supporters were also feeling the mounting pres-sures. Since Gall had reversed his position on the 1889 Sioux Act, Sitting Bull's hostility toward him had increased. Gall, whose band only num-bered thirty-nine in 1885, allied with John Grass's nearby band, hoping there would be more safety in numbers.[12] Gall had worked assiduously to keep the church members of St. Elizabeth's Episcopal Mission from joining the Ghost Dancers. He also labored to keep the mission's teach-ers and students in school; this was the best place for them to stay out of trouble. His decisiveness showed that he was still an effective leader; his efforts even convinced another band, headed by Running Horse, to break with Sitting Bull.[13]

But Gall's people still felt intimidated. Although Sitting Bull's camp in the Grand River Valley was about eighteen miles southwest of Gall's home in the Oak Creek area, there was still a great deal of apprehension. Gall and Grass's fear that the Ghost Dance movement would spread as fast as it had on the Pine Ridge and Rosebud reservations during the months of October and November had produced strong feelings of un-ease among both men. In fact, on December 15, the day of Sitting Bull's bungled arrest, Gall and John Grass sent an urgent message to Major McLaughlin; they wanted ten guns so that they could defend themselves and their people. Claiming that their bands were camping together at Oak Creek, they wanted to know the whereabouts of the Ghost Dancers at Standing Rock. They also wanted instructions as to what they should do if Sitting Bull's more numerous followers were to intrude into their part of the reservation.[14]

McLaughlin felt the same sense of urgency that Gall and Grass did. He appreciated the support of both men during this crisis just as he did the sup-port of most of the Yanktonais and Blackfoot Lakotas on the reservation. But Sitting Bull's announced intention to go to Pine Ridge and consult with the most fanatical of the Ghost Dancers made prompt action essen-tial. Always sensitive about the scope of his authority, McLaughlin had al-ready headed off a friendly arrest of the Hunkpapa leader by Buffalo Bill Cody.

In late November, Cody had agreed, at the behest of General Miles, to take his old friend from their Wild West show days into custody.

McLaughlin, however, feeling that his jurisdiction was being violated, was able to plant false tracks on the road from Fort Yates to the Grand Valley so that Buffalo Bill could not find Sitting Bull. After a prolonged debate in Washington over Sitting Bull's arrest, General Miles, who had prevailed in this jurisdictional dispute with McLaughlin, ordered the apprehension of the old chief, but in as peaceable a manner as possible.

The weeks of debate over Sitting Bull's impending arrest finally resulted in the army's decision on December 20 to let Lieutenant Colonel William F. Drum perform this potentially dangerous duty. When McLaughlin received word from his Indian police on December 13 that Sitting Bull's followers were beginning to corral their horses for his controversial Pine Ridge visit, however, McLaughlin sent forty-two of his police officers to make the arrest on December 15.

Headed by First Lieutenant Bull Head, these Indian law enforcers, who enjoyed McLaughlin's trust, surrounded Sitting Bull's cabin before dawn.[15] They all wore white handkerchiefs around their necks so that they could distinguish themselves from Sitting Bull's people, many of whom had been awakened by the incessant barking of dogs that ultimately revealed the enforcers' presence.[16] Nevertheless, they entered Sitting Bull's silent cabin and ordered the surprised leader to get dressed and follow them out. As the old chief was being escorted from his home by Lieutenant Bull Head and sergeants Red Tomahawk and Shave Head, one of Sitting Bull's loyal followers, Catch-the-Bear, fired his Winchester at Bull Head, a man whom he had long despised. The wounded Bull Head shot Sitting Bull in the chest as he was falling, while Red Tomahawk shot the chief in the back of the head, killing him instantly.[17]

The result of Sitting Bull's shocking death was a furious exchange of gunfire. The outnumbered Indian police fired from Sitting Bull's cabin and from the sheds and corrals located behind it. Showing equal determination, the enraged Hunkpapa followers of the dead chief fired at the Indian police from the top of a knoll and from a nearby timbered area. Upon the army's arrival, Captain E. G. Fechet, who was in charge of Colonel Drum's cavalry unit, responded to the confusion by using his Hotchkiss gun to bombard Sitting Bull's angry partisans.

Fechet eventually forced some four hundred of Sitting Bull's followers to flee. When his troopers finally reached the dead chief's cabin, they discovered, "within a radius of 50 yards from the door," the bodies of eight Indians, including Sitting Bull's and Catch-the-Bear's. Inside the cabin, they found four dead Indian policemen and three injured ones, including the fatally wounded Bull Head and Shave Head. The tragic scene was made more bizarre by the wailing of Sitting Bull's crestfallen wives.[18]

Given Sitting Bull's great prominence since the Little Bighorn, his death became a major national news story. Most westerners were probably relieved, given the aging chief's intransigent resistance to reservation life. Easterners, however, were more divided. Many supporters of the Mohonk movement were chagrined and embarrassed, probably not recognizing their inadvertent role in the Ghost Dance crisis that resulted in his death. But Thomas A. Bland of NIDA, long critical of the deteriorating conditions at Standing Rock, denounced the entire affair. Some of his followers tied the aggressive activities of those land grabbers who helped bring about the Sioux Act of 1889 to Indian agents like McLaughlin, who had the power to incite Indian policemen anxious to exercise their authority.

These more damning allegations of Sitting Bull's demise were eventually picked up by the country's more sensational newspapers. Some of them even hinted that the old chief's death was the result of a conspiracy between Colonel Drum and Agent McLaughlin. Regardless of the true causes of this tragedy, the violent outcome of the botched arrest was certainly another example of how factionalism among reservation Indians can be manipulated by civil and military authorities with devastating results.[19]

McLaughlin's role in Sitting Bull's fatal arrest would remain controversial for some time. A December 1 telegram from Washington instructed him in the most forceful terms to "co-operate with and obey the orders of the Military Officers Commanding on the reservation." McLaughlin was also reminded that his basic responsibility was to "carry into effect the educational" purposes of the agency. Five days later, the acting commissioner of the Office of Indian Affairs, R. V. Belt, insisted that McLaughlin "make no arrests whatever except under orders of the Military or upon an order of the Secretary of the Interior." Yet McLaughlin would justify his actions in a December 16 letter to commissioner of Indian Affairs Thomas J. Morgan by claiming that an "immediate arrest" was necessary in order to prevent Sitting Bull and his followers from joining the most fanatical of the Ghost Dancers at Pine Ridge.[20]

Sitting Bull's death had an unsettling effect on all Lakotas, whether they identified themselves as supporters or critics of the chief in life. Gall was certainly in the critic category. Although his once close relationship with Sitting Bull had been marked by hostility since their sharp disagreement over the controversial Sioux Act of 1889, he could not entirely forget those early years when Sitting Bull was his mentor. Nor could he ignore altogether those years when he was Sitting Bull's chief lieutenant, but the decade following Gall's surrender had resulted in significant changes. Gall had decided to take a different road than Sitting Bull; he had vowed in the early 1880s to live as a white man because he saw no other feasible alternative. Yet the circumstances of Sitting Bull's death greatly disturbed him.

Nine months after Sitting Bull's controversial demise, Gall and one of his wives were visiting the once hostile Grand River valley where they were observed by Ethel C. Jacobson, niece of the famous Congregational missionary Mary C. Collins. Jacobson was surprised at how big Gall had become. "He is perfectly immense, I should think could weigh little less than 300 pounds."

Gall's unexpected appearance, so far from his home at Oak Creek, reminded her of a recent conversation she had had with Agent McLaughlin's wife. Marie Louise, a mixed-blood from Minnesota who could speak Dakota as well as English, had become "a real mother to the Indians" because of her warmth and personality. She described Gall, who probably felt more relaxed around her than with her supremely confident husband, as seeming greatly agitated. He had expressed his alarm to the agent's understanding wife over the tales of brutality surrounding the disastrous effort to arrest Sitting Bull.

The once formidable warrior's concern, however, was met with a verbal chastisement that only a person with Mrs. McLaughlin's unique qualities could administer. "Gall, I am fairly disgusted with you. You have known me for over ten years now, and did I ever tell you a lie? . . . And here you believe all the lies you hear about *Ateyapi* [Agent McLaughlin] and all the things these runaway Indians tell, and you feel half inclined to join them yourself."[21] She concluded her scolding by telling Gall that he should have learned some lessons from the serious difficulties that had plagued his people during the past year, admonishing him in the process not to fall in with those who would make more trouble. Gall was apparently impressed with her stinging remarks because he stayed loyal to McLaughlin.

Marie Louise McLaughlin's reference to "runaway Indians" in her lecture to Gall included those four hundred Hunkpapas who had fled the

carnage of Sitting Bull's death after Captain Fechet arrived with his reinforcements. The great fear of Standing Rock's authorities was that these
runaways would join the most dedicated Ghost Dancers at the Stronghold. To prevent this from happening, McLaughlin sent emissaries southward to persuade the frightened fugitives to return to Standing Rock.
The agent's promise of fair treatment convinced 160 of them to return,
but another 89 elected to remain a little longer at their Cheyenne River
Reservation encampment along the Moreau River.

The rest of them, however, sought asylum with Big Foot's Miniconjou
band on the Cheyenne River. Their decision was especially alarming to
federal authorities because Big Foot (or Spotted Elk) had embraced many
of the promises of the Ghost Dance religion to restore the old way of life.
Although not a great warrior, Big Foot had earned the respect of many
Lakota leaders because of his ability to reconcile the differences among
Lakota tribes that emerged from time to time.[22]

Because of Big Foot's reputation as a diplomat, a number of Oglala
leaders had asked him to come to Pine Ridge and help them reconcile
those disagreements among Indians and federal authorities caused by the
Ghost Dance. These peacemakers included Red Cloud, Big Road, Young-
Man-Afraid-of-His-Horse, Calico, and No Water. They were willing to
offer Big Foot and his band one hundred horses if they would come to
Pine Ridge for such peace discussions. Having his own misgivings about
the divisiveness caused by the Ghost Dance, Big Foot decided to go to
Pine Ridge with his band, which had now swelled to 350. Its members
included some of Sitting Bull's disgruntled followers, along with those
most ardent Miniconjou converts to Wovoka's new faith.

When Big Foot headed south with his frenzied followers on December
23, the army units brought into the Dakotas because of the Ghost Dance
began an intense search for them. For five days soldiers patrolled the frozen
Dakota plains to find the elusive Big Foot. But their search was too far to
the west. They had believed all along that this fugitive band was moving toward the Stronghold to join the most zealous adherents of the Ghost Dance.
Instead Big Foot was heading for a rendezvous with Red Cloud and the
other peacemakers, who were located at the Pine Ridge Agency south and
east of the Stronghold.

On December 28, a squadron of the Seventh Cavalry finally located
Big Foot's bedraggled band near Porcupine Butte, north of the agency.
Big Foot and his people were promptly ordered to encamp along nearby

Wounded Knee Creek. At this wintry site they remained overnight, peacefully huddled in their well-worn tipis.[23]

On December 29, the following morning, Big Foot, tired and suffering from pneumonia, appeared ready to surrender. His people, surrounded by five hundred soldiers under the command of Colonel James W. Forsyth of the Seventh Cavalry, were tired and hungry. But before Forsyth could accept their surrender, he was under orders to search the members of Big Foot's band for weapons. During this tense inspection, a rifle accidentally went off while two soldiers were trying to take it from a deaf and unbalanced young man named Black Coyote. Almost instantaneously, a half-dozen young Lakotas dropped their blankets, revealing Winchesters ready to fire. The ensuing exchange of gunfire was murderous, as both sides fired point blank at one another. Moreover, on a nearby hilltop, four small Hotchkiss cannons spewed destruction, flattening Miniconjou and Hunkpapa tipis and killing women and children as well as warriors.[24]

When the unexpected battle was over, 150 of Big Foot's followers were dead, including the ailing chief himself, and 50 were wounded. Of the soldiers, 25 were killed, while 39 were wounded.[25] Many of these desperate Miniconjous and Hunkpapas attempted to flee this bloody scene; some of their bodies were later found as far away as three miles from Big Foot's hastily assembled encampment. General Miles insisted on a court of inquiry for Colonel Forsyth on the basis of his misconduct at Wounded Knee. Ironically, twenty-three of Forsyth's men would eventually be awarded the Medal of Honor for their "heroic" conduct during this encounter.[26] That night, following the battle, a cold snow fell, revealing a grotesque sight the morning after of frozen bodies scattered along a creek where the last major battle of the Indian wars had been fought.

Unquestionably the Battle of Wounded Knee Creek was part of Gall's discussion with McLaughlin's wife in September 1891. This bloody clash, which further humbled Gall's people at a time when everything seemed to be going wrong, was an event that no proud Lakota could easily forget. Although Gall would continue to walk the white man's road, his misgivings regarding the violent results of federal policy pertaining to the Sioux must have troubled him.

The death of Sitting Bull and the Battle of Wounded Knee Creek, occurring as they did within a two-week period, probably did have some effect on Gall's close link with McLaughlin. Two of Gall's descendants recall stories of a gradual cooling off of Gall's once close and interdependent relationship with Standing Rock's willful agent. Gall became more reluctant to respond to McLaughlin's frequent calls upon him to discharge certain duties for the good of the reservation. As he got older, he preferred to stay home and work on his farm during the day and peacefully smoke his pipe at night.[27] His voluntary trips to the agency headquarters at Fort Yates also became less frequent.

In fact, McLaughlin's "favorite chief" openly revealed a deep resentment when McLaughlin built a fine frame house for John Grass but not one for Gall. Grass had been more effective than Gall in fulfilling McLaughlin's purposes during the bitter debate over the Sioux Act of 1889, yet McLaughlin usually extolled the virtues of Gall; he was the hero at the Little Bighorn who could best appeal to most of Standing Rock's Indians. But Gall, famous for his quick temper, was so angry with Grass over this incident that he swore he would kill him; Grass was wise enough to become too ill to leave his new home for weeks.[28] Whether Gall ever approached McLaughlin on this contentious matter is uncertain. It must have put yet another strain on their relationship, but there is no evidence of any serious or permanent rift between the two as a result of it.

These photographs show some of the personalities and an environment that were part of Gall's historical legacy. Starting with Rain-in-the-Face in the lower left corner and moving clockwise are Gall, Sitting Bull's camp, Sitting Bull, and Crow scout Curly, who was with Custer at the Little Bighorn. In the center is John Grass, a major Lakota leader and Gall ally at the Standing Rock Reservation. Courtesy of the Denver Public Library, Nate Salsbury Collection, N5-71.

Colonel Nelson A. Miles neutralized Crazy Horse's followers at Wolf Mountain and pursued the Lakotas under Sitting Bull and Gall across the Canadian border in 1877, all but ending the Great Sioux War. As a result of Miles's tenacity following the army's defeat at the Little Bighorn, the Lakotas remained in exile in Saskatchewan, Canada, for four years. Courtesy of the Little Bighorn Battlefield National Monument.

Northwest Mounted Police inspector Major James Walsh exercised effective control over the defeated Lakotas during much of their Canadian exile. He was one of the few white men Sitting Bull trusted because of his fairness toward the Lakota chief's people. Courtesy of Glenbow Archives, NA-1234-5, Calgary, Alberta, Canada.

One Bull became the closest confidant and chief lieutenant of his uncle Sitting Bull during the Lakotas' Canadian exile. Gall assumed a rather low profile until his band, along with other Lakota bands, began to face starvation because of the diminishing numbers of buffalo in Canada. Courtesy of the W. H. Over Museum, Vermillion, South Dakota.

This rather forlorn encampment of twenty tipis was the temporary home of Chief Gall's band at Fort Buford after Gall's surrender at the Battle of Poplar River in 1881. Gall's tipi is in the foreground on the left. Courtesy of State Historical Society of North Dakota, B0179.

This photograph by F. Jay Haynes of five Lakota Sioux leaders was taken at the Standing Rock Agency in 1881. From left to right: Gall, Sitting Bull's old friend Crawler, Oglala chief Low Dog, aging Hunkpapa shirt wearer Running Antelope, and Rain-in-the-Face, who was made famous by one of Henry Wadsworth Longfellow's best-known poems. Courtesy of Haynes Foundation Collection, Montana Historical Society, Helena.

Gall, clad in a business suit in this 1888 photo, became agent James McLaughlin's favorite Indian leader at Standing Rock. He adopted many of the white man's ways, serving as a district farmer and a judge on the Court of Indian Offenses. Courtesy of the State Historical Society of North Dakota, 1017-04.

Gall's appearance in this photograph was probably more typical of how he dressed and looked during his reservation years. Wearing his hair loose without the customary feather to represent his once proud status as a warrior, he looks like the successfully assimilated Indian farmer that the federal government worked so hard to make of him. Courtesy of the State Historical Society of North Dakota, 0022-H-126.

Longtime Indian agent James McLaughlin, called White Hair during his later years, was effective because of his strong will and the support of his Sioux wife and the Roman Catholic Church. Courtesy of the State Historical Society of North Dakota, 0036-134.

Posing in this photograph is Gall's fourth wife, Martina Blue Earth. Already married, Gall made an unsuccessful effort to gain Indian agent James McLaughlin's approval to take another wife, possibly Martina, whom he wed shortly before his death. Courtesy of the State Historical Society of North Dakota, B0175.

Gall poses with a nephew, William Hawk, during his reservation years. There is some controversy over the gigantic cross around his neck. Many assume that it represents Christ's crucifixion, Gall having become an Episcopal convert before his death in 1894. Others assume that the cross represents the sacred four directions, or winds, of the Lakota world. Courtesy of the State Historical Society of North Dakota, A1624.

David F. Barry took this photograph of reservation Indians gathered at Standing Rock for a federal census in the 1880s. Gall is standing in the middle, holding a cane, while Agent McLaughlin is seated at the table to Gall's right. Courtesy of the State Historical Society of North Dakota, A4392.

CHAPTER FOURTEEN

His Final Years

During the early 1890s, Gall's flagging energies and his strong preference to stay home and plow his fields became more noticeable. This slowdown was probably due more to his deteriorating health than any disagreement he might have had with McLaughlin. His descendants insist that his old war wounds slowed him down and ultimately shortened his life.[1] High blood pressure and heart trouble, compounded by a weight problem, were other reasons; during the last five years of his life, his weight ranged from 250 to perhaps as high as 300 pounds.[2] Poor health probably hampered his efforts to wage such all-consuming fights as the ones he had over the controversial Sioux bills of 1888 and 1889. These infirmities made Gall's efforts to discourage his people from embracing the Ghost Dance more arduous. They may have accounted for the stress he felt trying to limit Sitting Bull's influence during the Ghost Dance movement. Indeed by 1892, it was becoming increasingly obvious that Gall's struggle against poor health would become his final battle in a life crowded with life-threatening challenges.

The first significant signs of Gall's ill health surfaced after the age of fifty. Prior to 1892, starting during his early years at Standing Rock, he had been an active culture broker. His service as a district farmer from 1883 to 1892 had provided a convincing example that a nomadic Lakota warrior could become a successful farmer. Although he served only one term as a judge on the court of Indian offenses, he rendered verdicts that most of his people could understand and appreciate. He also helped to establish and support St. Elizabeth's Episcopal Mission, sending his children to the mission's school and attending mass at the mission with some regularity.[3]

Throughout his reservation years, Gall had used his influence as a culture broker, honestly attempting to bring the races together. But he was limited by the aggressive opposition of his old mentor, Sitting Bull. There was an ongoing and bitter factionalism at Standing Rock that prevented Gall from achieving the successes of such Indian leaders as the Comanche Quanah Parker in promoting the culture of assimilation that had been so energetically advanced by the Mohonk movement. Spotted Tail was another chief who tried to bridge the cultural divide. What successes he enjoyed, however, were partially negated upon his death in 1883; the legacy of his often inflexible leadership resulted in a factionalism that deeply divided his Brulés at the Rosebud Agency. At Pine Ridge, Young-Man-Afraid-of-His-Horse and George Sword worked to bring about cooperation among the Oglalas and the reservation staff, but their efforts toward acculturation were sometimes blunted by the more ambivalent Red Cloud.[4]

Gall's deteriorating health, however, did not prevent him from traveling around the reservation during his final years. He, along with the members of his band, could still attend the biweekly gatherings of the Sioux at Fort Yates, where Standing Rock's Indian residents would collect their government beef rations. He continued farming his own plot of land. An indication that Gall's intense efforts to be a good farmer had been vital to the welfare of his family became evident after his death; his family had to sell Gall's land allotment to a presumably white farmer named Jackson.[5] Gall also enjoyed getting around the reservation whenever he could. For instance, in fall 1891, Gall went as far south as the Moreau River on the Cheyenne River Reservation to monitor one of those fearful prairie fires that periodically swept the Standing Rock and Cheyenne River reservations.[6]

As Gall's health problems mounted, he grew closer to the Episcopal Church, thus assimilating even more of the white culture that McLaughlin and his colleagues had persistently promoted. His association with St. Elizabeth's mission had been a halfway one for many years, as evident in his sitting in the back of the church, acting more as an observer than a participant, during attendance at Sunday masses. He enjoyed discussing the Bible with St. Elizabeth's priests, deacons, and catechists, even becoming a good friend of Bishop Hare's first appointee as the mission's rector.[7] His attitude toward the conversion efforts of St. Elizabeth's clergy was one of approval and understanding mixed with confusion over why they were telling him who the Great Creator was when he already knew. Like so many Lakotas, he retained some of his old religious beliefs and values and synchronized some of them with his new Christian ones.[8]

As his once legendary vigor began to wane, however, he grew much closer to the Christian faith. On July 4, 1892, he was baptized as an Episcopalian under the name of Abraham Gall. (He also went by the Christian name John during his reservation years.) On November 12, 1894, three weeks before his death, he sanctified his marriage to Martina Blue Earth in an Episcopal Church ceremony.[9]

When it became evident that he was terminally ill, Gall surrounded himself with those band members and friends who also had made their full conversion to Christianity. According to Josephine Waggoner, who served as an interpreter at St. Elizabeth's from 1888 to 1889, "The bible was read to him each day, as he never tired of hearing the word of God."[10] As he lay dying in his log cabin at Wakapala in the Oak Creek valley, only a third of a mile from St. Elizabeth's, his favorite daughter, Nancy, was there. As he neared the end, she desperately tried to revive him by "filling her mouth with water and squirting it over him as a Chinaman does when ironing a shirt."[11]

The decline in Gall's health became irreversible during the final months of 1894. In December of that year he died. The exact date is in dispute. According to the Episcopal Church records, he died on December 5 of heart disease, but according to the Friday, December 14, edition of the *Bismarck Weekly Tribune*, he had died the previous Saturday, which would have placed his death on December 8. Although the *Tribune's* obituary did not give a cause for his death, it did hint that this once powerful warrior, whom Libbie Custer had described as the "finest specimen of a warrior" she had ever seen, had a weight problem. It characterized Gall as being "quite short and stout" at the time of his death.

In fact, the catalyst for Gall's demise, according to his friend and admirer David F. Barry, was a fat-reducing medicine some of his friends had recommended. After methodically taking this antifat remedy for a week, with few promising results, the ailing Gall, demonstrating his growing faith in white medicine as well as white technology, took the full bottle. The results were fatal. The once formidable chief died at the age of fifty-four and was buried in nearby St. Elizabeth's cemetery.[12]

Gall's career had been dogged by controversy during much of his life. His enemies, and even some of his friends, dismissed him as an opportunist. The muscular Hunkpapa war chief was indeed a singularly independent person. He would lead his band in raids on enemy villages in times of war and visit them on trading expeditions in times of peace. He had survived the vicious bayonet attack instigated by Bloody Knife and a detachment of soldiers during one of these visits to a village of presumably friendly Arikaras, Hidatsas, and Mandans.[13]

In another act of independence, Gall, serving as Sitting Bull's emissary, put his mark of approval on the Treaty of Fort Laramie during an 1868 conference with federal authorities at Fort Rice. Curiously, prior to this approval, Gall had thoroughly denounced the treaty in one of his most famous orations. Yet Sitting Bull, who was also opposed, was not upset when Gall brought back presents for his people as a reward for endorsing this treaty. As Sitting Bull, who was about to become chief of all the nontreaty Indians, put it: "You must not blame Gall. Everyone knows that he will do anything for a square meal."[14]

Despite Gall's sometimes frivolous nature, it would be most unfair to characterize him as a shallow opportunist. This pragmatic war chief was very loyal to Sitting Bull and his people on the issues that really counted. In the numerous battles and skirmishes the Hunkpapas fought with the army, he gave Sitting Bull his unwavering support for almost a quarter of a century. At Killdeer Mountain, at sites along the Yellowstone, and at the Little Bighorn, just to provide a few examples, the Fighting Cock of the Sioux played a prominent role. He only broke with Sitting Bull after a sharp disagreement in Canada over his mentor's unwillingness to surrender to the federal government, even though most of the Lakota exiles were near starvation.

After choosing to walk the white man's road at Standing Rock, Gall found in Agent James McLaughlin a new mentor. The cooperative Gall served this paternalistic symbol of authority as loyally as he had Sitting Bull. His unusually strong commitment to assimilation seemed sincere as witnessed by his tireless role as a district farmer and his one term as a judge on the court of Indian offenses. Gall appeared to thrive as McLaughlin's major Indian supporter at Standing Rock. He was apparently satisfied to assume once again the role of chief lieutenant for yet another powerful mentor.

But Gall apparently did believe that cooperation with the authorities at Standing Rock was the best way to advance the welfare of his people.

Given the power and strength of the United States government and its large military presence, he felt that cooperation was the only viable option open to the Lakotas. In essence, he was a realist, a pragmatic realist. In his view, it was necessary for the Hunkpapas, Blackfoot Lakotas, and other heretofore defiant Lakotas to learn to farm, a controversial position because it meant giving up a traditional way of life based on hunting the now-vanishing buffalo.

Gall also felt that his Hunkpapa kin needed to be educated so that their children could compete with subsequent generations of the dominant white culture. The once intransigent warrior had even convinced himself that he could live in harmony with the Anglo-American governmental structure that had been foisted on the Hunkpapas. Indeed, he, along with John Grass and other like-minded Indians, exercised his recently granted political rights by resisting those efforts to reduce the size of the Great Sioux Reservation, even though federal negotiators outmaneuvered them in the end. He clearly showed a willingness to live with the new legal system being imposed on the Indians at Standing Rock. As a judge, he tried to temper the more stringent legal measures affecting his people.

Gall's conversion to Christianity, gradual but eventually complete enough for him to be baptized, married, and buried by the Episcopal Church, was not that unusual. In fact, leaders like Red Cloud, Crow King, and John Grass became Roman Catholics, yet, like Gall, they kept many of their old Indian beliefs. Black Elk, one of the inspiring voices of the Lakota people, went even further; in 1904 he became a catechist for the Catholic Church.[15]

Yet Gall would later be criticized for being too extreme in embracing the values of acculturation. One prominent scholar of the American Indian, Duane Champagne, claimed that Gall had "adopted a way of life more European than Indian.[16] This patriot chief, who was one of the most important Indian leaders in resisting the tide of white encroachment prior to the 1880s, was indeed a complex man. He refused to join Buffalo Bill's Wild West Show as Sitting Bull had, because he thought it would be demeaning to him as a Hunkpapa warrior, yet he became actively involved after his surrender with most facets of white assimilation. Perhaps his break with Sitting Bull, who for many years symbolized Indian resistance among the Lakotas, made Gall's opposition to the policies of his old mentor look like a betrayal of the Lakota cause.

One aspect of Gall's life often overlooked was the amount of attention he paid to the members of his band, or tiospaye. He seemed determined to help them fulfill their needs, whether they be economic or social; this obligation was regarded as the major duty of a headman, according to Lakota tradition. The Hunkpapa leader tended to exercise his leadership through persuasion and reason. He could also be democratic, a necessary virtue given the independent nature of most Lakota warriors. For instance, when he left the Standing Rock Agency in late 1875 to join Sitting Bull and his defiant nontreaty bands, he gave his own band members the right to decide whether they would accompany him. When he surrendered at the Poplar River Agency in 1881, he refused to agree to any peace terms until he had discussed them with his people. During the Ghost Dance crisis, he, along with John Grass, pleaded for guns to protect both their bands against the more zealous Ghost Dancers.

Gall's prominence in Standing Rock's more responsive Indian faction did, however, bring him great rewards. McLaughlin and his like-minded associates praised him as a great hero, the bellwether at the Little Bighorn. At the same time, they worked diligently to denigrate Sitting Bull in every possible way because of his opposition to McLaughlin's policies. The editors of the *Bismarck Daily Tribune*, representing the views of many of the white settlers in the Standing Rock area, added to the criticism of Sitting Bull, whom they once called that "sly old trickster." The Standing Rock agent's version of Gall's exploits would in the long run alienate Gall from many of his old war comrades. Because the relentless war chief was the first major Lakota warrior to give the Indian side of the Battle of the Little Bighorn, Gall's more modest version of his role was confused with the exaggerated versions of such Gall partisans as McLaughlin, Burdick, and Barry. Admittedly, Gall did focus on his own role, but such an approach was typical of most warriors when describing their participation in a battle.[17]

Gall's descendants feel that his historical legacy should be based primarily on his record as a warrior. Whether fighting under Sitting Bull or acting with him to coordinate their battle movements, this war chief, usually clad in red, would often terrify his opponents. On September 3, 1864, seven weeks after his participation at the Battle of Killdeer Mountain, the twenty-four-year-old Gall was one of the war chiefs who led an attack on Captain James L. Fisk's wagon train after Sitting Bull was wounded and taken out of action. Demonstrating his skills as both a tactician and strategist, he led a separate band against the army during the Yellowstone Campaign of 1872. Army units were needed to protect Northern Pacific Railroad surveyors, who were anxious to locate a transcontinental rail route through the Yellowstone country. Gall was the first of Sitting Bull's warriors to warn him of the arrival of one of these army units, Colonel David S. Stanley's imposing infantry force. Near the end of that campaign, Gall left a lasting impression on Stanley's men as well as much of the nation when he defiantly dangled the scalps of at least two of his band's victims from a hillock near Fort Rice. One of those slain by Gall's men was Second Lieutenant Louis Dent Adair, a cousin of President Grant's wife, Julia Dent. This death not only elevated Gall to a new prominence but also helped influence General Sheridan to increase the size of the army for the 1873 Yellowstone Campaign, which pitted Sitting Bull and Gall against Custer for the first time.

Although Gall's participation at the Little Bighorn was a tardy one, this conflict cost him two of his wives and three of his children. Notwithstanding his grief, he became an active participant at Custer's legendary Last Stand and led a significant attack against Captain Myles W. Keogh. In this latter action, he and his men scattered Keogh's horses and deprived the captain's dismounted troopers of their mobility.

Indeed, the omnipresent war chief was credited by one Lakota war comrade as earning twenty coups during his years as a warrior. It is most doubtful, however, that this number included all the soldiers he fought and vanquished. The U.S. Army's fighting style simply did not emphasize the required personal valor stressed by Lakota warriors to qualify for these coveted coups.[18] Nevertheless, Gall was a familiar figure to many blue-coated soldiers because his powerful frame clad in red would be conspicuous in many of the mounted Lakota war parties they encountered.

Perhaps the most vivid glimpse of Gall as a warrior was provided by Samuel J. Barrows, a correspondent for the New York *Tribune*. He observed Gall up close during the 1873 Yellowstone campaign, when an unsuccessful Hunkpapa cavalry charge was waged against Custer's troopers. Barrows was particularly awed by one fearless warrior wearing a conspicuous red blanket, undoubtedly Gall. The war chief jumped from his horse, which had been shot dead, and leaped on a fresh one so he could continue the fight and later make his escape. Like Custer, Gall knew no fear, and like Custer, he could be flamboyant.

Gall would mellow during his last years, showing gentleness and warmth, particularly toward the members of his family and his band. Characteristic of his Lakota heritage, kinship continued to be important to him. Moreover, the rage and vengeance he showed against enemies like Bloody Knife understandably became less evident during his reservation years. His once volatile temper was largely replaced by a quiet stoicism; yet his passive approach could be very intimidating because of the respect he enjoyed. His old reputation for ferocity remained; however, this was not an unusual criticism for a warrior as formidable as Gall.

The survival culture that marked the Great Plains during much of the nineteenth century often depended on a fighting style among warriors in which no quarter was given. Red Cloud, like Gall, was also reprehended for his cruelty in some of the skirmishes and battles in which he participated.[19] One conclusion about this Hunkpapa war chief does seem indisputable. His life was a difficult and challenging one that required unquestionable courage and great savvy in warfare. Gall's outstanding implementation of these traits made him one of the best-known Lakota warriors of his day.

There was a certain charisma about Gall that drew to him not only white friends like Burdick and Barry but many Indians as well. Even some of the more traditional Lakotas who disagreed with him liked him; indeed, many were in awe of him. His role as a culture broker actively taking on the new challenges he faced at Standing Rock brought him praise from many of those living outside the reservation too. The publishers of the *Bismarck Daily Tribune* recognized his significant role in history when they published his obituary on December 14, 1894. They acknowledged Gall's opposition to the encroachment of settlers in the 1860s and 1870s; indeed, this "implacable foe of the whites" fought the U.S. Army at such historic places as the Little Bighorn before becoming one of the last of his people to make peace. "His stoicism, courage and ability rendered him a conspicuous character in his tribe and an object of interest to all who knew of his history."

A willingness to assimilate into the white culture at Standing Rock and urge the Indians there to do likewise also won Gall favorable recognition in the *Tribune*. Even though he cooperated with reservation authorities, the veteran Hunkpapa leader was not easily manipulated. "He differed from many of his tribesmen in that he was impervious to flattery or cajoling, and his reserve and silence resembled the ideal Indian as pictured in fiction."[20] Although Major McLaughlin did succeed in influencing Gall at crucial times, the respected Hunkpapa headman appeared to believe in his agent's perception of what the future held for his people. Of course, their close relationship did prove to be beneficial for both of them.

By 1890 Gall's fame came close to matching Sitting Bull's.[21] He enjoyed the respect of many Lakotas from the Sioux reservations that had been created by the Sioux Act of 1889 as well as the respect of many white inhabitants from the Dakotas. Sixteen years after his death in 1894, for instance, a town was named after him; ironically, it was built on a branch of the Northern Pacific, a railroad Gall had bitterly opposed during the Yellowstone campaigns of 1872–1873. Its tracks extended from Mandan, North Dakota, southward, straddling the Cannonball River along the northern boundary of the Standing Rock Reservation and terminating at the town of Flasher, some forty miles southeast of Bismarck. Although the town, which had a post office, lasted only three years, giving it Gall's name was a singular honor. The Northern Pacific Railroad tended to name its towns after company personnel; for example, the railhead at Bismarck was originally designated Edwinton to honor the Northern Pacific's chief engineer, Edwin F. Johnson, but was later renamed after the famous Prussian leader Otto von Bismarck to attract needed capital from the German empire.[22] During subsequent years, however, Gall's fame was significantly eclipsed by Sitting Bull's as the dominant Indian leader among the Hunkpapas during the Sioux wars of the late nineteenth century. Today Sitting Bull's name is as well known in the country's popular culture as Crazy Horse's and Geronimo's. Gall's role has not been forgotten, but it has been largely undervalued in recent years.

It does seem just as unfair to underestimate Gall's importance as it is to overstate it. Whether Gall was the bellwether at the Little Bighorn or not, his conception of what happened to the luckless Custer and his men became one of the dominant interpretations of this battle, which has only been rivaled in western history by the legendary defense of the Alamo. Gall was also the key leader in ending the Canadian exile, which had become by 1880 a starving time for most of the Lakotas and their allies; his resolve was an act of strong conviction because he had to defy his old ally in war, Sitting Bull.

Gall deserves a second look. He was both a formidable warrior and a reservation leader prominent for his favorable views on assimilation. In his former role, he often terrified the officers and men of the U.S. Army. In his latter role, he proudly bowed to the inevitable fate of his people by adjusting to reservation life and attempting to be a conscientious culture broker in a time of great stress and discouragement.

Notes

CHAPTER 1. LIKE A ROMAN WARRIOR

1. Dispatch from Major Ilges to Brigadier General Alfred H. Terry as quoted in a telegram from Terry to the Adjutant General, Division of the Missouri in Chicago, January 8, 1881, roll 32, McLaughlin Papers. For many of the military sources cited in the McLaughlin Papers, see U.S. Army, "Sioux Campaign."

2. Telegram from Sherman to Terry, February 3, 1881, McLaughlin Papers.

3. Utley, *The Lance and the Shield*, 217, 218. Gall acquired the nickname "Fighting Cock of the Sioux" because he was probably involved in as many major battles against the army as any other warrior on the northern plains, according to Winsell, "Gall," 155.

4. Utley, *The Lance and the Shield*, 182.

5. The famous visionary and one of the oft-quoted voices of the Lakotas, Black Elk, who spent at least a couple of seasons with the exiled Sitting Bull and Gall, called Canada Grandmother's Land, as did many of the Lakotas at this time. The term was a tribute to the durable English monarch Queen Victoria. See Black Elk, *Black Elk Speaks*, 101, 112, 115, 136.

6. Mangum, "Gall," 33–34; Manzione, *"I Am Looking to the North,"* 144. There is conflicting documentation regarding the number of lodges Gall allowed to return to the United States (see chap. 10, n. 33).

7. Hedren, *Traveler's Guide*, 103.

8. Ilges to Assistant Adjutant General, January 31, 1881, McLaughlin Papers.

9. Ibid.

10. Allison, *The Surrender of Sitting Bull*, 36, 53–55; Mangum, "Gall," 34. The numbers of those who stayed with Sitting Bull and those who left with Gall remain in dispute. The two-thirds majority Allison claimed for Gall has been challenged by Utley. See *The Lance and the Shield*, n. 379.

11. As quoted in Ilges to Assistant Adjutant General, January 31, 1881, McLaughlin Papers.

12. Ibid. Utley, *The Lance and the Shield*, 219–20. Crow King did not entirely satisfy Major Ilges when he suggested at the conference that the trip to Fort Buford should be slowed. The delay would allow the warrior and his people to hunt along the way for skins to clothe their women and children. Crow King later broke with Sitting Bull on January 11, 1881, in a heated quarrel over when the Lakotas in Canada should surrender.

13. As quoted in Ilges to Assistant Adjutant General, January 31, 1881, McLaughlin Papers.

14. Ibid. Utley, *The Lance and the Shield*, 220–21.

15. Ilges to Assistant Adjutant General, January 31, 1881, McLaughlin Papers.

16. Shumate, *Chief Gall*, 93; Utley, *The Lance and the Shield*, 220. According to a presumably erroneous account by photographer David F. Barry, an old friend of Gall, the use of Gatling guns, not the Howitzer and the Rodman, compelled the surrender. See Burdick, *David F. Barry's Indian Notes* (1937), 19.

17. Utley, *The Lance and the Shield*, 221.

18. Dispatch from Ilges to Terry, as quoted in a telegram from Terry to the Adjutant General, Division of Missouri, January 8, 1881, McLaughlin Papers.

19. By command of Terry to Ilges, January 10, 1881, McLaughlin Papers.

20. Dispatch from Ilges to Terry, as quoted in a telegram from Terry to the Adjutant General, Division of the Missouri, January 8, 1881, McLaughlin Papers; Utley, *The Lance and the Shield*, 221.

21. Terry to Brotherton, January 10, 1881, McLaughlin Papers.

22. Hedren, "Sitting Bull's Surrender," 3; Diana Avans interview, May 19, 2001, at Fort Buford. Unless otherwise stated, all interviews were conducted by the author.

23. Charles M. Stalnaker, site supervisor at Fort Buford for the State Historical Society of North Dakota, emphasized the term "detained" in characterizing the nature of Gall's stay at Fort Buford. Telephone interview, May 31, 2001. Carole Barrett, associate professor of American Indian Studies at the University of Mary, Bismarck, believes, on the basis of her research, that conditions were much harsher. Barrett interview, May 16, 2001, at the State Historical Society of North Dakota.

24. Hedren, "Sitting Bull's Surrender," 3.

25. Undated (1931) news clipping from the *Fargo Forum*, by Usher L. Burdick, Fiske Papers.

26. Neil Mangum referred to the relatively short stature of Gall in his June 21, 1991, Custer Symposium article, but he claimed that this fact was belied by the Hunkpapa warrior's fearsome "grizzly bear countenance." See Mangum, "Gall," 30.

27. Taylor, "Bloody Knife and Gall," 165.

28. The description of this potentially dangerous incident was found in one of Barry's advertisements, titled "Chief Gall, Photo from Life, by D. F. Barry, Photographer of Noted Indians." The advertisement, donated to the state of North Dakota by Usher L. Burdick in March 21, 1934, is found in the D. F. Barry Papers. A hand-tinted copy of this first photo of Gall is stored with other historical treasures in a locked room at the State Historical Society of North Dakota, Bismarck. For a longer account of Barry's dispute with Gall over this first photograph, see Heski, *The Little Shadow Catcher*, 44–45.

29. A photo of Gall's head was usually located on the top left side of the advertisement, while another prominent Lakota leader would be located on the top right side. In Barry's favorite pose of Gall, the warrior usually wore no feather but allowed his thick black hair to hang loosely about his neck. See D. F. Barry Papers.

30. Barry was convinced that Fiske was violating the copyrights of his photos of such Lakota leaders as Gall and Sitting Bull. See Barry to M. Stephen, July 8, 1921, D. F. Barry Papers.

31. See Burdick, *David F. Barry's Indian Notes* (1937), 7–16.

32. As quoted in Mangum, "Gall," 34. See also Heski, *The Little Shadow Catcher*, 44–45.

CHAPTER 2. LITTLE CUB BEAR

1. See Standing Rock Mission Records, vol. A-1. DeLorme W. Robinson, in his article "Pi-zi," gives the year 1838 for Gall's birth, while Marquis, in his *Sitting Bull and Gall, the Warrior*, gives the year 1846. See Mangum, "Gall," 39.

2. Standing Rock Reservation was created by the Sioux Act of 1889 from what had been the Standing Rock Agency. It was originally called the Grand River Agency before it was renamed in 1873 and moved north to its new site on the Missouri River. The reservation was one of six partitioned from the Great Sioux Reservation. It ministered to the needs of the Hunkpapas, Blackfoot Lakotas, and the Yanktonais, while the Cheyenne River Reservation, created by the same law, ministered to the needs of the Miniconjous and the Sans Arcs. Utley, *The Lance and the Shield*, 88, 268–69. For a description of the boundaries of the Great Sioux Reservation, which incorporated both the Standing Rock and Cheyenne River agencies, see Kappler, *Indian Affairs*, 998.

3. On the early life of a Lakota boy, see Doane Robinson, "The Education of an Indian Boy," Robinson Papers. Robinson expanded chronologically on this theme of an Indian boy's education by focusing on Red Cloud in "The Education of Redcloud," 156–78.

4. Red Cloud, "Red Cloud, Chief of the Sioux," 4, Nebraska State Historical Society. This invaluable manuscript was authenticated and edited by R. Eli Paul. See Paul's *Autobiography of Red Cloud*, 34.

5. The names of Gall's parents were found in his baptism and marriage records, Standing Rock Mission, vol. A-1, 210–11, 408–409. Their translation into English was provided by Ambrose Little Ghost, in a telephone interview with LaDonna Brave Bull Allard by the author, arranged by Richard E. Collin, State Historical Society of North Dakota, October 28, 2002. The interpretation of these names was provided over the telephone by LaDonna Brave Bull Allard, October 29, 2002. Walks-with-Many-Names could also be translated as Many Names, according to Standing Rock Lakotas interviewed by Carole Barrett, Barrett to Larson, September 21, 2002. See also Vestal, *New Sources of Indian History*, 71–72.

6. Letter on Internet from Jeanine Standing Bear to Mark E. Gray, October 10, 2001, in Gray's possession.

7. One early twentieth-century historian of the Hunkpapas, Usher L. Burdick, insists that Gall was raised by his widowed mother; such scholars as Neil Mangum, Herbert T. Hoover, and Frederick Webb Hodge, editor of the *Handbook of American Indians North of Mexico*, have pretty much accepted this assertion. Other evidence regarding the presence of Gall's mother in his life is a purported photograph of her in the extensive photo collection at State Historical Society of North Dakota. Burdick, *The Last Battle of the Sioux Nation*, 69; Mangum, "Gall," 28; Hoover, "Gall (Sioux)," 590–91; Hodge, *Handbook of American Indians North of Mexico*, 482.

8. Vernon Iron Cloud and his wife, Theo, interview, May 21, 2001, Standing Rock Reservation. The late Lavora Jones, Gall's great-granddaughter, expressed surprise that Gall's widowed mother, along with his maternal uncles, allegedly raised him. "That's new to me." Telephone interview, February 26, 2001. Upon his death, Gall had at least three daughters, Nancy Shave Elk, his eldest, Sarah Shoots, and Jenny Gall. Chapman, *Remember the Wind*, 210–11; Linda Jones, telephone interviews, April 26 and May 5, 2005.

9. Eastman, *Indian Heroes and Great Chieftains*, 70. Although Charles A. Eastman, a Dakota of mixed blood who became a medical doctor, utilized Indian sources for his accounts of Indian leaders, his accuracy has been questioned. James C. Olson believes his work has been "generally discredited." See Olson, *Red Cloud and the Sioux Problem*, 18–19. George E. Hyde, an earlier historian writing in 1937, used the term "appalling" to describe the validity of much of Eastman's writings. See Hyde, *Red Cloud's Folk*, 54. Carole Barrett, whose ties to the Standing Rock Reservation are close, believes that Eastman's observations regarding the Hunkpapas might be more accurate than most of his others, given the length of time he spent on the reservation. Telephone interview, February 16, 2002.

10. Mangum, "Gall," 28; Vestal, *New Sources of Indian History*, 220. Gall is listed as Abraham Gall in his baptism, marriage, and burial records. See Standing Rock Mission, vol. A-1.

11. The practice of multiple names continues today. Russell Means, the noted Lakota activist, has four names, representing each stage of his life. Larson, *Red Cloud*, 34.

12. Mangum, "Gall," 28. One of Gall's red saddle blankets is stored at the State Historical Society of North Dakota.

13. *The Sioux or Dakota Nation*, 1–3; Larson, *Red Cloud*, 6–7. For a list of all seven tribes, properly accented with English translations, see Howard, *The Dakota or Sioux Indians* (1980), 3. Much like early Christian tradition, seven was an important number for many Indian tribes. The Pawnees, longtime enemies of the southern Lakota tribes, used the position of the Seven Stars, called the Pleiades by Europeans, to ascertain the beginning of their ceremonial year. The concept of wisdom for the Seneca people far to the east was distinguished by seven talents. Moreover, many North American tribes have felt a great responsibility for the welfare of all future generations down to the seventh generation. Zimmerman and Molyneaux, *Native North America*, 138.

14. *The Sioux or Dakota Nation*, 1; Larson, *Red Cloud*, 9.

15. Waldman, "Gall (Pizi)," 222–23. *The Sioux or Dakota Nation*, 1–2. In recent years, the use of the name Nakota for the Yanktons and Yanktonais has largely fallen out of favor, the two tribes preferring to be called Dakotas. Howard, *The Dakota or Sioux Indians*, 4.

16. Hyde, *Red Cloud's Folk*, 5–7.

17. Larson, *Red Cloud*, 11–14.

18. Ibid., 20–21; According to the winter count of the Oglala warrior American Horse, the most important event of the winter of 1875–76 was the discovery of the Paha Sapa, which translates as "Hills that are Black," by a party of Oglala warriors led by Standing Bull. The Lakotas' major rivals for control of these hills were the Kiowas, whom the Lakotas eventually drove southward into Oklahoma. Cloud Shield claimed that the discovery occurred during the following year. A winter count is a pictographic representation of what Lakota record keepers felt was the most important event of any given year. With foreign sources being scanty at this time and tribal sources being exceedingly scarce, winter counts have become invaluable to historians. See also Hyde, *Red Cloud's Folk*, 22–23.

19. Josephy, "Crazy Horse, Patriot of the Plains" in *The Patriot Chiefs*, 261–62.

20. Larson, *Red Cloud*, 9–10, 12, 16–17.

21. Anderson, "An Investigation," 88, 93.

22. Bray, "Teton Sioux," 182–83.

23. Other English translations for the Hunkpapa name are Campers at the Horn and End of the Camp Circle. See Howard, *The Dakota or Sioux Indians*, 20.

24. Larson, *Red Cloud*, 12–13, 14–16, 17; *The Sioux or Dakota Nation*, 3.

25. Larson, *Red Cloud*, 17–18. The noted anthropologist John C. Ewers believed that the white man's diseases were "more numerous and wreaked more havoc . . . than scholars have demonstrated today." Quoted in Washburn, *The Indian in America*, 106.

26. White, "The Winning of the West," 325.

27. Bray, "Teton Sioux," 174. In his statistical study, Bray reveals the disparities in counting the Lakotas. He questions the accuracy of the 1881 Sioux census, which led to a reassessment of the 1875 count, in which the Lakota population had reached 34,651. Later estimates, however, stabilized by new census procedures, concluded that there were 16,000 Lakotas by the late nineteenth century. In 1931 the Indian Office census, counting Dakota and Nakota as well as Lakota Sioux, computed the total population of all three at 33,168, making the Sioux the second largest tribe in the nation. *The Sioux or Dakota Nation*, 1.

28. Larson, *Red Cloud*, 18–19.

29. The success of the Oglalas in particular made them the fastest growing of the seven Lakota tribes in terms of actual numbers. During the nineteenth century, they enjoyed a growth of 385 percent over a seventy-six-year period. See Bray, "Teton Sioux," 181.

30. Larson, *Red Cloud*, 21–22; Hyde, *Red Cloud's Folk*, 22.

31. Hyde, *Red Cloud's Folk*, 28.

32. Larson, *Red Cloud*, 33, 34.

33. Ibid., 23–24, 27–28.

34. White, "The Winning of the West," 334–35. White discusses the four neutral hunting grounds most important to the Sioux: the Powder River (which he calls the Yellowstone drainage), the forks of the Platte, the Medicine Bow–Laramie plains country, and the Republican River valley.

35. Ibid., 336–39; Larson, *Red Cloud*, 26–27.

36. Gall would almost lose his life at the hands of U.S. Army soldiers and Arikara enemies, Custer's future Indian Scout Bloody Knife being an especially vengeful foe. Innis, *Bloody Knife*, 46–47.

37. Larson, *Red Cloud*, 21, 99, 138–39, 203–041. One tale, which emerged from the Lakota oral tradition, was related to anthropologist Ella Deloria by an old Oglala named Left Hand. According to Left Hand, an Oglala band, pursuing a herd of buffalo during the mid-eighteenth century, got stranded on the west bank of the Missouri. Because of melting ice, they could not return to the other side. The desperate band fortunately encountered two Cheyenne scouts riding some very strong horses. The two scouts led the Oglala band to a large Cheyenne encampment, where horses grazed nearby. The Cheyennes treated the Oglalas "royally" and gave their headman horses to allow them more mobility. This act of kindness molded a strong alliance between all Lakotas and Cheyennes and even such Cheyenne allies as the Arapahoes. Howard, *The Dakota or Sioux Indians* (1980), 20–21.

CHAPTER 3. PROVING HIMSELF

1. Robinson, "The Education of an Indian Boy." 2, Robinson Papers.

2. Howard, *The Dakota or Sioux Indians* (1980), 22.

3. Vestal, *New Sources of Indian History*, 233. Vestal's book, much of which comprises documents found in the Walter S. Campbell Collection at the University of Oklahoma Library, makes reference to Lone Man as one of the organizers of the Silent Eaters Society, which was composed of veteran warriors and leaders of the tribe. See no. 26 in Vestal's book, titled "The Silent Eaters," 231–233.

4. Ibid., 220. A description of the elaborate ceremony is included in no. 25, "The 'Treaty of Laramie' at Fort Rice," 219–30.

5. This arrangement would harmonize with the belief of some students of the Sioux that the Lakota world was matrilocal in its family practices. But there is no solid consensus on this subject; indeed, certain scholars have insisted that newly married wives in particular tended to move to their husband's homes, a practice that can hardly be characterized as matrilocal. Pertinent references to the tiospaye system of kinship are found in Hassrick, *The Sioux* (1964), 11–12, 108–09, 113–14; Anderson, *Kinsman of Another Kind*, ix–xii. For an especially thorough analysis of the tiospaye, see DeMallie, "Teton Dakota Kinship," 110–14.

6. Utley, *The Lance and the Shield*, 3, 8–9. Like Gall, a number of different birth years have been attributed to Sitting Bull. Utley feels that 1831, nine years before Gall's birth, is the most likely year for Sitting Bull's birth.

7. Hassrick, *The Sioux* (1964), 14, 25, 32, 53–54.

8. Eastman, *Indian Heroes and Great Chieftains*, 69–74.

9. Robinson, "The Education of an Indian Boy," 3, Robinson Papers.

10. Utley, *The Lance and the Shield*, 10.

11. Eastman, *Indian Heroes and Great Chieftains*, 74–75.

12. Robinson, "The Education of an Indian Boy," 2–3, Robinson Papers.

13. Eastman, *Indian Heroes and Great Chieftains*, 77–79. Roman Nose was not an uncommon name among the Cheyennes, Lakotas, and Arapahoes. John Monnett interview, October 7, 2004, Denver. The most prominent warrior with that name was the Northern Cheyenne leader who distinguished himself at the Battle of the Platte Bridge in 1865 and was later killed at Beecher Island in 1868. He was probably the one who wrestled Gall that day. Another prominent Roman Nose was an Oglala warrior who was involved in the Battle of Slim Buttes in 1876. See Greene, *Slim Buttes, 1876*, 49, 50–51.

14. Larson, *Red Cloud*, 36–37.

15. Ibid., 41; Utley, *The Lance and the Shield*, 14.

16. Utley, *The Lance and the Shield*, 5, 14–15. One Sitting Bull descendant questioned whether Sitting Bull was ever called Jumping Badger. Isaac Dog Eagle, telephone interview, July 14, 2001.

17. Robinson, "The Education of an Indian Boy," 2. Robinson Papers.

18. In Mari Sandoz's classic biography of Crazy Horse, there are references to the importance of visions in his life. See *Crazy Horse*, passim. See 41–44 for one especially good example.

19. Eastman, *Indian Heroes and Great Chieftains*, 76–77.

20. Olson, *Red Cloud and the Sioux Problem*, 6–8; Larson, *Red Cloud*, 667. For a copy of the 1851 Treaty of Fort Laramie, see Kappler, *Indian Affairs*, 594–596.

21. Utley, *The Lance and the Shield*, 8. According to Edwin Thompson Denig, an observant employee of the American Fur Company at Fort Union from 1837 to 1856, the separation of the Assiniboines from the Yanktonais occurred around the year 1760. The Sioux called the Assiniboines Hohes, or Fish Eaters, because fish had become the principal item in the Assiniboine diet when they lived near the Crees in British Canada. See Denig, *The Assiniboines*, 395–396.

22. Utley, *The Lance and the Shield*, 15–16, 99–100.

23. Ibid., 8. One Mandan, Amy Mossett of New Town, North Dakota, claimed to be the descendant of one of only thirty-one Mandan warriors who survived the 1837 epidemic that many Mandan and Hidatsa tribal members call "the Holocaust." *The Denver Post*, October 13, 2002. The *Post* article used the headline "Smallpox 'Holocaust' Haunts Indians" and was prompted by modern fears of a return of smallpox through terrorist actions.

24. Innis, *Bloody Knife*, 19–20, 22–23, 27. Bloody Knife and his mother joined her Arikara people at Fort Clark, an important trading post near present-day Stanton, North Dakota. A visit to his old Hunkpapa band encamped at the mouth of the Rosebud River in 1860 only exposed Bloody Knife to more abuse. Gall was again the major instigator. Collin, "Bloody Knife," 4.

25. Larson, *Red Cloud*, 41; One Bull, box 104, folder 11, Campbell Collection. Frank Grouard, a mixed-blood adopted by Sitting Bull, who later won the Hunkpapa leader's wrath by leaving his village to fraternize with the whites, had to admit that Sitting Bull was a most formidable warrior; Grouard claimed that Sitting Bull had earned as many as sixty-three coups. Utley, *The Lance and the Shield*, 94, 163–64.

26. Hassrick, *The Sioux* (1964), 16–17.

27. Utley, *The Lance and the Shield*, 21–22.

28. Larson, *Red Cloud*, 35–36. For a more thorough discussion of Lakota religious practices, including the role of the medicine man, see Price, *The Oglala People*, 2–11, passim. There were different kinds of medicine men and even medicine women. Some of these people practiced herbal medicine, while others, the *wakan*, or holy people, interceded with the sacred to ensure success in both important and everyday matters affecting the tribe or its individual members. Their power to interpret the natural or sacred signs of the universe made them es-

pecially important to the tribe. One of the most comprehensive examinations of these influential tribal leaders is found in Powers, *Oglala Religion*, 56–67.

29. Tim Mentz, Sr. (Red Bull), interview, May 21, 2001, Fort Yates.

30. Utley, *The Lance and the Shield*, 22.

31. Larson, *Red Cloud*, 35, 44–45, 49, 76, 213; Price, *The Oglala People*, 160–63. For a helpful account of Crazy Horse's tragic death following his failure to cooperate enough with the federal authorities at Camp Robinson, see Hedren, *Fort Laramie in 1876*, 231–32.

32. Utley, *The Lance and the Shield*, 16–17, 18. There were many different kinds of akicitas who exercised various powers and duties. For a detailed analysis, see DeMallie, "Teton Dakota Kinship," 128–33.

33. Utley, *The Lance and the Shield*, 16–18, 338. The Strong Heart Society should not be confused with the Christian society of Sioux Indians with the same name, who were influenced by Father DeSmet's kindness toward the Sioux at Fort Pierre in 1852, where he treated many of them for cholera. Many Lakotas called these Christian Indian defenders of law and order Foot Soldiers after they made their arduous November journey in 1863 from Bad River to Sitting Bull's encampment on the Grand River to rescue some white captives. See the biographies of Mad Bear, Four Bear, and Swift Bear in the Waggoner Papers. Some of these biographies were made available to the author by James F. Strouse during an interview with him in Golden, Colorado, on January 8, 2003.

34. Lone Man was one of the organizers of the Silent Eaters Society, according to Vestal, *New Sources of Indian History*, 233.

35. White Bull, box 105, notebook 53, Campbell Collection; Mangum, "Gall," 28, 30, 34; Utley, *The Lance and the Shield*, 18, 19–20, 22. Sitting Bull often splashed red paint on other parts of his body, indicating that red was indeed his color of choice.

CHAPTER 4. THE NEW ENEMIES

1. Anderson, *Kinsmen of Another Kind*, 240–44, 246–51, 252–54, 255–59, 260–64, 274, 277–78; Utley, *The Indian Frontier*, 78–81. For insights into the unlikely leadership role of Little Crow, see Andrist, *The Long Death*, 35–36.

2. Anderson, *Kinsmen of Another Kind*, x–xii, 228, 232, 236–37, 240–43, 250–52.

3. Severn "Pete" Pederson interview, December 3, 2002, Douglas County, Colorado. Pederson has a fine collection of weapons, clothing, beadwork, and artifacts of the Plains tribes, particularly for the Lakotas, Cheyennes, and Arapahoes.

4. Olson, *Red Cloud and the Sioux Problem*, 8–9. John Grattan was a young lieutenant whose attack on Conquering Bear's Brulé encampment in 1854 resulted in Grattan's death and the demise of the twenty-nine men under his command; Conquering Bear was also a victim. Harney's attack on Little Thunder's Brulés a year later not only ended in the deaths of many Indians but also led to their enforced transfer to Fort Laramie in chains. For a new monographic account of the Blue Water Creek fight, often called the Battle of Ash Hollow, see Paul, *Blue Water Creek*, 88–110.

5. Andrist, *The Long Death*, 59–60. Little Crow survived the Battle of Wood Lake only to be killed on July 3, 1863, after being caught picking berries and stealing corn near Hutchison, Minnesota. Sundbloom and Ubl, letters to the editor in the December 2006 issue of *Wild West*, 9. Interestingly enough, Sibley had social, or fictive, kinship ties with Little Crow, having fathered Dakota children. Anderson, *Kinsmen of Another Kind*, 273.

6. Utley, *The Lance and the Shield*, 52–55, 343n. When Sully reached Fort Pierre on September 3, 1863, it had been abandoned as a military post for six years because of the lack of timber, grass,

and hay. The original Fort Pierre, located some three miles north of the present capital of South Dakota, had been established as a trading post on the west side of the Missouri River as early as 1831. It was purchased by the government as a military fort in 1855 and occupied until May 16, 1857. Its location on the southern flank of Hunkpapa country made its utilization by Sully a more immediate threat after the Minnesota Sioux war. See Frazer, *Forts of the West*, 136.

7. Utley, *The Lance and the Shield*, 53. One of the survivors of Whitestone Hill was the young Hunkpapa warrior, Bull Head, who would later shoot Sitting Bull in the chest during the Hunkpapa leader's fatal arrest in 1890. Bull Head, who was only sixteen in 1863, was assigned to look after the horses during the battle. His presence at the Battle of Whitestone Hill is a sure sign that Sitting Bull and probably Gall were also present. Bull Head's biography, Waggoner Papers.

8. Both trading posts were once owned by the American Fur Company, Fort Union since 1828 and Fort Berthold since 1862. Frazer, *Forts of the West*, 109–110, 115–16. Another trading post that had been important to this region was Fort Clark, located on the west bank of the Missouri above the mouth of Knife River. This post, built on the site of veteran trader James Kipp's earlier post, was taken over by the American Fur Company in 1831 and was important to the buffalo robe trade, which existed primarily with the nearby Mandans and Hidatsas. This fort fell into disuse during the smallpox epidemic of 1837, three years before Gall's birth. D. J. Wishart, *The Fur Trade*, 59; Hart, *Tour Guide to Old Western Forts*, 112–13.

9. One particular observation regarding the Indian concept of combat drawn from Stanley Vestal's research and interviews sums it up best: "all he [the warrior] cared about was his own *coups*." See Vestal, *New Sources of Indian History*, 61.

10. Utley, *The Lance and the Shield*, 55.

11. Gall's biography, Waggoner Papers. Waggoner, a mixed-blood who became a close friend of Gall during his last years, was an interpreter at Standing Rock during the late nineteenth century. Utilizing this position, she was able to interview many Sioux warriors about their past experiences.

12. Utley, *The Lance and the Shield*, 55–56.

13. Inkpaduta was described by one of Vestal's sources as the "hero of half a dozen battles." Vestal, *New Sources of Indian History*, 56. See also Inkpaduta's biography in the Waggoner Papers and more information about him in Anderson, *Kinsmen of Another Kind*, 216–17, 226.

14. Utley, *The Lance and the Shield*, 55–56.

15. Ibid., 56; Vestal, *New Sources of Indian History*, 56; Inkpaduta's biography, Waggoner Papers. For a more detailed account of Inkpaduta's role at Killdeer Mountain, see Van Nuys, *Inkpaduta*, 313–39.

16. Utley, *The Lance and the Shield*, 56, 57; Vestal, *New Sources of Indian History*, 57.

17. Quotation from Vestal, *New Sources of Indian History*, 56. A captive white woman, Fanny Kelly, was with the retreating Sioux women during this attack. When she returned after four months of captivity, she wrote about this chaotic episode.

18. Ibid., 57; Utley, *The Lance and the Shield*, 57. Feelings of vengeance and outrage were strong among the Sioux. On the following night, July 29, a hundred avenging warriors cut off a picket post established by Sully's men during their march back to the Heart River corral, where the gold seekers they were escorting to Montana had stayed during the battle. Two soldiers were killed; each had a dozen arrows embedded in his body.

19. Vestal, *New Sources of Indian History*, 58.

20. Numerous Lakota warriors regarded with hostility Inkpaduta and "his unpopular gang, [who] . . . had caused all this trouble," ibid. For additional specifics on Inkpaduta's controversial role at Killdeer Mountain, see Inkpaduta's biography, Waggoner Papers.

21. Utley, *The Lance and the Shield*, 57–59; Vestal, *New Sources of Indian History*, 59–60. The Indian sources used in Vestal's chapter "The Battle of the Badlands" tend to minimize the Indian losses and emphasize the misery felt by Sully's soldiers as they made their way through the Badlands.

22. Utley, *The Lance and the Shield*, 59–62; Gall's biography, Waggoner Papers. The unfortunate Fisk party, after three days of travel in their quest for safety, finally stopped and circled their wagons in preparation for negotiations with their Hunkpapa tormentors. Captain Fisk was willing to give the Indians three horses, and some coffee, sugar, and flour in exchange for peace and the return of the white captive Fanny Kelly. When the Sioux warriors insisted on four wagons loaded with food, negotiations broke down. Gall's participation in the Fisk Wagon Train Fight is confirmed in his biography in the Waggoner Papers.

23. Frazer, *Forts of the West*, 110; 113, 114.

24. Utley, *The Lance and the Shield*, 62–63. Bear's Rib's father was one of the Hunkpapas who was converted to Catholicism by Father Pierre Jean DeSmet. He was also an organizer of the Christian Society of Strong Hearts. The elder Bear's Rib was killed in 1862 after apparently reneging on an agreement to take such Indian goods as fifty-eight buffalo hides from Sitting Bull's band to the trading post at Pierre. There, he was to exchange these hides for trade items sought by the Hunkpapa band. His failure to return from Pierre prompted a party of Hunkpapas to go to the post, where a violent incident occurred in which Bear's Rib was fatally shot. See Bear's Rib's biography, Waggoner Papers.

25. Pictographs of Running Antelope winning coups against Arikara warriors in combat are found in Powell, *Bureau of Ethnology*, 208–14. For more information about Running Antelope's life, see his biography in the Waggoner Papers.

26. Utley, *The Lance and the Shield*, 67.

27. Larson, *Red Cloud*, 80–83, 85.

28. Indians who hung around a military fort were generally held in low esteem by the Lakotas. The name given to those tribesmen who insisted on living near Fort Laramie to beg for food on the Oregon Trail during the 1850s and 1860s was Laramie Loafers, or Waglukhe. See ibid., 71, 73, 83, 125.

29. Utley, *The Lance and the Shield*, 67–68, n. 346.

30. Ibid., 68.

31. Larson, *Red Cloud*, 85.

32. Hyde, *Life of George Bent*, 235–36; Utley, *The Lance and the Shield*, 69.

33. Utley, *The Lance and the Shield*, 69; Gall's biography, Waggoner Papers. Bull Head, the teenager who also fought at Whitestone Hill and Killdeer Mountain, was fatally wounded while arresting Sitting Bull on December 15, 1890. Bull Head's biography, Waggoner Papers.

34. Hyde, *Life of George Bent*, 236–42. George Bent, the mixed-blood son of Colonel William Bent, elected to live with his mother's people, the Cheyennes. He was a participant in this Powder River war, along with Northern Cheyenne and Lakota warriors living in the area. For the Cheyenne perspective of General Connor's 1865 expedition, see the new 2004 biography of George Bent, Halaas and Masich, *Halfbreed*, 194–99. Fort Reno was named after Major Jesse Reno, who had been killed during the Civil War in the Battle of South Mountain on September 14, 1862. Frazer, *Forts of the West*, 184.

35. White Bull, box 105, notebook 8, and One Bull, box 104, folder 11, Campbell Collection.

36. Innis, *Bloody Knife*, 32–33, 40–41. In 1936 a formal alliance was established among the Arikaras, Hidatsas, and Mandans in which they were designated the Three Affiliated Tribes.

37. Taylor, "Bloody Knife and Gall," 170; Collin, "Bloody Knife," 5.

38. Innis, *Bloody Knife*, 33, 41–42, 43, 46; Taylor: "Bloody Knife and Gall," 170.

39. Innis, *Bloody Knife*, 46–47; Utley, *The Lance and the Shield*, 74–75. Innis's and Utley's versions of this incident that almost ended Gall's life are essentially the same, but Innis states that Bloody Knife's gun was swept aside by the officer's arm, while Utley claims the soldier kicked it aside.

40. Innis, *Bloody Knife*, 47; Taylor, "Bloody Knife and Gall," 171–72. Polygamy being common among Lakota leaders particularly, Gall had two wives at this time. According to a contemporary of Gall, Joseph Henry Taylor, the wife Gall was closest to placed him under the care of this capable woman. Vestal has another version of this near-fatal attack. According to him, Gall ran off the horses of a Sioux Indian named Long Mandan when the latter had gone to an Arikara village to take a wife. Some time thereafter, Long Mandan saw Gall and his band encamped near Fort Berthold and, seeking revenge, quickly went to Fort Stevenson, where a detachment of one hundred soldiers was recruited. They made a hasty trip to Fort Berthold, and on the morning of the following day, surrounded Gall's camp. Gall was badly wounded trying to escape and was left for dead. Although his band had already departed, Gall, despite his wounds, was able to walk twenty miles to the lodge of his best friend, Hairy Chin, who slowly nursed him back to health. See Vestal, *Sources of Indian History*, 221–23.

41. Innis, *Bloody Knife*, 47.

CHAPTER 5. IN SEARCH OF A TREATY

1. Pope to Major Frank Wheaton, commander of the District of Nebraska, August 23, 1865, as quoted in Larson, *Red Cloud*, 88.

2. Utley, *The Lance and the Shield*, 70–71.

3. Warner, "A History of Fort Buford," 41–43; Frazer, *Forts of the West*, 110–11.

4. Frazer, *Forts of the West*, 114–15.

5. E. B. Taylor, head of the 1866 presidential commission, as quoted in Larson, *Red Cloud*, 9.

6. Colonel Carrington took command of Fort Reno, on the left bank of the Powder River, on June 28, 1866. It had been established by General Connor on August 14, 1865, during his disappointing campaign in the Powder River country. Carrington built Fort Phil Kearny at the edge of the Bighorn Mountains between the Big and Little Piney creeks on July 13, 1865. He later dispatched two infantry companies ninety-two miles northward to establish Fort C. F. Smith on August 12, 1865. Ibid., 97, and Fraser, *Forts of the West*, 83–84.

7. Interview with Red Cloud by Judge Eli S. Ricker, November 24, 1906, Ricker Collection.

8. According to historian Herbert T. Hoover, Gall's name first appeared in federal records as one of the Hunkpapa warriors who cooperated with Red Cloud in the December 1866 ambush of Fetterman's column near Fort Phil Kearny. "Gall (Sioux)," 590. References to Gall's presence in Red Cloud's War are also found in such sources as *Notable Native Americans*, the *Biographical Dictionary of Indian History to 1906*, and *The Native North American Almanac*, and in such secondary accounts as Fielder's *Sioux Indian Leaders*. Gall insisted in an interview with Josephine Waggoner years later that he had played an active role in Red Cloud's War. Winsell, "Gall," 155; Waldman, "Gall (Pizi)," 138; Champagne, "Gall (Pizi)," 1059; Fielder, *Sioux Indian Leaders*, 58. For Gall's own testimony, see Gall's biography, Waggoner Papers.

9. Vestal, *New Sources of Indian History*, 221.

10. Larson, *Red Cloud*, 97, 103. Olson lists all the members of the Sanborn-Sully Commission, including Colonel Ely S. Parker, who later became President Grant's commissioner of Indian Affairs. See his *Red Cloud and the Sioux Problem*, 53.

11. Larson, *Red Cloud*, 110–113. One of the older but still important accounts of Red Cloud's War is Hebard and Brininstool, *The Bozeman Trail*.

12. Jones, *The Treaty of Medicine Lodge*, 17–19 and passim.

13. Larson, *Red Cloud*, 116–17, 118, 119, 120, 122–24. Red Cloud gave the treaty his approval after compelling Major William Dye, the new commandant at Fort Laramie, to read the provisions of the treaty item by item. Throughout these proceedings, the willful and intelligent Indian leader managed to keep government negotiators off balance much of the time with his sharp questions and aggressive demeanor. James Mooney, author of *The Ghost Dance Religion and the Sioux Outbreak of 1890*, summed up his evaluation of Red Cloud with this sentence: "Red Cloud was a warrior and a diplomat, and knew how to be an Indian while keeping favor with the government." Mooney to Doane Robinson, February 20, 1904, Robinson Papers.

14. Treaty reprinted in Kappler, *Indian Affairs*, 998–1007, and later reproduced in Olson, *Red Cloud and the Sioux Problem*, 341–49.

15. Carriker, *Father Peter John DeSmet*, 237–44.

16. Utley, *The Lance and the Shield*, 1–2, 79.

17. A number of these more peaceful Sioux had been converted by Father DeSmet. For instance, the father of Bear's Rib had become a Roman Catholic because of this priest's pious example and kindly persuasiveness. In fact, the senior Bear's Rib organized the Christian Society of Strong Hearts and was, until his assassination by more warlike Hunkpapas in 1862, the leader of the Lakota peace movement. See Bear's Rib's biography, Waggoner Papers.

18. Galpin had longstanding contacts with the Sioux, going back to the 1830s. He and a fellow trader named John Sabille had traveled to the sacred Lakota landmark Bear Butte to convince the Oglala chief Bull Bear to lead his people to Fort William for trade on the site of what would later become Fort Laramie. But Bull Bear needed little persuasion to go to the rich buffalo country along the North Platte. In 1834, he migrated there with approximately one thousand of his tribesmen. Larson, *Red Cloud*, 54.

19. Utley, *The Lance and the Shield*, 78–79; Carriker, *Father Peter John DeSmet*, 220–23. DeSmet would call this conference he was about to have with the Hunkpapas the Great Powder River Council.

20. Vestal, *Sitting Bull*, 100–101.

21. Ibid., 101–104; Utley, *The Lance and the Shield*, 78–80.

22. As quoted in Utley, *The Lance and the Shield*, 80.

23. Sitting Bull obviously did not want to offend DeSmet, whom he truly respected. In later years some Lakotas still believed that DeSmet had baptized Sitting Bull during this conference. What the priest actually did was give the Hunkpapa war chief a crucifix of brass and wood, which became a treasured possession of Sitting Bull's family. The Jesuit priest did, however, convert Lone Man and a number of other Sioux at this often tense meeting. Vestal, *Sitting Bull*, 109.

24. Vestal, *New Sources of Indian History*, 220, 224.

25. Ibid., 228.

26. Ibid., 223.

27. Ibid., 221. Because of Gall's later break with Sitting Bull, some of the testimony solicited from Indian sources by Vestal is critical, if not hostile.

28. Ibid., 226; Indian Peace Commission, "Council of the Indian Peace Commission," 97. Quotations from Gall's speech are from the "Council of the Indian Peace Commission," which vary slightly from Vestal's account.

29. Vestal, *New Sources of Indian History*, 226–27. Harney, whose Sioux nickname Mad Bear was not a term of endearment, had been one of the Lakotas' most resolute adversaries since

his bloody attack in 1855 on a largely Brulé village during the Blue Water Creek fight, often called Battle of Ash Hollow.

30. Vestal, *New Sources of Indian History*, 91–92, 220; Indian Peace Commission, "Council of the Indian Peace Commission," 97.

31. See the 1972 edition of Kappler, *Indian Affairs*, 1006, for Gall's use of the name Man-that-Goes-in-the-Middle. For a time historians did not know that Gall headed the Hunkpapa delegates to Fort Rice because he had used this name instead of Gall.

32. Support for this position is found in the first two provisions of article 11: 1) "That they [the Sioux] will withdraw all opposition to the construction of railroads now being built on the plains" and 2) "That they [the Sioux] will permit the peaceful construction of any railroad not passing over their reservation as herein defined." 1972 edition of Kappler, *Indian Affairs*, 1002.

33. Vestal, *New Sources of Indian History*, 230; Frank, "Chief Gall," 31.

CHAPTER 6. THREATS ALONG THE YELLOWSTONE

1. Utley, *The Lance and the Shield*, 85.

2. Ibid., 84.

3. U.S. Congress, House, *Report of the Secretary of War*, 56, 58.

4. Warner, "A History of Fort Buford," 47. Inkpaduta, or Scarlet Point, has been underrated as a steadfast and surprisingly ubiquitous warrior. He fought in Minnesota, in the Dakota Territory, and in Montana at such battles as the Little Bighorn. See Inkpaduta's biography, Waggoner Papers.

5. Utley, *The Lance and the Shield*, 84–56.

6. The woman was Red Cloud's niece, Black Buffalo Woman, who had a passionate courtship with Crazy Horse until it was shattered by her marriage to No Water. In 1860, thereabouts, No Water, feigning a toothache, had left a raiding party in which Crazy Horse was a member. Using the time he gained by this ruse, he convinced Black Buffalo Woman to marry him. Eventually, Crazy Horse and Black Buffalo Woman, still very much in love, ran off together. In retaliation, an angry No Water shot Crazy Horse in the jaw. Although Crazy Horse recovered from his wound, the Lakota elders made him give up his shirt because his conduct in this affair was not up to that expected of a shirt wearer. Sandoz, *Crazy Horse*, 131–36, 225–44.

7. Vestal, *New Sources of Indian History*, 92.

8. Ibid., 91, 92; Utley, *The Lance and the Shield*, 87.

9. Vestal, *Sitting Bull*, page 92–93.

10. Description of Sitting Bull's inaugural ceremony and quotation in ibid, 94.

11. Ibid., 94–95. Another detailed account of this Rosebud meeting is found in an undated clipping from the *Mobridge Tribune* of Mobridge, South Dakota, near the Standing Rock Reservation, Fiske Papers. For Gall's elevation as a war chief, see Robert P. Higheagle, box 104, folder 22, Campbell Collection.

12. Other leaders at this conference who would distinguish themselves at the Battle of the Little Bighorn include the Hunkpapa Crow King, a worthy rival of Gall in many ways, the Miniconjou Lame Deer, and the Northern Cheyenne Ice.

13. Larson, *Red Cloud*, 144–56. The new Red Cloud Agency, sometimes called the White River Agency, was located on the White River, approximately seventy miles above the North Platte.

14. Mangum, "Gall," 30.

15. Despite the much greater threat posed by the U.S. Army and the white settlements, Sitting Bull's band, encroaching on the edge of Crow hunting lands, attacked a Crow village in winter 1869–70 in the Thirty-Crows-Killed Battle. Several months later, during summer 1870, the new supreme chief's band, employing the familiar decoy stratagem of the Lakotas, drew a force of one hundred Bitterroot Salish out of their village in the Musselshell River valley. The Lakotas' casualties were light because their strategy worked so well. Utley, *The Lance and the Shield*, 97–100.

16. Four Horns once counseled Sitting Bull to be "a little against fighting, but when anyone shoots be ready to shoot back." Sitting Bull apparently listened, because there were no recorded full-scale attacks on such army posts as Fort Buford after 1870. Robert P. Higheagle manuscript, box 104, folder 21, p. 3, Campbell Collection.

17. Utley, *The Lance and the Shield*, 91, 93–95; Frank, "Chief Gall," 32–33.

18. Frost, *Custer's 7th Cav*, 1–3.

19. Billington, *Westward Expansion*, 560.

20. Frost, *Custer's 7th Cav*, 15–16.

21. Ibid., 3; Lubetkin, "The Forgotten Yellowstone Surveying Expeditions," 1, 3, 7.

22. Utley, *The Lance and the Shield*, 106–07.

23. Ibid., 107; Frost, *Custer's 7th Cav*, 3.

24. Utley, *The Lance and the Shield*, 107.

25. Utley has called this battle, or skirmish, the Battle of Arrow Creek, while the historians and archeologists working for the Frontier Heritage Alliance have called it Baker's Battle on the Yellowstone. Ibid., 107–09. See "Baker Battle: Analysis is completed on shell casings recovered. Project completion date is slated for September, 2002," Frontier Heritage Alliance, hereafter cited as Baker Battle Report. Arrow Creek is the Crow name for this tributary of the Yellowstone. This battle site, according to the Baker Battle Report, is the only positively identified battlefield of the Yellowstone Expedition of 1872. Howard Boggess, telephone interviews, June 25, 2003, and March 21, 2005. Other members of the alliance interviewed about the Baker Battle are Mary Ellen McWilliams, June 24, 2003 (telephone), and Richard E. Collin, June 24, 2003 (State Historical Society of North Dakota).

26. Utley, *The Lance and the Shield*, 107–09; Vestal, *New Sources of Indian History*, 129–30. According to one of Vestal's Indian sources, Sitting Bull initiated this bold action to prove that, while he was no longer as robust as such younger warriors as Crazy Horse and Gall, he could still demonstrate his exceptional courage by this kind of act. Crazy Horse, not to be upstaged, insisted on circling the enemy lines one more time only to have his horse shot out from under him.

27. Boggess interview, June 25, 2003. Some of the same rifles used in this battle were also used at the Battle of the Little Bighorn, according to the results of a shell-casing examination made by Douglas Scott, National Parks Service archeologist, in behalf of the Frontier Heritage Alliance. See also Baker Battle Report.

28. Baker Battle Report; Boggess interview, June 25, 2003; Utley, *The Lance and the Shield*, 109.

29. Gall's discovery of Colonel Stanley's presence on O'Fallon Creek also provides convincing evidence that Gall was not a participant in the Baker Battle, as some historians have argued. Neil Mangum made this point in his article on Gall. See "Gall," 31, n. 41. Ben Innis in his *Bloody Knife*, 91, was one of those who believed Gall was present at the Baker Battle. Little Bighorn veteran Edward S. Godfrey, who later became a brigadier general, was another one, according to Mangum. See also Godfrey's 1923 version of "Custer's Last Battle," 159, and Graham, *The Custer Myth*, 131.

30. Stanley, who hoped to find Major Baker's party at the mouth of the Powder River, had his artillerymen fire their cannons in a vain attempt to signal the engineers with the Baker expedition. Utley, *The Lance and the Shield*, 110.

31. Ibid.; Innis, *Bloody Knife*, 91–92. Stanley's facial hair was especially full at a time when flourishing beards were commonplace. See Frost, *Custer's 7th Cav*, 4, and the striking photographs in his book. Also see Lubetkin, "An Ambush That Changed History," 75, 76.

32. Quotation from the *Journal's* October 19, 1872, edition in Lubetkin, "An Ambush That Changed History," 77.

33. Quoted in "Indian Policy of the President," *Philadelphia Inquirer*, October 20, 1872, as cited in Lubetkin, *Jay Cooke's Gamble*, 160–61, n. 326. For other sources regarding Gall's 1872 escapades, see Lubetkin, "An Ambush That Changed History," 78–81; Innis, *Bloody Knife*, 92; Mangum, "Gall," 31. One of Gall's victims, the one-armed lieutenant Eban Crosby, whose scalp was probably displayed in this incident, had his other arm removed by Gall as a trophy of the Lakota leader's vengeance for the deaths of his followers. Vestal, *New Sources of Indian History*, 132.

34. Helena *Daily Herald*, August 21, 1873, as quoted in Frost, *Custer's 7th Cav*, 96.

35. Frost, *Custer's 7th Cav*, 6, 41, 43, 48–49, 61. During the 1872 survey, Stanley's heavy drinking often made him an indecisive leader, resulting in procrastination that frustrated his men. On one occasion an officer under his command, Major W. S. Wentworth, found him on the ground dead drunk. When Stanley was not drinking, he could be a perfect gentleman, but when he was, he could be most erratic. He once put Custer under arrest for a short time and then released him with profuse apologies. See also Utley, *Cavalier in Buckskin*, 119. Lubetkin discounts the importance of Stanley's drinking problem on the progress of the expedition. "An Ambush That Changed History," 81. He also provides insights into Major Baker's equally destructive drinking problem. See "The Forgotten Yellowstone Survey Expeditions," 6–7, 14–15.

36. Frost, *Custer's 7th Cav*, 64, 66.

37. Ibid., 66; Utley, *Cavalier in Buckskin*, 119–20. Frost claims that the fire set by Lakota warriors on August 4 failed to spread because the grass was too green, not because of any lack of wind. For another detailed account of the August 4th battle, see Lubetkin, "Clash on the Yellowstone," 12–31.

38. Frost, *Custer's 7th Cav*, 66, 68, 77, 131, 143; Lubetkin, "Clash on the Yellowstone," 24–25. Rain-in-the-Face, who later escaped from an army jail to participate in the Battle of the Little Bighorn, eventually admitted that he killed Baliran and Honsinger. See also Burdick, *David F. Barry's Indian Notes* (1937), 37–41.

39. Utley, *Cavalier in Buckskin*, 121; Frost, *Custer's 7th Cav*, 81.

40. Utley, *The Lance and the Shield*, 112.

41. Frost, *Custer's 7th Cav*, 84.

42. Gerry Groenewold, telephone interview, July 9, 2003.

43. Frost, *Custer's 7th Cav*, 84; Lubetkin, "Strike Up Garry Owen,'" 8.

44. As quoted in Frost, *Custer's 7th Cav*, 84.

45. Innis, *Bloody Knife*, 92. Gall often fought in red clothing during the Yellowstone campaign, according to Innis. In 1975 historian Stephen E. Ambrose published a study in which he compared the fighting prowess of Custer and Crazy Horse as warriors of great renown. A similar study comparing Custer to Gall would not be inappropriate. General George Crook once expressed the belief that Gall was more effective in fighting the U.S. Army than Crazy Horse was. The performance of Custer and Gall in the Battle of the Yellowstone would be a good case study. See Ambrose, *Crazy Horse and Custer*, passim. Hoover, "Gall (Sioux)," 590.

46. Frost, *Custer's 7th Cav*, 85.

47. Ibid., 86; Utley, *Cavalier in Buckskin*, 122.

48. Frost, *Custer's 7th Cav*, 85.

49. Utley, *Cavalier in Buckskin*, 123.

50. Billington, *Western Expansion*, 560. For a detailed analysis of the downfall of Cooke's banking enterprise and its impact on the nation, see Lubetkin, *Jay Cooke's Gamble*, 368–93.

51. Helena *Daily Herald*, August 21, 1973, as cited in Frost, *Custer's 7th Cav*, 96.

CHAPTER 7. THE PATH TO WAR

1. Utley, *Cavalier in Buckskin*, 134–36, and *The Lance and the Shield*, 115–16.

2. See articles 2 and 16 of the 1868 Treaty of Fort Laramie in the 1972 edition of Kappler, *Indian Affairs*, 998–99, 1002–03.

3. Utley, *The Lance and the Shield*, 115; Larson, *Red Cloud*, 20–21.

4. *Bismarck Daily Tribune*, June 21, 1876; Olson, *Red Cloud and the Sioux Problem*, 173, 199–200.

5. The Oglalas began to winter at Bear Butte, a favorite haunt of the Cheyennes, in the years following 1805. It was at Bear Butte that Galpin and Sabille persuaded the Oglala chief Bull Bear to bring his large band to the Platte country for trading purposes in 1834 and 1835. In 1857, all seven of the Lakota tribes purportedly met at Bear Butte for a major council on how to deal with the growing threat of white encroachment on their lands. See Larson, *Red Cloud*, 26, 54, 75. The belief that the Black Hills were considered sacred by the Lakotas has been questioned. The economic motivation may have been stronger; Sitting Bull once declared the Black Hills as a "food pack" that should be protected. Years later, Black Elk declared that Harney Peak, the highest mountain in the hills, was the center of the earth, the focal point of his people's sacred hoop. Research recently done at Sinte Gleska College, on the Rosebud Reservation, has led to the conclusion that the Black Hills have been the center of the Lakotas' spiritual world for three thousand years. Worster, *Under Western Skies*, 146–47, 149.

6. Utley, *The Lance and the Shield*, 102, 116–20; Groenewold interview, July 9, 2003. According to Groenewold, a number of rogue traders operated at Fort Union and Fort Berthold, where Gall continued to trade even as Indian-white relations deteriorated.

7. Boggess interview, June 25, 2003. See also Baker Battle Report.

8. Gall's Winchester is located in the archives of the State Historical Society of North Dakota, Bismarck. Other possessions of the Hunkpapa war chief held at the society include two pipes, a beaded and quilled pipe bag, a dark blue stroud blanket, a saddle blanket, leggings, and a tinted photo of Gall. Information about these items was presented by Mark J. Halvorson, curator of research collections, in a tour and through an interview on May 17, 2001.

9. Frank, "Chief Gall," 44, 47–48. Agents at the Red Cloud Agency tended to regard these nontreaty Indians as troublemakers. By the fall of 1873 the population at Red Cloud doubled with the arrival of many "Northern Indians" who had never been to an agency before. Indian agent J. J. Saville characterized these people as being "exceedingly vicious and insolent." Miniconjous from the north were especially controversial. According to one Red Cloud agent, J. W. Daniels, in a letter to Commissioner of Indian Affairs Edward P. Smith on August 1, 1873, they were all "impudent and saucy." All cited in Olson, *Red Cloud and the Sioux Problem*, 159–60, 162–63.

10. Innis, *Bloody Knife*, 46–47.

11. Larson, *Red Cloud*, 160–62, 163–67. For a thorough analysis of Red Cloud's charges against Saville, see Olson, *Red Cloud and the Sioux Problem*, 189–98.

12. See Office of Indian Affairs (now called Bureau of Indian Affairs), *Report of the Special Commissioner.*

13. Larson, *Red Cloud,* 186–94.

14. Utley, *The Lance and the Shield,* 125–26. The small attendance of nontreaty Indians at the Black Hills negotiations, notwithstanding the persuasiveness of Red Cloud's couriers, was recognized as a serious concern for those promoting the conference. William Garnett, interview by Eli S. Ricker, January 18, 1903, Ricker Collection.

15. Utley, *The Lance and the Shield,* 127; Larson, *Red Cloud,* 196–98.

16. Watkins to E. P. Smith, Commissioner of Indian Affairs, U.S. Congress, House, *Military Expedition,* 8–9. General Sherman agreed with Watkins's recommendation for a winter campaign but cautioned that the army "should have timely notice of the object to be accomplished, and the means for its attainment." Sherman to Adjutant General's Office, January 7, 1876, H. Exec. Doc. 184, 11.

17. Chandler to Secretary of War William W. Belknap, December 3, 1875, H. Exec. Doc. 184, 10.

18. Frank, "Chief Gall," 53; Larson, *Red Cloud,* 198. Sitting Bull's nephew White Bull questioned whether Sitting Bull ever received the January 31 ultimatum from the Commission of Indian Affairs. White Bull, box 105, notebook 8, Campbell Collection.

19. Hutton, *Phil Sheridan and His Army,* 298–303. Preparations for General Crook's role in the winter campaign were known in the press two and a half months prior to the January 31 deadline. On November 20, 1875, the *Bismarck Weekly Tribune* reported a story carried in the *Inter Ocean* of Chicago that frenzied activities were occurring in "Russell, Laramie and Cheyenne, and other frontier points for a winter campaign against Sitting Bull's hostile band, to be led by Gen. Crooks [*sic*]."

20. Utley, *The Lance and the Shield,* 129–36, 131–32; C. M. Robinson, *A Good Year to Die,* 72–83.

21. C. M. Robinson, *A Good Year to Die,* 82, 91. Two Moon's Cheyennes, along with Oglala warriors like He Dog, were the chief occupants. Vestal, *Sitting Bull,* 140.

22. As quoted in Marquis, *A Warrior Who Fought Custer,* 171–72.

23. According to section 2 of article 11, the Lakotas "will permit the peaceful construction of any railroad not passing over their reservation." Kappler, 1972 edition, *Indian Affairs,* 1002.

24. Inkpaduta's son allegedly stunned Custer with a tomahawk early in the Battle of the Little Bighorn, knocking the surprised leader off his horse. Inkpaduta's biography, Waggoner Papers. For a more detailed account regarding the number of nontreaty lodges, see Utley, *The Lance and the Shield,* 133, 134–35.

25. McLaughlin to Commissioner of Indian Affairs J. D. C. Atkins, September 3, 1887, responding to charges made by Sebastian Beck, a longtime white settler on the northern plains, cited in Frank, "Chief Gall," 142.

26. In some Cheyenne accounts of the Battle of the Little Bighorn, there is a romantic notion that the Cheyennes played their major role in this bloody fray in order to kill Custer for breaking his promise, after the Washita fight, to maintain everlasting peace with them. In reality, the invasion of their hunting grounds by the U.S. Army and the unfair treatment of Lakotas who had chosen reservation life motivated them the most. Graham, *The Custer Myth,* 107.

27. Vestal, *New Sources of Indian History,* 157.

28. Robert P. Higheagle manuscript, p. 20, Campbell Collection. Sitting Bull's role as a visionary medicine man is still revered by many on the Standing Rock Reservation. Mentz, Sr., interview, May 21, 2001.

29. Marquis, *A Warrior Who Fought Custer*, 191–92.

30. Utley, *The Lance and the Shield*, 138.

31. Quotation from Sitting Bull's nephew White Bull, box 108, folder 8, Campbell Collection.

32. Robinson, *A Good Year to Die*, 120, 128–30, 136–48; Utley, *The Lance and the Shield*, 139–43. For a detailed account of the battle, see Mangum, *Battle of the Rosebud*. White Bull, who claimed five coups at the Rosebud, insisted that there were Arikara scouts as well as Crow and Shoshone scouts at the battle. He was especially impressed with the fighting qualities of the Shoshone warriors, whom he characterized as the "bravest and the best" he had ever fought. Vestal, *Warpath*, 185, 188–89.

33. Mangum, *Battle of the Rosebud*, 53.

34. Lieutenant John D. Bourke, one of Crook's aides-de-camp, later expressed his belief that the Battle of the Rosebud was a trap in which Crook became distracted, chasing Indians from one ridge to another. Bourke, *On the Border with Crook*, 311.

35. *Bismarck Daily Tribune*, July 5, 1876.

36. Mildred Fielder insisted Gall had been second in command under Crazy Horse at the Rosebud. See her *Sioux Indian Leaders*, 66. Herbert T. Hoover and Keith A. Winsell in their encyclopedia articles on Gall have asserted that Gall played an important role in the battle and was praised by Crook as being Crazy Horse's equal in warfare. See Hoover, "Gall (Sioux)," 590 and Winsell, "Gall," 155. Gall claimed to be a participant at the Rosebud in his interview with Josephine Waggoner. See Gall's biography, Waggoner Papers.

37. Interviews with Neil Mangum and Jerome A. Greene, February 23, 2002, at the 2002 Denver Symposium on Custer. See bibliography for some of their most pertinent studies. Sitting Bull's Hunkpapas were at Slim Buttes when Crook's men attacked a large number of Lakotas there. Because of their closeness, Gall might have been at Slim Buttes with Sitting Bull, along with other Hunkpapa leaders such as Four Horns and Black Moon. Utley, *The Lance and the Shield*, 166.

38. Lakota custom suggested that sun dance participants should rest after they dance and continue in a prayerful way for four days. Barrett, "One Bull," 7; Barrett, telephone interview, October 5, 2002. The Sioux's closest allies, the Cheyennes, used the term "great medicine dance" rather than sun dance for their ceremony. Marquis, *A Warrior Who Fought Custer*, 191.

39. Vaughn, *With Crook at the Rosebud*, 45.

CHAPTER 8. THE LITTLE BIGHORN

1. First accounts of the Battle of the Little Bighorn report that as many as four thousand warriors were involved. *New York Times*, July 7, 1876. Neil Mangum estimated that the number could have exceeded three thousand. "Gall," 32. Robert M. Utley presents the more modest figures of from eight hundred to eighteen hundred fighting men, but he also documents the explosive growth of the village caused by the late arrival of agency Indians. See *The Lance and the Shield*, 142.

2. Marquis, *A Warrior Who Fought Custer*, 204–05.

3. Estimates of the size of this nontreaty village have stirred up considerable controversy. Lieutenant George D. Wallace, who fought under Reno at Reno Hill, testified four years later at a military inquiry into Reno's conduct that the village was three miles long. Baird, "Into the Valley," 97. One of the leading photographers of the Sioux, David F. Barry, estimated that it was over two miles in length. Burdick, *David F. Barry's Indian Notes* (1937), 9. Gregory F. Michno, in a careful study using geometric techniques and time and motion models, has concluded

that the nontreaty village was much smaller. He estimated that the encampment, as it stretched along the river, was only a mile and a half in length, and its width was about three hundred yards from the river's bank. Michno, *Lakota Noon*, 18.

4. Marquis, *A Warrior Who Fought Custer*, 210. Early news dispatches after the Battle of the Little Bighorn place the number of Indians there at ten thousand. *New York Times*, July 7, 1876.

5. One Bull was one of those who had tended his horses before Reno's attack; Barrett, "One Bull," 7.

6. Marquis, *A Warrior Who Fought Custer*, 208–210.

7. Michno, "Revision at the Little Bighorn," 21. For a more detailed account of Gall's activities that day, including his readiness for any surprise attack, see Michno, *Lakota Noon*, 37–38.

8. Holley, *Once Their Home*, 275.

9. Custer, who had criticized Orvil Grant for his brazen role in a scandal involving accusations that Belknap illegally sold post traderships at frontier forts, was deprived of his command of the Dakota Column. Indeed, the president opposed any involvement on Custer's part in the campaign against the Sioux. General Terry, who had no experience in Indian campaigning, however, needed Custer's experience and aggressiveness for his mission to succeed. He therefore dictated a telegram for Custer to send, in which the proud officer virtually begged Grant to relent and allow him to at least go on the expedition and be with his men. Utley, *Cavalier in Buckskin*, 152–53, 160–63.

10. Baird, "Into the Valley," 85–86.

11. Crook got the nickname Three Stars because as a brigadier general he could wear one star on his hat and one on each shoulder. Curiously, though, he usually wore a canvas suit and pith helmet, particularly when campaigning. He was also called Gray Eagle, probably because of his braided blond beard with its distinctive gray tint. Larson, *Red Cloud*, 201.

12. Utley, *Cavalier in Buckskin*, 174–77; Baird, "Into the Valley," 86.

13. Utley, *The Lance and the Shield*, 140–41.

14. Fox, *Archaeology, History*, 25–28; Baird, "Into the Valley," 88.

15. According to a paper by Ronald H. Nichols, "A Brief Analytical Study of the Reno Fight in the Valley," Reno fully expected Custer to follow him as he approached the southern end of the large nontreaty village. He was apparently not informed about Custer's move northward along the bluffs east of the Greasy Grass. For more insights in Reno's unsuccessful attack on Gall's village, see Nichols's *In Custer's Shadow*.

There are a plethora of good studies on the Battle of the Little Bighorn, some of which provide valuable insights into Gall's role. Historian Robert M. Utley's favorite is Gray, *Centennial Campaign*, which he feels is the best syntheses of the battle. Neil Mangum, former superintendent of the Little Bighorn Battlefield National Monument, believes that Stewart, *Custer's Luck*, has withstood the test of time as the best single account of the battle. One of the early groundbreaking accounts of the battle is Kuhlman, *Custer and the Gall Saga*. Michael J. Koury, whose Old Army Press reprinted Kuhlman's book, feels that Kuhlman, of all the Custer historians of the 1940s and 1950s, best understood the battlefield terrain at the Little Bighorn. Another older study with good insights into the battle is Marquis, *Sitting Bull and Gall*. Both Kuhlman's and Marquis' accounts, which are now rather difficult to find, are located in the library of the State Historical Society of Nebraska at Lincoln.

A study that has challenged many of the prevailing interpretations of the battle is Fox, *Archaeology, History*. Employing archaeological as well as historical methods, Fox challenges many of the battle's traditional conclusions, such as Custer's legendary Last Stand. An analysis that tries to relate Fox's provocative study with these earlier standard accounts is Halaas

"Reflections on a Theme." Another significant revisionist study is Michno, *Lakota Noon*. As all students of the Battle of the Little Bighorn know, any discussion of the battle's numerous studies is bound to omit many important monographs and articles.

16. Hardorff, *Hokahey!*, 35–37; Baird, "Into the Valley," 88–89.

17. Hardorff, *Hokahey!*, 35–39.

18. As quoted in ibid., 32. See page 127 in this chapter for another account, in which the breakdown of fatalities is six women and ten children.

19. One Bull, in his account of the attack on the Hunkpapa circle, claimed that a warrior named Fat Bear rode into camp as early as the morning of June 25 to warn his people that the soldiers were coming. Prior to Fat Bear's arrival, moreover, a father and his boy, who had gone out to search for a stray horse, also encountered a party of soldiers; these troopers chased them, killing the boy. See Barrett, "One Bull," 7.

20. Michno, "Revision at the Little Bighorn," 21; Baird, "Into the Valley," 88–90, 93–94. Gall's delay in retaliating against Reno's troopers was not that uncommon. Many Oglala and Northern Cheyenne warriors were still waiting for their ponies one and a half hours after they received word of Reno's attack. Bray, *Crazy Horse*, 239.

21. Innis, *Bloody Knife*, 155–58, 172–73. Bloody Knife's sister, who like Bloody Knife was part Hunkpapa and part Arikara, believed that Gall had killed Bloody Knife. According to her testimony, her two daughters went to the battlefield after the conflict and found Bloody Knife's body. Recognizing it as one belonging to the enemy, they cut off their uncle's head and carried it back to the Hunkpapa camp to their mother's horror. See page 159 of the Innis study. Five Lakota scouts, apparently Hunkpapas married to Arikara women, also rode with Custer at the Little Bighorn. Calloway, "Army Allies or Tribal Survival?," 67.

22. Michno, "Revision at the Little Bighorn," 21. Several historians have insisted that Gall played a major role in the Reno fight. Neil Mangum, for example, argues that Gall not only helped to blunt the progress of Reno's attack on his village, but even pursued the major's demoralized troopers across the river. Mangum "Gall," 32–33.

23. Hardorff, *Hokahey!*, 31–32.

24. Michno, "Revision at the Little Bighorn," 21; Michno, *Lakota Noon*, 68–69.

25. Fox, *Archaeology, History*, xv–xvi.

26. Cooke note quoted Utley, *Cavalier in Buckskin*, 186.

27. Ibid., 186–87.

28. Godfrey, "Custer's Last Battle," *Century Magazine*, 379, and Godfrey's more detailed version, "Custer's Last Battle," *Contributions*, 144–45, 193–94.

29. Godfrey, "Custer's Last Battle," *Century Magazine*, 379–80, and *Contributions*, 144–45.

30. Vestal, *New Sources of Indian History*, 180–82.

31. Michno, *Lakota Noon*, 86–87.

32. Utley, *Cavalier in Buckskin*, 182.

33. Michno, *Lakota Noon*, 87.

34. As quoted in Burdick, *David F. Barry's Indian Notes* (1937), 13. See also Michno, "Revision at the Little Bighorn," 22, n. 15

35. Michno, *Lakota Noon*, 114.

36. Gall's efforts to find his family and his actions throughout the rest of the battle have been traced by historian Gregory F. Michno. Michno used Lakota and Cheyenne accounts in a time and motion study that followed, in ten-minute intervals, the movements of Gall and many other Indian participants. See *Lakota Noon* and "Revision at the Little Bighorn." Michno used, with his own modifications, the approach of John S. Gray in his time and motion study. See *Custer's Last Campaign*.

37. White Bull, box 108, folder 8, Campbell Collection. See also Michno, *Lakota Noon*, 148.

38. Michno, *Lakota Noon*, 155.

39. Hardorff, *Hokahey!*, 34–35; Graham, *The Custer Myth*, 260. The loss of Gall's family members at the Little Bighorn has been questioned. The Hunkpapa war chief had been offered, according to one rumor, a large sum of money to tell this story at the 1886 reunion held at the battlefield. However, a Captain Cummings, who was married to one of Sitting Bull's nieces, has challenged this assertion. He was told by his wife's relatives that after Gall returned with his ponies, following the Reno attack, he saw the dead bodies of his wife and one of his children lying in front of his lodge. Despite the discrepancies in Cummings' account of the number of family members killed, Hardorff feels that this version argues powerfully for the crushing personal losses incurred by Gall at the Little Bighorn. See Hardorff, *Hokahey!*, 32.

40. Office of Indian Affairs, "Census of Hunkpapa Indians of Standing Rock Agency." To identify the names of Gall's family members who were killed at the Little Bighorn, I interviewed Gall descendants such as great-grandson Vernon Iron Cloud and his wife, Theo, May 21, 2001; great-granddaughter Lavora Jones, February 26, 2001, and her daughter-in-law Linda Jones, April 26 and May 5, 2005; great-granddaughter Gladys Hawk, September 28, 2006 (telephone); and great-grandson Mike Her-Many-Horses, September 20, 2006 (telephone), and his nephew Leo Her-Many-Horses, September 21, 2006 (telephone), both of whom are now members of the Oglala Tribe. None of them knew the names of the family members killed at the Little Bighorn. Mike and Leo Her-Many-Horses and Linda Jones attributed this lack of information to a longstanding Lakota tradition of adults not talking to their children about adult matters of this nature, feeling it was not appropriate or necessary.

41. Little Sioux related this incident to Orin G. Libby. Hardorff, *Hokahey!*, 32–33. See also Libby's study, *The Arikara Narrative*, passim. The killing of women and children was an act that many of Reno's troopers and white scouts felt they were above. It was, however, an unfortunate wartime reality for many Indian tribes. Southern Cheyennes who fought against Custer told their Indian agent upon their return from the Little Bighorn that some of the women and children there were killed at the outset of the battle. Hardorff, *Hokahey!*, 34.

42. Graham, *The Custer Myth*, 90, 260; Michno, *Lakota Noon*, 155.

43. Michno, *Lakota Noon*, 161. Bray agrees with Michno that Gall arrived at the Medicine Tail ford late, but not as late as Michno maintains. *Crazy Horse*, 442, n. 37.

44. Baird, "Into the Valley," 88, 91–92.

45. Ibid., 91–92; Fox, *Archaeology, History*, 20, 31–32, 280–86, 295–98.

46. Utley, *Cavalier in Buckskin*, 185–87.

47. Ibid., 187–88, 191; Baird, "Into the Valley," 90–91.

48. Shortly after the battle, General Terry listed the number of known fatal casualties for both Custer's and Reno's forces at 251, with another 51 listed as wounded, making for a total of more than 300. C. M. Robinson, *A Good Year to Die*, 211–12. More up-to-date figures not only place the deaths of the men under Custer's command at 210 but list the number of casualties among troopers who fought in the valley and on the bluffs as 52 killed and 60 wounded. Utley, *The Lance and the Shield*, 160–61. Indian casualties are more difficult to determine. White Bull, who counted seven coups at the battle, claimed that there were only twenty-nine Indian deaths as a result of the battle, a figure probably about a dozen short of the actual number. Vestal, *New Sources of Indian History*, 182.

49. Some Indian sources declare that Custer was either wounded or killed at the mouth of the Medicine Tail Coulee and was carried to the spot where his body was found. Utley, *Cavalier in Buckskin*, 189.

50. Michno, *Lakota Noon*, 242–47. See also Michno, "Crazy Horse," 42–53.

51. *St. Paul Pioneer Press*, as quoted in Graham, *The Custer Myth*, 92.

52. As quoted in Utley, *Cavalier in Buckskin*, 189.

53. Ibid., 190; Fox, *Archaeology, History*, 227–28. Fox questioned the sincerity of Gall's praise for the courage of Custer's men at the tenth anniversary reunion of the Custer battle, believing he was too anxious to please the Seventh Cavalry officers at this gathering. Moreover, Gall was allegedly given money for speaking at this reunion, and this was another plausible reason for his praise.

54. Kuhlman, *Custer and the Gall Saga*, 34–35. Kuhlman's accounts of Gall's bloody deeds at this point in the battle seem somewhat ironic, because on the same pages where they are discussed, he also criticizes Gall's exaggerated exploits at the Little Bighorn. Crazy Horse biographer Kingsley M. Bray, on the other hand, believed that Gall's involvement in the attack on Keogh's position allowed Crazy Horse to exercise "tactical initiative" to drive Custer's surviving troopers up Last Stand Hill, where they were killed in about five minutes. *Crazy Horse*, 239–40.

55. *Bismarck Weekly Tribune*, July 12, 1876.

56. Utley, *Cavalier in Buckskin*, 191. An account of the almost forgotten exploits of the Suicide Boys is found in Thackery, "Suicide Boys," in the newsletter of the Friends of the Little Bighorn Battlefield, sent by John Doerner, chief historian of the Little Bighorn Battlefield National Monument, after a telephone interview with him on April 19, 2006.

57. Fox, *Archaeology, History*, 32, 77–79, 218–19. The archaeological discoveries of Fox and Scott, however, did more than challenge the standard interpretations of this bloody fray. In their perusal of the metallic and human remains of the Seventh Cavalry's luckless troopers, they discovered that the Indians carried twenty-nine different types of firearms, including Henry and Winchester repeating rifles, along with a number of older trade muskets. The troopers, on the other hand, carried only Springfield single-shot breechloading carbines, which were more accurate for distance firing but provided little advantage against those Lakota and Cheyenne warriors who were able to creep up on them for close combat. See also the discussion on firepower at the Little Bighorn in Baird, "Into the Valley," 93–96.

58. Willis Rowland, box 106, notebook 52, Campbell Collection.

59. White Bull, box 105, notebook 4, p. 38, Campbell Collection. Also quoted in Michno, "Revision at the Little Bighorn," 24.

60. Vestal, *New Sources of Indian History*, 180–82.

61. McLaughlin, who hated Sitting Bull, believed that Gall was the "chief architect" of the victory his people had won at the Little Bighorn. He even persuaded the Hunkpapa war leader to participate in the ten-year anniversary reunion of the battle in 1886. Mangum, "Gall," 35. See also Burdick's *David F. Barry's Indian Notes* (1937), 9–17. Barry was one of the participants in the 1886 reunion.

62. White Bull's outstanding feats at the battle have been carefully chronicled in Utley, *The Lance and the Shield*, 155–59. Despite the prominence Rain-in-the-Face gained from Longfellow's poem, it is difficult to know whether this maverick warrior belongs in this shortened list of war heroes. He certainly did not kill Custer and cut his heart out at the battle as Longfellow claimed. Burdick, *David F. Barry's Indian Notes* (1937), 31. One historian claims that Rain-in-the-Face was hunting buffalo with a warrior named Kills Eagle at the time of the battle, while Gall barely arrived on time to participate in the Seventh Cavalry's doomed fight on Custer Hill. Milligan, *Dakota Twilight*, 71.

63. As quoted in Innis, *Bloody Knife*, 160, from frontiersman Joseph Henry Taylor's *Frontier and Indian Life and Kaleidoscopic Lives*, 297.

64. Utley, *Cavalier in Buckskin*, 192.

CHAPTER 9. THE ZEALOUS PURSUIT

1. Utley, *The Lance and the Shield*, 165.

2. As Sitting Bull's nephew White Bull put it, the seasoned warrior and medicine man had been an akicita for "two terms." White Bull, box 105, notebook 8, Campbell Collection.

3. Utley, *The Lance and the Shield*, 165–66. Crook and Terry did not work well together. In fact, just before the Battle of the Little Bighorn, Crook made no effort to communicate with Terry, leaving Terry to presume that Crook's men were on their way northward as the third force in Sheridan's three-pronged attack. Thus, Crook inadvertently contributed to the setback at the Little Bighorn. Robinson, *General Crook and the Western Frontier*. 165.

4. Utley, *The Lance and the Shield*, 166. The continual rain during the past several days had tightened the now swollen leather lacings of the elk hide tipis to such an extent that the Indians had to cut their way out to escape, according to C. M. Robinson, *A Good Year to Die*, 248.

5. American Horse and He Dog biographies, Waggoner Papers. Although one of Crook's officers heard his commander tell Captain Mills to avoid any Indian fight if possible, Mills insisted that, as he departed toward the Black Hills for provisions, General Crook gave him verbal orders to attack any Indian village he encountered. Greene, *Slim Buttes, 1876*, 48. According to Mills's own words in an article published later, "Crook had told me to pitch into anything I found on my route that I could handle." Clements and Mills, "The Starvation March," 112.

6. C. M. Robinson, *A Good Year to Die*, 246, 252, 253; Schmitt, ed., *General George Crook*, 206, 208. American Horse, better known as Iron Plume, was shot through his intestines and died without complaint after much pain.

7. Larson, *Red Cloud*, 205–07.

8. Ibid., 205, 207–09. The seizure of the Lakota ponies caused a greater commotion among the Oglalas than the replacement of Red Cloud as their main chief. Red Cloud was soon restored to his leadership position, and Spotted Tail, to his credit, never tried to assume it. But the legal struggle to be compensated for the horses that Mackenzie had seized went on for seven decades. In the late 1880s, for instance, the Indian position was recognized when the U.S. Congress appropriated $28,200 to recompense the affected Oglalas for their losses. For a list of the claimants, see Office of Indian Affairs, "Pony Claims of Red Cloud."

9. Greene, *Battles and Skirmishes*, 116.

10. C. M. Robinson, *A Good Year to Die*, 272; Greene, *Yellowstone Command*, 83.

11. C. M. Robinson, *A Good Year to Die*, 272–73; Gall's biography, Waggoner Papers.

12. C. M. Robinson, *A Good Year to Die*, 274. Bear's Face, or Bear Face, as some called him, claimed that he was accompanied by two peace emissaries. One was Crow Feather, not Long Feather, and the other was Charging Thunder. Bear's Face's biography, Waggoner Papers.

13. Greene, *Yellowstone Command*, 92–94. Both Greene and Hedren stress the importance of Sitting Bull's meeting with Miles, who was acting as the chief representative of the federal government. See also Hedren's *Traveler's Guide*, 90.

14. Utley, *The Lance and the Shield*, 168, 177–78. John Bruguier was tried because he had intervened in a fight in which his brother was allegedly being choked to death by a much larger man. Bruguier had picked up a poker and fatally struck his brother's assailant on the head. His work as a translator at Sitting Bull's conference with Colonel Miles did pay off. Miles appeared as a character witness in behalf of Bruguier at Bruguier's murder trial in December 1879. Bruguier was acquitted. Bruguier began serving as a scout and interpreter for Colonel Miles several weeks after the Miles–Sitting Bull conference. John Bruguier's biography,

Waggoner Papers. Lazy White Bull gave a concise but insightful account of the dialogue between Sitting Bull and Miles to Walter M. Camp on July 23, 1910. See Long Feather et al., "The Cedar Creek Councils and the Battle of Cedar Creek" in Greene, *Lakota and Cheyenne*, 112.

15. Utley, *The Lance and the Shield*, 171–72.

16. Greene, *Yellowstone Command*, 99.

17. Bear's Face's biography, Waggoner Papers. For the army's view of these two conferences, see Pope, "The Battle of Cedar Creek," 134–39.

18. Utley, *The Lance and the Shield*, 172; Greene, *Yellowstone Command*, 100–101.

19. Hedren, *Traveler's Guide*, 91.

20. Ibid.

21. Greene, *Yellowstone Command*, 106–09.

22. Ibid., 111–12; Utley, *The Lance and the Shield*, 173, 176–77, 178. For more information about Gall's role in the Red Water area, see Gall's biography, Waggoner Papers.

23. For a good account of Mackenzie's attack on this Cheyenne village, see C. M. Robinson, *A Good Year to Die*, 288–303.

24. Gall specifically mentioned Baldwin's aggressive pursuit of his and Sitting Bull's bands at this time. Gall's biography, Waggoner Papers.

25. Hedren, *Traveler's Guide*, 94–96; Utley, *The Lance and the Shield*, 178–79; Gall's biography, Waggoner Papers. For Baldwin's account of the encounters at Bark Creek and at Ash Creek, see Baldwin, "The Fights at Bark Creek and Ash Creek."

26. Utley, *The Lance and the Shield*, 179.

27. According to Captain Edmund Butler of Miles's Fifth Infantry, the Indians were primarily armed with Winchesters, but they did fire a number of Sharps rifles on that day. Ammunition was not a problem. "For people who were supposed to be short of ammunition, they used it rather lavishly." Tilton and Butler, "The Wolf Mountains Expedition," 201.

28. Hedren, *Traveler's Guide*, 97–98.

29. Olson, *Red Cloud and the Sioux Problem*, 235–39.

30. Lame Deer had almost killed Miles during the army's attack on his encampment on the Muddy River, one of the tributaries of the Rosebud. Lame Deer and Iron Star, the other headman of the camp, were in the process of laying down their arms when one of Miles's civilian scouts opened fire at them. A startled Lame Deer stepped back about five yards and deliberately fired at Miles, but his bullet killed a private standing near the colonel instead. As Sergeant John L. McBlain put it, "How the bullet missed the one it was fired at is one of those mysterious things that happen in all battles." McBlain, "The Lame Deer Fight," 209.

31. Robert Higheagle, an astute Hunkpapa observer, claimed that his people called the Queen of England grandmother, the president of the United States grandfather, and the agents at Standing Rock father. Higheagle manuscript, box 104, folder 22, Campbell Collection.

32. Utley, *The Lance and the Shield*, 181–82.

33. Spotted Tail's biography, Waggoner Papers.

34. Inkpaduta's biography, Waggoner Papers.

CHAPTER 10. THE CANADIAN EXILE

1. Buffalo were particularly plentiful in the Cypress Hills, but there were signs of decline in Canada's buffalo population, causing concern among such Canadian tribes as the Blackfeet, who would later blame the Lakotas for the animal's gradual demise in the grasslands of Saskatchewan. B. Wishart, "Grandmother's Land," pt. 1, 19.

2. Robert M. Utley compared Major Walsh to Custer in terms of his self-confidence and courage. See Utley's *The Lance and the Shield*, 186.

3. Ibid., 181, 183–85, n 370; B. Wishart, "Grandmother's Land," pt. 1, 18–20.

4. Relations would not always be smooth between Sitting Bull and Major Walsh. In summer 1879, Sitting Bull, Four Horns, and Black Moon visited Walsh with a large group of Indians to demand more provisions as times were becoming increasingly difficult. Walsh did not like their tone of voice and exploded with anger. An insulted Sitting Bull reached for his gun, inciting Walsh to throw him out the door. Fortunately, Sitting Bull's companions intervened to prevent a truly violent scene from occurring. The two men did, however, reconcile shortly thereafter. B. Wishart, "Grandmother's Land," pt. 3, 24.

5. B. Wishart, "Grandmother's Land," pt. 2, 27; Utley, *The Lance and the Shield*, 185–86.

6. Utley, *The Lance and the Shield*, 200.

7. Crazy Horse was killed by soldiers as he resisted an effort to incarcerate him in the guardhouse at Camp Robinson, near Nebraska's Red Cloud Agency. He received more than one bayonet wound, the mortal one probably being administered by Private William Gentiles. Crazy Horse did draw a knife to resist imprisonment, but Little Big Man grabbed him by the arms so he could not defend himself. Little Big Man claimed he was just trying to restore order, but one Indian observer, Turning Bear, insisted that Little Big Man had urged Crazy Horse to resist as a matter of pride: "Crazy Horse, do not disgrace yourself by entering a prison." Quotation from Turning Bear's undated biography in the Waggoner Papers. For informative accounts of Crazy Horse's arrest and death, see Bray, *Crazy Horse*, 374–90; Hedren, *Fort Laramie in 1876*, 231–32; and Buecker, *Fort Robinson*, 111–18. Historian Stephen E. Ambrose believed that a jealous Red Cloud was the master manipulator whose efforts to discredit Crazy Horse led to the independent-minded warrior's arrest and death. See Ambrose, *Crazy Horse and Custer*, 427.

8. Larson, *Red Cloud*, 220–21.

9. Utley, *The Lance and the Shield*, 200.

10. Ibid., 201–04. For a detailed analysis of the diplomatic maneuvering of the British and American governments over the Lakota migration to Saskatchewan, see Joyner, "The Hegira of Sitting Bull," 6–18.

11. As quoted in B. Wishart, "Grandmother's Land," pt. 2, 32. Eastern newspapers remained critical of Sitting Bull's hardline position at the Terry conference for weeks, some of them regarding him as an insulting and probably unwelcomed Canadian guest. See *New York Times*, December 14, 1877.

12. Although the Lakotas sympathized with the Nez Percés, Sitting Bull did not want to get actively involved in their plight for fear of compromising the precarious position of his own people with their Canadian hosts. "This is your fight not mine," he allegedly informed a hopeful Nez Percé courier. Joyner, "The Hegira of Sitting Bull," 12.

13. Utley, *The Lance and the Shield*, 193.

14. One Bull, box 105, folder 15, Campbell Collection.

15. One Bull, whom Sitting Bull was obviously grooming for a leadership role in the Lakotas' new Canadian home, was placed at the head of a one-hundred-man policing unit to keep order and enforce tribal law. Barrett, "One Bull," 9.

16. Gray Eagle's biography, Waggoner Papers; Utley, *The Lance and the Shield*, 211–12. One Bull's account of the Gray Eagle incident differs from Gray Eagle's. One Bull claims that Gray Eagle's steed was actually a "gentle horse" and that Lakota Indians, as well as Canadian Mounted Police, were part of the "crowd" allowed to shoot over his head. One Bull, box 105, folder 16, Campbell Collection.

17. Utley, *The Lance and the Shield*, 201–02; Joyner, "The Hegira of Sitting Bull," 8.

18. Journalists, such as John Stillson of the *New York Herald* and Charles Diehl of the *Chicago Times*, who encountered Sitting Bull at the Terry Commission meetings, and John S. Finerty, also of the *Chicago Times*, created word pictures of Sitting Bull that featured his powerful role among the nontreaty bands in Canada and gave the old leader realistic dimensions the public could understand. Utley, *The Lance and the Shield*, 194, 197, 210; Manzione, *"I Am Looking to the North,"* 136–37.

19. Utley, *The Lance and the Shield*, 203–04.

20. Manzione, *"I Am Looking to the North,"* 142–43.

21. B. Wishart, who insisted that Gall kept a very low profile in Canada, also denied that Gall and Sitting Bull ever had a serious quarrel or falling out in Canada. See "Grandmother's Land," pt. 4, 29.

22. Utley, *The Lance and the Shield*, 208–09.

23. Long Dog regaled almost everyone in Miles's camp with his humor and his colorful language. In summing up Miles's successful use of artillery at the Milk River encounter, he simply said: "Heap shoot! Bad Medicine! God damn." Ibid., 209.

24. Manzione, *"I Am Looking to the North,"* 142.

25. Utley, *The Lance and the Shield*, 214. The Canadian prime minister, John A. McDonald, refused to permit Walsh to take Sitting Bull's case to President Hayes, remaining convinced that starvation would eventually force the Lakotas to return to the United States.

26. Walsh also tried to weaken Sitting Bull's central leadership by dealing with lesser chiefs individually, but not in the sometimes brutal manner employed by Crozier. B. Wishart, "Grandmother's Land," pt. 4, 28–29.

27. Utley, *The Lance and the Shield*, 216; Manzione, *"I Am Looking to the North,"* 141. About the same time that White Eagle, Rain-in-the-Face, and Big Road were considering surrender, there was a big council of prominent Lakota leaders in which White Eagle and Big Road expressed a desire to return to the United States. Supporting their position were such war chiefs as Gall, Crow King, No Neck, Running Horse, Fool Bull, Turning Bear, He Dog, and Fools Heart. The council, according to One Bull, had been approved and permitted by Sitting Bull. One Bull, box 104, folder 11, Campbell Collection.

28. The difficult winter of 1880–1881 probably did more to break down Sitting Bull's intransigence regarding surrender than did any of the diplomatic pressures applied by governmental authorities in Ottawa, London, and Washington. Joyner, "The Hegira of Sitting Bull," 16.

29. As early as 1878, Gall and about forty of his band attempted to reach the Powder River country to hunt because game was already becoming scarce in Canada. He was, however, forced back over the border by blue-coated troopers under Captain William P. Clarke. Gall's biography, Waggoner Papers.

30. Allison, *The Surrender of Sitting Bull*, 9–10. Although Allison claimed in his published account that he and his companions were driving their herd to Bismarck, in background information for an autobiography he was preparing to write, he identified Fort Buford as the cattle drive's destination. See Edwin H. Allison autobiography. See also Manzione, *"I Am Looking to the North,"* 142.

31. Allison, *The Surrender of Sitting Bull*, 13, 14, 22–26.

32. Ibid., 36. Although Allison in his published work on Sitting Bull's surrender claimed he had insisted that Gall send twenty lodges to Fort Buford, he maintained in his proposed autobiography that only eighteen of Gall's followers actually became involved; they were sent to the fort as "voluntary prisoners." See background information for Edwin H. Allison auto-

biography. Mangum, in his article on Gall, claims that Allison wanted the Lakota war chief to send twenty lodges "of mostly women and children." Mangum used another source provided by Allison in the *South Dakota Historical Collection*. Mangum, "Gall," 34, n. 42.

33. Allison, *The Surrender of Sitting Bull*, 56. During the last dreary days of the Lakota exile in Canada, there was a growing defiance of Sitting Bull's leadership. Another Lakota war chief, Crow, or Patriarch Crow as Allison called him, angrily compelled Sitting Bull to move his lodge to a small clearing in the timber a few hundred yards from the main camp. Only forty-three families joined Sitting Bull in this clearing, while three hundred remained with Crow. The aging chief, once the supreme leader of all the nontreaty bands, was ultimately forced to leave the camp with his still loyal followers. See Manzione, *"I Am Looking to the North,"* 146–49. This alleged incident has become part of the historical tradition at Fort Buford, where both Gall and Sitting Bull eventually surrendered. Stalnaker interview, May 31, 2001.

34. Vestal, *New Sources of Indian History*, 248. Bruce Wishart regards the alleged quarrel between Gall and Sitting Bull as a myth concocted by Allison. According to Campbell, Allison was called "Fish" because he was a "slippery customer" and a liar. See B. Wishart, "Grandmother's Land," pt. 4, 29.

35. Utley, *The Lance and the Shield*, 217, 379n.

36. Allison, *The Surrender of Sitting Bull*, 53–55, 84.

37. Mangum, "Gall," 34; Manzione, *"I Am Looking to the North,"* 145. Mangum estimates that two-thirds of the Lakota exiles left for Canada, while Manzione estimates that "roughly half" of them did.

38. For detailed information about these Canadian authorities, see Utley, *The Lance and the Shield*, 188–89, 215–16, 217, 221–23, 227–28, 231–32, and Joyner, "The Hegira of Sitting Bull," 16.

39. Adjutant General's Office, Fort Buford Post Returns, July 1881.

40. Utley, *The Lance and the Shield*, 226–32. When Sitting Bull arrived he was as poor as any of his followers. Just to survive, he had to sell nearly everything he owned, including his horses. Higheagle manuscript, p. 53, box 104, folder 22, Campbell Collection. Part of Sitting Bull's poverty was due to the unusual generosity he showed his people, a trait regarded as one of the four cardinal virtues of the Lakotas.

41. One Bull, who was with Sitting Bull at the time of his surrender, insists that Sitting Bull did not hand his rifle over to his son, nor did he ever claim to be the last Lakota to give up his gun. According to One Bull, Sitting Bull said absolutely nothing during the surrender ceremony. Barrett, "One Bull," 9–10. A good account of the popular version of Sitting Bull's meeting with Brotherton, involving Sitting Bull's son and the surrender of his rifle, is in Ewers, "When Sitting Bull Surrendered his Winchester."

42. The fort was located on the west side of the Missouri River, almost eight miles above the border between North Dakota and South Dakota. Fiske Papers, State Historical Society of North Dakota, Bismarck.

43. Utley, *The Lance and the Shield*, 227.

CHAPTER 11. STANDING ROCK

1. McLaughlin, *My Friend the Indian*, 35.

2. Pfaller, *James McLaughlin*, 76.

3. Office of Indian Affairs, Record of Rations Issued 1885, Standing Rock Agency.

4. Items listed in ibid.

5. Vestal, *New Sources of Indian History*, 287, 289.

6. Pfaller, *James McLaughlin*, 3; Vestal, *New Sources of Indian History*, 244.

7. Larson, *Red Cloud*, 137–69, 298–304, passim. Office of Indian Affairs, *Report of the Special Commissioner*.

8. Olson, *Red Cloud and the Sioux Problem*, 217–48. For the terms of the Black Hills agreement, see U.S. Congress, *An Act to Ratify an Agreement with Certain Bands*. For the signatures of the headmen and chiefs who gave their approval, such as Red Cloud, Running Antelope, and Bear's Rib, see 257–64.

9. Pfaller, *James McLaughlin*, 3–4, 194.

10. Utley, *The Indian Frontier*, 206. McLaughlin's Catholicism at a time when the country was so strongly Protestant did not help him in his efforts to seek promotion. Because of his effectiveness as an Indian agent, he might have even become commissioner of Indian Affairs if he had not been a Catholic. See Barrett, *"Into the Light,"* 4.

11. From the proceedings of the fifth annual meeting of the 1887 Lake Mohonk Conference, as quoted in Utley, *The Indian Frontier*, 215.

12. Ibid., 203–07, 209; Prucha, *American Indian Policy in Crisis*, 138–43.

13. Behrens, "In Defense of 'Poor Lo,'" 165; Larson, *Red Cloud*, 240–41.

14. As quoted in Barrett, *Major McLaughlin's March*, 30.

15. Larson, *Red Cloud*, 225.

16. Pfaller, *James McLaughlin*, 76–77.

17. Excerpt from McLaughlin's September 5, 1882, annual report to the commissioner of Indian Affairs, as cited in Vestal, *New Sources of Indian History*, 291.

18. Correspondence approving of McLaughlin's appointments of Gall to assistant farmer and to district farmer from the commissioner of Indian Affairs on May 15 and September 4, 1883, Office of Indian Affairs, Appointment Approval Letters..

19. Gall's appointment-approval letters for district farmer from 1884 through 1889 and his February 13, 1889, appointment as a judge on the court of Indian offenses, along with his February 13, 1889, resignation as district farmer, Office of Indian Affairs, Appointment Approval Letters.

20. Appointment approval letters for 1890 through 1893 and Gall's December discharge, along with those of other district farmers, approved by the Office of Indian Affairs on May 4, 1893, Office of Indian Affairs, Appointment Approval Letters.

21. One scholar, in writing about a Northern Ute cultural broker named William Wash, contends that some academics have persisted in perpetuating the traditional and progressive dichotomy to "generalize about the social, economic, and political nature of reservation factionalism." The weakness in using this dichotomy becomes apparent, in his opinion, in the attempts to categorize individuals [possibly like Gall], particularly "the intermediators, the middlemen, and the culture brokers . . . who operate on the cultural margins." Lewis, "Reservation Leadership," 125–26. Historians have been slower than anthropologists in dealing with contemporary Indian affairs that better reflect the generations of intercultural contacts since the close of the western frontier. For varied testimony from several prominent scholars regarding the successes of culture brokers from the colonial period to the modern period, see Szasz, *Between Indian and White Worlds*, 1–20 and passim.

22. Running Antelope's appointment approval letters from 1883 to 1888, Office of Indian Affairs, Appointment Approval Letters. See also Utley, *The Lance and the Shield*, 238–39, 251.

23. John Grass's biography, Waggoner Papers; Vestal, *Sitting Bull*, 274, 309, 312.

24. Grass's brother-in-law liked to tease him about his bald spot, once facetiously urging him to cut what remained of his hair and proudly polish his bald pate like those congressmen and senators in Washington do. Vestal, *New Sources of Indian History*, 341.

25. As quoted in White Bull, box 105, notebook 7, Campbell Collection.

26. Appointment approval letters from 1887 to 1889 and Grass's February 13, 1889, appointment as judge on the court of Indian offenses along with his February 13, 1889, resignation as district farmer, Office of Indian Affairs, Appointment Approval Letters.

27. Vestal, *New Sources of Indian History*, 290–91.

28. John Grass's biography, Waggoner Papers.

29. Pfaller, *James McLaughlin*, 70–71. The hunt in spring 1882 was so important to the Lakotas that it was recorded in the winter count of that year as one of the great events in Lakota history. Because McLaughlin joined the hunt, he is shown riding down a buffalo in that year's traditional Lakota pictograph.

30. Annie Goodreau McLaughlin's "The Last Buffalo Hunt," McLaughlin Papers, as quoted in Frank, "Chief Gall," 112. A detailed account of the buffalo hunt is found on 110–15.

31. Utley, *The Lance and the Shield*, 245–46. Lincoln had earlier supported the idea of keeping Sitting Bull separated from his Hunkpapa brethren. He even wanted to increase the size of the military garrison at Fort Yates for fear of future Indian agitation on the part of the controversial chief. Lincoln to the Secretary of the Interior, September 27, 1881, McLaughlin Papers.

32. Utley, *The Lance and the Shield*, 248–56.

33. Vestal, *New Sources of Indian History*, 290–91.

34. McLaughlin's August 15, 1883, annual report to the commissioner of Indian Affairs as quoted in Utley, *The Lance and the Shield*, 250.

35. McLaughlin, *My Friend the Indian*, 35, 180.

36. Vestal, *New Sources of Indian History*, 288–89.

37. McLaughlin, *My Friend the Indian*, 34.

38. Grass, unlike Gall, was also perceived as being quite an egotist: "Grass doesn't like to come down. He likes to praise himself and stay up[,] whereas Gall is not ashamed to tell of his failures." Higheagle manuscript, box 104, folder 22, 37, Campbell Collection.

39. DeMallie and Parks, *Sioux Indian Religion*, 11.

40. Vestal, *New Sources of Indian History*, 247.

41. Utley, *The Lance and the Shield*, 239. Vestal even claimed that Gall was the "first man to meet and embrace" Sitting Bull when he arrived at Fort Yates. *New Sources of Indian History*, 247.

42. Utley, *The Lance and the Shield*, 251.

43. Vernon Iron Cloud and Theo interview, May 21, 2001; Barrett, *"Into the Light,"* 4; Gall's biography, Waggoner Papers.

44. Sitting Bull's traditional religious beliefs and practices still have adherents at Standing Rock, notwithstanding the number of them who have synchronized their Christian beliefs with their tribal ones. Mentz, Sr., interview, May 21, 2001. For more information about Bishop Marty and Collins, see Utley, *The Lance and the Shield*, 244, 255.

45. Standing Rock Mission Records, vol. A-1; Barrett, *"Into the Light,"* 5; Gall's biography, Waggoner Papers; Frank, "Chief Gall," 134–40.

46. Barrett, *"Into the Light,"* 4–5.

47. Larson, *Red Cloud*, 227–28. Spotted Tail reacted to this affront by pulling his children out of the school, much to the consternation of its founder, Captain Richard Henry Pratt.

48. Prucha, *Americanizing the American Indian*, 201.

49. Deloria, *Custer Died for Your Sins*, 152–53; Barrett, *"Into the Light,"* 9. Training native catechists gave the Episcopal Church an advantage over the Roman Catholic Church in some parts of the Standing Rock Agency where the Catholic Church felt it had a governmental

mandate to proselytize Indians. For more information about the Reverend Deloria, see DeMallie and Parks, *Sioux Indian Religion*, 91, 97–98, passim. For an insightful evaluation of Vine Deloria, Jr., and the controversy he sparked with his book *Custer Died for Your Sins*, see Szasz, *Between Indian and White Worlds*, 12–13.

50. February 13, 1889, appointment approval letter for Gall's judgeship, Office of Indian Affairs, Appointment Approval Letters.

51. Barrett, telephone interview, June 15, 2002.

52. Burdick, *David F. Barry's Indian Notes* (1937), 33; Milligan, *Dakota Twilight*, 125.

53. Barrett, *Major McLaughlin's March*, 8.

54. According to the records, Gall was discharged as a district farmer on December 31, 1892. Because of his good relations with McLaughlin, the choice to leave this position was probably his because there is no evidence of dissatisfaction on McLaughlin's part. See May 4, 1893, appointment and discharge approval letter, Office of Indian Affairs, Appointment Approval Letters.

55. *Washington Post*, October 15, 1888, as cited in Utley, *The Lance and the Shield*, 275.

56. McLaughlin, *My Friend the Indian*, 64–65.

57. Office of Indian Affairs, "Census of Hunkpapa Indians of Standing Rock Agency"; Standing Rock Mission Records, vol. A-1.

58. Barrett, *Major McLaughlin's March*, 9.

59. McLaughlin, *My Friend the Indian*, 62–64.

60. Vernon Iron Cloud and Theo interview, May 21, 2001; Linda Jones interviews, April 26 and May 5, 2005. See also Office of Indian Affairs, "Census of Hunkpapa Indians of Standing Rock Agency"; Frank, "Chief Gall," 208–09. Frank found evidence that Gall had another wife whom he gave to one of Standing Rock's Indian policemen, Bloody Knife. One prominent North Dakota historian, Frank Zahn, compiled a list of Hunkpapa bands in 1887–1888 and counted thirty-nine members in Gall's band. Census schedule, Zahn Collection.

61. Utley, *The Lance and the Shield*, 264–65. A couple of new biographies of Annie Oakley have been published recently. See Riley, *The Life and Legacy of Annie Oakley*, 26, 145–46, 148–49, and Kasper, *Annie Oakley*, 25–28.

62. The single most costly defeat of the U.S. Army in an Indian battle, however, occurred on November 4, 1791, when Major General Arthur St. Clair lost more than six hundred men in a disastrous fight with the Miami chief Little Turtle along the Mississenewa River in northern Indiana.

63. Godfrey, "Custer's Last Battle," *Century Magazine* probably had the biggest impact.

64. Burdick, *David F. Barry's Indian Notes* (1949), 21.

65. McLaughlin, *My Friend the Indian*, 122, 133.

66. Michno, *Lakota Noon*, 305–06.

67. *The Last Battle of the Sioux Nation*, 69.

68. Burdick, *David F. Barry's Indian Notes* (1949), 29.

69. "Three Noted Chiefs of the Sioux."

70. Barrett D. Randall to Mossman, no date, Decimal Correspondence File 053.0.

71. Mossman to Randall, January 21, 1932, ibid.

72. Reid to Mossman, ibid.

73. For an analysis based on the old progressive versus traditional model of factional politics on the Great Sioux Reservation and the involvement of some of the more prominent Indian agents, see Larson, "Lakota Leaders and Government Agents," 47–57.

74. A reproduction of Kicking Bear's pictographic version of the Little Bighorn is found in Josephy, *Book of Indians*, 368–69.

CHAPTER 12. THE SIOUX BILLS

1. Larson, *Red Cloud*, 88.

2. Ibid., 236–38; U.S. Congress, Senate, *Letter from the Secretary of the Interior, Transmitting, in Compliance with the Resolution of the Senate of December 6, 1883*. Hereafter cited as the Edmunds Report. Utley, *The Lance and the Shield*, 234–35.

3. Utley, *The Lance and the Shield*, 257; Frank, "Chief Gall," 119–26, especially 121–22; Barrett, *"Into the Light,"* 4.

4. Edmunds Report, 39. When a special commission headed by Captain Richard Henry Pratt arrived at Standing Rock in 1888 to persuade the Indians to support the implementation of the Dawes Act in the Sioux bill of 1888, one of the commission members, Judge John V. Wright, reminded Grass, Gall, Mad Bear, and Big Head that they had supported the plans of the 1882 Edmunds Commission, along with one hundred and thirty-eight other Indians. See Office of Indian Affairs, Minutes of the Sioux Commission of 1888.

5. McLaughlin to Agent J. A. Stephen of the Standing Rock Agency, October 31, 1878; Lieutenant Colonel W. P. Carlin to Standing Rock's Indian agent, May 21, 1879, Office of Indian Affairs, Miscellaneous Correspondence Received (1864–1910), 1878–79 folder. Indictment for murder against Brave Bear signed by A. J. Edgerton of the Second Judicial District and also chief justice of the Territorial Supreme Court; Chief Justice Edgerton to the members of the Second Judicial District, affirming the proposed execution of Brave Bear on May 18, 1882, and a writ of error to the Second Judicial District, May, 1882; Edgerton to U.S. Marshal Harrison Allen, acting in behalf of President Chester A. Arthur, June 12, 1882; Governor of Dakota Territory to U.S. Marshal Allen, September 12, 1882; U.S. Marshal Allen to Chief Justice Edgerton, informing him of Brave Bear's execution, November 15, 1882. U.S. District Courts for the Territory of Dakota. Case 101, Appellate Case Files (1867–1886). See also Pfaller, "Brave Bear Murder Case," 121–36. Interestingly enough, one of the key figures in the eventual apprehension of Brave Bear was Edward H. "Fish" Allison, the man who talked Gall into surrendering in 1880. See especially 130–33, 136.

6. Grass once characterized the pressures put on him and his tribal colleagues by Edmunds and the other commissioners as follows: "Those men fairly made my head dizzy, and my signing it was an accident." At the August hearing, Sitting Bull, who had just been transferred to Standing Rock from Fort Randall, provoked the ire of Illinois Senator John A. Logan, who chastised him in a most disrespectful manner. For the heated dialogue between Sitting Bull and Senator Logan, see U.S. Congress, Senate, *Dawes Report*, 79–81. See also Utley, *The Lance and the Shield*, 257–59.

7. Utley, *The Indian Frontier*, 213–15. For a copy of the Dawes Act, see Washburn, *The Assault on Indian Tribalism*, 68, 73. See also Larson, *Red Cloud*, 252.

8. Behrens, *"In Defense of 'Poor Lo,'"* 161.

9. Prucha, *American Indian Policy in Crisis*, 248–57; Larson, *Red Cloud*, 252.

10. For a comprehensive view of the political developments in Dakota Territory at this time, see Lamar, *Dakota Territory*.

11. Utley, *Last Days of the Sioux*, 44–45.

12. Captain Pratt strongly reiterated this rationale for the committee's decision to start at Standing Rock with an appeal to the pride of this agency's Indians. "This is one reason why we came here first. And another was because you stand well in Washington, and your Agent stands very high there." Office of Indian Affairs, Minutes of the Sioux Commission of 1888, 257.

13. Ibid., 2; *Bismarck Weekly Tribune*, July 24, 1888.

14. Office of Indian Affairs, Minutes of the Sioux Commission of 1888, 2. Running Antelope, who was sixty-eight years old at the time, had done many things to please McLaughlin. He founded the village of Little Eagle in 1884, where the Congregationalists had built a church one year later. He became a devout Christian who went out of his way to be cooperative. Running Antelope's biography, Waggoner Papers. For a copy of Vilas's letter to McLaughlin, see U.S. Congress, Senate, *Letter from the Secretary of the Interior, Transmitting, In Response to Senate Resolution of December 13, 1888*, 34, hereafter cited as Pratt Report.

15. Office of Indian Affairs, Minutes of the Sioux Commission of 1888, 197, 201–02. Gall and other Indian leaders were emboldened by letters Red Cloud sent to the commission expressing his determination to oppose the 1888 Sioux bill not only at Pine Ridge but at other agencies as well. *Bismarck Weekly Tribune*, July 25, 1888.

16. Office of Indian Affairs, Minutes of the Sioux Commission of 1888, 257; Utley, *Last Days of the Sioux*, 46.

17. Office of Indian Affairs, Minutes of the Sioux Commission of 1888, 202, 258.

18. Ibid., 258–59; Utley, *The Lance and the Shield*, 274; Utley, *Last Days of the Sioux*, 46–47. For a full discussion of Gall's sometimes heated exchange with the Pratt Commission, see Pratt Report, 266–68. Rumors were rife during the Pratt Commission's visit to Standing Rock. One Dakota newspaper reported rumors that both Sitting Bull and White Bull had agreed to the 1888 Sioux bill. As it turned out, the journal was only half right. *The Daily Argus* (Fargo), August 23, 1888.

19. Two good studies on Indian visits to Washington are Turner, *Red Man Calling* and Viola, *Diplomats in Buckskin*.

20. Larson, *Red Cloud*, 254–55. Because Red Cloud had been recognized as the Lakotas' major spokesman for twenty years, his omission was particularly significant.

21. Utley, *The Lance and the Shield*, 274–77; Utley, *The Last Days of the Sioux Nation*, 49–54.

22. The Springer Omnibus bill was sponsored by Congressman William M. Springer of Illinois, chairman of the House Committee on Territories. Springer, a Democrat, wanted New Mexico included in the bill because it was the only one with Democratic voting tendencies. Under the original Springer bill, Dakota Territory would have been only one state. See Larson, *New Mexico's Quest for Statehood*, 147–48. For a comprehensive account of the final days of the statehood movements in Dakota Territory, see Lamar, *Dakota Territory*, 244–72.

23. Utley, *Last Days of the Sioux*, 48–49.

24. Larson, *Red Cloud*, 257–59. Chapter 16 of Olson's study of Red Cloud has an especially detailed account of the ratification fights over both Sioux bills. Olson, *Red Cloud and the Sioux Problem*. See also *Bismarck Weekly Tribune*, June 21 and July 26, 1889.

25. McLaughlin, *My Friend the Indian*, 284–85. The abrupt turnabout of the Standing Rock leaders on the 1889 Sioux bill must have been particularly difficult for John Grass because he had posed to the Crook Commission some of the toughest and most potentially embarrassing questions about the contents of this controversial measure. See *Bismarck Weekly Tribune*, August 2, 1889.

26. U.S. Congress, Senate, *Message from the President of the United States*, 297, 302, hereafter cited as Crook Report.

27. Ibid., 285–87. McLaughlin set up the voting so that after the rolls were signed, the qualified adult male Indians could walk through the back door of a warehouse near the poll site and exit that building from the front. The Lower Yanktonai semicircle formed around the speaker's platform near the back door of the warehouse.

28. Sitting Bull quoted in Barrett, *Major McLaughlin's March*, 26; Greene, "The Sioux Land Commission," 62–63. See also *The Daily Argus* (Fargo), August 6, 1889.

29. McLaughlin, *My Friend the Indian*, 287–88; Utley, *The Lance and the Shield*, 279. For an overall view of the thirty-nine provisions of the Sioux Act of 1889, see U.S. Congress, *Act of Mar. 2, 1889*, 888–99.

30. McLaughlin, *My Friend the Indian*, 288. McLaughlin, of course, did not regard his selection of Gall, Grass, and the others to this new delegation as being part of a payoff.

31. Utley, *Last Days of the Sioux*, 55–58.

CHAPTER 13. THE DEATH OF SITTING BULL

1. Hyde, *A Sioux Chronicle*, 239–42; Utley, *The Lance and the Shield*, 64–67, 69–71. Raymond J. DeMallie compares the Ghost Dance with existing Lakota beliefs and practices to show that there were points of harmony between Wovoka's new faith and the religion of the Sioux. "The Lakota Ghost Dance," 385–405.

2. Larson, *Red Cloud*, 265–67. Kicking Bear and Short Bull, both members of Crazy Horse's militant camp during the Great Sioux War, became fanatical believers in the Ghost Dance movement. They started these controversial dances at Pine Ridge, but later Kicking Bear went to the Cheyenne River Reservation and Short Bull to the Rosebud, where he enjoyed more success than Kicking Bear. Hyde, *A Sioux Chronicle*, 241–42.

3. Pine Ridge clerk Robert O. Pugh's interview by Eli S. Ricker, August 21, 1907, Ricker Collection; Utley, *Last Days of the Sioux*, 102–03, 110–11; Jensen, Paul, and Carter, *Eyewitness at Wounded Knee*, 12.

4. Larson, *Red Cloud*, 271–72. For more information about Red Cloud's ambivalent attitude toward the Ghost Dance, see Mooney, *The Ghost Dance Religion and the Sioux Outbreak of 1890*, 183, 210, 214.

5. For a time Grass, along with Gall, identified with the Episcopalians, but he was never entirely happy with that church. Grass was eventually converted by Father Strassmaier of the Benedictine order sometime after the priest came to Dakota Territory in December 1866. Upon his death, Grass was buried in a Catholic cemetery. Frank, "Chief Gall," 209–10; Vestal, *New Sources of Indian History*, 72–73; Utley, *The Lance and the Shield*, 269, 291–9.

6. Higheagle manuscript, box 104, folder 22, p. 51, Campbell Collection.

7. Utley, *The Lance and the Shield*, 283–84; Utley, *Last Days of the Sioux*, 97–98; Vestal, *New Sources of Indian History*, 341.

8. Vestal's *New Sources of Indian History*, 43–44.

9. Carignan to McLaughlin, December 14, 1890, Office of Indian Affairs, *Report by James McLaughlin*. Carignan reported on another occasion that two hundred men and their families were dancing daily and that only three of his ninety students showed up for classes while the Ghost Dance was in progress. Hoover, "Sitting Bull," 167–68. See also Utley, *Last Days of the Sioux*, 152–53.

10. Campbell had to admit that McLaughlin, whom he often criticized, was an efficient and honest agent, much respected by his peers. His competence eventually resulted in his promotion to the job of U.S. inspector of the Indian Office. Vestal, *New Sources of Indian History*, 287–88.

11. Utley, *Last Days of the Sioux*, 152–53.

12. See Office of Indian Affairs, "Census of Hunkpapa Indians of Standing Rock Agency." The size of Gall's band varied just as those of the other chiefs and headmen did. It could have

increased in numbers, but this is doubtful with the difficult economic conditions at Standing Rock and the prevalence of epidemics at this time.

13. Gall's biography, Waggoner Papers; Vestal, *New Sources of Indian History*, 56–57; Utley, *Last Days of the Sioux*, 151.

14. December 15, 1890, letter to McLaughlin from Gall and John Grass as reprinted in Vestal, *New Sources of Indian History*, 56.

15. Utley, *Last Days of the Sioux*, 123–30, 148–50. McLaughlin's daughter-in-law added three chapters on Sitting Bull's controversial arrest to her deceased father-in-law's book, *My Friend the Indian*, in 1931, twenty-one years after the book's first edition. These chapters tended to praise the role of the Indian police while denigrating Sitting Bull's. See McLaughlin, *My Friend the Indian or Three Heretofore Unpublished Chapters*, 5–30. A good account of the importance and effectiveness of the Indian police at this time is Hagan, *Indian Police and Judges*, 154–68.

16. Shoots Walking, box 104, folder 5, Campbell Collection.

17. For McLaughlin's account of Sitting Bull's death, see Office of Indian Affairs, *Report by James McLaughlin*. See also the three new chapters added to McLaughlin, *My Friend the Indian,* in his book's 1931 edition regarding McLaughlin's version of Sitting Bull's death, particularly chapter thirteen, 5–15. See also Red Tomahawk's biography, Waggoner Papers.

18. Captain Fechet's description of the aftermath of this bloody affair is found in Utley, *Last Days of the Sioux*, 158–62.

19. Ibid., 167–169. Josephine Waggoner claimed that her husband, a soldier from the Twelfth Infantry and a carpenter by trade, was ordered to make Sitting Bull's coffin. She also claimed that Sitting Bull, on McLaughlin's orders, had stopped attending the Ghost Dance gatherings before his attempted arrest. Sitting Bull's biography, Waggoner Papers. According to an October 21, 1932, letter to Frank Bennett Fiske from Edward Forte, one-time first sergeant from Troop D, Seventh Cavalry, it was Forte who built Sitting Bull's coffin. Fiske, as a seven-year-old boy living at Fort Yates, was an eyewitness to some of the events surrounding Sitting Bull's death. See his *Life and Death of Sitting Bull*, 52–57. For McLaughlin's response to the press's allegedly unfair barrage against him, see the 1931 edition of his *My Friend the Indians*, 6, 12–13.

20. See December 1 telegram and Belt's December 5 telegram, along with McLaughlin's December 16 report to commissioner of Indian Affairs Thomas J. Morgan in Office of Indian Affairs, *Report of James McLaughlin*.

21. Jacobson, "Life in an Indian Village," 68–69.

22. Utley, *Last Days of the Sioux*, 169–73; Spotted Elk (Big Foot) biography, Waggoner Papers.

23. Big Foot band member Joseph Horncloud's interview by Eli S. Ricker, October 23, 1906, Ricker Collection. See Danker, "The Wounded Knee Interviews," 151–243, for a good overview of Big Foot's misunderstood migration and its tragic outcome. See also Larson, *Red Cloud*, 276–77.

24. For good account of the battle, see Utley, *Last Days of the Sioux*, 200–230; Hyde, *A Sioux Chronicle*, 294–303; Coleman, *Voices of Wounded Knee*, 279–310.

25. Utley, *The Indian Frontier*, 257. The number of Indian casualties has been in dispute from the very beginning. Utley's numbers are at variance with other estimates. One source placed Indian deaths at Wounded Knee as high as forty men and two hundred women and children. Powers, *Oglala Religion*, 122. See also W. A. Birdsall's interview by Eli S. Ricker, February 2, 1907, Ricker Collection.

26. Powers, *Oglala Religion*, 122; Coleman, *Voices of Wounded Knee*, 35; Vestal, *New Sources of Indian History*, 27.

27. Vernon Iron Cloud and Theo interview, May 21, 2001.

28. Vestal, *New Sources of Indian History*, 275.

CHAPTER 14. HIS FINAL YEARS

1. Vernon Iron Cloud and Theo interview, May 21, 2001.

2. These are only estimates of Gall's weight. Ethel C. Jacobson's calculation that he weighed almost 300 pounds is probably too high, but there is no question that he became more corpulent the older he got. No longer leading the strenuous life of a nomadic warrior and hunter is no doubt one reason for this obesity. Jacobson, "Life in an Indian Village," 68.

3. Barrett, *"Into the Light,"* 4; Gall's biography, Waggoner Papers.

4. Larson, "Lakota Leaders and Government Agents," 50–53; Larson, *Red Cloud*, 159, 227, 233–34, 238–39, 241, 244, 248–49, 291, 303; Hagan, *Quanah Parker*, 125–33; Steltenkamp, *Black Elk*, 158, 162–63.

5. Vernon Iron Cloud and Theo interview, May 21, 2001.

6. Jacobson, "Life in an Indian Village," 69–70.

7. Gall's biography, Waggoner Papers; Barrett, *"Into the Light,"* 4.

8. Mentz, Sr., interview, May 21, 2001. Gall's great-granddaughter Gladys Hawk, inspired by the writings of Vine Deloria, Jr., was convinced that Gall already knew that God was the Great Creator before Christian clergymen told him. Telephone interview, September 28, 2006.

9. Standing Rock Mission Records, vol. A-1.

10. Gall's biography, Waggoner Papers.

11. Chapman, *Remember the Wind*, 211; Carole Chapman, telephone interview, December 1, 2002. Two of Gall's young daughters, Nancy and Sarah, were very devoted to their ailing father, who had become a more thoughtful and benign person during his last years. It was probably difficult for them to realize how fierce he had once been as a warrior.

12. Burdick, *David F. Barry's Indian Notes* (1937), 35; *Bismarck Weekly Tribune*, December 14, 1894. White Bull's remarks about Gall's death were really quite casual: "1894—No grass winter. Gall died. This year all WB [White Bull] knows is [Gall] got sick and died." White Bull, box 105, notebook 23, Campbell Collection. Reference to Gall's death being caused by heart disease is found in burial records of Standing Rock Mission Records, vol. A-1.

13. Vestal, *New Sources of Indian History*, 224.

14. Ibid., 230.

15. Black Elk, a strongly religious man who had observed the carnage at Wounded Knee and at one time had embraced the Ghost Dance religion, became a Catholic so devout that the Jesuits took him to other tribes, such as the Arapahoes, Omahas, and Winnebago, to preach the Gospel. Another Christian convert from the Oglalas, George Sword, who became an Episcopalian like Gall, claimed that in his wars with white people, he found their "Wakan Tanka the Superior." Thus, he joined the Episcopal Church, became a deacon, and remained a Christian until he died. Steltenkamp, *Black Elk*, 27, 62–63, 96–97, 158–59.

16. Champagne, "Gall," 1059–60.

17. A good example of an Indian war leader focusing on his own exploits is Red Cloud. In recounting his years as a warrior in numerous battles and skirmishes, he tended to concentrate on his own deeds. Paul, *Autobiography of Red Cloud*, 29–187; *Bismarck Daily Tribune*, July 24, 1888.

18. One Bull listed the coups of famous Sioux war leaders as follows: Gall, twenty; Sitting Bull, thirty; and Crazy Horse, forty-eight. Although he implies that they included "both white + Red" opponents, his estimates were probably low. One Bull, box 104, folder 11, Campbell Collection. Utley insisted that Sitting Bull had as many as sixty-three coups, while Red Cloud claimed as many as eighty. These two older leaders earned more coups than Gall because they had much longer careers as warriors. Moreover, when their warrior years started, the major opponents of the Lakotas were enemy tribes, whose style of warfare stressed personal valor as opposed to the group discipline and tactics emphasized by the U.S. Army. Although Sitting Bull's nephew White Bull counted coups when fighting soldiers, one suspects that Gall and many other warriors did not. A good insight into how willing Lakota warriors were to throw their lives into dangerous hand-to-hand combat for the sake of honor was ably provided by John D. McDermott in his paper "The Indian War of 1865."

19. Larson, *Red Cloud*, 45–48.

20. Although Gall's name was spelled "Gaul" in this *Bismarck Tribune* obituary, the error was not indicative of any lack of respect for this Hunkpapa leader. Throughout his life, many journalists and military rivals spelled his name this way.

21. Barry, who not only photographed such famous Indians as Sitting Bull, Red Cloud, Spotted Tail, and Chief Joseph but also such frontiersmen and military officers as Buffalo Bill, Charlie Reynolds, General Nelson A. Miles, General George Crook, and Lieutenant Colonel George Armstrong Custer and his brother Tom, once admitted that the widespread fame of Gall had been a real boon to him. Gall's "face has been a money maker for me." Barry to Albert W. Johnson, May 20, 1929. On his business envelopes he put the names of more than thirty famous people, most of whom had been connected with the epochal struggle of the Lakotas to preserve their way of life. David F. Barry Papers.

22. Mark J. Halvorson, telephone interview, September 20, 2006. For maps and descriptions locating the town of Gall, see map titled "Railroad Commissioners' Map of North Dakota—1914" and the map in the 1917 *Atlas of Morton County, North Dakota*, 58. There is some discrepancy regarding the exact location of the town of Gall between the Morton County atlas and the more recently published Wick, *North Dakota Place Names*, 72. Photocopies of the pertinent maps were supplied to the author by James A. Davis, North Dakota State Archives.

Bibliography

MANUSCRIPT COLLECTIONS

Allison, Edwin H., Autobiography. William L. Clements Library, University of Michigan, Ann Arbor.

Baker Battle Report. Frontier Heritage Alliance, Sheridan, Wyoming.

Barry, D. F., Papers. Small Manuscripts Collection. State Historical Society of North Dakota, Bismarck.

Barry, David F., Papers. Western History/Genealogy Department, Denver Public Library, Denver.

Campbell, Walter S. (Stanley Vestal), Collection. University of Oklahoma Library, Norman.

Electronic Text Center, University of Virginia Library, Charlottesville.

Fiske, Frank B., Papers. State Historical Society of North Dakota, Bismarck.

Frontier Newspaper Collection. Western History/Genealogy Department, Denver Public Library, Denver.

McDermott, John D., File. Collection of articles and newspapers about Gall in McDermott's possession.

McLaughlin, Major James. Correspondence and Miscellaneous Papers, 1855–1937. State Historical Society of North Dakota, Bismarck.

Red Cloud. "Red Cloud, Chief of the Sioux." Autobiography. Nebraska State Historical Society, Lincoln.

Ricker, Eli S., Collection. Nebraska State Historical Society, Lincoln.

Robinson, Doane, Papers. South Dakota State Historical Society, Pierre.

Waggoner, Josephine, Papers. Museum of the Fur Trade, Chadron, Nebraska.

Zahn, Frank, Collection. State Historical Society of North Dakota, Bismarck.

PUBLIC AND CHURCH RECORDS

Adjutant General's Office. Fort Berthold Post Returns, May 1865 to June 1867. Records of the Adjutant General's Office, RG 94, microfilm publication 617, roll 110. National Archives and Records Administration, Washington, D.C.

———. Fort Buford Post Returns, June 1866 to September 1895. Records of the Adjutant General's Office, RG 94, microfilm publication 617, rolls 158 and 159. National Archives and Records Administration, Washington, D.C.

Indian Peace Commission. "Council of the Indian Peace Commission with the Various Bands of Sioux Indians at Fort Rice, Dakt. T., July 2, 1868." In *Papers Relating to Talks and Councils Held with the Indians in Dakota and Montana Territories in the Years 1866–1869.* Washington, D.C.: Government Printing Office, 1910.

Kappler, Charles J., comp. *Indian Affairs: Laws and Treaties.* Vol. 2. Washington, D.C.: Government Printing Office, 1904.

Mooney, James. *The Ghost-Dance Religion and the Sioux Outbreak of 1890.* 14th Annual Report of the Bureau of Ethnology, 1892–1893, pt. 2. Washington, D.C.: Government Printing Office, 1896. Reprint, North Dighton, Mass.: JG Press, 1996.

Office of Indian Affairs [now called Bureau of Indian Affairs]. Appointment Approval Letters. Standing Rock Correspondence from 1865, Records of the Bureau of Indian Affairs, RG 75; National Archives and Records Administration—Central Plains Region, Kansas City).

———. "Census of Hunkpapa Indians of Standing Rock Agency, Dakotah Territory, July 1st, 1885" [handwritten]. State Historical Society of North Dakota, Bismarck.

———. Circular to Superintendents of Indian Affairs and Indian Agents for the 1860s. Records of the Dakota Superintendency, 1861–1870 and 1877–1878, and Wyoming Superintendency, 1870, Records of the Bureau of Indian Affairs, RG 75, microfilm publication 1016, roll 3. National Archives and Records Administration, Washington, D.C.

———. Decimal Correspondence File 053.0. Genealogy–Family History, Etc., Standing Rock, Records of the Bureau of Indian Affairs, RG 75. National Archives and Records Administration—Central Plains Region, Kansas City.

———. Minutes of Sioux Commission of 1888 [handwritten ledger]. Standing Rock, Records of Bureau of Indian Affairs, RG 75. National Archives and Records Administration—Central Plains Region, Kansas City.

———. Miscellaneous Correspondence Received (1864–1910). Standing Rock, RG 75, box 25. National Archives and Records Administration—Central Plains Region, Kansas City.

———. "Pony Claims of Red Cloud, Pine Ridge (Red Cloud Band) Pony Claim No. 1." South Dakota State Historical Society, Pierre.

———. Record of Rations Issued 1885, Standing Rock Agency, Fort Yates, North Dakota. Records of the Bureau of Indian Affairs, RG 75, roll 5A. National Archives and Records Administration—Central Plains Region, Kansas City.

———. *Report by James McLaughlin, U.S. Indian Agent, Standing Rock Agency, on the Death of Sioux Chief Sitting Bull, December 15, 1890.* Records of the Bureau of Indian Affairs, 1793–1989, RG 75, Special Case 188. National Archives and Records Administration, Washington, D.C.

———. *Report of the Special Commissioner Appointed to Investigate the Affairs of the Red Cloud Indian Agency, July 1875.* Washington, D.C.: Government Printing Office, 1875.

Powell, J. W. *Bureau of Ethnology to the Secretary of the Smithsonian Institute, 1882–83, by J. W. Powell, Director.* Washington, D.C.: Government Printing Office, 1886.

Standing Rock Mission Records. Vol. A-1. Augustana Collection, Center for Western Studies, Augustana College, Sioux Falls, South Dakota.

U.S. Army. *Sioux Campaign, May–September 1879 and January–September 1881.* In Special Files, Military Division of the Missouri, Records of the U.S. Army Continental Commands, 1821–1920, RG 393, roll 5. National Archives and Records Administration, Washington, D.C., 1988.

U.S. Congress. *Act of Mar. 2, 1889. U.S. Statutes at Large* 25 (1889) 888, ch. 405, 888–99. Washington, D.C.: Government Printing Office.

————. *An Act to Ratify an Agreement with Certain Bands of the Sioux Nation of Indians and also the Northern Arapaho and Cheyenne Indians. U.S. Statutes at Large* 19 (1877), ch. 72, 254–64. Washington, D.C.: Government Printing Office.

U.S. Congress. House. *Military Expedition Against the Sioux Indians, July 15, 1876.* 44th Cong., 1st sess., 1875–76, H. Exec. Doc. 184.

————. *Report of the Secretary of War.* 41st Cong., 2nd sess., 1869, H. Exec. Doc. 1.

U. S. Congress. Senate. *Letter from the Secretary of the Interior, Transmitting, in Compliance with a Resolution of the Senate of December 6, 1883, Report of the Commissioner of Indian Affairs Submitting Copies of Sioux Agreements to Cession of Land to the United States, with Correspondence Connected Therewith* [Edmunds Report]. 48th Cong., 1st sess., 1884, S. Exec. Doc. 70, serial 2165.

————. *In the Senate of the United States, March 7, 1884 — Ordered to be printed. Mr. Dawes, from the Select Committee to Examine into the Condition of the Sioux and Crow Indians, submitted the following report* [Dawes Report]. 48th Cong., 1st sess., 1884, S. Rep. 283, serial 2174.

————. *Letter from the Secretary of the Interior, Transmitting, in Response to Senate Resolution of December 13, 1888, Report Relative to Opening a Part of the Sioux Reservation* [Pratt Report]. 50th Cong., 2nd sess., 1888, S. Exec. Doc. 17, serial 2610.

————. *Message from the President of the United States, Transmitting, Reports Relative to the Proposed Division of the Great Sioux Reservation, and Recommending Certain Legislation* [Crook Report]. 51st Cong., 1st sess., 1890, S. Exec. Doc. 51, serial 2682.

U.S. District Courts for the Territory of Dakota. Case 101, Appellate Case Files (1867–1886). Second Judicial District, Yankton, Dakota Territory, Records of the U.S. District Courts for the Territory of Dakota, RG 21 National Archives and Records Administration— Central Plains Region, Kansas City.

NEWSPAPERS AND MAGAZINES

Bismarck Daily Tribune, 1875–1894
Bismarck Weekly Tribune, 1875–1894
The Daily Argus (Fargo), 1888–1889
Denver Post, 2002
Fargo Forum, 1931
Harper's Weekly, 1890
Mobridge Tribune (Mobridge, South Dakota), undated
New York Times, 1876–1877
St. Paul Pioneer Press, 1886

PUBLISHED PRIMARY SOURCES

Allison, Edwin H. *The Surrender of Sitting Bull.* Columbus, Ohio: Walker Lithograph and Printing, 1891.

Baldwin, Frank D. "The Fights at Bark Creek and Ash Creek, December 1876." In *Battles and Skirmishes of the Great Sioux War, 1876–1877: The Military View*, compiled, edited, and annotated by Jerome A. Greene, 157–66. Norman: University of Oklahoma Press, 1993.

Black Elk, Nicholas. *Black Elk Speaks: Being the Life Story of a Holy Man of the Oglala Sioux.* As told through John G. Neihardt (Flaming Rainbow) by Nicholas Black Elk. Lincoln: University of Nebraska Press, 2000.

Bourke, John Gregory. *On the Border with Crook*. New York: Charles Scribner's Sons, 1891. Reprint, Alexandria, Va.: Time-Life Books, 1980.

Burdick, Usher L., ed. *David F. Barry's Indian Notes on "The Custer Battle."* Baltimore: The Proof Press, 1937. Reprint, Baltimore: Werth Brothers, 1949 (found in the John D. McDermott File).

Clements, Bennett A., and Anson Mills, "The Starvation March and the Battle of Slim Buttes." In *Battle and Skirmishes of the Great Sioux War, 1876–1877: The Military View*, compiled, edited, and annotated by Jerome A. Greene, 96–115. Norman: University of Oklahoma Press, 1993.

Danker, Donald F., ed. "The Wounded Knee Interviews of Eli S. Ricker." *Nebraska History* 62 (Summer 1981): 151–243.

Denig, Edwin Thompson. *The Assiniboines*. Edited by J. N. B. Hewitt, with introduction by David R. Miller. Norman: University of Oklahoma Press, 1984. (Originally an unpublished manuscript titled "A Report of the Hon. Isaac I. Stevens, Governor of Washington Territory, on the Indian Tribes of the Upper Missouri, by Edwin Thompson Denig.")

Eastman, Charles A. *Indian Heroes and Great Chieftains*. Boston: Little, Brown, 1920.

Fiske, Frank Bennett. *Life and Death of Sitting Bull*. Fort Yates, N.Dak.: Pioneer-Arrow Print, 1933.

Godfrey, Edward S. "Custer's Last Battle." *Century Magazine* 43, no. 3 (January 1892): 358–87.

———. "Custer's Last Battle." *Contributions to the Historical Society of Montana* 9, 144–212. Helena: Montana Historical Library, 1923.

Greene, Jerome A., ed. *Battles and Skirmishes of the Great Sioux War, 1876–1877: The Military View*. Norman: University of Oklahoma Press, 1993.

———. *Lakota and Cheyenne: Indian Views of the Great Sioux War, 1876–1877*. Norman: University of Oklahoma Press, 1994.

Holley, Frances Chamberlain. *Once Their Home or Our Legacy from the Dahkotahs: Historical, Biographical and Incidental from Far-Off Days, Down to the Present*. Chicago: Donohue and Henneberry, 1892.

Hyde, George E. *Life of George Bent: Written from His Letters*. Edited by Savoie Lottinville. Norman: University of Oklahoma Press, 1968.

Jacobson, Ethel C. "Life in an Indian Village." *North Dakota History* 26 (Summer 1959): 45–92.

McBlain, John L. "The Lame Deer Fight, May 7, 1877." In *Battles and Skirmishes of the Great Sioux War, 1876–1877: The Military View*, compiled, edited, and annotated by Jerome A. Greene, 204–12. Norman: University of Oklahoma Press, 1993.

McLaughlin, James. *My Friend the Indian*. Boston: Houghton Mifflin, 1910.

———. *My Friend the Indian or Three Heretofore Unpublished Chapters of the Book Published under the Title My Friend the Indian*. Edited and prefaced by Usher L. Burdick, Baltimore: The Proof Press, 1931.

Paul, R. Eli, ed. *Autobiography of Red Cloud: War Leader of the Oglalas*. Helena: Montana Historical Society Press, 1997.

Pope, James W. "The Battle of Cedar Creek, October 21, 1876." In *Battles and Skirmishes of the Great Sioux War, 1876–1877: The Military View*, compiled, edited, and annotated by Jerome A. Greene, 134–39. Norman: University of Oklahoma Press, 1993.

Robinson, DeLorme W. "Pi-zi (Gall)." *South Dakota Historical Collections* 1 (1902): 151, 153–54.

Schmitt, Martin F., ed. *General George Crook: His Autobiography*. Norman: University of Oklahoma, 1960.

Taylor, Joseph Henry. "Bloody Knife and Gall." *North Dakota Historical Quarterly* 9, no. 1 (October 1929): 165–73.

"Three Noted Chiefs of the Sioux." *Harper's Weekly* 34 (October 20, 1890): 995. (Available at the Electronic Text Center, University of Virginia Library, Charlottesville.)

Tilton, Henry R., and Edmund Butler. "The Wolf Mountains Expedition and the Battle of Wolf Mountains, January 8, 1872." In *Battles and Skirmishes of the Great Sioux War, 1876–1877: The Military View*, compiled, edited, and annotated by Jerome A. Greene, 186–203. Norman: University of Oklahoma Press, 1993.

Vestal, Stanley [Walter S. Campbell]. *New Sources of Indian History, 1850–1891.* Norman: University of Oklahoma Press, 1934.

SECONDARY SOURCES

Ambrose, Stephen E. *Crazy Horse and Custer: The Parallel Lives of Two American Warriors.* Garden City, N.Y.: Doubleday, 1975.

Anderson, Gary Clayton. *Kinsmen of Another Kind: Dakota-White Relatives in the Upper Mississippi Valley, 1650–1862.* Lincoln: University of Nebraska Press, 1984.

Anderson, Harry. "An Investigation of the Early Bands of the Saone Group of Teton Sioux." *Journal of the Washington Academy of Sciences* 46 (March 1956): 87–94.

Andrist, Ralph K. *The Long Death: the Last Days of the Plains Indians.* New York: Collier Books, 1969.

Baird, Andrew T. "Into the Valley Rode the Six Hundred: The 7th Cavalry and the Battle of the Little Bighorn." *Vulcan Historical Review* 4 (Spring 2000): 83–104.

Barrett, Carole. "*Into the Light of Christian Civilization*": *St. Elizabeth's Boarding School for Indian Children (1886–1967).* Bismarck: North Dakota Humanities Council, 2004.

———. *Major McLaughlin's March of Civilization.* Bismarck: North Dakota Humanities Council, 1989.

———. "One Bull: A Man of Good Understanding." *North Dakota History: Journal of the Northern Plains* 66 (Summer/Fall 1999): 3–16.

Behrens, Jo Lea Wetherilt. "In Defense of 'Poor Lo': National Indian Defense Association and Council Fire's Advocacy for Sioux Land Rights." *South Dakota History: South Dakota State Historical Society Quarterly* 24 (Fall/Winter 1994): 153–73.

Billington, Ray Allen, with James Blaine Hedges. *Westward Expansion: A History of the American Frontier.* 4th ed. New York: Macmillan Publishing, 1974.

Bray, Kingsley M. *Crazy Horse: A Lakota Life.* Norman: University of Oklahoma Press, 2006.

———. "Teton Sioux Population History, 1655–1881." *Nebraska History* 75, no. 2 (Summer 1994): 165–88.

Buecker, Thomas R. *Fort Robinson and the American West, 1874–1899.* Lincoln: Nebraska State Historical Society, 1999.

Burdick, Usher L. *The Last Battle of the Sioux Nation.* Stevens Point, Wisc.: Worzalla Publishing, 1929.

Calloway, Collin G. "Army Allies or Tribal Survival? The 'Other Indians' in the 1876 Campaign." In *Legacy: New Perspectives on the Battle of the Little Bighorn*, edited by Charles E. Rankin, 63–81. Helena: Montana Historical Society Press, 1996.

Carriker, Robert C. *Father Peter John DeSmet: Jesuit in the West.* Norman: University of Oklahoma Press, 1995.

Champagne, Duane. "Gall (Pizi) (1840–94): Hunkpapa Sioux Tribal Leader." In *The Native North American Almanac: A Reference Work on Native North Americans in the United States and Canada*, edited by Duane Champagne, 1059–60. Detroit: Gale Research, 1994.

Chapman, William McK. *Remember the Wind: A Prairie Memoir.* Philadelphia: J. B. Lippincott Company, 1965.

Coleman, William S. E. *Voices of Wounded Knee*. Lincoln: University of Nebraska Press, 2000.

Collin, Richard E. "Bloody Knife: Custer's Favorite Scout." *Greasy Grass Magazine* 13 (May 1997): 2–9.

Connell, Evan S. *Son of the Morning Star*. New York: Harper and Row, 1984.

Deloria, Vine, Jr. *Custer Died for Your Sins*. Norman: University of Oklahoma Press, 1988.

DeMallie, Raymond J. "The Lakota Ghost Dance: An Ethnohistorical Account." *Pacific Historical Review* 51 (November 1982): 385–405.

———. "Teton Dakota Kinship and Social Organization." PhD dissertation, Department of Anthropology, University of Chicago, 1971.

DeMallie, Raymond J., ed. *The Sixth Grandfather: Black Elk's Teachings Given to John G. Neihardt*. Lincoln: University of Nebraska Press, 1984.

DeMallie, Raymond J., and Douglas R. Parks. *Sioux Indian Religion*. Norman: University of Oklahoma Press, 1987.

Ewers, John C. "When Sitting Bull Surrendered His Winchester." In *Indian Life on the Upper Missouri*, 175–81. Norman: University of Oklahoma Press, 1968.

Ewers, John C., ed. *Indian Life on the Upper Missouri*. Norman: University of Oklahoma Press, 1968.

Fielder, Mildred. *Sioux Indian Leaders*. Seattle: Superior Publishing, 1975.

Fox, Richard Allan, Jr. *Archaeology, History, and Custer's Last Battle*. Foreword by W. Raymond Wood. Norman: University of Oklahoma Press, 1993.

Frank, James R. "Chief Gall and Chief John Grass: Cultural Mediators or Sellouts?" Master's thesis, Department of History, University of Montana, 2001.

Frazer, Robert W. *Forts of the West: Military Forts and Presidios and Posts Commonly Called Forts West of the Mississippi River to 1898*. Norman: University of Oklahoma Press, 1972.

Frost, Lawrence A. *Custer's 7th Cav and the Campaign of 1873*. Vol. 3 of Montana and the West. El Segundo, Calif.: Upton and Sons, 1986.

Graham, W. A. *The Custer Myth: A Source Book of Custeriana*. Introduction by Brian C. Pohanka. Mechanicsburg, Pa.: Stackpole Books, 2000.

Gray, John S. *Centennial Campaign: The Sioux War of 1876*. Fort Collins, Colorado: Old Army Press, 1976. Reprint, Norman: University of Oklahoma Press, 1988.

———. *Custer's Last Campaign: Mitch Bouyer and the Little Bighorn*. Lincoln: University of Nebraska Press, 1991.

Greene, Jerome A. *Morning Star Dawn: The Powder River Expedition and the Northern Cheyennes, 1876*. Norman: University of Oklahoma Press, 2003.

———. *Slim Buttes, 1876: An Episode of the Great Sioux War*. Norman: University of Oklahoma Press, 1993.

———. "The Sioux Land Commission of 1889: Prelude to Wounded Knee." *South Dakota History* 1, no. 1 (Winter 1970): 41–72.

———. *Yellowstone Command: Colonel Nelson A. Miles and the Great Sioux War, 1876–1877*. Lincoln: University of Nebraska Press, 1991.

Hagan, William T. *Indian Police and Judges: Experiments in Acculturation and Control*. New Haven, Conn.: Yale University Press, 1966.

———. *Quanah Parker, Comanche Chief*. Norman: University of Oklahoma Press, 1993.

Halaas, David Fridtjof. "Reflections on a Theme: Indians, Custer, and History." *Colorado Heritage* (Spring 1994): 38–44.

Halaas, David Fridtjof, and Andrew E. Masich. *Halfbreed: The Remarkable Story of George Bent: Caught Between the Worlds of the Indian and the White Man*. Cambridge, Mass.: Da Capo Press, 2004.

Hardorff, Richard G. *Hokahey! A Good Day to Die*. Lincoln: University of Nebraska Press, 1993.

Hart, Herbert M. *Tour Guide to Old Western Forts*. Boulder, Colo.: Pruett Publishing, 1980.

Hassrick, Royal B. *The Sioux: Life and Customs of a Warrior Society*. 1964. Reprint, Norman: University of Oklahoma Press, 1989.

Hebard, Grace Raymond, and E. A. Brininstool. *The Bozeman Trail*. Cleveland: Arthur H. Clark, 1923. Reprint, Lincoln: University of Nebraska Press, 1990.

Hedren, Paul L. *Fort Laramie in 1876: Chronicle of a Frontier Post at War*. Lincoln: University of Nebraska Press, 1988.

———. "Sitting Bull's Surrender at Fort Buford: An Episode in American History." *North Dakota History: Journal of the Northern Plains* 62 (Fall 1995): 2–15.

———. *Traveler's Guide to the Great Sioux War: The Battlefields, Forts, and Related Sites of America's Greatest Indian War*. Helena: Montana Historical Society Press, 1996.

Heski, Thomas M. *The Little Shadow Catcher*. Seattle: Superior Publishing Company, 1978.

Hodge, Frederick Webb. "Gall (Pizi)." In *Handbook of American Indians North of Mexico*, pt. 1, edited by Frederick Webb Hodge, 482. New York: Rowman and Littlefield, 1971.

Hodge, Frederick Webb, ed. *Handbook of American Indians North of Mexico*. Pt. 1. New York: Rowman and Littlefield, 1971.

Hoover, Herbert T. "Gall (Sioux)." In *Encyclopedia of the American West*, vol. 2, edited by Charles Phillips and Alan Axelrod, 590–91. London: Simon and Schuster and Prentice Hall; New York: Macmillan, 1996.

———. "Sitting Bull." *American Indian Leaders: Studies in Diversity*. Edited by R. David Edmunds, 152–74. Lincoln: University of Nebraska Press, 1980.

Howard, James H. *The Dakota or Sioux Indians: A Study of Human Ecology*. Anthropological Papers 2. Vermillion: Dakota Museum, University of South Dakota, 1966. Reprint, Lincoln: J. and L. Reprint Company, 1980.

Hutton, Paul A. *Phil Sheridan and His Army*. Lincoln: University of Nebraska Press, 1985.

Hyde, George E. *Red Cloud's Folk: A History of the Oglala Sioux Indians*. Norman: University of Oklahoma Press, 1937.

———. *A Sioux Chronicle*. Foreword by Raymond J. DeMallie. Norman: University of Oklahoma Press, 1993.

Innis, Ben. *Bloody Knife: Custer's Favorite Scout*. Edited by Richard E. Collin. Bismarck, N.Dak.: Smoky Water Press, 1994.

Jensen, Richard E., R. Eli Paul, and John E. Carter. *Eyewitness at Wounded Knee*. Lincoln: University of Nebraska Press, 1991.

Jones, Douglas C. *The Treaty of Medicine Lodge: The Story of the Great Treaty Council as Told by Eyewitnesses*. Norman: University of Oklahoma Press, 1966.

Josephy, Alvin M., Jr., ed. *Book of Indians*. New York: American Heritage Publishing, 1961.

———. *The Patriot Chiefs: A Chronicle of American Indian Resistance*. New York: The Viking Press, 1972.

Joyner, Christopher C. "The Hegira of Sitting Bull to Canada: Diplomatic Realpolitik, 1876–1881." *Journal of the West* 13 (April 1974): 6–18.

Kasper, Shirley. *Annie Oakley*. Norman: University of Oklahoma Press, 1992.

Kuhlman, Charles. *Custer and the Gall Saga: Some Interesting Deductions Regarding the Battle of the Little Bighorn[,] June 25–26, 1876*. Billings, Montana: privately printed, 1940. (Available at State Historical Society of Nebraska, Lincoln)

Lamar, Howard R. *Dakota Territory, 1861–1889*. New Haven, Conn.: Yale University Press, 1956.

Lamar, Howard R., ed. *The New Encyclopedia of the American West*. New Haven, Conn.: Yale University Press, 1998.

Larson, Robert W. "Gall: 'The Fighting Cock of the Sioux.'" *Wild West* 19, no. 1 (June 2006): 26–32.

———. "Lakota Leaders and Government Agents: A Study of Changing Relationships." *Nebraska History* 82, no. 2 (Summer 2001): 47–57.

———. *New Mexico's Quest for Statehood, 1846–1912*. Albuquerque: University of New Mexico Press, 1968.

———. "Red Cloud: The Reservation Years." Part 2. *Montana The Magazine of Western History* 47, no. 2 (Summer 1997): 14–25.

———. "Red Cloud: The Warrior Years." Part 1. *Montana The Magazine of Western History* 47, no. 1 (Spring 1997): 22–31.

———. *Red Cloud: Warrior-Statesman of the Lakota Sioux*. Norman: University of Oklahoma Press, 1997.

———. "The Warrior Gall: War Chief of the Hunkpapa Sioux." *Greasy Grass Magazine* 23 (2007): 16–29.

Lewis, David Rich. "Reservation Leadership and the Progressive-Traditional Dichotomy: William Wash and the Northern Utes, 1865–1928." *Ethnology* 38, no. 2 (Spring 1991): 124–48.

Libby, Orin G. *The Arikara Narrative of the Campaign Against the Hostile Dakotas[,] June, 1876*. New York: Sol Lewis, 1973.

Lubetkin, M. John. "An Ambush That Changed History: Thomas L. Rosser, David S. Stanley, Gall and the 1872 Eastern Yellowstone Surveying Expedition." *Journal of the West* 43, no. 1 (Winter 2004): 74–83.

———. "Clash on the Yellowstone: Monday, August 4, 1873." *Research Review: The Journal of the Little Big Horn Associates*, February 2004, 12–31.

———. "The Forgotten Yellowstone Surveying Expeditions of 1871: W. Milnor Roberts and the Northern Pacific Railroad in Montana." *Montana The Magazine of Western History* 52, no. 1 (Winter 2002): 32–47.

———. *Jay Cooke's Gamble: The Northern Pacific Railroad, the Sioux, and the Panic of 1873*. Norman: University of Oklahoma Press, 2006.

———. "'No Fighting Is to Be Apprehended': Major Eugene Baker, Sitting Bull, and the Northern Pacific Railroad's 1872 Western Yellowstone Surveying Expedition." *Montana The Magazine of Western History* 56, no. 2 (Summer 2006): 28–91.

———. "'Strike Up Garry Owen,' August 11, 1873: Custer's Second Battle on the Yellowstone." *Research Review: The Journal of the Little Bighorn Association*, Summer 2006, 2–16.

Mangum, Neil C. *Battle of the Rosebud: Prelude to the Little Bighorn*. El Segundo, Calif.: Upton and Sons, 1987.

———. "Gall: Sioux Gladiator or White Man's Pawn?" in *Fifth Annual Symposium [,] Custer Battlefield Historical & Museum Assn., Inc.*, 28–44. Hardin, Mont.: Custer Battlefield Historical and Museum Association, 1987.

Manzione, Joseph. *"I Am Looking to the North for My Life": Sitting Bull, 1876–1881*. Salt Lake City: University of Utah Press, 1991.

Marquis, Thomas B. *Sitting Bull and Gall, the Warrior*. Hardin, Mont.: Custer Battle Museum, 1934. (Available at State Historical Society of Nebraska, Lincoln)

———. *A Warrior Who Fought Custer*. Minneapolis, Minn.: The Midwest Company, 1931.

McDermott, John D. "The Indian War of 1865." Paper presented at the Denver Symposium: G. A. Custer and/or the Plains Indian Wars, September 13, 2003.

Michno, Gregory F. "Crazy Horse, Custer, and the Sweep to the North." *Montana The Magazine of Western History* 43, no. 3 (Summer 1993): 42–53.

———. *Lakota Noon: The Indian Narrative of Custer's Defeat.* Missoula, Mont.: Mountain Press Publishing, 1997.

———. "Revision at the Little Bighorn: The Fall of Gall." *Research Review: The Journal of the Little Big Horn Associates* 10, no. 2 (June 1996): 19–25.

Milligan, Edward A. *Dakota Twilight: The Standing Rock Sioux, 1874–1890.* Hicksville, N.Y.: Exposition Press, 1976.

Nichols, Ronald H. "A Brief Analytical Study of Reno's Fight in the Valley." Paper presented at the Denver Symposium: G. A. Custer and/or the Plains Indian Wars, September 13, 2003.

———. *In Custer's Shadow: Major Marcus Reno.* Introduction by Brian C. Pohanka. Norman: University of Oklahoma Press, 2000. First published 1999, Old Army Press.

Olson, James C. *Red Cloud and the Sioux Problem.* Lincoln: University of Nebraska Press, 1965.

Paul, R. Eli. *Blue Water Creek and the First Sioux War, 1854–1856.* Norman: University of Oklahoma Press, 2004.

Pfaller, Louis. "Brave Bear Murder Case." *North Dakota History: Journal of the Northern Plains* 36, no. 2 (Spring 1996): 121–39.

———. *James McLaughlin: The Man With an Indian Heart.* Richardson, N.Dak.: Assumption Abbey Press, 1992.

Phillips, Charles, and Alan Axelrod, eds. *Encyclopedia of the American West.* London: Simon and Schuster and Prentice Hall International, 1996.

Powers, William K. *Oglala Religion.* Lincoln: University of Nebraska Press, 1975. Reprint, Bison Book Edition, 1982. Page references are to the 1982 edition.

Price, Catherine. *The Oglala People, 1841–1879: A Political History.* Lincoln: University of Nebraska Press, 1996.

Prucha, Francis Paul. *American Indian Policy in Crisis: Christian Reformers and the Indian.* Norman: University of Oklahoma Press, 1976.

———. *Americanizing the American Indian: Writings by the "Friends of the Indian," 1880–1900.* Lincoln: University of Nebraska Press, 1978. First published 1973, Harvard University Press.

Rankin, Charles E., ed. *Legacy: New Perspectives on the Battle of the Little Bighorn.* Helena: Montana Historical Society Press, 1996.

Remele, Larry, ed. *Fort Buford and the Military Frontier on the Northern Plains, 1850–1900.* Bismarck: State Historical Society of North Dakota, 1987.

Riley, Glenda. *The Life and Legacy of Annie Oakley.* Norman: University of Oklahoma Press, 1994.

Robinson, Charles M., III. *A Good Year to Die: The Story of the Great Sioux War.* Norman: University of Oklahoma Press, 1996.

———. *General Crook and the Western Frontier.* Norman: University of Oklahoma Press, 2000.

Robinson, Doane. "The Education of Redcloud." *South Dakota Historical Collection* 12 (1924): 156–87.

Sandoz, Mari. *Crazy Horse: The Strange Man of the Oglalas.* Lincoln: University of Nebraska Press, 1992. First published, Knopf, 1942.

Shumate, Jane. *Chief Gall: Sioux War Chief.* North American Indians of Achievement series, edited by W. David Baird. New York: Chelsea House Publishers, 1995.

The Sioux or Dakota Nation: Divisions, History and Numbers. Leaflet 41. 1932. Reprint, Denver: Denver Art Museum in cooperation with the Denver Public Schools, 1967.

Steltenkamp, Michael F. *Black Elk: Holy Man of the Oglala*. Norman: University of Oklahoma Press, 1993.

Stewart, Edgar I. *Custer's Luck*. Norman: University of Oklahoma Press, 1955.

Sundbloom, Loren, and Elroy E. Ubl. Letters to the Editor. *Wild West* 19, no. 4 (December 2006): 9

Szasz, Margaret Connell, ed. *Between Indian and White Worlds: The Cultural Brokers*. Norman: University of Oklahoma Press, 1994.

Thackery, Lorna. "Suicide Boys: Warriors' Act Kept Secret for Decades." *Friends of the Little Bighorn Battlefield*, April 14, 2006, 1–4.

Turner, Katherine C. *Red Man Calling on the Great White Father*. Norman: University of Oklahoma Press, 1951.

Utley, Robert M. *Cavalier in Buckskin: George Armstrong Custer and the Western Military Frontier*. Norman: University of Oklahoma Press, 1988.

———. *The Indian Frontier of the American West, 1846–1890*. Albuquerque: University of New Mexico Press, 1984.

———. *The Lance and the Shield: The Life and Times of Sitting Bull*. New York: Henry Holt, 1993.

———. *The Last Days of the Sioux Nation*. New Haven, Conn.: Yale University Press, 1963.

Van Nuys, Maxwell. *Inkpaduta—The Scarlet Point: Terror of the Dakota Frontier and Secret Hero of the Sioux*. Denver: privately printed, 1998.

Vaughn, J. W. *With Crook at the Rosebud*. Harrisburg, Pa.: Stackpole, 1956.

Vestal, Stanley. *Sitting Bull, Champion of the Sioux: A Biography*. Boston: Houghton Mifflin, 1932.

———. *Warpath: The True Story of the Fighting Sioux Told in a Biography of Chief White Bull*. Edited by Raymond J. DeMallie. Lincoln: University of Nebraska Press, 1984.

Viola, Herman J. *Diplomats in Buckskin: A History of Indian Delegations in Washington*. Washington, D.C.: Smithsonian Institution Press, 1981.

Waldman, Carl. "Gall (Pizi) Hunkpapa Lakota (Sioux) (1840–1894) Leader in the Sioux Wars; War Chief of Sitting Bull." In *Biographical Dictionary of American Indian History to 1900*, 138–39. New York: Checkmark Books, 2001.

Waldman, Carl, ed. *Encyclopedia of Native American Tribes*. Illustrations by Molly Brown. New York and Oxford: Facts on File Publications, 1988.

Warner, Ronald Phil. "A History of Fort Buford, 1866–1895." In *Fort Buford and the Military Frontier on the Northern Plains, 1850–1900*, edited by Larry Remele, 41–55. Bismarck: State Historical Society of North Dakota, 1987.

Washburn, Wilcomb E. *The Assault on Indian Tribalism: The General Allotment Law (Dawes Act) of 1887*. Edited by Harold M. Hyman. Philadelphia: J. B. Lippincott, 1975.

———. *The Indian in America*. New York: Harper and Row, 1975.

White, Richard. *Roots of Dependency: Subsistence, Environment, and Social Change Among Choctaws, Pawnees, and Navajos*. Lincoln: University of Nebraska Press, 1983.

———. "The Winning of the West: The Expansion of the Western Sioux in the Eighteenth and Nineteenth Century." *Journal of American History* 65, no. 2 (September 1978): 319–43.

Wick, Douglas A. *North Dakota Place Names*. Fargo, N.Dak.: Prairie House, 1988.

Winsell, Keith A. "Gall[,] 1840–1894[:] Hunkpapa Lakota Sioux Warrior and Tribal Leader Also Known as Pizi." In *Notable Native Americans*, edited by Sharon Malinowski, 155–57. New York: Gale Research, 1995.

Wishart, Bruce. "Grandmother's Land: Sitting Bull in Canada." *True West* 37, part 1, "Arrival of the Warrior" (May 1990): 14–20; part 2, "Time of Power" (June 1990): 26–32; part 3, "The Time of Defeat" (July 1990): 20–26; part 4, "Surrender" (August 1990): 28–32.

Wishart, David J. *The Fur Trade of the American West, 1807–1840: A Geographical Synthesis.* Lincoln: University of Nebraska Press, 1979.

Worster, Donald Eugene. *Under Western Skies: Nature and History in the American West.* New York: Oxford University Press, 1992.

Zimmerman, Larry J., and Brian Leigh Molyneaux. *Native North America.* Norman: University of Oklahoma Press, 1996.

INTERVIEWS

Allard, LaDonna Brave Bull, Standing Rock Reservation, North Dakota, October 29, 2002 (telephone).

Avans, Diana, maintenance supervisor, Fort Buford, State Historical Society of North Dakota, Bismarck, May 19, 2001.

Barrett, Carole, associate professor of American Indian Studies, University of Mary, Bismarck, May 16, 2001 (at the State Historical Society of North Dakota); June 23, 2001 (telephone); February 16, June 15, and October 5, 2002 (all by telephone).

Boggess, Howard, project coordinator, Frontier Heritage Alliance, Billings, Montana, June 25, 2003; March 21, 2005 (both by telephone).

Chapman, Carole, December 1, 2002 (telephone).

Collin, Richard E., communications director, State Historical Society of North Dakota, Bismarck, and member of the Frontier Heritage Alliance, June 24, 2003.

Doerner, John. Chief historian, Little Bighorn Battlefield National Monument, April 19, 2006 (telephone).

Dog Eagle, Isaac, Standing Rock Reservation, North Dakota, July 14, 2001 (telephone).

Greene, Jerome A., National Park Service, February 23, 2002 (Denver, Colorado).

Groenewold, Gerry, president, Frontier Heritage Alliance, and director, Energy and Environment Center, University of North Dakota, Grand Forks, July 9, 2003 (telephone).

Halvorson, Mark J., curator of research collections, State Historical Society of North Dakota, Bismarck, May 17, 2001; September 20, 2006 (telephone).

Hawk, Gladys, Gall's great-granddaughter, September 28, 2006 (telephone).

Her-Many-Horses, Leo, Gall's great-great-grandson, September 21, 2006 (telephone).

Her-Many-Horses, Mike. Gall's great-grandson, September 20, 2006 (telephone).

Iron Cloud, Vernon, Gall's great-grandson, and wife, Theo, Standing Rock Reservation, North Dakota, May 21, 2001.

Jones, Lavora, Gall's great-granddaughter, February 26, 2001 (telephone).

Jones, Linda, daughter-in-law of Lavora Jones. April 26 and May 5, 2005 (telephone).

Little Ghost, Ambrose, spiritual leader at Spirit Lake Reservation, Fort Totten, with LaDonna Brave Bear Allard, October 28, 2002 (telephone). Arranged by Richard E. Collin, communications director, State Historical Society of North Dakota, Bismarck.

Mangum, Neil, former superintendent, Little Bighorn Battlefield National Monument, February 23, 2002 (Denver, Colorado).

McWilliams, Mary Ellen, coordinator, Frontier Heritage Alliance, Sheridan, Wyoming, June 24, 2003 (telephone).

Mentz, Tim, Sr. (Red Bull), tribal historic preservation officer, Standing Rock Reservation, North Dakota, May 21, 2001 (at Fort Yates).

Monnett, John, professor of history, Metropolitan State College, Denver, October 7, 2004.

Pederson, Severn "Pete," collector of Indian artifacts, Douglas County, Colorado, December 3, 2002.

Stalnaker, Charles M., site supervisor at Fort Buford, State Historical Society of North Dakota, Bismarck, May 31, 2001 (telephone).

Strouse, James F., collector of Indian artifacts, Golden, Colorado, January 8, 2003.

Thompson, Harry, curator, Center for Western Studies, Augustana College, Sioux Falls, South Dakota, June 18, 2001 (telephone).

CORRESPONDENCE

Barrett, Carole, to Robert W. Larson, May 16, 2001, and September 21, 2002.

Collin, Richard E., to Robert W. Larson, October 29, 2002.

Standing Bear, Jeanine, to Mark E. Gray, October 10, 2001, in Gray's possession.

Index